Masquerade and Civilization

MASQUERADE AND CIVILIZATION

The Carnivalesque in Eighteenth-Century English Culture and Fiction

TERRY CASTLE

Stanford University Press, Stanford, California

Stanford University Press
Stanford, California
© 1986 by the Board of Trustees of the
Leland Stanford Junior University
Printed in the United States of America
Original printing 1986
Last figure below indicates year of this printing:
96   95   94   93   92   91   90   89   88   87

CIP data appear at the end of the book

Frontispiece
Masquerade scene at the King's Theatre in the
Haymarket, by Giuseppe Grisoni, ca. 1724

To Kristin Midelfort

Preface

This book aims at two things: to re-create the historical phenomenon of the English masquerade and to outline its literary history, particularly in fiction, roughly between 1720 and 1790.

I have been lucky in my subject. There is something inherently appealing in the idea of the masquerade—an ineluctable charm in the notion of disguising oneself in a fanciful costume and moving through a crowd of masked strangers. Here "*Indian Kings*, with *Turkish* Sultans stand, / Gyants and Fairy Queens walk Hand in Hand," wrote Susannah Centlivre in a poem on the masquerade in 1713. The eighteenth-century masquerade is particularly evocative—a subject for reverie and fantasia, a utopian image, the set piece of an age.

I have not wished to dispense entirely with the aura of phantasmagoria that lingers around the masquerade in the modern imagination. At the same time, however, I have tried to ground the masquerade firmly in its eighteenth-century cultural setting and to provide an account of its concrete social and artistic functions. From the start I attempted to produce what might be called a phenomenology of the English masquerade—some intuition of the meaning it held for its participants, as well as for those who merely observed or wrote about it from afar.

The historical and literary aspects of the book were inseparable from the beginning. To grasp the complex part the masquerade played in eighteenth-century English culture one must necessarily turn to the prose and poetry of the age. To its contemporaries the masquerade represented diverse things: the decay of civilization, frivolity and freedom, sexual and moral chaos, a liberating escape from decorum. It would be hard indeed to get much sense of this protean phenomenon without consulting Walpole's letters, the writings of the popular essayists, the satiric poems and pamphlets of the anti-masquerade writers, the flamboyant set pieces in eighteenth-century comic drama, and the memorable masquerade scenes in the novels of Richardson, Defoe, Fielding and Burney. Given the masquerade's evanescence and the paucity of other sorts of documentation, we must often rely on the rich devices of literature to supply us with a notion of what the occasion was like.

But the history of the masquerade likewise offers a remarkable insight into the imaginative life of the period. If descriptions of masquerades are ubiquitous in eighteenth-century writing, their importance has seldom been acknowledged. To understand the historical significance of the masquerade is also to understand the workings of a classic literary topos. True, masquerades in eighteenth-century literature may seem at first glance as ambiguous or idiosyncratic as the occasion that gave rise to them, but they can tell us much about literary representation. For the topos invariably reflected the disruptive power the masquerade held in contemporary civilization. I concentrate here on early fiction, where the masquerade episode had a particularly charismatic role. Though typically presented as a moral emblem, the image of a corrupt and pleasure-seeking populace, the masquerade was also an indispensable plot-catalyst, the mysterious scene out of which the essential drama of the fiction emerged. All the ambivalence that the masquerade aroused in English public life—where it was at once the sign of depravity and freedom, corruption and delight—was thus replicated in its fictional representation. Indeed I will argue in what follows that the novel, above all other genres, registered most symptomatically the paradoxical carnivalization of eighteenth-century society.

In writing this book I have benefited greatly from the recent growth of theoretical interest in carnival and its offshoots. (As the reader will discover, I include the masquerade under the general rubric of the carnivalesque.) Since Bakhtin's magisterial *Rabelais and His World* first appeared in the 1960's, the idea of carnival has attracted widespread attention from scholars in many different disciplines. By its very nature the subject may invite attempts at all-inclusiveness. Bakhtin's own work is encyclopedic, encompassing the history of the carnivalesque in Western literature from the Middle Ages through the eighteenth century. I focus here, however, on a single period and a single national experience. This book is not an account of masquerades in Europe, or even, at many points, an overview of popular-cultural elements in literature. The catalyst for the book was my interest in a single work: Fielding's satiric poem on the masquerade written in 1728. My curiosity about this little-read piece gradually led me to other writings on the subject, and ultimately to the history of the English masquerade itself. My impulse throughout the book has likewise been to start with the specific—the historical detail or discrete set piece—and move from there to more general considerations. The method of investigation is similar in some respects to the psychoanalytic case history or anthropological field study, two theoretical models I value especially highly. But the final effect, I hope, might also be compared with the masquerade itself, which drew its life from the richness—and strangeness— of its particulars.

I could not have finished this book without assistance from a number of quarters. I would like to thank first of all the Society of Fellows at Harvard University, under whose generous auspices I wrote the first chapters. I am similarly grateful to Stanford University for nominating me for an NEH summer grant in 1983 and for providing research funds in 1984 so that I might complete the manuscript.

Preface

My scholarly and personal debts are many. To Paul Alkon, John Bender, Bliss Carnochan, and especially Herbert Lindenberger I owe many thanks for their inspirational support, as well as for the rigorous and helpful criticisms each has given my work over the past two years. While I cannot say I have met all their objections, I have tried to take their advice to heart. I am likewise grateful to Ronald Paulson and John Richetti for inviting me to present my research on the masquerade at sessions they organized at meetings of the American Society for Eighteenth-Century Studies and the Modern Language Association in 1983, and for the encouragement, again, that each has given me. I thank the editors of *PMLA* and *Eighteenth-Century Studies* for granting me permission to reprint material that originally appeared in those journals, as I do the many colleagues who supplied much-needed "masquerade intelligence"—references to masquerades in fact and fiction: Paula Backscheider, Marshall Brown, Liz Cohen, Jackson Cope, Chris Cullens, Margaret Doody, Robert Hume, Kelly Hurley, Jeslyn Medoff, Thomas Moser, Dorothea von Muecke, Harriet Napier, Felicity Nussbaum, Ruth Perry, Susan Staves, Wilfred Stone, and Richard Wendorf. Aileen Ribeiro (whose study of masquerade costume has been an invaluable resource) was kind enough to assist me in finding some of the illustrations. And in the past year I have benefited immensely from the outstanding editorial advice of Helen Tartar of Stanford University Press. Finally, I would like to thank Dennis Allen, Susan Blaustein, George Dekker, Ingrid Gifford, Arturo Islas, Diane Middlebrook, Kristin Midelfort, Nancy Miller, Rob Polhemus, Don Reid, Leon Wieseltier, and especially Doree Allen for help of other, less translatable kinds.

T.C.

Contents

1. The Masquerade and Eighteenth-Century England   1

2. Travesty and the Fate of the Carnivalesque   52

3. Literary Transformations: The Masquerade in English Fiction   110

4. The Recarnivalization of Pamela: Richardson's *Pamela*, Part 2   130

5. Masquerade and Allegory: Fielding's *Amelia*   177

6. Masquerade and Utopia I: Burney's *Cecilia*   253

7. Masquerade and Utopia II: Inchbald's *A Simple Story*   290

8. Epilogue:
The Masquerade Topos After the Eighteenth Century   331

Notes   349   Works Cited   371

Sources of Illustrations   383   Index   387

Masquerade and Civilization

1

The Masquerade and Eighteenth-Century England

The history of human pleasures—of festivity, games, jokes, and amusements—has seldom met with the same dignified attention accorded the history of human suffering. Wars, plagues, and collective miseries of all kinds have always been conventional historical and philosophical topoi; laughter, as Mikhail Bakhtin observed in his monumental work on carnival, has not.[1] This imbalance reflects a standard interpretation of experience: that suffering is perpetual, fundamental to human life, and hence worthy of discourse. Pleasures, felt to be discontinuous and fleeting (not to mention morally and theologically problematic), remain trivial. In Goethe's words, "the most lively and exquisite delights are, like horses racing past, the experience of an instant only, which leaves scarcely a trace on our soul."[2] How to write a history of such instants?

Approaching the eighteenth-century masked assembly, one confronts a similar ideological problem. For along with snuff-boxes, beauty patches, follies, and fêtes champêtres, the masquerade inescapably figures in the stereotypic imagery of eighteenth-century frivolity. In our collective reconstructions of the age, we tend to think of masquerades either in purely decorative terms—as part of an operatic, mythic eighteenth century, an imaginary ancien régime—or only slightly less reductively as an uncomplicated sign of the licentiousness and social disengagement of the upper classes of the period. We inherit this attitude in large part from the eighteenth century itself. For though the masquerade was an established and ubiquitous feature of urban public life in England from the 1720's on, it was universally condemned by contemporary moralists and satirists as a foolish, irrational, and corrupt activity perpetrated by irresponsible people of fashion. The literary and visual references to the masquerade most familiar to us now reinforce this view. Addison's *Spectator* essays on the "Midnight Masque"; Pope's references in *The Rape of the Lock* and *The Dunciad*; Hogarth's attacks in *Masquerades and Operas*, the satirical *Masquerade Ticket*, *A Harlot's Progress*, and *Marriage à la Mode*; Johnson's plea, in *London*, for a return to a time "ere masquerades debauch'd"—all paradoxically deny intellectual significance to the masquerade at the same time that they commemorate its excesses and suffuse its representation with an aura of excitement and moral danger. For the Augustans and their heirs the masquerade is a trope not just for the corruption of taste but for inanity.

I would like to make more complex historical and intellectual claims for the masquerade. Throughout the eighteenth century the masked assembly, that "promiscuous Gathering," was at once a highly visible public institution and a highly charged image—a social phenomenon of expansive proportions and a cultural sign of considerable potency. It is easy to forget the pervasiveness and magnitude of these events. During the second and third decades of the century, Count Heidegger's elaborate masquerades at the Haymarket drew up to a thousand antic "masks" weekly. Later, public masquerades at Vauxhall and Ranelagh, the Dog and Duck Gardens, Almack's, and the Pantheon, Mrs. Cornelys's extravaganzas at Carlisle House, and those prodigious costumed assemblies held in celebration of special events—the Jubilee of 1749, the King of Denmark's visit in 1768, the Shakespeare Jubilee of 1769—attracted crowds num-

bering in the thousands.[3] London newspapers regularly advertised subscription masquerades, as well as costume warehouses
at which fancy dress designs—of nun, Turk, or scaramouche—
could be purchased. In the second half of the century, the newspapers ran columns of "masquerade intelligence," lengthy descriptions of particularly elegant masquerades.* The modern
reader is jarred by the surrealistic prominence of these accounts,
which are juxtaposed quite unself-consciously to reports of
troop movements, Parliamentary sessions, and other more somber public doings. The hint is suggestive: on some level the masquerade was news as much as any other public occasion. Indeed,
an odd blurring sometimes takes place in the eighteenth century
between the masquerade and politics: they absorb similar kinds
of public attention. The frequent refrain in Horace Walpole's
correspondence—that "balls and masquerades supply the place
of politics," and "histories of masquerades" take up "people's
thoughts full as much" as national events—suggests something
of the masquerade's intrusive force.[4] The popularity of these
gatherings fluctuated from time to time during the century,
often in response to civil or religious censure, but did not wane
until the 1780's and 1790's.

Beyond its local manifestation, however, the masked assembly
figured powerfully in the symbolic order as part of the imagery
of urbanity itself. For the eighteenth-century Londoner the idea
of the masquerade, with its erotic, riotous, and enigmatic associations, was at least as compelling as the actual event. The voluminous literature that grew up around the public occasion suggests as much: pamphlets, sermons, squibs, and moral essays on
the masquerade abound. These typically deplore its invention
while lingering over its scenes of promiscuity and impropriety.
Writers of popular fiction, such as Eliza Haywood in *The Masqueraders; or, Fatal Curiosity* (1724), quickly came to exploit the
masquerade's sensational association with sexual license and lib-

---

*Most accounts were anonymous. Boswell is believed, however, to have written the
account of the Shakespeare Jubilee masquerade that appeared in *London Magazine*, September 1769. Boswell devoted much attention to the "gallant" Corsican chief seen on
this occasion, who was of course himself. On "masquerade intelligence," see Ribeiro,
The Dress Worn at Masquerades in England, p. 7.

ertinage, while playwrights, initiating a theatrical tradition that would persist through the nineteenth century, adopted the masquerade as a favorite setting for dramatic imbroglio and intrigue. In the visual realm a host of popular prints, like those depicting Miss Chudleigh's notorious deshabille at the 1749 Jubilee assembly at Ranelagh, illustrated unusual costumes worn at real or imaginary masquerades.[5] By the time the "Midnight Masque" makes its ambiguous appearance in the polite art of the period—in Pope, Fielding, Addison, and the rest—it has already become a familiar popular topos, a modern emblem, carrying multiple, indeed protean, metaphoric possibilities.

All this activity suggests that the pleasures (and dangers) of the masquerade were of a particularly revelatory kind. And indeed, the masquerade broached in a peculiarly stylized way certain issues we have come to locate at the heart of eighteenth-century culture. The notion of the self—so crucial in the artistic and philosophical idiom of the period, so endlessly problematic—must be invoked in any discussion of the masquerade. The masked assemblies of the eighteenth century were in the deepest sense a kind of collective meditation on self and other, and an exploration of their mysterious dialectic. From basically simple violations of the sartorial code—the conventional symbolic connections between identity and the trappings of identity—masqueraders developed scenes of vertiginous existential recombination. New bodies were superimposed over old; anarchic, theatrical selves displaced supposedly essential ones; masks, or personae, obscured persons. (In a revealing eighteenth-century usage, one attending a masquerade was referred to, not just in synecdoche, as a "mask.") One became the other in an act of ecstatic impersonation. The true self remained elusive and inaccessible—illegible—within its fantastical encasements. The result was a material devaluation of unitary notions of the self, as radical in its own way as the more abstract demystifications in the writings of Hume and the eighteenth-century ontologists. The pleasure of the masquerade attended on the experience of doubleness, the alienation of inner from outer, a fantasy of two bodies

4

simultaneously and thrillingly present, self and other together, the two-in-one. If, as one commentator has suggested, the eighteenth century was an "age of disguise," the masquerade—with its sensuous, exquisite duplicities, its shimmering liquid play on the themes of self-presentation and self-concealment—must take its place among the exemplary phenomena of the period.[6]

The nature of masquerade costume helps to explain some of the intense symbolic meaning these assemblies held for contemporaries. Theatricality had its formal patterns, and one may detect an underlying system of transformation in the travesties of the age. The masquerade crowd was a shifting, disorienting visual mass, Ovidian in the luxurious proliferation of its forms, but not entirely unregulated. While it was certainly true, as Addison wrote in *Spectator* 14, that "People dress themselves in what they have a Mind to be, and not what they are fit for," at the same time a subtle, nonetheless insistent, logic governed these scenes of collective metamorphosis. As in those "rites of reversal" described by modern anthropologists, a logic of symbolic inversion informed the masquerade. If the masked ball was a kind of anarchy, it was paradoxically a systematic anarchy, a *discordia concors*. "Everyone here wears a Habit which speaks him the Reverse of what he is," wrote the author of the *Universal Spectator* after a masquerade in 1729.[7] Costume ideally represented an inversion of one's nature. At its most piquant it expressed a violation of cultural categories. If one may speak of the rhetoric of masquerade, a tropology of costume, the controlling figure was the antithesis: one was obliged to impersonate a being opposite, in some essential feature, to oneself. The conventional relationship between costume and wearer was ironic, one that replicated a conceptual scandal. Contemporary accounts inevitably focus on the antithetical surprises generated by the masquerade crowd: duchesses dressed as milkmaids, footmen as Persian kings, pimps as cardinals, noblemen as ancient bawds, young ladies of the court as "trowser'd" hussars. "I found nature turned topsy-turvy," wrote a correspondent in the *Guardian*, "women changed into men, and men into women, children in leading-strings, seven-foot high, courtiers transformed into clowns, ladies of the night into saints, people of the first quality into beasts or birds, gods or goddesses."[8]

Like the world of satire, the masquerade projected an anti-nature, a world upside-down, an intoxicating reversal of ordinary sexual, social, and metaphysical hierarchies. The cardinal ideological distinctions underlying eighteenth-century cultural life, including the fundamental divisions of sex and class, were broached. If, psychologically speaking, the masquerade was a meditation on self and other, in the larger social sense it was a meditation on cultural classification and the organizing dialectical schema of eighteenth-century life. It served as a kind of exemplary disorder. Its hallucinatory reversals were both a voluptuous release from ordinary cultural prescriptions and a stylized comment upon them.

We will return to the theme of classification and what one might call the metacritical functions of masquerade inversion. The rebellious element in the masquerade, its gay assault on cultural categories, is in many ways the most intriguing and baffling feature of the phenomenon. One may wonder how such a potentially subversive event retained, however precariously, its institutional hold, and what collective impulses, conscious or unconscious, it may have satisfied. The problem is double-edged, moreover, for any theory of the masquerade's popularity must also seek to explain its gradual disappearance at the end of the century. Why the spectacular efflorescence of carnivalesque activity in early eighteenth-century England, and why its subsequent end?

Before approaching these problems—which may after all admit only increasingly refined description rather than solution—one must start with the known, the contemporary record. Having invoked anthropology and the theory of carnival, I will begin by commenting on the matter of origins and reconstructing, as far as possible, the phenomenology of these gatherings. Such an account must of necessity have its gaps and elisions, for like similarly estranging and ephemeral moments in human life, the masquerade resists containment in discourse. It follows no plot; its spirit is profoundly antitemporal, and its exemplary liberties a spectacular rebuff to all ordering forces, including those of historical encapsulation. The masquerade evokes a world of *temps perdu*; it tends to elude all but the most nostalgic and distorting forms of recuperation. This is a difficulty eighteenth-century commentators faced—the unsusceptibility of the masquerade to programmatic inquiry—and to some degree it will also be ours.

Eighteenth-century observers were convinced, on the whole, that the masquerade had no English precedent. To those who opposed it, and this included virtually everyone who spoke publicly about it, the masquerade was an entirely novel plot against decency, a shocking cultural surprise, a gratuitous and offensive offshoot of the modern world of "fashion." Though the masquerading impulse had doubtless been seen earlier elsewhere— in the Garden of Eden perhaps, at the moment Satan disguised himself before Eve, or in unregenerate Popish countries like France and Italy—it had certainly never appeared before in England, and was taken as a sign of the pervasive decay of English morals. Throughout the century, not surprisingly, masquerades were persistently associated with diabolical foreign influence, imported corruption, the dangerous breach of national boundaries, contamination from without. To its most vociferous critics, the masquerade was a kind of cultural influenza, a foreign sickness that, having invaded English shores, undermined every aspect of national life.

Thus the Bishop of London, preaching his famous sermon against masked assemblies in 1724, blamed their appearance on the machinations of a certain "Ambassador of a neighboring Nation," and exposed them as a French plot to enslave "true Englishmen" by encouraging in them "Licentiousness and Effeminacy."[9] Following the contemporary impulse to analyze on the basis of climatic influence, a writer for the *Weekly Journal* of April 19, 1718, claimed that masquerades were imported from "hot Countries (notorious for Lewdness)" and were an English imitation of the carnivals of "Venice, Roam, and Spain." Only

7

slightly facetiously a writer for the same newspaper noted on January 25, 1724, that "this Diversion . . . has been propagated amongst us, since the Nation has been honour'd with the Residence of a Number of Foreigners," and that it was all part of a Continental conspiracy to neutralize the superior beauties of English women by forcing them to hide their charms under masks. This same critic added that the masquerade did not sit well with the "native Stupidity" of the English, who were ill-equipped for the sorts of wit and repartee the costumed assembly demanded—a drollery that echoes feebly throughout the century. For all its exotic derangements, the masquerade was thought to provide little remedy for that gelid national disorder, the spleen.

These impressions are useful in one sense and reductive in another. Foreign fashions did play a part, and it is true, technically speaking, that nothing generally recognized as a masquerade, in the eighteenth-century sense of the word, took place in England before the 1700's. Similar events had been known elsewhere, however. The word *masquerade* is of foreign origin, and was originally applied only to Continental festivals. Its etymology is ambiguous: the *Oxford English Dictionary* suggests either an Arabic source, *maskhara*[h], meaning "laughing-stock" or "buffoon," or a connection with the Old French *mascurer* (*mascherer*), "to blacken (the face)," and perhaps more distantly, the Latin *macula* or "spot." The early forms *mascarado* and *mascurado* appear in English in the late sixteenth and the seventeenth century, but only in the context of foreign custom. In his *Introduction to Practicall Musicke* of 1597, Thomas Morley speaks of the Italian "mascaradoes," and in 1660, in a translation of Vincent Le Blanc's *Travels*, Francis Brooke mentions the Spaniards' "Mascuradoes," at which they disguised themselves as devils. In the decades following the Restoration, *masquerade*, as Dryden's writing attests, is used to speak of the lavish masked entertainments at the court of Charles II. (I will return later to the related yet distinctive term *masque*.) The *Oxford English Dictionary* lists a reference in one of Walpole's letters (1742) as the first application of *masquerade* to a popular public diversion, yet this attribution is far too late: the word had come into local use by the second decade of the eighteenth century, when the masquerade was itself established in London as a fashionable commercial entertainment. Masquerades are topical from roughly 1710 on. Witness Addison's *Spectator* pieces of 1711, or Pope's letter to Mary Wortley Montagu in 1717: "For the news in London, I'll sum it up in short; we have masquerades at the theatre in the Haymarket, of Mr. Heideker's institution."*

And from one perspective it does look as though masquerades were, as the critics held, introduced into England from without. A number of notable foreign visitors (some, like Heidegger, associated with the emigré court of Hanover) had much to do, superficially at least, with popularizing the masked assembly in the first decades of the century. Louis, Duc d'Aumont, the French ambassador to England (and undoubtedly the same ambassador to whom the Bishop of London referred in his sermon) held some of the earliest masquerades at Somerset House in 1713. These were private diplomatic affairs, and since the duke was eager to ingratiate himself with the English aristocracy, the charges of political motivation were not perhaps entirely unfounded. One of the first poems on the subject of the masquerade, Mrs. Centlivre's, is dedicated to the Duc d'Aumont.[10]

But the English taste for masquerading was also encouraged by other, more obviously opportunistic, entrepreneurs from abroad. The two most famous masquerade promoters of the

---

*Montagu, *Letters and Works*, pp. 428–29. Contemporary dictionaries define *masquerade* variously, and often connect it with foreign carnival. In John Kersey's *New English Dictionary* (London, 1737), "Mascarade or Masquerade" is defined as "a Company of Persons, having Masks or Vizards on, and dancing to divert themselves; especially on some Festival; Whence one that is fantastically dress'd, as if he intended to disguise himself, is said *To walk in Masquerade*." In Nathan Bailey's *Dictionarium Britannicum*, 2d ed. (London, 1736), "Masquerade" is listed as "an assembly of persons mask'd and in disguised habits, meeting to dance and divert themselves." E. Chambers's *Cyclopedia*, 7th ed. (London, 1752), has the following definition: "an assembly of persons masqued or disguised; meeting to dance, and divert themselves. This is now much in use with us, and has been long a very common practice abroad, especially in carnival time." And in Johnson's *Dictionary*, 4th ed. (London, 1773), "Masquerade" is defined, succinctly enough, as "a diversion in which the company is masked." Johnson's illustrative quotation is from Swift: "I find that our art hath not gained much by the happy revival of *masquerading* among us."

century, John James ("Count") Heidegger (1659?–1749) and Theresa Cornelys (1723–97), both had somewhat mysterious and distinctly un-English origins. Heidegger, ridiculed by Pope and Fielding for encouraging the new taste in Italian opera (he was an early supporter of Handel) as well as for his frightening personal ugliness, was Swiss. He became manager of the Haymarket in 1713, and began orchestrating weekly masked assemblies there by 1717, on the nights when operas were not performed. These were the first major public masquerades in England. Admission was by ticket (sold in coffee houses and at the Haymarket itself), and the "Midnight Masque" grew steadily in popularity. In spite of civil and religious opposition, including a presentment from the Middlesex Grand Jury in 1729 that described him as "the principal promoter of vice and immorality," Heidegger continued to hold masquerades into the 1730's. He served as Master of the Revels to George II, who despite being forced at one point after much public outcry to issue a proclamation denouncing masquerades, was himself an occasional incognito guest at various London masked assemblies.[11]

Mrs. Cornelys succeeded Heidegger as the main sponsor of masquerades in London in the second half of the century. She was Venetian-born, an opera singer and friend of Casanova. After a number of adventures she emigrated to England in 1746 and sang at the Haymarket as "Madame Pompeati." (A connection between the masquerade and opera persisted throughout the century.) She managed her first subscription masquerades at Carlisle House in Soho Square in 1760. Described by Walpole as the "Heidegger of the age," she drew in "both righteous and ungodly" and "made her house a fairy palace, for balls, concerts, and masquerades."[12] Her assembly rooms remained successful through the 1770's, despite competition from Almack's (opened in 1765) and the Pantheon (1771), also popular sites for masquerades. But a series of financial reverses, brought about mainly by overly lavish renovations to her ballroom, forced Mrs. Cornelys into bankruptcy in 1772, and she lost her position thereafter as London's doyenne of the masquerade.

Both Heidegger and Cornelys were accused of being foreign

adventurers—out to put the "Bite" on the gullible English public—and anti-masquerade pamphlets throughout the century often contained personal attacks on one or the other, as well as general criticism of the entertainment they sponsored.[13] It would be unwise, certainly, to discount the importance of such entrepreneurs, Heidegger in particular. However one may choose to regard it, he was in fact responsible for the development of the public masquerade in England as a capitalist venture. He had the foresight to see the profit-making potential of such occasions, and under his hand masquerade pleasure became a commodity. The masquerade ticket—later, in sentimental fiction, the fetishized corrupter of virgins—was his fortuitous invention, an easily purchased entrée into a world of fashionable phantasmagoria.

To acknowledge the role of impresarios like Heidegger is not, however, to settle entirely the matter of origins. For we are left with the event itself, which though encouraged and to some degree institutionalized by the promoters, was not wholly created by them. The English masquerades of the eighteenth century had the shape, from one angle, of a business enterprise, and were part of the new capitalist world of public entertainment that was coming into being.[14] But however commercialized and stylized they became, they were always something else too. Above all, they were a vestige of the ancient and powerful world of carnival.

It is impossible to speak of the masquerade without reference to the carnival and the carnivalesque. Indeed, much of the remainder of this study will be devoted to exploring the larger question of the meaning of the carnivalesque in eighteenth-century English cultural life, and in particular its function in fictional works of the period. The classic features of the masquerade—sartorial exchange, masking, collective verbal and physical license—were traditional carnival motifs, and hint, if at first obscurely, at an historical connection with such phenomena as the Saturnalia of Roman antiquity, the medieval Feast of Fools and charivari, and similar "festivals of misrule" popular throughout Europe in the early modern period. Sir James Frazer documented many of these seasonal outbursts in *The Golden Bough*; they have lately attracted new interest from historians, anthropologists, and literary critics.[15] Yet here certain problems of characterization confront us. Though unmistakably akin to traditional European carnivals (many of which survived into the eighteenth century), the English masquerade was also in many ways an exceedingly impure, even bastardized, phenomenon. Its impurity was reflected not just in its commercial and secular aspect; commercialization and secularization were forces, after all, that affected virtually all forms of popular culture in the eighteenth century. Rather, it inhered most in the ambiguous, hybrid shape of the event itself—its peculiar mixture of Continental and English elements, its simultaneous allusion to foreign and native popular traditions. The detractors of the masquerade, as we have seen, thought it an entirely inauthentic phenomenon, a deracinated second-hand imitation of foreign custom, and the Italian carnival in particular. (A commentator in *Gentleman's Magazine*, May 1750, wrote disparagingly, for example, of the "mock-Carnivals" held at Ranelagh House.) The first historical issue is plain: whether such was in fact an accurate assessment of this new and highly visible cultural institution.

The proper response can only be an ambivalent one. Undoubtedly the rage for masquerades was shaped in part by foreign models. The Grand Tour and foreign travel generally had made Continental customs familiar to the educated English public; along with the Italian palaces, museums, and ruins, the picturesque festivals of Rome, Venice, and Florence were an indispensable part of the peripatetic English gentleman's itinerary. As one historian has pointed out, the Mediterranean carnival had itself become increasingly commercialized by the eighteenth century. With the influx of northern visitors into Catholic countries, traditional festivals were gradually denatured and became tourist attractions. Thirty thousand visitors attended the Venetian carnival of 1687; English travelers figured here, as well as in carnival crowds recorded in the next century.[16] Contemporary accounts register the confrontation of the English upper classes with the Italian carnival. Addison, though opposed to the English masquerade, spoke appreciatively of the Venetian carnival

1. Figures in traditional European carnival costumes. Jacob Gheyn II, *The Masks* (no. 3), late 16th century.

in his *Remarks on Italy* (1718), describing the pleasure of "dressing as a false personage."[17] In his *Letters from the Grand Tour* (1732), Joseph Spence celebrated the Italians' "noble art of mimicking" (see Fig. 2). In 1741 Walpole's friend Horace Mann described grand masked parties on the bridges of Florence.[18] And

Mary Wortley Montagu, always a devotee of disguise and masquerade, wrote of the congeniality of the Mediterranean carnival season, and the freedom it offered, particularly for women.[19]

English masquerades were sometimes advertised as being after the Continental manner. The Jubilee masquerade at Ranelagh in 1749 was designed "in the Venetian manner," though as Walpole dryly observed, "it had nothing Venetian in it."[20] Indeed, this particular masquerade, with its "Maypole dressed with garlands" and assortment of royal guests adorned in "Old English" costumes, seems to have had little of the Italianate about it, apart from a solitary gondola "rowing about" on the canal. When one turns to accounts of more typical English masquerades, how-

2. Italian masqueraders. *The Ridotto*, by Giuseppe de Gobbis, mid-18th century.

3. Outdoor carnival scene. *The Minuet,* by Giandomenico Tiepolo, 1754.

ever, Continental influences are obvious. Many costume types
were drawn from non-English tradition. Dresses based on commedia characters—Harlequin, Punchinello, and the rest—created a kind of second-order carnival atmosphere, mediated by
an imported imagery of diversion and theatrical fantasy. Likewise, the wearing of ecclesiastical garb—the habits of priests
and nuns—seems a direct borrowing from the *parodia sacra* of
the Catholic carnivals. Finally, the "domino," a neutral cloak
worn by those masqueraders who did not wish to appear in
more specific disguises, was of Mediterranean origin. Nathan
Bailey's *Dictionarium Britannicum* (1736) defines the domino as a
"Venetian cloak"; this is probably what Mrs. Garrick, described
in *Gentleman's Magazine* for June 1769 as making "a very fine
figure in the Venetian Carnival Habit," wore at the Duke of
Bolton's grand masquerade in that year. Dominos, along with
other masquerade accessories, were regularly depicted in those
popular Venetian scenes by Francesco Guardi and Pietro Longhi

4. An engraving by Remigius Parr commemorating the Royal Jubilee masquerade at Ranelagh Gardens, April 26, 1749. According to Walpole, no fewer than eight masquerades were held at Ranelagh during the Jubilee festivities.

and their followers that made their way into eighteenth-century English collections.

At the same time, almost in spite of what one might think of as its "bad faith," its mediation from without, the masquerade seemed from the start to draw on vestiges of English festive life. England had always had its own traditions of the carnivalesque, dating from the Middle Ages. The Shakespearean scholar C. L. Barber was one of the first modern commentators to call attention to this multifaceted ritual past—to the diverse assortment of "morris-dances, sword-dances, wassailings, mock ceremonies of summer kings and queens and of lords of misrule, mummings, disguisings, masques," and the "bewildering variety of sports, games, shows, and pageants improvised on traditional models."[21] But others recently have enriched his description of English folk practice, notably Keith Thomas in *Religion and the Decline of Magic*.

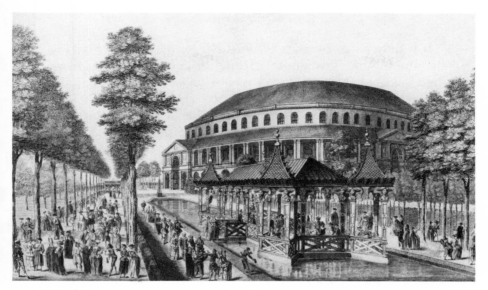

5. *The Chinese House, or Rotunda and the Company in Masquerade in Renelagh*
(sic) *Gardens*, by Carington Bowles, 1751. The first masquerades were held at
Ranelagh in 1742.

6. Interior of the Rotunda at Ranelagh, by Canaletto, 1754

It is difficult to estimate to what degree the archaic masking and mumming rituals of rural English communities—and all the associated ancient imagery of misrule—lingered in popular consciousness in the increasingly urbanized and denatured environment of eighteenth-century London. Certainly throughout the period, even in rural areas, the traditions of the Shrovetide game, of the May Day, Midsummer, and All Hallow's Eve festivals, were on the wane. The work of religious reformers, begun in the sixteenth century, had done much already to weaken traditional rural festivities: the Puritan (later Evangelical) attempt at the "reform of popular culture" was intensifying.[22] In addition the fragmentation of traditional agricultural communities, resulting from enclosure and the flight to the towns, contributed to a gradual displacement of folk practices.

Yet these same factors may explain in part some of the new saturnalian patterns taking shape in eighteenth-century urban society. Historians have lately begun to pay more attention to these contemporary manifestations of the urban carnivalesque: the celebratory behavior and atavistic magical beliefs surrounding public hangings in eighteenth-century London; the popular treatment of famous criminals, such as Wild and Shepherd, as traditional Lords of Misrule; the many processions, effigy-burnings, mock trials and rituals of the London mob throughout the century.[23] Even if, as Keith Thomas has suggested, English society witnessed a general "decline of magic" in this period—an attenuation of traditional belief and practice—it is still possible, on the basis of such evidence, to claim a continued vestigial life for popular festivity in the manifold rituals of the city. Traditional English society provided fewer and fewer outlets for cathartic behavior, though the emotional impulses and desire for symbolic expression that the old rituals satisfied may not have gone away. Throughout the period one senses these impulses returning, in displaced form, in otherwise alienating urban settings. With its liberating inversions and echoes of archaic revelry, the public masquerade might be counted, though admittedly with qualifications, among such late transformations:

it has both the peculiar fervor and the underlying pathos of a penultimate outburst.

Occasionally an eighteenth-century commentator makes a connection between masking and the English festive past. "Antiquarius," writing in *Lady's Magazine* for May 1775, describes the "Progress" of the masquerade in England from its primitive origins. Notably lacking is any reference to Continental custom. Rather, Antiquarius locates the origins of the masquerade in the "Christmas Gambol" and mummery of the time of Edward III. "Mumming," he claims, was again popular during the reign of Henry IV, and Henry VIII was certainly a "notorious masquerader" who first mingled "love affairs" with "the disguises of the night." The court of James I, Antiquarius avers, was a "continual masquerade" in which the Queen and her ladies "like so many sea nymphs or nereids, appeared in various dresses, to the ravishment of the beholders."

The reference here to court masque is suggestive, if slightly misleading. Certainly English royalty from the Tudor period on participated in various forms of seasonal masked revels: Barber notes again the popular aspect of such traditions, which had their origins in the harvest dinner and holiday feast. A Lord of Misrule was allowed to preside at the Christmas celebrations of the English court through the reign of Henry VIII; royal festivity mirrored, on a somewhat more magnificent scale, that of common people.[24] Later court entertainments lost some of this traditional quality. What is now generally referred to as a masque—the lavish musical and dramatic court performance of the seventeenth century—may have been an offshoot of older practice but was hardly traditional in nature. Such aristocratic fantasia—the elaborate allegorical productions of Inigo Jones and others—probably had little direct impact on the popular resurgence of carnivalesque behavior in the eighteenth century. The Jacobean masque was an expression of an elite aesthetic culture, and a highly articulated, self-conscious artistic fantasy. It was a performance, and a performance for the few. In contrast, the eighteenth-century public masquerade, like the earlier holi-

7. Maypole dancers at the Jubilee masquerade. Detail from *A View of the Rotunda, House, and Gardens at Ranelagh*, by Remigius Parr (after Canaletto), 1749.

day revel, was an eminently unscripted, unstaged event. There was no audience, no privileged group of beholders. All participated, and all shared in an equal verbal and gestural freedom. The spirit of theatricality, though reigning everywhere, followed no explicit program; it was individualized and anarchic. In this swerve away from scripted performance, the masquerade again betrayed an underlying connection—not with the tradition of high culture ultimately represented by the masque, but with older popular expression and the utopian liberated traditions of carnival.

The Victorian antiquarians and social historians, from whom we derive much anecdotal information regarding eighteenth-century public amusements, pursue in similarly intuitive and unscientific fashion the resemblances between the English masquerade and popular English ritual. Edward Walford, for instance, in his history of London, connects the eighteenth-century entertainment with the Christmas revels of Henry VIII, and treats them both as vestiges of traditional seasonal festivities.[25] In *The Amusements of Old London* William B. Boulton cites an account from Hall's *Chronicle* for 1513 describing a masked gathering "on the daie of Epiphany at night" as an example of an early English masquerade. The event recorded here, he suggests, is still imbued with traditional feeling, and yet is also a harbinger "on a small scale" of "the fashionable amusement of London in the eighteenth century."[26]

One may hesitate to make a great deal of such hypothesizing, particularly in light of the masquerade's persistently *raffiné* and stylized associations, but one cannot entirely dismiss it. For despite the masquerade's air of deracinated fashionability, it reflected English versions of the carnivalesque in sometimes quite specific ways. During much of the century the London masquerade season preserved a subterranean relation to the traditional festive calendar. Indoor masquerades took place in the carnival months, October through February, and clustered around Christmas and New Year's. Open-air balls and ridottos, such as the "mock-Carnivals" of Ranelagh, were likely to occur at the time of the old spring and summer festivals, May Day and Midsummer's Eve. In 1749, the year of the royal Jubilee, a number of masquerades took place on May Day. Walpole's description of a Ranelagh Jubilee masquerade, with its "Maypole dressed with garlands, and people dancing round it to a tabor and pipe and rustic music, all masked," points to the lingering influence of popular ritual (see Fig. 7).[27] Large masquerades like these frequently celebrated the ancient, quasi-magical rites of kingship, coinciding with coronations, royal birthdays, and jubilees.

The impresario Heidegger, such an important figure in the early development of the masquerade, seemed to awaken popular memories of the ancient Carnival King. His appointment as Master of the Revels to George II played a part here, but one suspects it was also the fact of his grotesque personal appearance that activated the association. Like a traditional Lord of Misrule, Heidegger presided over a scene of travesty, folly, and libidinous excess. Satirists hailed him as a mock authority, a comic satyr, whose distorted and ludicrous visage burlesqued every notion of majesty and noble demeanor. His huge nose seemed phallic in aspect, his other features gargoyle-like—a familiar picture of carnivalesque physiognomy. Fielding, in dedicating his poem *The Masquerade* (1728) to Heidegger, spoke of his face as a "natural masque" and referred to rumors that the impresario was a conjurer. Later he mockingly celebrated Heidegger in *The Author's Farce* (1730) as "Count Ugly" and in *Tom Jones* (1749) as a "Great High Priest of Pleasure." In each case Heidegger's popular reputation as "Cock-Bawd" and cuckold-maker lay just under the surface. In 1724, in a scurrilous aside on Heidegger's six mistresses and "extraordinary Genius," the author of the satiric *Seasonable Apology for Mr. H----g--r* likewise gave an unconscious hint of the Carnival King's traditional connection with sexuality and generation. Although in actuality an eminently modern specimen—the prototypical entrepreneur—Heidegger was immediately endowed, in the collective imagination, with all the attributes of this charismatic figure from the festive past.

In the realm of sartorial spectacle, masquerade costume revivified other aspects of folk tradition. Both transvestite and animal disguise (two of the most popular costume types throughout the century) were visual reminders of popular ritual. In medieval England at the feast of the Boy Bishop (Childermass), young boys had appeared "strangely decked and apparelled as counterfeit priests, bishops, and women," and similar rituals persisted well into the eighteenth century.[28] The she-male, or man dressed in women's clothes, was a prominent feature in the traditional festivity known as the hobby-horse or hoodening game, many versions of which survived in rural England in this period.[29] The figure of the burlesque female—or "disorderly woman," as Natalie Davis has called her—remained a droll and suggestive presence at English masquerades throughout the century. As in carnival imagery, the she-male was often linked with sexuality or parodic motherhood, for example when male masqueraders took the form of old women and bawds or oversized mothers and children. The *Connoisseur* (May 1, 1755) describes "one gentleman above six foot high, who came to the Masquerade drest like a child in a white frock and leading-strings, attended by another gentleman of a very low stature, who officiated as his nurse." *Gentleman's Magazine* (February 1771) mentions the appearance at a masquerade of "two great Girls, one in a white frock, with her doll."

As for animal disguises, these too had their archaic associations. Participants in the hooden horse games had impersonated horses and deer; both disguises reappeared in the masquerade crowds of the eighteenth century.[30] The *Connoisseur* account mentioned above describes a masquerader "pranc[ing] a minuet on his hobby-horse, with a dancing bear for his partner." Visual records of the masquerade suggest similar survivals. As Ronald Paulson has pointed out in *Hogarth's Graphic Works*, the antlers displayed on either side of the Haymarket assembly room in Hogarth's satiric *Masquerade Ticket* (Fig. 8) were the contempo-

8. Hogarth's satirical *Masquerade Ticket*, 1727. Heidegger's face appears on the clock above the crowd. The "lecherometers" on either side of the room measure "ye Companys Inclinations as they approach 'em."

23

rary emblem for cuckoldry (with which the masquerade was always associated) and hence part of Hogarth's joke; but antlers were also the classic accoutrement of the ancient morris dance, and were worn during such well-known rituals as the Horn Dance of Abbot's Bromley.[31] A mock "masquerade advertisement" in Steele's *Spectator* 22 mentions "morris dancers" in attendance at one of Heidegger's masquerades. Masqueraders also sometimes appeared as dragons, unconsciously borrowing from the old festivals of Saint George, such as that of "Snap the Dragon," held at Norwich until the nineteenth century.[32] The *Weekly Journal* for February 8, 1724, notes an appearance by the "Dragon" from the New Theatre, again at a Haymarket assembly.

One should note in passing, finally, a host of miscellaneous "character" costumes drawn, sometimes quite self-consciously, from popular folk types and England's mythic past. The company at one of Mrs. Cornelys's masquerades later in the century included a "Druid, with misseltoe."[33] But other assemblies featured masqueraders dressed as Mad Tom, Merry Andrew, Merlin, Somebody and Nobody, Punch, Tiddy-Doll, and in at least one instance that primeval figure from the English forest, the wodewose or Green Man. This "Wild Man, in a very fanciful dress, all covered with leaves of ivy" appeared at a masquerade in 1773.[34]

How then, given this complex total picture, to mediate between Continental and English influences on the masquerade? Though one may subsume the eighteenth-century occasion under the general rubric of the carnivalesque, it is more difficult to place it resoundingly within any single festive tradition. It represents a curious and often disconcerting mixture of native and Continental influences, a hodgepodge of traditional ritual allusions and crassly inauthentic borrowings. This ambiguity— the simultaneously English and non-English aspect of the masquerade—may be frustrating to the typologist, or to those in search of unadulterated cultural forms. But it is also eminently appropriate to an institution that celebrated so profoundly the hybrid and duplicitous nature of material appearances. The mysteriously double origins of the masquerade, which at every turn obstruct any simple historical or sociological characterization of the phenomenon, accord perversely with its essential nature, and with that relentless structural interplay it set up between self and other, the natural and the artificial, the familiar and the alien.

And what of the event itself—the "Midnight Masque" of spectacular, disreputable note? How to reconstruct those remarkable scenes of disorder the masquerade so disarmingly engendered? A report in the *Weekly Journal* for February 15, 1718, describing one of Heidegger's first masquerades, offers a starting point: it is an epitome of masquerade phenomenology. The account is particularly useful because of its moral neutrality; it lacks entirely that voyeuristic exaggeration characteristic of so much masquerade writing of the period. If anything, the writer here, like one of Defoe's narrators, quantifies a bit too disingenuously the sensual and social niceties of the occasion.

The Room is exceeding large, beautifully adorn'd, and illuminated with 500 Wax Lights; on the Sides are divers Beauffetts, over which is written the several Wines therein contain'd, as Canary, Burgundy, Champaign, Rhenish, &c. each most excellent in its kind; of which all are at Liberty to drink what they please, with large Services of all Sorts of Sweetmeats. There are also two Setts of Musick, at due Distance from each other, perform'd by very good Hands. By the vast Variety of Dresses (many of them very rich) you would fancy it a Congress of the principal Persons of all the World, as Turks, Italians, Indians, Polanders, Spaniards, Venetians, &c. There is an absolute Freedom of Speech, without the least Offence given thereby; which all appear better bred than to offer at any Thing prophane, rude, or immodest; but Wit incessantly flashes about in Repartee, Honour, and good Humour, and all kinds of Pleasantry. There was also the Groom Porter's Office, where all play that please, while Heaps of Guineas pass about, with so little Concern in the Loosers, that they are not to be distinguished from the Winners. Nor does it add a little to the Beauty of the Entertainment, to see the Generality of the Masqueraders behave themselves agreeable to their several Habits. The Number when I was there on Tuesday, last week, was computed at 700, with some Files of Musquetiers at Hand, for the preventing any Disturbance might happen by Quarrels, &c. so frequent in Venice, Italy, and other Countries, on such Entertainments. At Eleven o'Clock, a Person gives Notice that

Supper is ready, when the Company pass up into another large Room, where a noble cold Entertainment is prepared, suitable to all the rest; the whole Diversion continuing from Nine o'Clock till Seven next Morning. In short, the whole Ball was sufficiently illustrious in every Article of it, for the greatest Prince to give on the most extraordinary Occasion.

Postponing for the moment any discussion of masquerade costumes (which in any case are described in relatively little taxonomic detail), one may make a number of general sociological comments. The scene depicted here—the sumptuous ballroom, the night setting, the polymorphous, twisting crush of masqueraders, the overflow of food and drink, the somewhat hectic gaiety—is in many respects typical; it was replicated at public and private masquerades throughout the century. One notices immediately the proliferation of classic carnival motifs. The unrestrained eating, drinking, and gambling are of course traditionally carnivalesque activities. With their emphasis on biological and economic transformations, such activities symbolically reproduced the basic carnival theme of metamorphosis.[35] (The indistinguishability of "Loosers" and "Winners" at the gaming table also repeats in little the dizzying formal ambiguity reinscribed at every level of masquerade spectacle.) The noise of the scene is likewise reminiscent of older festivities. The conversational hubbub, the "flashes" of raucous laughter, the two orchestras playing simultaneously—all suggest auditory redundance, a saturnalian cacophony in which sense is lost in a general explosion of unregulated sound. The "500 Wax Lights" evoke the brilliant illumination of carnival nights. We may recall Goethe's description in the *Italienische Reise* of the *moccoli*, or candles, carried by maskers in the riotous evening processions of the Roman carnival. Here, as there, the intense lighting seems designed not only to disclose the fantastical intricacies of costume but to create a large-scale and unnatural effect of visual reversal, a false day in the midst of night. Such play upon symbolic polarities was typical of the eighteenth-century masquerade.

At the same time, however, one notices elements that jar with the idealized carnivals of Goethian or Bakhtinian discourse.

Most important among these is the bounded setting itself—the structural enclosure of the masquerade crowd within walls, and the somewhat sinister "Files of Musquetiers" on the periphery of the room. The confinement of the masked group, its relegation to an assembly room, or a similarly bounded space like the Ranelagh amphitheater, at once marks an interesting departure from carnivalesque tradition and a sociological paradox informing the institution of the masquerade throughout the century.

The classic European festivals of misrule took place, as Frazer pointed out, in the open air, in town streets or surrounding fields, with all social groups participating. They were scenes of unbounded license, lacking any spatial or sociological restriction. The English masquerades of the eighteenth century, by contrast, were for the most part physically set off from the surrounding urban macrocosm, and often made an interesting pretense of social exclusivity. This enclosure was entirely the design of the promoters. Impresarios like Heidegger and Cornelys never intended to re-create an authentically open carnival space for the London populace; such a plan would have been without commercial potential. Rather, they aimed to create an event with an "inside" and an "outside," and to make participation depend on the purchase of a ticket. The ticket gave access to a now-privileged inner realm, a private carnival hidden behind walls. In order to sell more tickets the promoters worked hard to maintain the illusion that the public masquerade was an exclusive, luxurious, elite form of entertainment—something open only to the "Quality." Heidegger and Cornelys both claimed that their proceedings were strictly genteel, and that undesirables were carefully refused admittance. Such claims were made, somewhat compromisingly, in those same puffs in the newspapers that advertised masquerades to the general London public.[36] Heidegger's line of dragoons (who, one suspects, may sometimes have comically resembled members of the masquerade crowd itself, with its assortment of imaginary hussars and quasi-military parodies) marked off, then, a physical and symbolic boundary. They represented a self-conscious attempt on Heidegger's part to maintain a separation—between inside and

27

outside, between paying customers and riffraff, and between the space of privileged license and the surrounding inchoate, potentially disruptive urban scene.

Much evidence suggests, however, that this attempt at enclosure, though maintained in the architectural sense, never entirely succeeded in a sociological one. Contemporary descriptions of the public masquerade universally call attention to the inclusiveness of the occasion, and the fact that the "Lower Orders" invariably did penetrate the inner sanctum. And herein lies a basic paradox of masquerade sociology: though on one level the masquerade advertised itself as a gathering of the upper classes, on another it was popularly recognized as the event, virtually unique among modern civil institutions, that did in fact "promiscuously" mingle the classes, bringing together men and women from all social ranks. Despite its superficial aura of fashionable exclusivity—the invention of the entrepreneurs—the masquerade actually drew upon a suggestively varied clientele. Up to a point, like the protean City itself (with which it was metaphorically connected), it was indeed a "strange Medley" of persons—a rough mix of high and low.

This is not to say that the gentry did not patronize the masked assembly in large numbers. They did—often their most distinguished members. The promoters' appeals to "Ladies and Gentlemen of Quality" did not go unheeded. The Edinburgh *Evening Courant* described a public masquerade in 1727, for example, that both the King and the Prince of Wales attended in disguise.[37] Likewise George II was said to have appeared at one of Heidegger's masquerades.* Later in the century masquerade intelligence columns were filled with references to the English peerage. Addison complained that masquerades took place "within the Verge of the Court" and catered to dissolute nobles (*Spectator* 101), and Defoe, in *Roxana* (1724), exploited the conventional association between the masquerade and the highest (and stereotypically most licentious) element of English society.

---

*Ireland and Nichols, *Hogarth's Complete Works*, pp. 229–30. At the Jubilee masquerade of 1749, according to Walpole, "the King was well disguised in an old-fashioned English habit, and much pleased with somebody who desired him to hold their cup as they were drinking tea." Walpole, *Correspondence*, IV (20), 49.

The general availability of tickets gave the lie to the myth of exclusivity, however. For the first half of the century, the price of masquerade tickets remained relatively low. A writer for the *Weekly Journal* (April 19, 1718) complained, for instance, that at only "five shillings and three shillings a piece," inferior persons, including "Common Women of the Town," could gain entrance to the masquerade and mingle impertinently with their betters. A surviving ticket from 1744 advertising a masked ball at Hickford's assembly room is marked "5s" (Fig. 9). Certainly some masquerades were more expensive than others: in *An Enquiry into the Causes of the Late Increase of Robbers* (1751), Fielding mentions the purchase by a man of his acquaintance of four masquerade tickets for "4 Guineas." The reference is apparently to current ticket prices at the Haymarket—in the 1740's still the most fashionable venue—though Fielding speaks too in another passage of "inferior Masquerades," where ticket prices were presumably not so high. In Richardson's *Sir Charles Grandison* (1753), after the hero condemns the "common" nature of the masquerade, another character remarks that he rejoices "when I see advertised an eighteen-peny masquerade, for all the pretty 'prentice souls, who will that evening be Arcadian shepherdesses, goddesses, and queens."[38] Whatever the cost, and despite dragoons, it does not seem to have been impossible to sneak in. Such a maneuver is described in an essay on masquerades in the *Weekly Journal* for April 18, 1724. The situation was somewhat more restricted at private masked parties held in the townhouses of the aristocracy, but even here—given the inevitable mystifications of disguise and the general confusion of the occasion—one may assume that some gate-crashers found entry.

The result was a "promiscuous Multitude" such as Addison mentions in *Spectator* 8. The "Company" at the masked assembly, says Ogle in Benjamin Griffin's play *The Masquerade; or, An Evening's Intrigue* (1717), "consists of all Degrees and Qualities; . . . the Great Ones to indulge themselves in the Follies of Life, without exposing their Characters or Persons, the Inferior Sort out of Emulation." Where else can one meet "a *Nobleman* [dressed] like a *Cynder-Wench*, a *Colonel of Dragoons* like a *Coun-*

9. Masquerade ticket for Hickford's Rooms, Panton Street, the Haymarket, with Scaramouche and Harlequin figures, 1744

try *Rat-Catcher*, a *Lady of Quality* in *Dutch Trowsers*, and a *Woman of the Town* in a *Ruff* and *Farthingale*?" A writer for the *Weekly Journal* (January 25, 1724) notes, "All state and ceremony are laid aside; since the *Peer* and the *Apprentice*, the *Punk* and the *Duchess* are, for so long a time, upon an equal Foot." In Christopher Pitt's satire "On the Masquerades" (1727),[39] "lost in one promiscuous whim,"

30

Valets adorned with coronets appear,
Lacquies of state and footmen with a star,
Sailors of quality with judges mix, —
And chimney-sweepers drive their coach-and-six. (35–38)

Again, in *The Old Maid* for January 24, 1756, Mary Singleton censures "the confused mixture of different ranks and conditions, which is unavoidable at a masquerade."[40]

Certain disreputable members of the lower orders—thieves, sharpers, and prostitutes—were thought particularly apt to infiltrate the "Midnight Masque" in order to ply their trades under the cover of secrecy. Common sense suggests the truth of the claim, but there is also considerable evidence for this subcultural presence. *Gentleman's Magazine* for March 1753 reports, for example, on the arrest of several highwaymen at a London masquerade, and their subsequent appearance before Justice Fielding. Professional gamblers and pimps were similarly attracted by the distracted gaming and frenetic sexual solicitation that went on in the masquerade rooms. As Fielding observes in his poetic satire *The Masquerade*, "Thus Fortune sends the gamesters luck, / Venus her votary a ——" (343–44).

As for prostitutes, their presence is ubiquitously acknowledged. It is difficult to find a description of a public masquerade, particularly before 1750, at which participants from the "Hundreds of Drury" are not mentioned. The satiric pamphlet attack of 1724, *A Seasonable Apology for Mr. H----g--r*, was in fact comically dedicated to the notorious bawd Mother Needham, whose presence was seen ruling over the entertainment.* Heidegger and Needham were often linked in this manner; a writer in the *Weekly Journal* for April 10, 1725, complained that "Mother Heyd----r" had run away "with all the Business" of "honest" Mother Needham. Another masquerade account in the *Weekly Journal* for January 25, 1724, asserted that on the night of a recent assembly "all about the Hundreds of *Drury*, there was not a *Fille de Joie* to be had that Night, for Love nor Money, being all engaged at the Masquerade; and several Men

---

*The dedication praises the various "masks" employed by prostitutes in order to practice their trade: "Paints and Washes," the "Mask of Sanctity," the "Mask of artificial Maidenhead," and "a little Machine, or masking Habit"—that is, prophylactics.

of Pleasure receiv'd Favours from Ladies who were too modest to shew their Faces, and many of them still feel the Effects of the amorous Flame which they received from the unknown Fairs." That, as here, prostitutes disguised themselves as "women of quality" and went about entrapping unsuspecting men was a commonplace. The periodicals were full of stories of naive men, like the Templar in *Spectator* 8, who mistook "a *Cloud* for a *Juno*" and formed accidental liaisons with whores. Such anecdotes inevitably had more the air of misogynist disingenuousness than of accurate reportage: it is far more likely that male masqueraders were entirely aware of the prostitutes in their midst, and often attended specifically with the intention of finding sexual partners. The acknowledged presence of prostitutes, one may assume, was part of the masked assembly's allure. As for the women themselves, some undoubtedly were there, like Defoe's Roxana, with an eye to the main chance. But the masquerade may have held other attractions too for London prostitutes, who were, after all, part of a wretchedly exploited underclass. Fielding's grotesquely naturalistic vignette in *The Masquerade* is unintentionally sympathetic:

> Below stairs hungry whores are picking
> The bones of wild-fowl and of chicken;
> And into pockets some convey
> Provisions for another day. (191–94)

Conventional opinion notwithstanding, some prostitutes may have been drawn to the masked assemblies as much by the prospect of lavish sideboards as by overweening concupiscence.

The abundance of contemporary comment on prostitutes at masquerades was at a deep level related to another essential aspect of masquerade sociology: women, including those of respectable position, were free to attend the masquerade unescorted. Of virtually no other eighteenth-century public activity, with the exception of churchgoing, can this be said. "The Women either come by themselves or are introduced by Friends, who are obliged to quit them upon their first Entrance," wrote Addison disapprovingly. The masquerade was thus "wonderfully contriv'd for the Advancement of Cuckoldom" (*Specta-*

tor 8). Masks and disguises protected the reputations of middle-
and upper-class women, and hence, as we shall see in more detail later, removed social restraints—including sexual ones.
Contacts that were otherwise impossible, given the pervasive
sexual segregation of much upper-class public and domestic life,
suddenly became possible.

Much of the fear the masquerade generated throughout the
century is related to the belief that it encouraged female sexual
freedom, and beyond that, female emancipation generally. Contemporary satire on masquerade "whores" was always double-
edged. Many anti-masquerade writers made an elision between
prostitutes and ostensibly "respectable" women at masquerades—implying that the latter attended solely to gratify sexual
desires and hence were no better than whores themselves. (That
prostitutes were driven to their trade by economic needs was
a point usually lost on such critics.) Masquerading women,
whether "Punks" or "Duchesses," invariably illustrated the
misogynist theme that every woman was at heart a rake. Any
woman at a masquerade might be viewed as a "prostitute in disguise"—at once hypersexualized, hypocritical, and an exploiter
of innocent men. The attack on masquerading prostitutes lent
itself to general antifeminist elaboration, and acted as a not-so-
discreet form of social control. By suggesting the ubiquitous
presence of whores at the masked assembly, and identifying any
other woman who attended such a gathering with the "Sis-
terhood of Drury," anti-masquerade writers no doubt discour-
aged women of higher and consequently more powerful social
position from experiencing the heady, liberating, and potentially disruptive pleasures of the masquerade.[41]

We will return to the theme of sexual and social disruption.
For the moment the main point is that for all the pretense of the
entrepreneurs at enclosure and homogeneity, the public masquerades of the eighteenth century were an institutional setting
in which different ranks (as well as the sexes) met with a level of
freedom seldom achieved elsewhere in eighteenth-century English society. As at the eighteenth-century public fair, another
vestige of popular tradition, the mingling of the social classes

against which critics of the masquerade so often railed indeed seems to have occurred. High and low met, as Christopher Pitt wrote, in one "facetious crowd"; and polite society consorted, if covertly, with some of the more raffish elements of the English underclass.[42] The saturnalian exchanges encoded in masquerade costume—dukes dressed as footmen, footmen dressed as dukes—were thus reinscribed in the makeup of the masquerade crowd itself, where dukes and footmen indeed rubbed shoulders in one "promiscuous" huddle. If this coupling of high and low was seldom acknowledged by the masquerade impresarios—or in a conscious way by those masqueraders mad in pursuit of the aura of "Quality"—it surely contributed, like the similarly improper congress that took place between the sexes, to the masquerade's powerful contemporary mystique and subliminal appeal.

Individual behavior was freer at the masquerade than at virtually any other public occasion where the classes and sexes mixed openly. The presence of masks and costumes, not surprisingly, was responsible for this collective sense of increased liberty. In the sociologist's terms, a new behavioral and bodily "idiom" took effect under the universal screen of disguise.[43]

As in the *Weekly Journal* description quoted earlier, "absolute Freedom of Speech" between strangers was the rule. Joking, giggling, flirting—everything encompassed by "raillery"— became acceptable. Walpole, describing his various impertinent remarks at a masquerade in 1742, says, "I took the English liberty of teasing whomever I pleased."[44] Women in particular enjoyed a conversational nonchalance not usually permitted them in public settings. Forms of speech usually representative of masculine sociolinguistic privilege—cursing, obscenity, loud joking—were usurped by women masqueraders. Addison complains, for instance, of women at the "Midnight Masque" everywhere using the "pert Stile of the Pit Bawdry" (*Spectator* 14). Respectable women likewise had the unprecedented right to start random conversation with an unknown man without necessarily ruining their reputations. In Fielding's *The Masquerade* talk between the poet and a "lady in a velvet hood" is inaugurated by the woman; in a similar scene in *Tom Jones*, conversation between Jones and Lady Bellaston at the masquerade is begun, quite abruptly, by the "domino'd" lady.[45]

Several unusual or bizarre features of verbal behavior appear frequently in contemporary descriptions. A sequence of set phrases—usually beginning "I know you" or "Do you know me?"—was often used to initiate conversation between masks. Watching a rake dressed as a "Friar Minor" at a masked assembly, the writer of the *Universal Spectator* for April 5, 1729, observed him "accost a Female in a Harlequin Habit, and with much Eloquence, squeak out, *I know you*. The Lady . . . answer'd with as much Wit, and in the same Tone, *No but you don't* and *I am sure you don't. Yes but I do*, replied the Gallant, *and will be better acquainted with you: That's as it happens*, said the odd Lady, and took to her Heels." A critic in the *Weekly Journal* (January 25, 1724) animadverted on the conversation at masquerades, which "consists in two or three silly Questions, with their Answers, which your Ears are stunn'd with the whole Night together."[46] These ritualized gambits are suggestive in more than one sense. The obsessive verbal return to the question of identity threw into relief the central enigma of masquerade phenomenology, the mysterious nature of the other. "Do you know me?" called teasing attention to the problem, and suggested at once smugly and flirtatiously one's pleasure in withholding identifying information. "I know you," on the other hand, asserted mastery of the enigma, and could be used— sometimes unpleasantly, one suspects—to insinuate a special intimacy with the object of one's erotic pursuit. But the use of conventional phrases also marked a certain perverse orderliness in the midst of verbal disorder; it was as if total conversational freedom were almost too great a burden, and speakers needed still some vestigial rules for discourse. The invention of new conventions at the same time that others were being shattered is, as we shall see later with regard to costume, characteristic of the eighteenth-century masquerade.

The interlocutors in the foregoing *Universal Spectator* excerpt are, we notice, "squeaking"—a reference to one of the more spectacular anti-conventions informing verbal behavior. Descriptions of masquerades frequently refer to the "caterwauling," "cat-calling," or peeping sounds made by a roomful of masks. According to a commentator in the *Weekly Journal* (January 25, 1724), "The first Noise which strikes your Ears upon your entering the Room is a loud confused Squeak, like a *Consort* of *Catcals*." The company "affect this unnatural Tone," it turns out, "to disguise their Voices." There are many references to the "masquerade squeak," which seems to have been employed by men and women alike. The disguised Lady Bellaston addresses Tom Jones in a "squeaking" tone; in Richardson's sequel to *Pamela* (1741; Letter 56) the masquerading heroine is harassed by people "squeaking" at her. "This Piece of ridiculous, squeaking Nonsense" is how an irate correspondent in the *Daily Advertiser* (February 19, 1740) referred to masquerades when he called for a return to "the old *English* manly Exercises."

Like costume, the distortion of vocal register was a kind of semiotic defamiliarization; just as one manipulated the visible signs of identity, so too one manipulated the auditory. On every level there was a shift away from the distinctive, a scrambling of personal affect. "Squeaking," of course, mystified gender. For men the use of a masquerade falsetto suggested comic emasculation: the ambiguous eighteenth-century figure of the castrato may have been parodied here.* At the same time the masquerade squeak had more than a little of the atavistic about it. For anti-masquerade writers of the century, the devolution of human utterance into confused, unnatural sounds was a sign of the masquerade's infantile and even bestial nature. It was simultaneously a descent from adulthood and from full humanity. And indeed, the squeak suggests a kind of collective reversion, at once ontogenetic and phylogenetic, to an earlier stage. Such vocal release,

---

*A satiric connection is made between the masquerade, operas, and the figure of the castrato throughout the century. In Plate 4 of Hogarth's *Marriage à la Mode*, the theme of sexual confusion is doubly indicated—one figure points to a decorative screen depicting the travesties of the masquerade while the castrato Francesco Bernardi serenades the other guests in Countess Squanderfield's morning-room. The scurrilous broadsheet *An Epistle to John James H--d--g-r on the Report of Signior F-r-n-lli's being with Child* (1736) links the masquerade promoter with the most notorious of contemporary castrati.

particularly when it dissolved, as it sometimes did, into inarticulate peeps, hoots, and squeals, seems to echo at its deepest level both the cries of infants and the cries of animals.

Restraints on physical contact eased along with the new verbal freedom. Masqueraders approached one another more closely and more intrusively than they would have in ordinary social settings. Again costume, with its estranging layers, permitted this: the presence of an encasing, impenetrable disguise caused the usual protective spatial bubble around individual bodies to shrink. The pent-up huddle of human forms depicted in Hogarth's *Masquerade Ticket* shows something of the general relaxation of personal boundaries at the masquerade and the jostling intimacy the occasion enjoined. A new, liberated vocabulary of gesture arose. Touching, embracing, fondling, impromptu dancing, and other forms of bodily contact ordinarily taboo between strangers in public—all were allowed. Interestingly, the eighteenth-century masquerade seems to have had its own version of "carnival blows"—those playfully violent attacks Bakhtin describes in connection with the European carnivals of the Middle Ages and Renaissance. In *Guardian* 154, Addison describes being tapped on the shoulder with the end of a sword by "a jackanapes of a scaramouch." The author of the *Universal Spectator* for April 5, 1729, reports being rapped, again on the shoulder, by a "brisk lady" with a fan at a masquerade. The mysterious hooded woman of Fielding's *The Masquerade* ("Not Hercules was ever bolder") slaps the poet to get his attention. Finally, in the great masquerade set piece in Fanny Burney's *Cecilia* (1782), the beleaguered heroine is repeatedly prodded, squeezed, and pulled about by a man disguised as the Devil. He concludes his assault by dancing wildly around her and gesticulating in a horrific manner. That such aggressive antics sometimes provoked a collective free-for-all seems likely enough; *Gentleman's Magazine* for April 1774 describes a Haymarket masquerade that at three o'clock in the morning degenerated into such a brouhaha that "the very instruments of harmony were not safe."

The hectic verbal and physical play—primary signs of that

paradoxical human contact possible when identity is obscured—undoubtedly resolved in many cases into sexual play. The libertinage of the masquerade was its most notorious popular association, and the idea that mass disguising inevitably resulted in licentiousness one of the stock assumptions of the century. "To carry on an Intrigue with an Air of Secrecy, to debauch a Citizen's Wife, or steal an Heiress," asks Reveller in Griffin's *The Masquerade*, "what Contrivance in the World so proper as a Masquerade?" Those "Lecherometers" placed above the masked crowd in Hogarth's *Masquerade Ticket* (calibrated Expectation, Hope, Hot Desire, and so on) comically materialize the masquerade's sexual connotations (Fig. 8).[47] Addison summarized conventional feeling when he wrote in *Spectator* 8 that "the whole Design of this libidinous Assembly seems to terminate in Assignations and Intrigues." To friend and foe alike the London masquerade seemed a kind of collective foreplay—the Dionysiac preliminary to indiscriminate acts of love.

Was this reputation justified? Because so much information about masquerade behavior must necessarily be drawn from hostile or satiric sources (sermons, for instance, and other hyperbolically antagonistic contemporary literature), it is difficult to estimate just how much sexual activity did take place during or after the "Midnight Masque." What is clear, however, is that masquerade spectacle was profoundly erotically charged, and that much of the occasion's popularity resulted from the aura of sexual danger and mystery—the air of "Intrigue"—that pervaded the scene.

The masquerade had its undeniably provocative visual elements: one took one's pleasure, above all, in seeing and being seen. With universal privileges granted to voyeurism and self-display, the masquerade was from the start ideally suited to the satisfaction of scopophilic and exhibitionist urges. Bodies were highlighted; other personal features were subsumed. The event put a premium on the sensuality of the visual.

Certain aspects of the masquerade intensified the eroticized atmosphere. Costume in general was believed to instigate sexual transgression. "The being in disguise," wrote the author of

Guardian 142, "takes away the usual checks and restraints of modesty; and consequently, the beaux do not blush to talk wantonly, nor the belles to listen; the one as greedily sucks in the poison, as the other industriously infuses it." But it was the mask in particular, that indispensable element of masquerade disguise, that was thought most powerfully aphrodisiacal—for wearer and beholder alike. Masks had always carried risqué associations. Conventional wisdom held that someone donning a mask, especially a woman, experienced an abrupt loss of sexual inhibition. Anonymity, actual or stylized, relaxed the safeguards of virtue. Thus one critic of masking wrote, "The mask secures the Ladies from Detraction, and encourages a Liberty, the Guilt of which their Blushes would betray when barefac'd, till by Degrees they are innur'd to that which is out of their Vertue to restrain."[48]

However invidiously put, there is a grain of truth here. Masks are an example of what one modern behavioral scientist has called the "involvement shield"—a portable bodily accessory that, by obstructing visual contact, promotes an unusual sense of freedom in the person wearing or using it. Anything that partially hides the face, writes Erving Goffman—whether mask, fan, newspaper, sunglasses—may act as a shield "behind which individuals safely do the kind of things that ordinarily result in negative sanctions."[49] The mask signified a certain physical detachment from the situation, and by implication a moral detachment also.

At the same time, by a somewhat Proustian logic the mask was thought to heighten the desire of one's partner. The mask mystified the object of desire; it symbolized the absence or withholding of connection. It was a kind of stylized evasion—a formal sign of resistance to full human exchange. Not surprisingly, masked individuals were seen as fetishistically exciting. "A Woman mask'd," Wycherley's Pinchwife somewhat uncouthly observes in *The Country-Wife* (1675), "is like a cover'd Dish, gives a Man curiosity, and appetite, when, it may be, uncover'd 'twould turn his stomack" (III,i). Prostitutes were known to exploit the mask's intriguing power. Ned Ward remarked approvingly on the masks worn by City prostitutes in *The London Spy* (1698); Hogarth's Harlot, in Plate 2 of *A Harlot's Progress*, displays a white silk mask on her table. By the eighteenth century the mask was thus a thoroughly compromised symbolic object. A classic prop in pornographic representation, it was as much a part of the subterranean sexual iconography of the period—a sign of perversely intensified eros—as it was, on a more refined and allegorical level, the conventional emblem of hypocrisy and moral duplicity.[50] Masqueraders undoubtedly both exploited and parodied these associations. Besides being innately uncanny, masks gave a flavor of the illicit to virtually every kind of masquerade activity.

In addition to masking, popular eighteenth-century costume types diffused the orgiastic mood. With some forms of dress it was a matter of symbolic association; with others, sheer exhibitionism. Transvestite costume was always symbolically charged, evoking realms of perverse and ambiguous sexual possibility. Its great popularity throughout the century, as numerous accounts make clear, was due in large part to that sexual frisson it invariably imparted. Ecclesiastical travesties were similarly charged with erotic meaning. The ironic disparity between the trappings of celibacy and the all-too-human body beneath held then as now a peculiarly inflaming power. In Charles Johnson's comedy *The Masquerade* (1719), for instance, when Lady Frances decides on her masquerade disguise for the evening, she comments on the sexually enticing nature of "prudish" dress: "I will be a Prude, a religious Prude; I will appear in all the gloomy inaccessible Charms of a young Devotee; There is something in this Character so sweet and forbidden" (II, ii). Again, underlying such bedroom philosophizing was eighteenth-century pornographic convention; works like Edmund Curll's *Venus in the Cloyster; or, The Nun in her Smock* (1725) had given new currency to old notions regarding the hypersexuality of nuns and priests, and to some extent masquerade costume alluded here to a world of subterranean erotic representation (see Fig. 21, p. 82).

"Prudish" dress drew its appeal, one suspects, from the interestingly muffled look it gave the human form; at the opposite extreme startlingly revealing costumes also contributed to the masquerade's libidinous air. That somewhat outré figure Miss Chudleigh, Maid of Honor to the Queen and afterward Duchess of Kingston, shocked onlookers at a royal masquerade in 1749 by appearing as a bare-breasted Iphigenia—"so naked," Mrs. Montagu dryly remarked, that "the high priest might easily inspect the entrails of the victim" (see Fig. 10).[51] In 1768 Miss Pelham dressed herself in the guise of a "blackamore," with artificially darkened legs entirely exposed.[52] Sexually explicit costume was not restricted to women: the *Connoisseur* for February 6, 1755, describes a gallant on his way to a masked "Frolick . . . with no breeches under his domino." In 1770 one Captain Waters, who seems to have possessed an inspired sense of dialectical play, appeared at Mrs. Cornelys's as Adam, in a flesh-colored silk body stocking, complete with "an apron of fig leaves worked in it, fitting the body to the utmost nicety." The result, *Gentleman's Magazine* (March 1770) regretfully observed, was a certain "unavoidable indelicacy."

Given such a visual aura, one may assume that sexual activity, if not taking place at the event itself, was in one sense or another stimulated by masquerading. Anonymity undoubtedly prompted the amorous. But certain masqueraders in particular may have found new freedom in the exemplary liberties of the night. Precisely those whom the anti-masquerade propagandists most often accused of masquerade debauchery—women certainly, but also, in more coded ways, homosexuals—seem to have had at the masquerade unusual opportunities for erotic experimentation and release. In the case of those members of eighteenth-century society for whom sexual expression was problematic—either heavily regulated by cultural rulings or taboo altogether—the masked assembly functioned as a paradoxical safe zone, a locale in which impulses suppressed or veiled in everyday life could be acted on, and illicit sexual contacts made. Among English cultural institutions the masquerade may have provided for such men and women a singular escape from large-scale sensuous deprivation.

The promiscuous freedom enjoyed by women at masquerades

10. Two anonymous prints commemorating Elizabeth Chudleigh's scandalous semi-nude appearance at the Jubilee masquerade in 1749 in the costume of Iphigenia. So indiscreet was her dress, wrote one observer, "the high priest might easily inspect the entrails of the victim."

is a constant theme in anti-masquerade writing throughout the century. Eighteenth-century critics pointed everywhere to the dangers of allowing respectable girls or women to venture into such gatherings, even when they were escorted by male relatives. An implicit double standard operated in such rhetoric: while male attendance at masquerades was never exactly condoned, it was somehow less heinous; the complicity of women in the "Midnight Masque" was invariably seen as criminal. In much writing of this sort, going to a masquerade is equated with the sexual act itself; the metonymic relation between masquerades and sex becomes a metaphoric one. Not surprisingly, the same contradictions that informed eighteenth-century sexual ideology generally were reinscribed in anti-masquerade discourse. Thus Eliza Haywood warned women readers in *The Female Spectator* (1750) that "women of honour" not only did not go to such entertainments, but shunned those depraved gentlemen who were so bold as to offer them tickets.[53] As for men, she warned them not against going, but against taking their wives or sisters, on the off chance that their mistresses might also be there.

That a woman who went to a masquerade put her virtue in danger was a given: witness that maxim reprinted in the *Weekly Journal* for April 18, 1724, "Fishes are caught with Hooks, Birds are ensnar'd with Nets, but Virgins with Masquerades." The satiric pamphlet *A Seasonable Apology for Mr. H----g--r*, ironically defending masquerade irregularities, cited the imaginary report of the "Committee of Matrons" led by the "Countess of Clingfast," who detailed approvingly innumerable cases of frigidity, obstruction, and green sickness (the classic ailment of postpubescent virgins) cured by attendance at masquerades. "An unspeakable Number of well-bred Ladies (restrained by their Characters from many convenient Liberties, enjoy'd by those in a lower Class) have been sadly oppress'd with Spleen and Vapours, 'till by frequenting these Masquerades, where they could assume the Liberty of talking, what pleas'd them best, without blushing, they have found Amendment of Health." These assumptions worked their way into the more memorable literature of the period as well. For Fielding, to cite one example, a fondness for masquerades is an index to female degeneracy. In *Tom Jones* Lady Bellaston demonstrates her moral irretrievability by attending the London masquerade, but Tom's character, though smirched on this occasion, is easily rehabilitated. Likewise, in Pope's *Rape of the Lock* the masquerade is an exemplary occasion at which a nymph may "break Diana's Law" (II, 105).

It is possible to interpret such pleasure-seeking in another way, however—as an altogether comprehensible reaction to the horrific erotic repression enjoined upon respectable women by eighteenth-century culture.[54] While eighteenth-century Englishmen of all classes had a set of social institutions designed for their sexual pleasure—brothels and bagnios, not to mention the institution of eighteenth-century marriage itself—women had virtually none. If middle-class women were expected to show few signs of sexual desire even within marriage, they were certainly not expected to show any outside it. Masquerades, one may speculate, provided a temporary if problematic release from such prescriptions. Under the effacements of costume women of the middle and upper classes had access to a unique realm of sexual freedom, and a kind of psychological latitude normally reserved for men. "I love a masquerade," wrote Harriette Wilson, "because a female can never enjoy the same liberty anywhere else." In her memoir of 1825 she summarized, only half-facetiously, that utopian pleasure a woman might take in masquerade anonymity: "It is delightful to me to be able to wander about in a crowd, making my observations, and conversing with whomsoever I please, without being liable to be stared at or remarked upon, and to speak to whom I please, and run away from them the moment I have discovered their stupidity."[55]

The risks remained high, of course; the repercussions of sexual activity initiated at the masquerade were inevitably more damaging for women than for men. A man hazarded at most an embarrassing case of the "French disease" after indiscreet masquerade indulgence; a woman in search of sensual fulfillment risked this too, as well as pregnancy, exposure, and consequent loss of reputation, and perhaps most frightening, brutalization at the hands of unscrupulous or violent partners. Literary evi-

44

dence provides a distressing clue to the last danger. In addition
to proliferating tales describing women caught in compromising situations at the masked assembly by male relatives, a number of contemporary masquerade narratives in periodicals and
elsewhere feature plots in which young women are abducted
from masquerade rooms and raped by unknown dominos. Pathetic convention demanded that an element of ghastly sartorial
accident intervene. The heroines of such tales usually mistake
their mysterious assailants for husbands or brothers (an interesting psychosexual theme in itself) and innocently accompany
them "home," where rape ensues. Typically insult is added
to injury: these unwitting victims of post-masquerade sexual
abuse are subsequently ostracized by their unsympathetic families. One may shudder, for example, at the fate of the unfortunate Matilda, described in an "Affecting Masquerade Adventure" in *Gentleman's Magazine* for December 1754. Not only is
Matilda taken away from a masquerade and raped by a man she
believes to be her husband, but when she at last returns home
in a bedraggled, hysterical state several days later, she is immediately exiled for life by her husband to his distant and gloomy
county seat. Likewise, in Haywood's very similar tale of Erminia
in *The Female Spectator*, the heroine, also kidnapped and ruined
by a masked stranger, has to leave her fiancé and family and reside
thereafter in "one of the most remote counties in *England*."[56] For
all the lubriciousness of such stories, one may assume that the
sexual violence encoded in them had its basis in fact. Inclusive
as it was, the masquerade made no exception for the sadistic
or psychopathic. In the face of such suggestive anecdotes, one
must grant to that woman willing to compromise herself at the
public masquerade a measure of courage and aplomb, as well as
a will toward sensual self-determination that was, under the circumstances, both radical and compelling.

Not surprisingly, given the utterly improper nature of the
subject, explicit accounts of homosexual behavior at masquerades are not as common as accounts of heterosexual behavior.
Yet judging by a number of oblique (and in some cases not-so-
oblique) references, one may infer that same-sex erotic contacts

took place. Anti-masquerade writers of the period often animadverted, if euphemistically, on homosexual activity at the masquerade. For example, the author of *Short Remarks upon the Original and Pernicious Consequences of Masquerades* (1721) denounces the fashion of transvestite costumes, claiming that such disguises led masqueraders into sexual "abomination." Citing Deuteronomic proscriptions against cross-dressing, he dwells upon what happens when "the distinguishing Mark of the Sexes" is removed: men and women now find "an Opportunity of conversing together with the most unlimited Freedom; and Shame . . . having here no Place, they greedily run into those Excesses, which otherwise they durst scarce have thought of . . . Heliogabalus, Sporus, Sardanapalus, Caligula" (a veritable rogue's gallery of homosexuals and libertines from antiquity)—all began their careers in vice, he writes, by dressing as women, and have been "justly branded in History as Monsters of Nature, the Scum, and Scandal, and Shame of Mankind." As for the masquerade itself, "These Sallies of Gallantry, I fear, will soon metamorphose the Kingdom into a *Sodom* for Lewdness."

The implication here—that sodomy follows from transvestism—became a standard notion in the eighteenth century: witness Ned Ward's early description of the "molly clubs" of the London subculture in *The History of the London Clubs* (1709).[57] Along with the fear of female rebellion (with which it was often linked), fear of homosexuality seems to underlie those numerous attacks on sartorial inversions—foppishly dressed men, women in periwigs or breeches—that one finds in contemporary periodicals. (As the *Universal Spectator* for December 14, 1728, had it, "In every Country, Decency requires, that the Sexes should be differenc'd by *Dress*, in order to prevent Multitudes of Irregularities, which otherwise would continually be occasion'd.") One might see this novel body of writing in Foucaultian terms as part of a new cultural discourse on homosexuality; the periodical chatter about "effeminate" men and "masculine" women contributed to a larger cultural articulation, hypostatizing a concept of sexual deviance.[58]

It is tempting to speculate on the degree to which the highly visible phenomenon of masquerade transvestism may have prompted this contemporary formalization of antihomosexual ideology. The *Short Remarks*—which is as much a piece of antihomosexual writing as it is a critique of masquerades—suggests as much, but one finds similar ideological overlapping elsewhere. In an attack on a "romping Hoyden" who adopts "Masculine Airs" and despises the scandal occasioned thereby, a writer for the *Weekly Register* (May 22, 1731) implies that she first practiced such irregularity at the public masquerade. In *The Masquerade* Fielding likewise blames masked assemblies for breeding a new "Amazonian race" of women and engendering sexual chaos. "For when men women turn—why then / May not women be chang'd to men?" (131–32). That sartorial travesty pointed the way, in Fielding's mind, to actual homosexuality seems to be borne out by his subsequent piece of anti–lesbian satire, *The Female Husband* (1746), in which a woman dresses as a man precisely in order to satisfy unnatural erotic desires.[59] The elision in Fielding's case, as in others, was clear: to don the garments of the opposite sex was to enter a world of sexual deviance. But it was the masquerade, preeminently among modern cultural institutions, that incited the initial vice. From the satirist's point of view the masquerade was the paradigmatic scene of transgression. It highlighted a new realm of sinful possibilities, all of which had to be enumerated and contained within a larger discourse of displeasure.

Less melodramatic but equally intriguing connections between masquerading and homosexuality appear elsewhere in the writing of the period. Several contemporary accounts describe scenes of homosexual flirtation, though usually between men only, and always in extremely coy terms. Typically a sartorial error is invoked to explain such incidents, but only after piquant images have been presented to the reader. As on the Shakespearean stage, men fall in love with "boys" at the masquerade who turn out to be women; "women" who are really men in disguise are approached by other men. Thus in Addison's *Guardian*

47

154 the narrator, who wears Luciferian but distinctly masculine garb, is accosted by a "Presbyterian parson" who tells him he is a "pretty fellow" and offers to meet him in Spring-gardens the next night. The sex of this person is never made clear, though Addison implies that it is a woman in disguise. Later, when the narrator is followed by an Indian king, "a tall, slender youth dressed up in a most beautiful party-colored plumage," he feels a host of disquieting sensations: "my heart leaped as soon as he touched me, and was still in greater disorder, upon hearing his voice." All is well, however: it is actually Leonora, his fiancée, playing a joke on him.

In an episode from James Boaden's account of the life of Elizabeth Inchbald, the scandal is reversed. Inchbald (who had played Bellario on the London stage) attended a masquerade in male dress in 1781 and was subsequently "charged with having captivated the affections of sundry witless admirers of her own sex." Boaden records that the experience put Inchbald in mind of "the beautiful equivoque in the character of Viola"—a reference to ambiguous female-female attractions in Shakespeare. Though distanced by literary mediation, the episode is nonetheless a self-conscious acknowledgment of the potential for female homoeroticism at the masquerade.[60]

Perhaps the most bizarre account of homosexual activity is that written by a masquerade "Spy" in the *Weekly Journal* for April 18, 1724. One hardly knows what to make of this chaotic little narrative—whether its peculiarities are unintentional or slyly disingenuous. In either case it is an interesting document from the prehistory of modern erotic sensibility. The Spy in question goes to one of Heidegger's masquerades ("to view the Follies of the Place") dressed as a "Female Quaker," though "padded out to the Size of Sir John *Falstaff*." He is accompanied by a diminutive male companion in harlequin dress and pumps who acts as his "Gallant." On their way to the Haymarket the two engage in silly yet oddly lascivious antics. "Feeling about the Sides of my Petticoat," writes the Spy, "[my companion] met with a Slit, thro' which he crep'd into my Pocket, which it seems was designedly made capacious enough to receive him."

After this "Matter of Mirth" they stop at a private masquerade, where "I drew my Lover out of my Pocket, and we danc'd a Minuet to the no small Diversion of the Company."

The harlequin hides again when they get to the Haymarket, and sneaks in without a ticket under the Spy's skirts. Once inside, "the little Fox" creeps out of "his Hole" and disappears. Conventional scenes of masquerade excess ensue. Eventually the Spy meets another "forward young Puppy," who—mistaking him for "a German Woman of Quality"—propositions him. The young domino pulls the narrator into an obscure alcove, where they tussle amorously until, says the Spy, "I was never so near being ravish'd in my whole Life." The Spy's mask conveniently falls off, however, disclosing a long beard, and the would-be ravisher runs off in a fright, "as if he apprehended Correction."

The Balzacian ambiguity of such a coda is that we never learn for sure whether the young man has in fact made a gender error or whether—surmising in advance the true sex of his inamorato and then being rebuffed—he flees in order to escape embarrassing or dangerous exposure. The account never rules out the latter possibility, and it adds yet another element of perversity to what is a highly perverse story to begin with.

If such fantastic tales encode masquerade homoeroticism on a subtextual level, Cleland's *Memoirs of a Woman of Pleasure* (1748–49) may serve finally to demystify the phenomenon. There, we may recall, Fanny Hill's fellow prostitute Emily attends a public masquerade dressed as a pretty boy and is soon approached by a man in a black domino. Though his courtship is "dash'd with a certain oddity," she attributes this to the "humour" of her disguise and not to any confusion about her sex. Needless to say, the man is a homosexual and has mistaken her for a boy. Along with clothes, mutual misapprehensions are removed at a nearby bagnio. Despite the unpromising material, Cleland gives the scene an otiose, pornographic expansion: the man halfheartedly tries to sodomize Emily, and must be politely redirected "down the right road." After this unsatisfying coupling, Emily and the stranger part, graciously if somewhat ruefully.

This passage, as so often with Cleland, renders comically explicit subterranean eighteenth-century sexual mores. Most to the point for our topic, however, is what the anecdote takes for granted: the masquerade as the stereotypical locale for homosexual seduction. Like the Bird-cage Walk in St. James's Park or the Covent Garden piazza, public masquerade rooms at the Haymarket, Soho Square, and elsewhere figured, one may conclude, in the clandestine erotic topography of the London male homosexual subculture.[61] And likewise, just as heterosexual men and women used the masked ball to make illicit sexual connections, so homosexuals made similar if more discreet use of the occasion.

That disguise gave rise, in Addison's phrase, "to abundance of love-adventures" was thus at once a commonplace of the age and a social phenomenon that can be at least indirectly documented. Certainly in the eighteenth-century imagination the physical and emotional license granted by such "midnight orgies" (*Connoisseur*, May 1, 1755) counted among the masquer-

11. An anonymous engraving of an all-male masquerade. The piping devil suggests the masquerade's satanic origins.

ade's most sensational features. The element of erotic theater, with its ironic echoes of bacchanal and fertility ritual, remains suggestive for modern students of the masquerade. It is a clue both to the carnivalesque origins of the event and the presence in eighteenth-century life of strong countercultural urges, some of which may have been validated by a self-conscious appeal to Continental models and England's festive past. Yet sexual liberty was only one aspect of the masquerade's implicit utopianism, and the transfigured relations of men and women merely one emblem of the universal escape from ordinary experience. Costume, we shall see, intimated the larger symbolic dimensions of the event—a metaphysics, as it were, of masquerade. In the philosophic as well as the behavioral sense, the overriding impulse was toward freedom. In the second part of the century, the masquerade became even more exquisite and spectacular, absorbing associations it has never lost—with voluptuousness, intrigue, and a kind of quintessentially "eighteenth-century" decorative sublime. Yet at the same time the event hinted at deeper transformations. One commentator called the masquerade the image of a "perfect Commonwealth."[62] Displaced though they were, the radiant travesties of the evening were also a charismatic meditation on human possibility. As the decades went by, the utopian space of the assembly room came increasingly to intimate, at the dense heart of eighteenth-century civilization, a new and sympathetic realm of the imagination—the "very Country of Liberty" itself.

2

Travesty and the Fate of
the Carnivalesque

 I have devoted considerable
space to the sociological violations taking place at the English
masquerade—the indiscriminate mingling of the social ranks
and the sexes, the collective return to various sorts of atavistic
behavior, the upsetting of erotic taboos—because they suggest
what one might call the general anti-decorum of the event. Not
all these elements were present at every masked assembly during
the century, obviously: private masquerades, sponsored by the
wealthy gentry, tended to be slightly less riotous. Even critics of
the masquerade sometimes acknowledged that with the proper
precautions—a guest list made up in advance and ritualized unmasking at some point in the evening (usually before supper)—
a masked ball might pass for tolerably respectable amusement.
Thus Haywood's admission that in contrast to the "mercenary
entertainments" of London (where "the most abandoned rake,
or low-bred fellow, who has the wherewithal to purchase a
ticket, may take the liberty of uttering the grossest things in the
chastest ear"), masquerades held in the private houses of great
families, "to which all the neighbouring gentry are invited,"
could be relatively genteel. An early letter of Fanny Burney's describes just such an occasion.[1]

At the classic eighteenth-century masquerade, however—the roiling, disreputable public assembly—a distinctly ungenteel liberty was the goal: liberty from every social, erotic, and psychological constraint. In this search after perfect freedom—a state of intoxication, ecstasy, and free-floating sensual pleasure—the eighteenth-century masquerade demonstrated its kinship, however distant, with those rituals of possession and collective frenzy found in traditional societies. Roger Caillois has argued that shamanistic rites and other so-called primitive forms of festive mania derive their power from the deeply gratifying bodily sensation participants experience—what he calls the feeling of *ilinx*, or vertigo. Ecstatic rituals transport their participants into another world, in which time and space are magically altered. In its most fervent stages the masquerade held a similarly labile and convulsive power. With its scenes of manic, impetuous play, the masquerade often seemed to contemporaries to induce a kind of hallucinatory state: a collective ilinx. Like its metaphoric counterpart the gaming den, the masquerade room was a symbolic space: that timeless place where "whirl is King," a world of dizzying transformation and intoxicating variety (see Fig. 12). Just as traditional ecstatic rituals work, in Caillois's words, to "destroy the stability of perception and inflict a kind of voluptuous panic upon an otherwise lucid mind," so too, in its most extreme forms, masquerade phenomenology resolved into surrender, that "spasm, seizure, or shock which destroys reality with sovereign brusqueness."[2]

Motifs of transport, surrender, "voluptuous panic," and self-alienation evoke the ideology of the sublime. It would not be amiss perhaps to connect the eighteenth-century fashion for masquerading with the contemporary intellectual fascination with sublime modes of self-transcendence. One might describe the masquerade spectacle, with its seething, grotesque, and paranormal forms, as a kind of chamber sublime—a condensed phantasmagoria, a bounded dreamscape of uncanny, disorienting power. Eighteenth-century commentators on the masquerade often fall into a descriptive language foreshadowing that of Edmund Burke and the phenomenologists of the sublime. In

Fielding's *The Masquerade*, for example, the satirist's struggling response to the masked multitude—

> O muse, some simile indite,
> To shew the oddness of the sight.
> As in a madman's frantic skull,
> When pale-fac'd Luna is at full,
> In wild confusion huddled lies
> A heap of incoherencies:
> So here in one confusion hurl'd
> Seem all the nations of the world. (61–68)

—prefigures in a comic register the sublime disorder that Burke later saw originating out of "obscure" shapes and entities: "the mind is hurried out of itself by a croud of great and confused

12. Masquerade *ilinx*. Charles White's *Masquerade Scene at the Pantheon 1773*.

images; which affect because they are crouded and confused."[3]
Likewise, Addison's description in *Guardian* 154 of "monsters"
cavorting at the masquerade—with its obligatory reference to
Miltonic apparitions ("Worse / Than fables yet have feign'd, or
fear conceived, / Gorgons and hydras, and chimeras dire")—at
once compares interestingly with his own analysis of sublimity
(*Spectator* 279 and 285) and anticipates Burke's comments on the
"horrible phantoms," "chimeras," and "harpies" that populate
the poetic sublime.[4]

Above all, it was the remarkable vision of the masquerade
crowd, a dense, shifting mass of costumed forms, that gave the
masquerade its radically unsettling aspect in the contemporary
imagination. To be sure, masquerade travesty had what one
might call its technological function: by ensuring anonymity, as
we have seen, it promoted a kind of group "Liberty," a psychological release. But it also accounted for the uncanniness of the
masquerade, its sheer, estranging power. Costume was inevitably freighted with disturbing symbolic potential. It bespoke the
possibility of astonishing transfigurations, and of a world perennially open to reconstitution. The exchange of garments was
that exemplary gesture on which everything turned—the gay
heart of the masquerade, its defining element, its *quidditas*. It is
time to examine the manifold fantasia of costume more closely,
and what such travesties may indicate about eighteenth-century
culture itself.

One might begin, at a slant, with the ancient analogy between clothing and language. The eighteenth century perceived
a deep correspondence between the two: not only was language
the "dress" of thought—that lucid covering in which the mind
decorously clothed its ideas—but clothing was in turn a kind of
discourse. Then, as now, dress spoke symbolically of the human
being beneath its folds. It reinscribed a person's sex, rank, age,
occupation—all the distinctive features of the self. Modern
semiotics has confirmed the force of the analogy: like language,
clothing is after all a system of signs, and a means of symbolic
communication. Like speech acts, different costumes carry conventional meanings; clothing opens itself everywhere to inter-

pretation by others, in accordance with prevailing systems of sartorial inscription. Clothing inescapably serves a signifying function within culture; it is in fact an institution inseparable from culture.[5]

Like the linguistic code, the code of dress may be subverted. Language, we know (as cases of untruth, false propositions, and literary "feigning" attest), can be stripped, drastically enough, of its referential functions; *res et verba* can be jarred apart, alienated from one another. The same might be said of the sartorial language. It too can be manipulated by its speakers, and made to serve other than referential functions. Because the meanings we read into clothing are always conventional—cultural rather than natural inscriptions—the system itself can be exploited. Fashion is endlessly separable from truth. Despite the existence of what one could call a sartorial social contract—an implicit agreement that individuals in society will wear revelatory, "communicative" garments—one is always free to wear misleading dress, dress that is either playfully or criminally inappropriate. Just as one may lie, so may one go "in disguise."

The massive instability of sartorial signs, and their susceptibility to exploitation, may account for that deep contempt in which clothing has been held in Western culture.[6] Clothing has always been a primary trope for the deceitfulness of the material world—a mutable, shimmering tissue that everywhere veils the truth from human eyes. Inherently superficial, feminine in its capacity to enthrall and mislead, it is a paradigmatic emblem of changeability. (Nietzsche notwithstanding, Western culture's metaphoric conflation of fashion with the tropological realm of the feminine has yet to find full explication.) None of this is to say, paradoxically, that human beings in daily intercourse with one another ever remember, as it were, cultural warnings about the untrustworthiness of dress. Though aware intermittently of the conventional nature of the sartorial code, we remain scandalized by its violation. In ordinary social exchange most of us respond to clothing in a pure, almost childlike way: we interpret it as if it were transparent; we try, in Anne Hollander's phrase, to "see through" it. A myth of the legible body informs most human contact: at the basic perceptual level, we naturalize sartorial signs, treat them as a perfectly readable script—indeed, as the fulfillment of a comforting tautology. Clothes seem to restate the self, to reaffirm, not obfuscate, its lineaments.

Disguise, when unveiled, is perceived as profoundly anti-social; witness the persistent association between the mask and criminality, travesty and treachery. The cheek of the masquerade was that it both sanctioned such deceit and suffused it with a kind of euphoria. Blatantly, joyfully, masqueraders subverted the myth of the legible body by sending false sartorial messages. The masquerade was a reveling in duplicity, a collective experiment—comical and arabesque—in semantic betrayal and violation of the sartorial contract.

The intense pleasure of the masquerade spectacle, as well as its intensely disturbing aspect, inhered at the deepest level, one suspects, in the hermeneutic disequilibrium it entailed. Masquerade dress demystified the sartorial code by exposing its arbitrariness. The travesties of the masquerade represented a collective "making strange"—a play, at once disorienting and compelling, on the instability of sartorial signs. In its power to dislocate, masquerade costume bore the same relation to everyday clothing, one could say, as literary language bears to everyday language. For like literary language—with its constant, incorrigible feignings (which in turn suggest the mythopoetic nature of all language)—masquerade disguise carried an éclat. It was a poetic, revelatory scrambling of the sartorial vocabulary. The conventions of disguise sanctioned that anti-decorum everywhere in effect at the English masquerade; but disguise was itself profoundly indecorous—the knowing bouleversement of a primeval informational system.

The rich variety of eighteenth-century masquerade costume types allowed masqueraders to choose among any number of false fronts. Costume institutionalized a multifarious whimsy. This is not to say that masqueraders were free to wear whatever they wished, for masquerade costume was to some degree conventionalized; that is, certain disguises appear again and again in descriptions throughout the century. Masquerade costume was

13. Trade card, Jackson's Habit Warehouse, 1770. Numerous masquerade costume warehouses flourished in 18th-century London, particularly in the theatrical district near Covent Garden.

14. Black silk domino, English, 1770–90

an institution, with its own pseudo-taxonomy, even as it parodied another, larger institution: the world of ordinary social appearances.

The eighteenth century divided masquerade costume into three generic types: the domino, or neutral costume; "fancy dress," in which one personated one of a general class of beings; and "character dress," in which one represented a specific figure, usually a historical, allegorical, literary, or theatrical character. (I borrow the typology from Aileen Ribeiro's exhaustive history of masquerade costume.[7]) The categories sometimes fused. That vaguely diabolical garb worn by some at masquerades—red and black robes, pitchfork, and so on—could be considered either fancy dress or character dress, depending on whether one saw it as representing *a* devil, one of the class of devils, or Mephistopheles himself. The categorization remains useful for descriptive purposes, however, and may tell us something again about masquerade phenomenology. For it calls attention to—indeed is organized around—variations in symbolic specificity. The masquerade crowd simultaneously presented costumes that offered complete, if false, messages about identity (character dress), partial or fragmentary messages (fancy dress), and no message at all (the blank, endlessly evasive domino). Undoubtedly much of the disorienting ambience of the occasion was due to this assortment of diverse messages. The observer's interpretative abilities were taxed different ways at once; the manifold disguises of the evening both invited and frustrated attempts at hermeneutic totalization. The crowd was composed of both overdetermined and underdetermined elements: some costumes conveyed too much (false) information, others not enough. In either case the observer remained at an alienating distance from the truth.

Of the domino little need be said. It was at once the most perfect and the least inspired of disguises—a simple loose cloak that totally enveloped the body in its folds. When the domino was worn with a mask (or sometimes a little hood known as a *baout* or *bahoo*),[8] the shape and sex of the person beneath were virtually obscured. Dominos were usually black, but could also come in colors, often white and blue. Dominos imposed an enigmatic uniformity on a masked crowd; when too many dominos appeared at a gathering, and too few of the more meaningful or picturesque dress types, connoisseurs were apt to complain of the dullness of the occasion. One Haymarket masquerade populated largely by dominos was described by *Gentleman's Magazine* (April 1774) as "not very numerous or brilliant." Certainly, for those without the imagination or the exhibitionistic élan needed to wear more spectacular costume, the domino was a convenient choice. At the same time, its somewhat sinister power of effacement, its utter incommunicativeness, was in its own way compelling. What Caillois has written of the archetypal black mask, "the mask reduced to its essentials, elegant and abstract," also applies to the domino.[9] It was disguise in its classic form—the quintessential sign of erotic and political cabal, the mark of intrigue itself. In Mozart's *Don Giovanni* (1787) the appearance of the Three Masks in simple black masks and dominos (Act I, scene iv) is a powerful visual emblem of the unearthliness and doom pervading the opera.

In contrast to the domino's cipherlike quality, its mute formalism, fancy dress and character dress were expressive: they allowed for the display of a host of fanciful, luxurious, and parodistic impulses. Both exuded symbolic information, albeit of an endlessly prevaricating, freakish sort. They were, one might say, voluble costumes, at once digressive and feigning.

The most popular subspecies of fancy dress was foreign or exotic costume. As the *Weekly Journal* said, the eighteenth-century masquerade did at times seem a veritable "Congress of Nations." Turks and pashas, Patagonian princesses and Polish queens, Spanish caballeros and Circassian maidens—each disported there. All nations met on the masquerade's enchanted (and enchanting) ground. Not surprisingly, English masqueraders typically impersonated members of national or ethnic groups with fashionably romantic associations. The fascination with exotic peoples was often indistinguishable from a fascination with their clothes; those groups considered most excitingly foreign in the eighteenth century were invariably those with the most unusual costumes. The spirit of Orientalism suffused masquerade representation: Persians, Chinese, and Turks remained exemplary subjects for sumptuous reconstruction throughout the century. American Indians, Polynesian islanders, Siberian Kamchatkas, "blackamores," and other supposedly savage races also offered interesting possibilities for impersonation.

Attesting to the popularity of the exotic, costume catalogues of the eighteenth century concentrated on foreign dress. John Tinney's *Collection of Eastern and Foreign Dresses* (1750) and Thomas Jefferys's *Collection of the Dresses of Different Nations, Ancient and Modern* (1757), both used as sourcebooks by masquerade dressmakers, suggest the prevailing emphasis on the Oriental and the primitive, though each also contains odd pictures here and there of historical personages and allegorical figures.[10] One hoping to pass for an Arabian sultana or a Turkish janissary could find the necessary visual information in such catalogs, as well as a measure of pseudo-anthropological detail suggesting ways to act one's unfamiliar part to perfection. Jefferys wrote of the "Tchingui," or Turkish dancers, for example, that though "they are accounted handsome," they "never mix with the men." Somewhat mysteriously, he added that "their dance is genteel, but their postures very indecent."[11]

A primitive ethnography is at work here; one should not be surprised at its crudeness. A similar impulse informed the masquerade itself. Granted, one might see in foreign costume a mere displacement of imperialist fantasy; the popularity of the masquerade coincided after all with the expansion of British imperialism, and the symbolic joining of races could conceivably be construed as a kind of perverse allusion to empire. Yet at a deeper level, such travesties were also an act of homage—to otherness itself (see Figs. 15 and 16). Stereotypical and innaccurate though they often were, exotic costumes marked out a kind of

15 (*left*). The vogue for Oriental masquerade costumes carried over into fancy-dress portraiture. John Montagu, 4th Earl of Sandwich, in Turkish dress, by Joseph Highmore, 1740.

16 (*right*). *Portrait of a Lady in Turkish Fancy Dress*, by Jean-Baptiste Greuze, late 18th century

symbolic interpenetration with difference—an almost erotic commingling with the alien. Mimicry became a form of psychological recognition, a way of embracing, quite literally, the unfamiliar. The collective result was a utopian projection: the masquerade's visionary "Congress of Nations"—the image of global conviviality—was indisputably a thing of fleeting, hallucinatory beauty.

Other kinds of fancy dress expressed other versions of alterity. If elaborate Oriental wear—silken robes, turbans, studded brilliants—suggested the sublime heights to which the masquerade spectacle might aspire, occupational costumes were its realization of the picturesque. Eighteenth-century masqueraders illustrated the dress of the working orders with considerable insouciance, creating a fantasy world of work made up of dairymaids and orange girls, shepherds and shepherdesses, millers, flower sellers, and gaily bedecked soldiers and sailors. Only the occasional chimneysweep hinted at a world of grimy urban labor, but he or she too—broom in hand and appearing interestingly sooty—could be made to seem picturesquely proletarian.

Again, one might view such impersonations cynically. For many observers in the twentieth century, the very idea of the masquerade brings to mind clichéd images of Marie Antoinette in milkmaid attire: the ultimate picture of ancien régime frivolity. Yet one should be careful not to generalize from such stereotypical and misleading anecdotes when speaking of the tremendously diverse and multifaceted English phenomenon. True, occupational costumes at the English public masquerades were seldom meant as a realistic representation of the working classes. Masqueraders re-created a purely ornamental world of labor. When performed by the upper classes, such parodies undoubtedly could be deeply patronizing, though one must never forget the challenging presence in the masquerade crowd of members of the "Lower Orders" themselves. Elite poetic convention played a part in such representations: particularly later in the century, when masquerades took on self-consciously literary and artistic associations, pastoral characters such as nymphs and shepherds became increasingly popular. Arcadia was always one of the masquerade's nostalgic dream landscapes—in part, one suspects, because the masquerade was itself an unremittingly urban (and urbane) phenomenon.

But as in the case of foreign fancy dress, the great and enduring emphasis of occupational costumes was on symbolic transformation, and the theatrical overthrow of difference. For every "garter'd small-coal merchant" and duchess "crying sprats," there was a counterfigure: the hairdresser turned alderman, the apprentice in magistrate's robes. Whether or not such reversals had subversive consequences is a matter to which we will return. Suffice it to say here that the provocative travesties of rank and occupation intimated a potentially disarming fluidity in the realm of social circumstance, as critics of the masquerade throughout the century were obsessively to point out.

Of ecclesiastical dress and transvestite costumes I have already spoken. The two genres of fancy dress are often mentioned together in contemporary descriptions, perhaps because they were generally perceived as the most scandalous forms of disguise. (In some cases, the types overlapped: men dressed as nuns, women as priests and cardinals.) In the ecclesiastical category, the costumes of the Catholic church were usually favored: the habits of various orders of monks and nuns, as well as the more extravagant and conspicuously luxurious vestments of bishop, abbess, and cardinal. Quakers, Methodists, and other "Fanatick" sects had their impersonators too. The custom of "supporting" a costume—that is, acting out the role it suggested—afforded those mimicking pious or sanctified personages considerable satiric leeway. A Mr. James appeared at the Duke of Bolton's masquerade in 1769 as the Pope and "supported that Character in a masterly manner." Likewise, at the same masquerade, Lord Littleton, in the character of a Methodist preacher, caused general levity by giving "very pathetic lectures to the ladies" while circulating through the assembly room.[12]

Transvestite garb began, necessarily, with a violation of the basic trouser/skirt opposition: as on the eighteenth-century comic stage, male masqueraders preened and glided in voluminous skirts, while their female counterparts strutted in breeches and jackboots. Simple cross-gender impersonation usually merged with occupational fancy dress: masquerade transvestites as a rule wore costumes suggesting professions or roles associated solely with the opposite sex. Women disguised themselves, thus, as hussars, pirates, bishops, and the like, while their male counterparts metamorphosed into milkmaids, spinsters, and wayward bacchantes. Given the peculiar metonymic connection between sexuality and the masquerade, the costume of procuress or bawd remained one of the more ironic choices open to male cross-dressers. A number of contemporary reports mention masqueraders disguised as Mother Needham, Mother Cole, and similar figures from the London netherworld of mercantile sexuality. The part of the disturbingly eroticized older woman was a favorite masquerade role of Horace Walpole.[13]

With its disorienting, dreamlike power, transvestite costume verged on the uncanny; yet other fancy dress types offered even more fantastical visions. Witches, conjurers, demons, hermaphrodites, and druids and other more or less marvelous beings crowded eighteenth-century masquerade rooms; the Devil was a ubiquitous presence. An account of one of Mrs. Cornelys's masquerades in *Gentleman's Magazine* (February 1771) lists not one but "three comical Devils, very tempting, and two dry Devils that every one avoided" in attendance. Satanic costume seems to be both a vestige of the *grand diablerie* traditions of the European carnival and a humorous acknowledgment of the Devil's paradigmatic role—witness events in Eden—in the invention of the masquerade. Steele observed in *Guardian* 142 that "the devil first addressed himself to Eve in a mask," and that "we owe the loss of our first happy state to a masquerade, which that sly intriguer made in the garden, where he seduced her."* In Hogarth's *Masquerades and Operas*, a cloven-hooved devil leads the deranged London populace into Heidegger's ballrooms (Fig. 17).

---

*References to the diabolical origins of the masquerade were numerous throughout the century. Defoe claimed not only that the Devil invented masquerading, but that many of those who attended masquerades were in fact diabolical apparitions. In the preface to *A System of Magick; or, A History of the Black Art* (1727), he observed that "the Devil's first Game, which he in *Eden* play'd," was "when he harangu'd to *Eve* in Masquerade." In *The Political History of the Devil* (1726), he adduced the fact that the Devil

17. Detail from Hogarth's *Masquerades and Operas*, 1724. The devil leads a crowd of masqueraders into the Long Room at the Haymarket while Heidegger watches from a window.

Whimsical two-in-one disguises suggested grotesque and un-natural fusions—the union of opposites in a single figure. A "lawyer" at a Pantheon assembly, reported in *Lady's Magazine* (February 1773), "had one side of his face black, with the word 'Plaintiff' wrote on it; the other white, with the word 'Defendant.'" A similar symbolic joke, as well as the same visual play on black and white, figured in another "double Man" at a 1770 masquerade, "half-Miller, half-Chimney-Sweeper." Also present here was a double figure conjuring up the world of folktale: "one side an old woman, the other a young one."[14] In Griffin's play *The Masquerade* Harriet attends as "a kind of Hermaphroditical Mixture; half Man, half Woman; a Coat, Wig, Hat, and Feather, with all the Ornaments requisite."

The corpse was another emblem of mutability. In *Guardian* 154, Addison mentions meeting a "walking coarse" at a masquerade—someone dressed in a shroud—who puts him in mind, somewhat chillingly, of "the old custom of serving up a death's head at a feast." An actual coffin sometimes figured as a macabre prop. A "dancing Corpse" carrying a coffin at Mrs. Cornelys's "alarmed numbers of the Ladies and Gentlemen" (see Fig. 18). His coffin, like Clarissa's, was inscribed, but with a comically gruesome, un-Richardsonian message:[15]

> Mortals, attend! this pale and ghastly spectre,
> Three moons ago was plump and stout as Hector!
> Cornelys', Almack's, and the Coterie,
> Have now reduc'd me to the thing you see:
> Oh! shun harmonic routes, and midnight revel,
> Or you and I shall soon be on a Level.

---

was fond of masked assemblies to support the belief that the Devil did not invariably display his cloven foot; if he did so, then "he could not go to the masquerade, nor to any of our balls; the reason is plain, he would always be discovered, exposed, and forced to leave the good company, or, which would be as bad, the company would all cry out, the Devil, and run out of the room as if they were frightened" (Part 2, chap. 6). Similar accounts of the Devil's masquerades appear in *A Seasonable Apology for Mr. H----g--r*. Eighteenth-century writers here implicitly followed Milton. Though Milton did not use the word itself, the concept of the diabolical masquerade does appear in *Paradise Lost*. In Book IV, in the celebration of Adam and Eve's conjugal lovemaking, he contrasts prelapsarian sexuality with that engendered by "court amours, / Mixed Dance, or wanton Mask, or Midnight Bal" (767–68).

18. An anonymous plate depicting one of Mrs. Cornelys's masquerades at Carlisle House, from *Oxford Magazine*, Feb. 1771. The artist has rendered the coffin and feet of the notorious "dancing corpse" present on this occasion.

Animal disguise, as I mentioned earlier, had its place too at the Engish masquerades, and suggested another sort of magical exchange. Eighteenth-century masqueraders metamorphosed into dancing bears, birds, donkeys, and apes. The *Weekly Journal* for February 8, 1724, reported only half-facetiously on "a perfect new Sort of Gentlemen Masqueraders," who dressed "some, in the shape of Monkeys and Baboons, others, of Bears, Asses, Cormorants, and Owls." Their female partners were transmogrified into "Apes, Bears, and Dromedaries." Occasionally masqueraders took the shape of mysterious beast/human hybrids. A fanciful guest at a Soho masquerade attended, like an avatar of Papageno, as a "feathered man." In Hogarth's *Masquerade Ticket*, a diminutive monkey in a surplice and a Capuchin with the face of an ape are seen cavorting—the grotesque *singerie* suggesting an unholy union of man and ape. Live animals were

67

sometimes brought into masquerade rooms, where they seem to have functioned as proto-dadaist accessories to costume. Sir William Watkins Wynne, who turns up in numerous masquerade intelligence columns in the 1770's in increasingly bizarre disguises, came to a masquerade at Almack's as "St. David, mounted on a goat." The same assembly witnessed "two girls with live chickens," as well as a somewhat mystifying "foreigner with a squirrel."[16] Human/plant combinations, finally, were not unknown: *Gentleman's Magazine* (April 1776) reported that a man at a Richmond masquerade appeared "in women's clothes with a head-dress four feet high, composed of greens and garden stuff, and crowned with tufts of endive nicely blanched"— the better to pursue, one supposes, a vegetable love.

Character dress, the impersonation of specific individuals, completed the taxonomy of eighteenth-century costume types. Such attire demanded a high degree of sartorial refinement, and it is not surprising that some of the more elaborate disguises seen at the masked assembly fell into this category. Things were made somewhat easier, however, by the fact that favorite characters represented were usually conventional; typically their images were fixed in the visual repertoire of popular eighteenth-century English culture already, through either artistic or theatrical representations.

Masqueraders in search of striking characters mined both high and low visual traditions. Court portraiture supplied models: the "Old English" costumes of Holbein, Hollar, Rubens, and Van Dyke were frequently copied. One of the most popular female masquerade characters throughout the century was "Rubens's wife," after the portrait (see Fig. 19).[17] Henry VIII, Richard III, and Mary, Queen of Scots, were likewise perennial subjects for masquerade representation. The appearance of each character had by this time been standardized, thanks to a series of well-known engravings. The rampant borrowing from portraiture had an interesting feedback later in the century, when it became the custom among English aristocrats to pose for portraits in sixteenth- and seventeenth-century fancy dress. The works of Reynolds, Zoffany, and Gainsborough offer numerous instances, the egregious *Blue Boy* being a particularly

19. Two plates from Thomas Jefferys's *Dresses of Different Nations*, 1757. The one on the left depicts "Old English" dress, and the other the popular masquerade character known as "Rubens's wife."

well-known example. Richardson's Clarissa, somewhat unexpectedly, owns a "whole-length" picture of herself done in the "Van Dyke" taste. In Goldsmith's *Vicar of Wakefield* (1766) the Primroses pose for a group portrait in a number of ill-assorted character dresses—a Venus, an Alexander, and so on. The result is a masqueradelike effect of visual confusion.[18]

On a less elevated plane, popular prints, book illustration, and theatrical representation inspired a wide range of masquerade characters. Emblematic figures taken from Ripa's *Iconologia* and other sources were popular: Fortune, Day, Night, Temperance, Liberty, and a host of similar abstractions circulated in

Tim Visard · Tom Fearidl · Lady Gadabout · Price Fighter · Bagpiper · Rope Dancer

20. Detail from a broadsheet showing 18th-century comic characters published by Bowles and Carver, ca. 1790. Masquerade costumes often drew upon popular iconography of this kind.

eighteenth-century assembly rooms. Literary and theatrical characters were ubiquitous. Extreme physical types like Falstaff and Don Quixote were obvious choices; but characters drawn from the ancient traditions of commedia and pantomime—Harlequin, Pierrot, Punch, Scaramouche, and the rest—were equally popular. I have already noted the costumes based on folk types such as Merry Andrew, John Bull, and Mad Tom; these figures too (the eighteenth-century equivalent, perhaps, of cartoon characters) had been fixed in the collective consciousness by engravings, catchpenny prints, and similar kinds of popular visual expression (see Fig. 20).[19]

Character costumes gave the masquerade, on top of everything else, the look of a chaotic tableau vivant. The scene, said contemporaries, resembled a hodgepodge of "speaking pictures," a phantasmagoric picture gallery in which the sitters had stepped from their frames and wandered free. The fanciful mixture of polite and popular iconographic styles was likewise a visual reinscription of the "mingling" and promiscuity present on every other level. The ordinary twentieth-century observer would undoubtedly be at a loss to identify all the characters in a typical masquerade crowd: we have for the most part lost touch with the world of representation upon which eighteenth-century fantasists drew. A list in *Lady's Magazine* (February 1773) of characters represented at a masquerade at Almack's suggests

something of the richness—and ultimate strangeness—of the masquerade's visual mélange. Here, in company: "Elfrida, her first virgin, Kitely, Momus, Henry VI, Cyrus, Jachimo, Falstaff, Touchstone, a wretched Richard, and several Pierots and Pantaloons," not to mention "Somebody, Nobody, Mungo, Merlin, and Angria, a pirate."

To hostile commentators masquerade spectacle, with its proliferation of incongruous, undulating, relentlessly fantastical forms, suggested nothing less than a return to universal chaos. The masquerade seemed the triumph of unreason itself. It embodied a kind of metaphysical as well as moral entropy, for it projected scenes—gaily, irresponsibly—that had no precedent in nature. It was a *discordia concors*, an anti-nature. Thus Fanny Burney wrote in *Cecilia* of "the ludicrous mixture of groups" to be seen at the masked assembly: men dressed as "Spaniards, chimney sweepers, Turks, watchmen, conjurers, and old women," women dressed as "shepherdesses, orange girls, Circassians, gypsies, haymakers, and sultanas."[20] The viewer was amazed by *adynata*, a farrago of impossibilities.

Critics expressed incomprehension that anyone could find such an occasion rewarding or entertaining. The writer of *The Connoisseur* for May 1, 1755, claimed that he could make no sense out of an event at which wit "chiefly consists in exhibiting the most fantastic appearances, that the most whimsical imagination can possibly devise." He was horrified by what he saw as the masquerade's assault on nature itself; "whimsy" was ever escalating into a profound threat against order. "A common person may be content with appearing as a Chinese, or a Turk, or a Friar; but the true genius will ransack earth, air, and seas, reconcile contradictions, and call things inanimate, as well as animate, to his assistance." His final judgment resonated with Augustan disapprobation: "The more extravagant and out of nature his dress can be contrived, the higher is the joke."

The ironic play on the "genius" and "imagination" of masqueraders is significant; the terms are used pejoratively, as code words for the perverse. Like many a product of modern poetic "fancy," the masquerade was seen as a random, frighteningly irrational flight out of nature, a consorting with the unnatural. Moreover, it derived much of its alarming power from the fact that it seemed so entirely gratuitous a violation of decorum. The masquerade meant nothing to the typical anti-masquerade writer of the eighteenth century, beyond the fact that it was meaningless; it could not be explained rationally, except by an unreconstructed humanity's desire for unreason. It signified nothing but that endless pleasure taken by human beings in the perverse, the skittish, the vicious.

The eighteenth-century masquerade poses a somewhat different problem for modern commentators. If we do not relegate it to the realm of the trivial, the operatic or ornamental, the historically uninteresting, we are apt to see in it not too little meaning, but too much. The sheer profligacy of the institution—its manifold inventions and visual excess—can seem overwhelming. The masquerade holds out too many messages, too much potential significance. It seems motivated on several levels at once. How to "read" it? How to sort out the implications of so rich, so polyphonic, a cultural enterprise?

Generally speaking, the masquerade as a historical phenomenon invites interpretation on at least two levels: the psychological, which reveals its meaning to the individual; and the anthropological, which reveals its meaning to eighteenth-century culture. To go masquerading in the eighteenth century was at once to enact a private vision of otherness, by plunging into an intensely self-absorptive state of fantasy and sensual gratification, and to participate in a cultural institution, by becoming part of a crowd, the anonymous collectivity of masks. It was both a personal abdication from the responsibilities of identity and a group abdication from the strictures of the social order itself.

In the all-important matter of costume (the crux of masquerade), the role of psychological determinants is easy to accept. Common sense suggests that acts of disguise and self-transfiguration include an element of wish-fulfillment. The idea that a specific masquerade disguise might betray the underlying nature of the person wearing it—that costume could be a way of acting out repressed desires—was not foreign to the eighteenth century. Addison, as we have seen, observed that masqueraders wore "what they had a Mind to be," and Fielding, in *The Masquerade*, offered the paradoxical wisdom that to "masque the face" was "t'unmasque the mind." The author of a bemused "Essay on Masquerades" in *Lady's Magazine* (December 1777) concluded that only at masquerades did people divest themselves of the "borrowed feathers" of social appearances and reveal their true natures. "Everyone humours his own genius so exactly, that whoever are well acquainted with the temper and disposition of our nobility in public life will have no difficulty in tracing them out." And in *Cecilia* Fanny Burney brilliantly exploited "fancy dress" as an index to hidden psychological states: in the great masquerade scene in that novel, costumes function allegorically, as the material emblems of veiled desire.

When we turn to particular historical figures and the costumes they are known to have worn at masquerades, our sense of this connection between sartorial fantasy and unconscious desire may intensify. In a number of cases recorded masquerade disguises seem transparently, even bathetically, revelatory. Miss Chudleigh's bare-breasted Iphigenia costume conveys something of that extravagant woman's self-destructiveness, as well as her sexual exhibitionism. Walpole's predilection for the costume of an old woman invites a psychoanalytic gloss, particularly in light of the distinctly homoerotic element in his character. (Lady Hervey described him undressing after a masquerade and standing for an hour in "stays and underpetticoat" before his footman.[21]) And Boswell's bedizened appearance at the Shakespeare Jubilee masquerade in the garb of a Corsican general, though admittedly an act of propaganda on behalf of General Paoli, reminds us of Boswell's persistent fantasies of self-enlargement and his somewhat ridiculous yearnings after exotic machismo.[22]

Freud's celebrated maxim that pleasure is the "fulfillment of a childhood wish" seems to have deep-seated relevance to the masquerade: much of the masquerade's popularity undoubtedly came from the fact that it offered a *Spielraum*, an environment where repressed impulses could be acted out safely, and where shame, inhibition, and social disapproval (at least of an immediate sort) found no quarter.

A strictly psychological approach to the masquerade is inadequate, however. Psychological determinism offers briefly titillating sidelights on masquerade participants about whom we already have considerable information, but tells us little about the masquerade, and in particular about the masquerade as a cultural institution. To treat the eighteenth-century masked assembly solely in terms of individual pathology is at once too difficult, for lack of psycho-biographical information, and too limiting.

More fruitful, if in other ways just as problematic, is an examination of the collective dimension of the masquerade—what one might call its cultural, rather than personal, eloquence. Masquerade disguise functioned as a communal *sotie*, a group flight into various forms of alterity. If the masquerade allowed repressed material to emerge in the individual, it did the same at the level of culture. It was a collective leap out of the everyday, a systematic embrace of that which was other, a mass escape into everything that eighteenth-century cultural categories ordinarily placed at a distance. Freud remains relevant here; but it is the Freud of *Civilization and Its Discontents* rather than the Freud of *The Interpretation of Dreams*. Even as the masquerade assumed its place in English society, it reified a sometimes devolutionary, sometimes revolutionary, anti-society founded on collective gratification. Its profuse, exquisite, difficult imagery symbolized a revision, not just of the psyche, but of culture itself.

To appreciate these implications, we must return to the fantastic specifics of costume. I have already spoken of the various rules, or anti-rules, informing masquerade phenomenology; in the matter of disguising, convention again played an essential paradoxical part. For all the multiplicity of costumes from which to choose, the masquerader was never entirely at liberty. At the most specialized or subliminal level—the level of the fetish—unconscious determinants no doubt entered in, but more generally, a set of implicit collective prescriptions served as a guide.

The overriding object of costume, obviously, was to gratify, horrify, or seduce others. It was the masquerader's duty to be beautiful or uncanny, but never insipid. Several anti-conventions defined how such a visual éclat was to be achieved. At the most banal level one was not allowed to come "disguised" as oneself. Wildean paradoxes did not figure in the eighteenth-century masquerade. At his public balls Heidegger, for instance, refused entry to anyone not attired in something clearly identifiable as costume: either a mask and domino or one of the other recognized costume types. The mask—that "particle of some other world," in Bakhtin's phrase—was the principal sign of self-alienation. In mask and costume one rejected "conformity to oneself."[23]

The costume's object was radical festivity, a violent transformation of everyday appearance. Subtle dislocations of one's ordinary appearance—a tiny yet significant detail askew, a vaguely unsettling wrongness about one's clothing—were not much appreciated. Masqueraders did not dress as themselves, nor did they dress as people like themselves. Dukes did not disguise themselves as marquises, or footmen as apprentices. At the moment of unmasking (if and when it came), one's disguise, seen suddenly in relation to one's real identity, was to excite the onlooker by its absolute impropriety. The conceptual gap separating true and false selves was ideally an abyss.

We can restate this sartorial anti-decorum as a single carnival convention: one was obliged to appear, in some sense, as one's opposite. As we have seen, masqueraders exploited a host of symbolic oppositions in their search after the outré: sexual, eco-

75

nomic, and racial incongruities; the oppositions between human and animal, natural and supernatural, past and present, the living and the dead. But the basic convention persisted underneath multiple reinscriptions: the relationship between costume and wearer expressed a conceptual antithesis, a secret paradox. One's disguise represented not just a skewing or modification of the truth, but its reversal. This was the endlessly repeated joke of disguise, its *sottisme*: that it held out a totalizing sartorial message, but falsified the subject in the most radical way possible. It defined a second self at the farthest remove from the actual. It was, in short, ironic.

However comically conceived the inversions of the masquerade, they had serious implications. Donning a costume brought into being a symbolic scandal. The costumed body posed a mysterious relationship between antinomies, connection where before there had only been separation. On the individual level the conventional alienation between self and other was phantasmagorically overcome. Masquerade disguise affirmed the appropriability of the shape, the very body, of the other: biological separateness itself was ritually revoked. Bodies seemed to fuse; the "two-in-one" became a momentary hallucinatory reality. In a single carnival gesture the Aristotelian principle of identity, the foundation of rationalism, was overthrown. Disguise was a glamorous, contradictory extension of the physical body—a capricious addition that suggested the body going beyond itself, metamorphosing before one's eyes, caught in the very moment of transformation from one pole to another. Like the "carnivalized" body of ancient festive tradition described by Bakhtin, the double body of masquerade "is not a closed, complete unit; it is unfinished, outgrows itself, transgresses its own limits."[24]

But the visible overthrow of the self-sufficient body, "the completely atomized being," was simultaneously, by symbolic implication, an overthrow of the itemized cosmos of eighteenth-century culture. Translated to a collective level, the level of ideology, the festive fusions of the masquerade suggested the breakdown of larger conceptual oppositions. By making magically available the body of the other, the body of dream and taboo, costume collapsed the boundary between individuals. But this collapse in turn hinted at another, greater indiscretion: the collapse of ideological polarities, those divisions around which culture itself was organized. For when the human body escaped its own boundaries, and disobeyed the laws of metaphysics by becoming its own opposite, the body politic, the civil body, was also affected. The fundamental logic of culture—the logic of categorical opposition—was subverted.

Thus masquerade metamorphosis insinuated a new global fluidity, not only between bodies but between states of being. Foreign costume breached ideological divisions between the indigenous and the exotic, European and Oriental, the light and the dark races, Northern and Southern. Occupational dress overthrew the hierarchy of rank and class, destroying distinctions between masters and servants, consumers and producers. Ecclesiastical disguise merged sacred and profane, celibate and noncelibate. Transvestite costume mysteriously negated the antinomy of gender, and animal disguise allowed one to pass out of the human realm altogether. The dress of devil, witch, corpse, and the like obviated ineffable distinctions between natural and supernatural, *heimlich* and *unheimlich*.

Even character costumes and the mute, effacing domino represented forms of conceptual transgression. The impersonation of historical figures subverted the separation between past and present, antiquity and modernity. In the place of temporal dialectic it substituted an eerie simultaneity, a palimpsest of epochs. Disguises based on literary, mythic, and allegorical figures enacted a similar movement between ontologically distinct realms—between those of real and unreal beings, living and fictive entities. Finally, the blank, obfuscating domino rendered perhaps the most drastic and unsettling dialectical play of all. With its shifting, undulating materiality, the domino represented on the one hand a kind of Ur-costume, a paradigmatic swatch of cloth from which any sartorial fancy might be formed: an emblem of potentiality. By its sheer incommunicativeness, it was on the other hand a sign of negativity, of the erasure or voiding of all form. It colonized either a region of becoming or a region of non-being. In both cases to wear a domino was to exempt oneself, after a fashion, from the realm of being—to cross symbolically from the realm of what "was" into the realm of what "might be" or of what "was not." This was Heideggerian play indeed.

At the deepest level the masquerade's work was that of deinstitutionalization. Eighteenth-century English culture was founded on a set of institutionalized oppositions: European and Oriental, masculine and feminine, human and animal, natural and supernatural, and so on. Each institution—each cultural category—depended for its existence on an opposite, and vice versa. As in one of Claude Lévi-Strauss's exemplary traditional societies, cultural classification, the collective ordering of experience, was at heart dialectical; the conceptual world of English society was founded on certain hypostatized binary pairs, or symbolic contraries.[25]

At the masquerade, however, counterposed institutions everywhere collapsed into one another, as did ideological categories: masculinity into femininity, "Englishness" into exoticism, humanity into bestiality. Without the principle of opposition, the ordering principle of civilization itself, the classification of entities became impossible. The whirling, saturnalian scene triumphed over cosmos; an anti-world of protean, oleaginous, constantly changing shapes came into being, replacing the rationalized world of eighteenth-century classification. As in a kind of cosmic opera buffa, order capitulated to imbroglio.

The visionary anti-society the masquerade projected was at heart utopian, for along with other oppositions, that of upper class and lower class was temporarily abolished. Roland Barthes's maxim, "Once the antinomy is rejected, once the paradigm is blurred, utopia begins," has its relevance here: the potent transformations of the masquerade implicitly challenged those hierarchical valuations built into the system of cultural oppositions.[26] When an equivalence, even a hallucinatory one, is proposed between two halves of an antithesis, when one pole can no longer be fully distinguished from the other, an ideological ranking of terms within the pair can no longer be performed.

78

In the moment of masquerade saturnalia, the archaic chain of being, with its value-laden system of interlocking vertical contrasts, was gloriously dismantled. That all-pervasive "Liberty" to which the masquerade aspired was not just political freedom of the sort articulated later in the century by various revolutionary movements, but an encompassing metaphysical libertinage—a convulsive negation of every form of ideological discrimination. The categories of domination folded endlessly into the categories of powerlessness, and vice versa. The venerated topoi of eighteenth-century culture (humanity, masculinity, adulthood, nobility, rationality) merged with their despised opposites (the bestial, effeminacy, childishness, servility, madness).

Those who observed the masquerade from the outside, without pleasure or liberality, unanimously castigated its disorienting anti-taxonomic force. To be sure, like anti-theatrical writing, anti-masquerade discourse often focused on dissimulation, finding in it the explicit sign of a society shot through with illusion and deception. The anti-masquerade complaint overlapped in many ways with the contemporary "anti-theatrical prejudice" that Jonas Barish has recently analyzed in such illuminating detail.[27] That eighteenth-century critics saw the masquerade and the theater as related was borne out in numerous works linking the two institutions. Examples of the double-barreled attack include *The Danger of Masquerades and Raree-Shows* (1718) by "C. R.," the anonymous *Conduct of the Stage Consider'd, with Short Remarks upon the Original and Pernicious Consequences of Masquerades* (1721), and the anonymous *Essay on Plays and Masquerades* (1724).

In such writing the masquerade was sometimes attacked even more sharply than the theater because it allowed not just a partial, but a universal feigning. "As the Entertainment is much meaner than that of the Theater," wrote *Gentleman's Magazine* (September 1771), "so it is something more hazardous to Virtue and Modesty. It does not so much as pretend to any such improvement of the mind, as the Theatre professes; while it lays a more dreadful snare to Modesty, and has made too often a dismal inroad on the morals of those that frequent it." Yet the ultimate focus of anti-masquerade attacks throughout the century was never just the general theatricality of the occasion, or its effeminacy. The offense ran deeper: the masquerade seemed to such critics to challenge the symbolic order of eighteenth-century culture. At its most profound level anti-masquerade rhetoric was directed against the masquerade's unholy mixing of things meant to remain apart—its impulse, as it were, toward an incest of forms.

Thus the insistent contemporary references to the occasion's dangerous, seemingly chimerical powers of fusion. The word that occurs again and again in such discussions, not surprisingly, is "promiscuity." Addison's epithet for the masquerade, the "promiscuous Multitude," is typical. Anti-masquerade writers saw promiscuity reinscribed at every level of masquerade phenomenology. It intruded at the level of origins: the masquerade was a promiscuous mixture of foreign perversion and native depravity; Continental panderers there cavorted with England's own worst, its degenerate aristocracy and vicious lower orders. Likewise, the masquerade crowd was promiscuous, an indiscriminate horde of high and low, male and female. The masquerade's tendency to put everyone—man and woman, gentry and riffraff—on a "Level" was the object of relentlessly anti-democratic invective. As one critic wrote, the masquerade did little but increase the insufferable impertinence of the lower orders: "It is possible the confused mixture of different ranks and conditions, which is unavoidable at a masquerade, may well be agreeable to the dregs of the people, who are fond, even at every price, of gaining admittance into a place where they may insult their superiors with impunity."[28]

And of course, as we have seen, promiscuity was sexual: other kinds of improper "Intercourse" resolved often enough into literal intercourse, the commingling of bodies. While anti-masquerade writers objected to the masquerade's licentiousness in general (the random coupling of strangers threatened the economic and class structure of society), they were particularly afraid of its tendency to produce liaisons "against Nature." The masquerade was to blame for inciting a host of tabooed physical contacts: between married women and men not their husbands, single women and men in general, members of the same sex, members of the same family.

Not surprisingly, incest took on figurative significance, standing for a whole range of transgressions. "By thee," the author of *A Seasonable Apology for Mr. H----g--r* wrote of the masquerade, "Sons aspire to the Wombs from whence they sprung; and Daughters wantonly embrace the Loyns that begot them." The writer of the *Short Remarks upon the Original and Pernicious Consequences of Masquerades* animadverted upon an unfortunate gentleman who "debauch'd his own Daughter" by mistake at a masquerade and died of horror at the discovery. In *The Masquerade; or, The Devil's Nursery* (1732), a "Virtuous Wife" is "an Incestuous Mother made" after another tragic masquerade mixup. Such fear was perfectly in keeping with the general direction of anti-masquerade complaint, for incest represented a violation of boundaries—kinship boundaries—and suggested a contradictory overlay of familial and sexual transactions. The child and the paramour became dangerously confused. "Who can think," thus asked the writer of the *Short Remarks*, "of the vile and unnatural Assignations made there, without being seiz'd with Horror?"

The paramount form of masquerade promiscuity, however—the form that sanctioned all the rest—was symbolic. The "joinings" metaphorically rendered in masquerade costume suggested a metaphysical assault on categories. Anti-masquerade writers typically dwelled on two symbolic outrages: the shocking coupling, in which two radically different costume types "paired off" in the masquerade crowd; and the deeper scandal of the individual costume itself, with its radical inauthenticity.

The masquerade Spy in the *Weekly Journal* (April 18, 1724) complained, for instance, of the impossible, dreamlike pairings he observed in the crowd at Heidegger's: "I overheard an Assignation made between a Lion and a Shepherdess; I also discover'd an extream Intimacy betwixt a Butterfly and a Prizefighter." The author of *Guardian* 154 described watching a nun embrace a heathen god at a masquerade. Another writer for the *Weekly*

Journal (January 25, 1724) found himself "transported to *Noah's Ark*," at a masquerade, "so fast did Figures of various Species come in by Pairs." Unlike those in Genesis, however, the "Pairs" were supremely, monstrously mismatched: "a Devil and a Quaker, Turk and female Rope-dancer, Judge and *Indian* Queen, and Friars of several Orders with *Fanatick Preachers*, all pair'd." Later he described a Presbyterian parson and a nun dancing a minuet, and a cardinal and a milkmaid "Arm in Arm, . . . very loving" (see Fig. 21).

But the surface incongruities concealed deeper paradoxes, for individual costume itself was a prolonged, scandalous deceit. Of the cardinal and milkmaid just mentioned, the former turns out to be "a pretty young Woman of good Friends" and the latter "one of the greatest Coxcombs about Town." In the *Guardian* piece the naive narrator is constantly assaulted by similar perverse discoveries. When he steps on the toe of a demure female Quaker, she unexpectedly cries out, "D--n you, you son of a -----!"; and later, after he bumps a shepherdess with his elbow,

21. Masquerade promiscuity. Detail of a nun and friar from Parr's *The Jubilee Ball After the Venetian Manner*, 1749 (see Fig. 4).

"she swore like a trooper, and threatened me with a very masculine voice." The typical masquerade epiphany is an unremitting parody of true spiritual insight. It reveals not the eternal and ineluctable rightness of things, and their perfected relation to one another, but a staggering, endlessly magnifying wrongness, the catastrophic disruption of meaningful relationship.

At times the anti-masquerade writers mingled, in their own rhetoric, the two kinds of promiscuous conjunction. Christopher Pitt's verse satire "On the Masquerades" creates a dizzying picture of confusion by juxtaposing various incongruously clad individuals next to shocking duos of one sort or another.

> So many various changes to impart,
> Would tire an Ovid's or a Proteus' art,
> Where, lost in one promiscuous whim, we see
> Sex, age, condition, quality, degree.—
> Where the facetious crowd themselves lay down,
> And take up ev'ry person but their own;
> Fools, dukes, rakes, cardinals, fops, Indian queens,
> Belles in tiewigs and lords in Harlequins,
> Troops of right honorable porters come,
> And garter'd small-coal merchants crowd the room,
> Valets adorn'd with coronets appear,
> Lacquies of state and footmen with a star,
> Sailors of quality with judges mix,—
> And chimney-sweepers drive their coach-and-six. . . .
> Idiots turn conjurers, and courtiers clowns,
> And sultans drop their handkerchiefs to nuns,
> Starch'd Quakers glare in furbelows and silk,
> Beaux deal in sprats and duchesses cry milk.
>
> (25–38, 45–48)

The sexual embraces that follow upon this whirling scene exceed polite description:

> But guard thy fancy, Muse! nor stain thy pen
> With the lewd joys of this fantastic scene,
> Where sexes blend in one confus'd intrigue,
> Where the girls ravish and the men grow big,—
> Nor credit what the idle world has said
> Of lawyers forc'd, and judges brought-to-bed,
> Or that to belles their brothers breathe their vows,

Or husbands through mistake gallant a spouse:
Such dire disasters, and a num'rous throng
Of like enormities, require the song;
But the chaste Muse, with blushes cover'd o'er,
Retires confus'd, and will reveal no more.   (49–60)

The implication is clear: the assembly room is a breeding ground for monsters. The unnaturally assorted mob at once prompts indiscriminate erotic coupling and foreshadows the chimerical offspring of such chaotic unions.

The all-encompassing "promiscuity" of the masked assembly, conceived as an offense against the cognitive order, was for the anti-masqueraders ultimately more horrifying than the general atmosphere of sinful self-indulgence. The masked assembly was of course "a Congress to an unclean end," where "the wanton Imagination is indulged to the last degree," and a host of ungodly activities—dancing, swearing, gambling, sexual exchanges—took place there.[29] But it posed a much deeper threat to the structure of human experience itself. That persistent, odd association throughout the century between devastating earthquakes and masquerading (English churchmen blamed both the Lisbon earthquake and another tremor at Leghorn in 1742, for example, on masquerades[30]) testifies on a metaphoric level to the hyperbolic, disruptive power contemporaries saw in masquerades. The way the masquerade rendered a dialectical fluidity between opposites, magic unities instead of differences, was a symbolic revocation of cosmos itself. At its worst the masquerade resembled a convulsive, unstoppable ripple through the core of things, a metaphysical shock wave.

Just as epidemic follows earthquake, the imagery of chaos expanded, finally, into the imagery of corruption and death. In their most apocalyptic moods anti-masquerade writers of the eighteenth century returned again and again to the occasion's contaminating, even pestilential nature. Like the plague, the corruptions of the masquerade threatened always to spread, to infect society at large with decay and death. Thus the author of the *Essay on Plays and Masquerades* described the masked assembly as a place where "the best Blood of the Nation is tainted with infection." The writer of the *Short Remarks upon the Origi-nal and Pernicious Consequences of Masquerades* warned his readers: "*Go not to the Pesthouse for Recreation.*" Fielding exploited the image too: speaking of masquerades in *An Enquiry into the Causes of the Late Increase of Robbers*, he observed that "bad Hab-its are as infectious by Example, as the Plague itself by Con-tact."[31] Such sentiments took a bathetic, literal form in Eliza Haywood's claim that masquerades caused those with "delicate constitutions" to "contract colds and various disorders, which hang upon them a long time, and sometimes never get rid of."[32]

When eighteenth-century satirists wished to depict a larger cultural sickness—the morbid state of civilization itself—the masquerade, not surprisingly, offered an image of universal cor-ruption. Writing of the world's abounding hypocrisy and deceit in "An Essay on the Knowledge of the Characters of Men" (1743), Fielding called human society "a vast Masquerade, where the greatest Part appear disguised under false Vizors and Hab-its."[33] In *Rambler* 75, Samuel Johnson scorned the way "the rich and powerful live in a perpetual masquerade, in which all about them wear borrowed characters."[34] Owen Sedgewick, in his compendium of modern vices, *The Universal Masquerade; or, The World Turn'd Inside Out* (1742), showed society entirely over-taken by masquerade deception, as did Goldsmith, in an epi-logue to Charlotte Lennox's *The Sister* (1769) spoken to "Boxes, Pit, and Gallery": "The world's a masquerade! the masquers, you, you, you."[35] Modern life, proclaimed a character in Hannah Cowley's *The Belle's Stratagem* (1781), had become "a mere chaos, in which all distinction of rank is lost in a ridiculous af-fectation of ease"; it was "all one universal Masquerade" with "all disguised in the same habits and manners" (II, i). For the eighteenth-century satirist the real world, in all its chicanery and bad faith, was ultimately indistinguishable from the masquer-ade; both resolved, pathologically, into a *mundus inversus*, where all pretended to be what they were not.

Yet the imagery of contagion, and the related notion that mas-querade vices had come to pollute society itself, confirmed again the masquerade's controversial role as a ritual of disorder.

Mary Douglas has described in some detail how in both traditional and modern societies, "pollution effects"—images of disease, filth, and corruption—cluster around cultural phenomena that somehow challenge metaphysical systems of order. A society may try to protect its conceptual order by attributing dangerous or polluting effects to categorical breaches or anomalous beings. As Douglas observes, pollution effects "inhere in the structure of ideas itself" and "punish a symbolic breaking of that which should be joined or a joining of that which should be separate." They strike "where form has been attacked."[36]

It is not hard to see how the masquerade excited such archaic responses. Its danger, as we have seen, lay precisely in the way it undermined articulated "lines of structure"—the system of oppositions on which eighteenth-century culture was founded. It created anomalies and monsters. Like the City and the Mob, the masked assembly appeared to its detractors as an unrecuperable event; it was a frightening jumble of contradictions, the dense site at which hybrids proliferated and taxonomy failed.

"Beauty, cleanliness and order," Freud writes in *Civilization and Its Discontents*, "obviously occupy a special position among the requirements of civilization."[37] What then of the grotesquerie, the danger and disorder of masquerade? How finally to characterize the masquerade's role in English civilization of the eighteenth-century—that epoch stereotypically commemorated as the model of pristine balance and rationalist hygiene?

As I suggested earlier, the prominence of motifs of reversal in the masquerade spectacle suggests an intriguing connection with a larger class of cultural events that anthropologists have come to call, variously, rituals of rebellion or rites of reversal. Defined more loosely, a "rebellious ritual" (the term is Victor Turner's) can be any collective event or activity that uses symbolic inversion for expressive purposes. It is "any act of expressive behavior which inverts, contradicts, abrogates, or in some fashion presents an alternative to commonly held cultural codes, values, and norms, be they linguistic, literary, artistic, religious, or social and political."[38] Seasonal carnivals fall within the category; as Frazer was among the first to point out, popular rituals like the Roman Saturnalia, medieval Feast of Fools, charivari, and so on are all fundamentally rituals of inversion. I have already suggested how the masquerade took its place (albeit a somewhat bastardized one) in the great family of carnivalesque outbursts, and preserved certain features of traditional English and Continental festivals of misrule. But we can now specify this connection even further. By its exemplary use of symbolic inversions (endlessly figured in the whimsical tropology of costume), the masquerade demonstrated a kinship with the traditional rite of reversal, and indeed with all those outbreaks of topsy-turvydom manifested in virtually every documented human culture.

Anthropologists have asserted the metacritical function of such rituals. Clifford Geertz and Victor Turner, for example, have proposed that institutionalized scenes of collective disorder serve an interpretive or heuristic purpose in culture: they help to make the social group's ordering categories known.[39] By posing a reversal of normal relationships, festivals of misrule implicitly comment on these relationships. By celebrating the negative, they clarify the positive. The logic here is the same that Freud applied to the psyche in his 1925 essay on negation ("Die Verneinung"): "by the help of the symbol of negation, the thinking-process frees itself from the limitation of repression and enriches itself with the subject-matter without which it could not work efficiently."[40] In the words of one critic, "the breaking of rules and the inverting of order implies that there *is* a rule to break and an order to invert."[41] A vision of the unnatural makes explicit our unconscious assumptions about the natural.

There is a similar instrumentality in the masquerade. The occasion was a *jeu* perhaps, but always a *jeu sérieux*. In much the same fashion as those quintessentially eighteenth-century forms satire and burlesque, the masquerade made hierarchies explicit by dramatically suspending them. It produced a kind of comic enlightenment, imparting knowledge about the real world while giving access to a numinous realm of dream and taboo. It offered contemporary society a negative of itself: the temporary collapse of structure intensified awareness of the structure being violated.

The cognitive éclat of the spectacle extended even further. Besides highlighting structure, rituals of inversion can demonstrate the fictionality of classification systems, exposing them as man-made rather than natural or divine. When members of a social group "turn round and confront the categories on which their whole surrounding culture has been built up," Mary Douglas writes, they can then "recognise them for the fictive, man-made, arbitrary creations that they are."[42] I suggested earlier that masquerade disguise enforced a radical awareness of the artificiality of the sartorial code; it also exposed those larger ideological distinctions to which clothing so blandly referred. The masquerade had powers of demystification. Its assault on hierarchy made cultural distinctions visible—as fashioned assessments of human experience. In Marxist terms masquerade inversions worked to unveil the false consciousness represented by ideology itself, and for a brief moment made the world "philosophical."[43]

To characterize the masquerade as a ritual of rebellion does create certain historical and intellectual puzzles. I have already had to modify my claim for the cognitive potency of the masquerade with a temporal qualification: "for a brief moment," perhaps no longer than its own duration, the masquerade effected an ecstatic liberation from the burdens of structure and hierarchy. To what extent its revelatory chaos disrupted actual social structures is ambiguous. The same ambiguity is characteristic of rites of reversal generally. A classic debate in social anthropology addresses just this question: whether symbolic rituals of disorder function within a culture as safety valves that reaffirm the status quo by exorcising social tensions, or are subversive events that explicitly threaten the prevailing order and encourage the formation of popular consciousness.[44] One proponent of the former view, Max Gluckman, has argued that while "rites of reversal obviously include a protest against the established order . . . they are intended to preserve and strengthen the established order."[45] His interpretation has recently been challenged, however, by social historians who, following Marx, have found in collective outbursts of saturnalian freedom very real challenges to authoritarian hierarchies. Emmanuel Le Roy Ladurie, Natalie Davis, and Peter Shaw have all suggested links between historical festivals of misrule and popular rebellion in early modern Europe and colonial America. A number of well-documented acts of popular insurgency occurring between the sixteenth and eighteenth centuries seem to have begun as spillovers of festive license. The Stonewall riots in New York City in 1969 offer a striking modern example of the phenomenon.[46]

To speak metaphorically, the basic question is whether an imagery of inversion—the World Upside-Down, for instance—has an inoculating or an infectious effect on collective consciousness. It is possible, Barthes has suggested, to "immunize" the collective imagination "by a small inoculation of acknowledged evil. . . . One thus protects it against the risk of a generalized subversion."[47] Others have held the view put forth most succinctly by Charles Lamb: "We dread infection from the representation of scenic disorder."[48]

I do not propose to adjudicate in any final way this complex dispute, though I tend to think that such rituals can never be entirely explained by appeals to a safety-valve or *Ventilsitten* theory. As far as the masquerade goes, both the reactions of contemporaries and the interesting fate of the institution in later eighteenth-century society intimate a far more provocative cultural role. As the eighteenth century progressed, contemporary critics became more rather than less concerned with the subversive possibilities of the masquerade, and increasingly linked it, quite self-consciously, with scenarios of actual rebellion.

For many participants the masquerade undoubtedly represented nothing more than an evening's entertainment: it was a brief, regressive moment of liberty and a respite, at once simple and fleeting, from the burdens of identity and history. For those inclined toward psychological explanations, it is always possible to treat the masquerade as a cathartic and hence basically conservative occasion. From such a perspective the masquerade

appears to be nothing more than nostalgia for an earlier devel-
opmental stage—for the state, perhaps, of polymorphous perversity, that pre-Oedipal moment before self and other have
been differentiated. The ancient Saturnalia was traditionally believed to revivify the Golden Age: it looked backward to a time
before classifications, before society had need of dialectic, of
masters and slaves. And often enough, particularly as one reads,
say, Walpole's shimmering descriptions, the eighteenth-century
masquerade has a similar aspect.* Like a collective fugue it
pointed back to a timeless moment before history—to a state
before states, a realm of informality, peace, and universal intimacy. Its energies, in Freudian terms, were oceanic, and recalled
a state before civilization's repressive separations and taxing demands on libido.

Yet the eighteenth-century masquerade was more than regressive, ahistorical play. From the beginning it had distinct political overtones. Early in the century, following the precedent
set by the Duc d'Aumont, the masquerade was sometimes an
occasion for playing out diplomatic and court intrigue; later it
became a natural stage for political satire. Masqueraders sometimes resembled walking political cartoons. In February 1770,
during the height of Wilkesite agitation, Walpole records a subscription masquerade (to which the House of Commons gaily
adjourned en masse) at which a man appeared as Wilkes—"with
a visor, in imitation of his squint, and a Cap of Liberty on a
pole" (Fig. 22). Another masquerade in that year featured a
madman "run mad for Wilkes and Liberty."[49]

In assessing the concrete social impact of the masquerade, one
must weigh the effects of two kinds of symbolic disruption: the
imitation of the powerless by the powerful (dukes masquerading
as footmen, for example, or men as women), and the reverse
(footmen disguised as dukes, women as men). The former sort

---

*"Nothing in a fairy tale," wrote Walpole, "ever surpassed" the Ranelagh Jubilee
masquerade of 1749: "The amphitheatre was illuminated, and in the middle was a circular bower, composed of all kinds of firs in tubs, from twenty to thirty feet high: under
them orange trees, with small lamps in each orange, and below them all sorts of the
finest auriculas in pots; and festoons of natural flowers hanging from tree to tree. . . .
There were booths for tea and wine, gaming tables and dancing, and about two thousand persons. In short it pleased me more than anything I ever saw." Walpole, *Correspondence*, I (17), 47.

22. Political satire at the masquerade. A masquerader holds up the Wilkesite Cap of Liberty in a detail from Charles White's *Masquerade Scene at the Pantheon 1773* (see Fig. 12).

of impersonation seems relatively devoid of incendiary effect. When power relations are fixed, "downward" travesty, however vulgar, is generally comic rather than provocative: witness the traditional burlesque appeal of male transvestism in patriarchal culture or the role of blackface in nineteenth-century American popular entertainment. The imitation of oppressed groups by their oppressors often excites laughter rather than complaint. Slumming is usually tolerated, unless a certain political consciousness has already taken hold among the oppressed themselves and they are in a position to protest. Indeed, in the Walpole account just mentioned, when the House of Commons makes its ludicrous progress across London to the masquerade (looking, to modern eyes, like nothing so much as a boobified Gilbert and Sullivan chorus), one detects something of the burlesque costume's vestigial power to amuse rather than outrage onlookers. The restive, potentially explosive rabble was seemingly magically pacified by the entrancing spectacle of oligarchs en travesti. Wrote Walpole: "The mob was beyond all belief: they held flambeaux to the windows of every coach, and demanded to have the masks pulled off and put on at their pleasure, but with extreme good-humour and civility. I was with my Lady Hertford and two of her daughters, in their coach: the mob took me for Lord Hertford, and huzzaed and blessed me! One fellow cried out, "Are you for Wilkes?" Another said, 'D--n you, you fool, what has Wilkes to do with a Masquerade?'"[50]

More unsettling are parodies of the powerful by the powerless. Borrowing again the terms of literary criticism, one could call these kinds of travesty mock-heroic rather than burlesque. Historically speaking, the appropriation of the trappings of authority by those without it has usually been perceived as a threat to social structure. In eighteenth-century England a number of sumptuary laws and regulations on proletarian attire still enforced the ancient view. The infamous Black Act of 1723 was in part a sumptuary law: directed at foresters and poachers, it authorized the apprehension of anyone "having his or their faces blacked, or being otherwise disguised." It was sometimes mentioned in debates about the public masquerade in the 1720's.[51] Presumably the fear underlying these proscriptions was that wearing the clothes of a higher rank, even in jest, incited a desire to join that rank and receive its perquisites. Luxurious costume might invest the lower orders with delusions of grandeur. Worse, it could lead to the revolutionary notion that rank itself could be altered as easily as its outward signs. Like the ideological prohibitions on women participating in masquerades, the attempts of eighteenth-century masquerade impresarios to bar members of the lower orders from their entertainments made perfect sense in light of common wisdom: "inferior" sorts had to be kept out of the clothes of their betters, in order to prevent them from getting rebellious ideas.

The anti-masquerade writers, not surprisingly, were firmly convinced of the political danger of letting the powerless dress up as the powerful. Often they explicitly linked masquerade disguise with social revolution. With its World-Upside-Down ambience, its leveling visual éclat, the masquerade raised the specter of past political upheavals. The Civil War is a common motif in anti-masquerade writing: the masquerade was sometimes seen as reanimating this most horrifying of national traumas. The author of *A Seasonable Apology for Mr. H----g--r*, for example, suggested that after the Devil, Cromwell was history's most notorious "masquerader"—one who posed improperly as a king. A writer in the *Weekly Journal* for November 21, 1724, made a similar link between masquerading and the Good Old Cause. The Puritans, he wrote, were perpetual masqueraders, "a sort of People always acting under a Disguise," who once committed "the greatest Villainies, *Rebellion*, *Sacrilege*, and *Murder*, under the specious Pretence of Reformation in Religion." Predictably the concept of sartorial transformation underlay these metaphoric connections: "short *Hair* and a *Round Head*," the same writer continued, "were certain Signs of Grace . . . and a plain Coat, was an infallible Token of *the Light Within*."

The provocative sartorial exchanges of the masquerade were also thought to fuel contemporary rebellion. Particularly later in the century—during the fitful 1760's and 1770's, when social unrest intensified—more and more political comment was directed against masquerades. The writer of a satirical "Essay on Masquerades" in *Lady's Magazine* for February 1777 began a backhanded attack with a charged topical reference: "Whoever knows the meaning and intention of a masquerade must be highly pleased to hear that the nation is this winter (notwithstanding the American war) blessed with its revival." He went on to praise "its tendency to diffuse a *spirit* of *liberty*, by reducing all men to an equality. . . . In this nocturnal assembly, rank and

93

distinction cease to insult us with their superiority; the noble peer is confounded with the ignoble peasant; the order of things is inverted; the first is put last and the last first." The masquerade's "innocent freedoms," he concluded, "must endear it to every lover of his country." The hidden charge, as always, was clear: the masquerade "diffused" a dubious equality, and by implication, created a dangerous taste for equality elsewhere—above all, as the American situation suggested, in real life.

How were the fluid travesties of the masquerade perceived by those in relatively powerless positions? As we know, in spite of restrictions members of the English underclass did penetrate the public masquerade, and respectable women did find their way into Heidegger's and Cornelys's forbidden entertainments. One wonders what effects such a potentially demystifying experience had on them, and whether any revocation, symbolic or otherwise, of the entrenched hierarchies of sex and class could remain innocent for long. Lack of information unfortunately makes these questions difficult to answer. Between the fundamentally detached remarks of privileged observers like Walpole and the lurid fulminations of the anti-masquerade writers, one finds relatively few first-hand accounts of the masquerade that are neither mere costume lists nor conventional complaints: the official animus against the event was simply too great. Few members of the "Lower Orders," one suspects, kept records of their participation. The ruling class documented working-class travesties only when an implicit moral warning could be drawn from them, as in an account in *Gentleman's Magazine* for January 1777 describing a masquerade held by "near forty persons, ladies and gentlemen of the hairdressing class." The floor literally fell in on these hapless revelers, killing one person and injuring many others. Women, likewise, were unlikely to publicize their masquerade exploits. The letters and memoirs of Mrs. Centlivre, Lady Mary Wortley Montagu, Fanny Burney, Margaret Leeson, and Elizabeth Inchbald, among others, hint at the appeal of masked nights and anonymous conversation, but few women approached the candor of the scandalous Harriette Wilson, who remarked baldly that she loved masquerades because women had more freedom there than anywhere else.[52]

"Many people, no doubt," the author of a plea for the prohibition of masquerades wrote in 1725, "will fancy it a chymerical, as well as a remote Fear, to imagine that the publick Good or Safety, any Way depends either upon a Masquerade, or no Masquerade. . . . But I believe, all people will allow that Vertue and good Manners may rise or fall according as these Assemblies are encouraged."[53] The author of the *Short Remarks upon the Original and Pernicious Consequences of Masquerades* put the matter even more bluntly: "Either you are pleased with the Indecencies and Obscenities of the Masquerade, or you are not." For much of the century those pleased and those not pleased with such "Indecencies" remained in an odd, tense standoff. On the one hand, there were those who saw, or claimed to see, the masquerade's innocence. They were its commercial promoters, aristocratic patrons, and the world of fashion—all the connoisseurs of piquant self-concealment and conspicuous indulgence. Lady Mary, Horace Walpole, Garrick, Boswell—the fashionable intelligentsia, in short—remained proponents of the masquerade throughout the century. But as we have seen, the masquerade had too its vocal opponents among clergymen, pamphleteers, satiric journalists, and others with schemes for the improvement of English morals. The eighteenth-century press stood always in dubious relation to the institution of masquerading, at once editorializing more or less smugly against it, and yet abetting its popularity with frequent advertisements and "masquerade intelligence" puff features. On a more thoughtful plane, though sometimes more ambiguously, the great middle-class moralists of the period, among them Fielding, Hogarth, and Richardson, also aligned themselves with the anti-masquerade forces, and registered their disapproval in complicated fictional and graphic works.

In response perhaps to this larger cultural ambivalence, the civil authorities alternated between uneasy toleration of masquerades and spasmodic efforts to suppress them. Almost from its inception the public masquerade was subject to civil harassment, but none that was really concerted or effective for more than a short time. In 1727, against his own inclination, George II was forced to issue a royal proclamation condemning Heidegger's assemblies; Heidegger responded by changing the name of the masquerade to the innocuous if somewhat vague "ridotto," sending it, as it were, temporarily underground. Heidegger likewise weathered the presentment issued against him in 1729 by the Middlesex Grand Jury as "the principal promoter of vice and immorality." Later attempts to ban "mock-Carnivals" met with only partial success. The longest continuous prohibition lasted a year; in 1750–51, after the devastation at Lisbon, masquerades were, in Walpole's words, "sacrificed to the idol earthquake" at the urging of the English bishops.[54] In her memoirs, published in 1797, the incorrigible demimondaine Margaret Leeson described an order against masquerades instituted in Dublin several decades earlier, following "some disturbances that had happened." This, she said, only "spirited me up to have one of my own, at my own house, to shew how much I disregarded all law or order, let the consequences be what they might."[55]

Sometimes masked parties were forcibly broken up by civil authorities, but usually only when the majority of those in attendance were thought particularly unfit to enjoy such amusements. The *Weekly Journal* for April 10, 1725, described an official crackdown on a London masquerade held by a group of "Chamber-Maids, Cook-Maids, Foot-Men, and Apprentices." The malefactors in question, the report observed, had just received their "Christmas-boxes," and under the influence of this sudden indulgence "resolved to be vicious in a very polite way." *Gentleman's Magazine* for June 1751 likewise described a raid on a private masquerade by the High Constable of Westminster. On this occasion "several idle persons of both sexes" were taken before Justice Fielding. "Being found," however, "to be persons of distinction under twenty, the justice not thinking proper to expose them, after a severe reprimand, dismissed them all."

Though attacks were occasionally mounted against it, the masquerade was never entirely stamped out by the forces of law and order. Though always ideologically suspect, the "promiscuous Assembly" retained its paradoxical hold on the eighteenth-century popular imagination, and for many decades withstood the persistent barrage of criticism and propaganda leveled against it (see Fig. 23). Clearly audible though they were, the animadversions of the virtuous ultimately did little, one suspects, to hinder those set on masquerading and its delights; they may even have added at times a desirable note of the illicit to such pursuits. For much of the eighteenth century one could say, as Hannah Cowley did, that the world had become "one universal Masquerade." The pleasure of an epoch was contained, it seemed, in the incandescent space of an assembly room, replete with swirling, enigmatic figures; and urbanity itself seemed defined by mask and domino, mystery and laughter.

23. An anonymous print from 1724 depicting the destruction of the masquerade by forces of law and order. Britannia, Wisdom, and Piety parade in triumph while Hercules chains a restive crowd of masqueraders and cudgels a supplicating Heidegger.

How then to explain what is surely among the most baffling facts about the English masquerade—its abrupt, virtually total eclipse by the end of the century? So long an axiom of eighteenth-century urban life, the public masquerade was none-theless moribund by the 1790's. The end came surprisingly swiftly, though the London press undeniably had been sound-ing the death knells earlier. After a subscription masquerade in 1779, for example, one relieved observer noted, "From the thin-ness of the Company at Monday night's Masked Ball, it is pretty clear that these kinds of exotic amusements are so much on the decline, as to promise a total and speedy extinction."[56] By the time of the French Revolution, the masquerade had fallen quite precipitately out of fashion. Apart from the odd Regency revival here and there, to which Byron's letters attest, it is difficult to find descriptions of large public masquerades held in England after 1790.[57]

The change was registered most poignantly perhaps in the fate of those buildings and public places connected with the masquerade, and in the dismal end of its most famous surviving champion. The Pantheon—described by Walpole in its heyday as a second "Baalbec," and the scene of London's largest mas-querades in the late 1770's and early 1780's—burned to the ground in 1792 and was not rebuilt. Vauxhall and Ranelagh Gar-dens, long associated with open-air masked entertainments, had lost their esprit by the last decades of the century, and were soon little more than forgotten landscapes, made up of dilapidated *al-lées* and droopy flowerbeds. As Sophie von la Roche wrote in her diary in 1796, "Ranelagh . . . is now quite forsaken."[58] Even Carlisle House, the scene of Mrs. Cornelys's greatest masked extravaganzas, was partially razed in 1788, and its grand saloon converted into a chapel. Abandoned by her former patrons, Mrs. Cornelys was herself reduced to opening breakfast rooms, which soon failed. After an ill-fated stint as a vendor of asses' milk, she died a bankrupt in Fleet Prison in 1797.[59]

There is something melancholy in all this, and again, a his-torical enigma. Why the abrupt change of spirit in the 1780's and 1790's? By the last decades of the century, it seemed as though

the pleasures of masking had been forgotten: the deinstitutionalization of the masquerade and the relegation of "costume parties" to the periphery of collective life were so rapid as to suggest a kind of cultural amnesia. The masquerade's duplicitous
fantasia were disavowed; its utopian spectacle was exorcised. By
the time the masquerade resurfaced in cultural memory, tenta-
tively, as part of that quaint, informal, anecdotal history of the
eighteenth century written by the nineteenth, it had been utterly transfigured. In the gossipy Victorian chronicles of James
Peller Malcolm, John Ashton, William Connor Sydney, and the
like, the Masquerade—along with the Club, the Pleasure Garden, the Opera—became a standard historical topos, but it was
also now seen as a fragment from another world, part of a ro-
manticized and stylish past of elegant yet obsolete amusements.
The masquerade was trivialized and distanced, becoming a part
of "Old Times"—a picturesque, vaguely titillating piece of Augustan local color, but one without compelling intellectual interest. Somewhere between epochs a break occurred: all sense of
the masquerade's cultural significance was mislaid; all sense of
that basically serious desire at its heart—for a second body, the
body of dream and taboo, vanished.[60]

Such a characterization, with its intimations of tristesse and
hint of Freudian pathos, may at first glance seem grandiose. We
may resist the metaphors of forgetting and repression; we may
be reluctant to encapsulate the masquerade within a psycho-
historical myth. At the same time the fact remains: the masquerade, and that organized infatuation with otherness it represented, had essentially run its course by the beginning of the
nineteenth century. (I speak, of course, only of England: on the
Continent, as the fictional landscapes of Balzac and Flaubert
suggest, the situation was somewhat different.) True, an etiolated masquerade imagery persisted in the nineteenth century: in
common figurative speech, as a metaphor for deception, and
here and there in literature. (Byron, again, was fond of images
of the masquerade and the carnivalesque.) But the metaphor had
lost its concrete grounding; the institution was dead.

The disappearance of the masquerade can be interpreted as a

symptom of larger cross-cultural changes, in particular the reform of popular culture that climaxed in Europe in the middle
and late eighteenth century. The work of moral reformers across
Europe was given impetus in the late eighteenth century by
new and powerful impersonal forces: industrialization and the
growth of towns, capitalist expansion, increasing literacy, the
fragmentation of traditional communities, the gradual rise of
class consciousness. The commercialization of popular culture
in the eighteenth century, a phenomenon that strongly influenced the development of the English masquerade, was one sign
of impending change. It marked a general decline of popular
tradition and a move toward new, diffused, capitalist forms of
mass entertainment. By the mid-nineteenth century the change
was complete: the culture of the carnival and fair had been fragmented, and its few vestiges relegated to the sentimental realm
of folkloristic "survivals." Though a somewhat compromised
and belated form of saturnalia, the masquerade shared the fate of
the European carnival generally. Its demise can easily be invoked to lend weight to a theory of the steadily attenuating role
of traditional culture in the modern world.

The fate of the masquerade can also be correlated with certain
distinctive changes in English cultural life in the last half of the
eighteenth century. Derek Jarrett has identified a "progress from
turbulence to regimentation" taking place in England between
1750 and 1800—a move from an age of neglect to an "age of
supervision." This shift, which became most striking after the
French Revolution, manifested itself in new bureaucracy, in-
creasing governmental intrusion into domestic life (the Marriage Act and the census being two examples), a growing insistence on the ethical and administrative role of the propertied
classes in national life, and the general ascendancy of bourgeois
ideology, with its preference for conspicuous work over pleasure, and duty over self-gratification. Late-eighteenth-century
English culture, Jarrett observes, represented a triumph of civilization over individual impulse. He uses Freudian (or perhaps
Wordsworthian) metaphors of socialization to encapsulate this
channeling of collective energy into "adult" cultural pursuits:

"England . . . was growing up: in the solemn atmosphere of the 1790's the rumbustious knockabout violence of the eighteenth century seemed like an irresponsible childhood that was being left behind." The process, he concludes, was not an altogether happy one: "Few dared to ask whether the tasks were really worthwhile or whether work was really an automatically ennobling activity," and to some, indeed, it seemed "the shades of the prison house were closing in on English society."[61]

Taboos on obvious frivolities—all the artificial pleasures of the preceding epoch, for instance—were a natural consequence of the new seriousness. The propertied classes led the way in rejecting fashionable excesses, and conspicuously embraced a new mode of discretion, caution, and respectability.[62] Moral "sincerity" displaced the easy, joyful theatricality that had reigned over so much of the former era. One detects a kind of collective anhedonia at the end of the eighteenth century—an inability or unwillingness, finally, to take pleasure. Self-indulgence had lost its charm.

This ideology of respectability, which J. H. Plumb has called the "intense moral vanity" of Englishmen after the French Revolution, held no quarter, clearly, for masquerades.[63] With its inevitable affirmation of childhood over adulthood, libido over constraint, duplicity over sincerity, and "promiscuity" over sexual, social, and metaphysical bureaucratization, the masquerade was a profound affront to modern life and its rigorous programs. And thus, even among those who before had been its most fervent supporters—the aristocracy, the fashionable avant garde—the masquerade lost, or appeared to lose, its emotional necessity. Masquerading had come to represent the morally and psychologically unacceptable, an infantile pleasure that must be abjured.

One might interpret the demise of masquerading somewhat more philosophically, not only as part of social history, and a superficial change in manners, but as a datum in the history of consciousness. For the denial of the masquerade, and of its projection of a universal mutability, was also the denial of a certain metaphysics. The masquerade, as we have seen, predicated the

hallucinatory merging of self and other; it set up magical continuities between disparate bodies. Miraculous transmogrifica-
tions were symbolically enacted; the metamorphoses of dream
and folklore became a temporary reality. As in Freud's logic of the
unconscious, the "either/or" had no place: only the "both/and."
Biological, social, and metaphysical taxonomies were overturned; the masquerade posited a return to primal unity.

I have suggested that the eighteenth-century anti-masquerade
writers were deeply aware of the institution's antitaxonomic
energy; more than anything else it was this feature of the masquerade that incurred their wrath. For much of the century their
persistent diatribe seemed nothing more than reactionary and
ill-tempered complaining, but it was also oddly prophetic. For
the philosophical assumptions of the anti-masqueraders, if not
their immediate pragmatic demands, were slowly being internalized on a collective scale. That world view typical of the anti-
masquerade authors, characterized everywhere by a fear of ontological promiscuity and a desire for firm conceptual boundaries,
was itself distinctly modern, and becoming increasingly pervasive in the eighteenth century. In effect, the anti-masquerade
writers celebrated a world made up of discrete forms, of rigid
categories and hygienically polarized opposites. They celebrated, in a word, the world of rationalism. And it was just this
vision of a classifiable cosmos that by the end of the eighteenth
century had come to assert its hegemony in Western culture.

Bakhtin's eloquent description of this new rationalist dispensation has its bearing on the fate of the eighteenth-century English masquerade. In his famous study of the carnivalesque, he
links the rise of rationalist epistemologies with the demise of the
traditional world of carnival. This world, he argues, was one of
endless, joyful fusions, inspired at the deepest level by an essentially religious perception of the hidden identity and connection
existing between all things. Carnival costumes disclosed "the
potentiality of an entirely different world, of another order, another way of life," and led human beings "out of the confines of
the apparent (false) unity, of the indisputable and stable." In the
moment of travesty and self-extension, the loneliness of subjec-

tivity was overcome and a magical dialectic established with the rest of creation. During the great festivals and *soties* of medieval and Renaissance Europe, "bodies could not be considered for themselves; they represented a material bodily whole and therefore transgressed the limits of their isolation. The private and the universal were still blended in a contradictory unity."[64]

And yet it was the very fluidity of carnival—the way it subverted the dualities of male and female, animal and human, dark and light, life and death—that made it so inimical to the new "atomizing" sensibility that heralded the development of modern bourgeois society. Rational individualism, the discourse of Descartes and Locke, predicates the discrete nature of bodies, their differentiation from one another and their classifiability. Within what Bakhtin calls the "new bodily canon" of rationalist ideology, the body is rendered impermeable, "merely one body; no signs of duality have been left. It is self-sufficient and speaks in its name alone. All that happens within it concerns it alone, that is, only the individual, closed sphere. Therefore, all the events taking place within it acquire one single meaning: death is only death, it never coincides with birth; old age is torn away from youth."[65] Ambiguous or hybrid forms, forms that reach beyond themselves and are neither one thing nor another, are rejected. With technological advance, industrialization, and the rise of consumer capitalism, the rigidly differentiated cosmos of bourgeois rationalism and "the petty, inert 'material principle' of class society" came to the fore.[66] The carnival was drained of its ancient religious and metaphysical meaning; its fantastic vision of the mutable, all-encompassing "double body" disavowed. It became marginal, anachronistic.

The process was already well advanced by the eighteenth century. For Bakhtin those forms of the carnivalesque that lingered in eighteenth-century culture were decayed and trivialized versions of the traditional vision. Contrasting carnival images in rococo art with those found in the art of earlier epochs, for instance, he suggests the ambivalent, vestigial quality of the former. Whereas the traditional imagery of carnival, still vivid in Rabelais, was unabashed, insistently corporeal, and grounded in a profoundly synthetic view of experience, rococo imagery is reduced and aestheticized. Eighteenth-century art retains only an intermittent consciousness of the philosophical meaning of carnival, and its fundamentally religious motivation.

Carnival forms serve a different role in rococo literature. Here the gay positive tone of laughter is preserved. But everything is reduced to "chamber" lightness and intimacy. The frankness of the marketplace is transformed into erotic frivolity, and gay relativity becomes skepticism and wantonness. And yet, in the hedonistic "boudoir" atmosphere a few sparks of the carnival fires which burn up "hell" have been preserved. In the setting of gloomy seriousness so widespread in the eighteenth century, rococo perpetuated after a fashion the traditional carnivalesque spirit.[67]

Ancient carnival motifs like the mask lost much of their symbolic power. Whereas the mask of folk tradition, Bakhtin suggests, "is connected with the joy of change and reincarnation, . . . transition, metamorphoses, the violation of natural boundaries," that of the modern period has been "stripped of its original richness and acquires other meanings alien to its primitive nature. . . . Now the mask hides something, keeps a secret, deceives." It has lost its comic and regenerative associations, and assumed a sinister, alienating aspect. Again, such meanings "would not be possible as long as the mask functioned within folk culture's organic whole."[68] Yet this culture, the culture of the carnivalesque, had been fragmented and diffused by the end of the eighteenth century.

Other writers have advanced similar historical arguments. Roger Caillois points out that forms of play organized around notions of mimicry, disguise, or transport from one body or state of being to another are essentially archaic, and lose their power when social groups develop the concept of a rationally ordered, quantifiable universe. The reign of mimicry "is indeed condemned as soon as the mind arrives at the concept of cosmos, i.e., a stable and orderly universe without miracles or transformations. Such a universe seems the domain of regularity, necessity, and proportion—in a word, a world of number." When cultures reach this stage of advanced civilization, individualizing games—games of competitive struggle or chance—take precedence over those of simulation and transformation:

> Whether it be cause or effect, each time that an advanced culture succeeds in emerging from the chaotic original, a palpable repression of the powers of vertigo and simulation is verified. They lose their traditional dominance, are pushed to the periphery of public life, reduced to roles that become more and more modern and intermittent, if not clandestine and guilty, or are relegated to the limited and regulated domain of games and fiction where they afford men the same eternal satisfactions, but in sublimated form, serving merely as an escape from boredom or work and entailing neither madness nor delirium.[69]

Whether or not one adheres fully to the intensely elegiac Bakhtinian myth of a modern fall away from the golden world of carnival (with bourgeois individualism cast as the satanic principle), or to Caillois's post-Freudian assertion that civilization represses the principles of transformation and vertigo, such hypotheses retain their suggestive force. In the fate of the masquerade one may indeed detect something like a historical paradigm. Already in the masquerades of the eighteenth century, that paradoxical "comic profundity" characteristic of the traditional carnival—its essentially religious spirit—has been somewhat diluted. The metaphysical content is there, symbolized in the rich phantasmagoria of costume, but it is often overlaid with a large admixture of self-regarding, even desperate hedonism. One uses the word with caution, but the eighteenth-century masquerade can be described as decadent, for it is at once the harbinger and the victim of cultural change. Its ultimate demise figured, on a small scale, the end of what one might call the organic perception of experience, an ancient, numinous sense of the connectedness of all things. In the largest sense, the decline of the masquerade was part of a pervasive "decline of magic" characteristic of Western culture after 1700—a symptom of changes in philosophy and the natural sciences, social organization, and the concept of human life itself.[70]

Seen in the light of a larger transformation in consciousness, the contemporary opponents of the masquerade emerge as the vanguard of a new ideology that was steadily gaining ascendancy in eighteenth-century culture and that, for better or for worse, is still with us. For excluding the recherché minority visions of literature and art, the carnivalesque has lost virtually all its immediacy and power in twentieth-century life. Its last major institutional manifestation, the public masquerade, never recovered from its late-eighteenth-century submersion.[71] Modern holidays, sporting events, and political conventions represent the last distorted vestiges of older festive traditions. As for purity, taxonomy, the absolute separation of self and other—these remain part of a modern desideratum. One need only think of the cartoonish racial and sexual dichotomies of our own time, our proliferating bureaucracies and fetishized commodities, or those genocidal wars we have waged in the name of boundary and prophylaxis.

"The dramatic combination of opposites," Mary Douglas has written, "is a psychologically satisfying theme full of scope for interpretation at varying levels." In her view those rituals that enact allegories of combination, "the happy union of opposites," serve a therapeutic role in culture. They are signs, at once material and spiritual, of "men's common urge to make a unity of all their experience and to overcome distinctions and separations in acts of at-onement."[72]

The chapters that follow, devoted to several English masquerade novels written before 1800, explore further the implications of the eighteenth-century masquerade, and in particular its rebellious, enchanting meditation on separation and unity, purity and impurity. Contemporary fictional representations of the masquerade, not surprisingly, preserve the multiple paradoxes of the social phenomenon. In the works of Fielding, Richardson, and Burney, for example, the masquerade episode is at once a gay, chaotic, exciting eruption into narrative—the very image of an ecstatic anti-society—and an intrusion that must ultimately be renounced or ideologically contained within the narrative. A moment of revelatory, atemporal impurity, the masquerade is both daemonically interesting and an affront to *Bildung*, the great plot of socialization at the heart of classic eighteenth-century fiction. The "Midnight Masque" is troped both as seduction and as danger—both as a gratifyingly atavistic chapter in the text of human experience, and as something that must be foresworn in order for the necessary channeling of collective libido to take place. Its narrative role is thus duplicitous, and always textually and ideologically problematic.

One could add by way of coda that the same ambiguity afflicted the masquerade itself. The masquerade remains an emblem of a peculiarly eighteenth-century paradox. On the one hand, it satisfied archaic, irrational cultural dreams—for new bodies, new pleasures, new worlds. (One could claim the same dreams haunted even those who called for the masquerade's extirpation, so lovingly, always, did they itemize its offenses.) But on the other hand, it was a phenomenon already belated. The masquerade was the last brilliant, even brittle eruption of an impulse inexorably on its way to extinction. The anti-masquerade rhetoric of the period offered a clue to the masquerade's ultimate demise when it exposed the masquerade as a threat to bourgeois decorum and rationalist taxonomies. Mask and costume, the signs of a joyful exchange between self and other, had to be laid aside, and more sober pursuits embraced. By the end of the eighteenth century, this transvaluation of pleasure had in fact been achieved: pleasure resided no longer in a magical incorporation of the other, but in the sentimental objectification of the other. In the rationalized moral cosmos of Richardson and Burney (two authors particularly concerned to enclose and neutralize the unstable realm of masquerade), otherness remains the object of charity, but never of identification.

The eighteenth-century masquerade was in many ways a nostalgic occasion; it inevitably awakens nostalgia in the modern sensibility. Reading of the decay of the great assembly rooms, of Walpole's masquerade dresses locked up, after 1770, in an old trunk ("I shall probably never go to another," he wrote in that year), one may feel a vague melancholia: the masquerade speaks to us, indeed, from the realm of *temps perdu*. The experience is utterly lost. Not only is the masquerade's phenomenological reality lost—the giddy, estranging visual play, the exquisite "comedies of the body" informing the occasion—so also is its

24. *Embarkation from the Island of Cythera*, by Jean-Antoine Watteau, 1717

deeper philosophic dimension, its dream of a perfected human community, free of the ravages of difference and alienation. For despite its occasional infatuation with perversity, and its some-time complicity with the merely fashionable, the eighteenth-century masquerade still invoked this utopian spirit. Its promis-cuity was at heart joyful rather than degrading; its sensual delights revelatory and life-enhancing rather than cynical or satiating.

Eighteenth-century critics often associated the masquerade, negatively, with "Love." Love was here a dangerous, insinuating deity whose only concern was to overthrow human reason and cast mortals down to the crude plane of the body. One coupled under Love's influence, but that was all. Thus a commentator in *Lady's Magazine* (December 1777) wrote, modern masqueraders

"make their offerings at the altar of beauty" and sacrifice themselves to a new goddess of Love, "*Venus Libatrix.*" In the *Weekly
Journal* (January 25, 1724) another writer described the masquerade as "a kind of Festival, dedicated to the Goddess of *Wantonness.*" The "Chevalier" Heidegger, officiating over this random fornication, was but "the *lovely Priest of Venus.*"

One might think of this Love-worship less pejoratively, however, and more humanely. For the celebration of Venus can be
more than the emblem of pagan sensual gratification; it can
stand as an allegory for ecstatic union. Worshiping at the altar of
Love is also a deeply human metaphor for intimacy and sensuous warmth. It was in this reconstructed sense that Watteau
invoked the image in his luminous fantasia *Embarkation from the
Island of Cythera* (1717; see Fig. 24). It should not surprise us that
Watteau's shimmering figures, about to leave the island of delight, wear masquerade disguise. As Michael Levey has written,

[Watteau's] people are dressed in masquerade costume, pilgrims of the
only god the eighteenth century really believed in, and set on a dream
island to which they have been brought in a gilded boat. These things,
like the rose-hung statue of Venus where the lovers pay their vows, become part of the allegory. Love's power is strongest at that place where
the kneeling man and seated woman whisper, oblivious of the cupid
(also in pilgrim costume) who tugs at the woman's skirt in an attempt
to recall her to reality. In every way, the picture is imbued with a poignant sense of the losing battle love fights against the reality of time.[73]

The "intimations of dispersal" in Watteau's painting—the fact
that it depicts a departure from the world of passionate mutu-
ality—suggest a compelling analogy with our topic. For the ultimate departure from the world of the masquerade, which had
indeed stood like a fantastical, beautiful island at the heart of
eighteenth-century culture, was also in a sense a revocation of
Love itself—that love conceived as a profound mingling of opposites, an absorptive, endlessly satisfying embrace of self and
other.

3

Literary Transformations:
The Masquerade in English Fiction

The literary history of the masquerade in England could be said to begin, not with a novelist at all, but with John Dryden. The following dialogue from *Marriage à la Mode* (1673) celebrates the birth of a topos:

PALAMEDE. We shall have noble sport tonight, Rhodophil; this masquerading is a most glorious invention.

RHODOPHIL. I believe it was invented first by some jealous lover to discover the haunts of his jilting mistress, or perhaps by some distressed servant to gain an opportunity with a jealous man's wife.

PALAMEDE. No, it must be the invention of a woman: it has so much of subtlety and love in it.

RHODOPHIL. I am sure 'tis extremely pleasant, for to go unknown is the next degree to going invisible.

PALAMEDE. What with our antique habits and feigned voices—do you know me? and I know you?—methinks we move and talk just like so many overgrown puppets.

RHODOPHIL. Masquerade is only vizor-mask improved, a heightening of the same fashion.

PALAMEDE. No, masquerade is vizor-mask in debauch, and I like it the better for't: for with a vizor-mask we fool ourselves into courtship for the sake of an eye that glanced or a hand that stole itself out of a glove sometimes to give us a sample of the skin. But in masquerade

there is nothing to be known; she's all *terra incognita* and the bold dis-
coverer leaps ashore and takes his lot among the wild Indians and sav-
ages without the vile consideration of safety to his person or of beauty
or wholesomeness in his mistress.   (IV, i, 121–45)

Here, in the form of a cosmogony, are all the later themes of the
masquerade: pleasure, women, sex, the unknown. Likewise the
scene that follows is archetypical enough—a comic imbroglio
involving mistaken identity and transvestism, erotic and political intrigue, deceit, commotion, and badinage. With Dryden,
the "glorious invention" of the masquerade, that terra incognita
at the heart of civilized life, becomes part of the scenery of English literature.

But Dryden is merely a symbolic point of origin, and a somewhat distant one at that. To be sure, *Marriage à la Mode* directly
influenced the eighteenth-century literature of the carnivalesque
in at least one respect. The play was produced in original form
until 1700; adaptations by Colley Cibber and others gave it continued life through the 1750's. It is likely that Dryden's masquerade scene provided a model for similar episodes in eighteenth-
century comic drama. A century of masquerade plays, farces,
and operas—from Shadwell's *The Virtuoso* (1676) to Sheridan's
The Duenna (1773) and Cowley's *The Belle's Stratagem* (1781)—
bear witness to the prototype.[1] In each play we find the same
exploration of the masquerade's comic potential, the same identification of the scene with error and plot complication, fantasia
and laughter. The masquerade seemed made for dramatic representation, and its "intrigues of the night" a perfect metaphor for
the playful mystifications of the eighteenth-century comic theater itself.

What Dryden did not anticipate, however, were subsequent
changes in the nature of masquerading, and the pressing ideological issues that came to surround the institution in the first
decades of the eighteenth century. *Marriage à la Mode* re-creates
the masquerade in its primeval, late-seventeenth-century English form—that of ornate, imitative, somewhat enigmatic
court entertainment. Dryden's idealized Sicilians resemble members of the court of Charles II, and their travesties the character-

25. Masquerade mayhem in art and literature. In Hogarth's *Marriage à la Mode* (1745), the adulterous Countess Squanderfield and her lover retire to a bagnio after a masquerade and are found there by her husband. The lover is shown escaping after mortally wounding the husband. The couple's masquerade paraphernalia lies strewn about the floor.

istic pleasures of a newly liberated aristocracy. These merry "frolics," mentioned in the chronicles of Gilbert Burnet and others, themselves imitated of course the lavish masked fêtes of Paris and Versailles.[2] In a large sense the Restoration masquerade belonged to the art world of the European courts, and Dryden appropriately stresses the aesthetic and aristocratic context. True, there are hints in *Marriage à la Mode* of quasi-democratic possibilities in the masquerade: Melantha and Palamede participate despite any official court connection; Melantha, in particular, here attempts to efface her status as a mere "town" lady. Masquerading coincides at least implicitly with the subversive theme of social climbing. But Dryden's main emphasis is on the masquerade as "heightened" fashion, a shimmering imago of high life.

What occurred during the early 1700's, however, was a basic change in the place the masquerade occupied in society, and its popularization as a form of public commercial entertainment. No longer strictly the predilection of royalty and hangers-on, the masquerade was transformed, in the second decade of the century, into a public event, a diversion of the "Town"—accessible, like Vauxhall or the theater or the opera, to anyone with aspirations after fashionability. It became a part of a new and burgeoning industry of public pleasures.[3] This democratization of the masquerading impulse, on which Heidegger and others capitalized so adroitly, had a critical significance in the literary history of the carnivalesque. For as the "Midnight Masque" became more and more deeply lodged in eighteenth-century popular consciousness, so too its tremendous symbolic potential, for both good and bad, emerged. The masquerade entered the repertoire of cultural emblems. This process, as we have seen,

26. David Garrick as Ranger and Mrs. Pritchard as Clarinda in a scene from Benjamin Hoadly's *The Suspicious Husband*, by Francis Hayman, ca. 1747

27. Anonymous engraving, *Couple in Masquerade*, French(?), ca. 1750

resulted in a wealth of moralizing literature—an anti-masquerade complaint of considerable proportions. But the masquerade's new visibility also led to its most significant literary manifestation: its representation in contemporary fiction.

It was fitting that one form of entertainment should be absorbed into another—that the masquerade should find a place within the new genre of eighteenth-century realistic fiction. Both were the products of an increasingly self-conscious, novelty-seeking public. Yet the masquerade was ripe for fictional exploitation for other reasons too. Early on, Addison had intimated the narrative potential of the carnivalesque: in his *Remarks on Italy* (1718), following descriptions of the Italian carnival and the pleasures of dressing "as a false personage," he commented with prescience that "the secret history of a carnival would make a collection of very diverting novels."[4] Because of the masquerade's classic association with mystification and intrigue, masquerade scenes in fiction, as in the drama, provided diverting opportunities for plot development. Early works such as Haywood's *The Masqueraders; or, Fatal Curiosity* (1724) exploited the melodramatic possibilities of the occasion. But at the same time the masquerade's characteristic themes—social mutability and sexuality, luxury, pleasure, and transgression—mirrored some of the early novel's deeper moral and ideological concerns. By mid-century, not surprisingly, the masquerade set piece had become a commonplace in English fiction. Notable masquerade scenes appear in Defoe's *Roxana* (1724), Richardson's *Pamela*, Part 2 (1741) and *Sir Charles Grandison* (1753), Fielding's *Tom Jones* (1749) and *Amelia* (1751), Cleland's *Memoirs of a Woman of Pleasure* (1749), Smollett's *Adventures of Peregrine Pickle* (1751), Burney's *Cecilia* (1782), Inchbald's *A Simple Story* (1791), and Edgeworth's *Belinda* (1801). In addition, significant references to the world of public travesty occur in Smollett's *Roderick Random* (1748), Goldsmith's *The Vicar of Wakefield* (1766), Burney's *Evelina* (1778), Radcliffe's *The Mysteries of Udolpho* (1794), and a host of minor works of the period.[5] In the guise of presenting a faithful record of modern manners, English novelists had fortuitously revivified the ancient literary imagery of the carnivalesque, and found in the process a way of giving life to certain compelling, specifically novelistic imaginative concerns.

Which is not to say that the masquerade did not make a paradoxical addition to the scenery of the novel. All the contradictions surrounding the masquerade in eighteenth-century culture, where it was seen as both delightful and pernicious, are replicated in contemporary fiction. Indeed, the intense cultural ambivalence regarding the carnivalesque is displayed perhaps more prominently here than anywhere else. Eighteenth-century novelists responded to the institution of the masquerade with moral concern—the scene is usually presented as part of a stereotypical urban topography of vice or dissipation—yet they drew upon it, sometimes disingenuously, for a host of provocative and memorable effects.

The topos exposed certain fundamental tensions at the heart of the genre itself. The novel, as Tony Tanner has brilliantly demonstrated in *Adultery in the Novel*, has always dramatized a larger cultural conflict between moralistic and transgressive imperatives, equanimity and adventure, the desire for bourgeois stability and the subversive human fascination with change and novelty. For Tanner the prescriptive moral and ideological elements of English fiction have been profoundly at odds with those currents of rebelliousness and disorder that from the beginning have implicitly animated the genre. While acknowledging the eighteenth- and nineteenth-century novel's overt celebration of the bourgeois values of marriage, social stability, and "the securing of genealogical continuity," he also notes how the genre "gains its particular narrative urgency from an energy that threatens to contravene the stability of the family on which society depends." The orphans, prostitutes, and adventurers of early fiction incarnate for Tanner "a potentially disruptive or socially unstabilized energy that may threaten, directly or implicitly, the organization of society, whether by the indeterminacy of their origin, the uncertainty of the direction in which they will focus their unbonded energy, or their attitude to the ties that hold society together and that they may choose to slight or break." So potent and interesting are these destabilizing forces that the novel "becomes a paradoxical object in society, by no means an inert adjunct to the family décor, but a text that may work to subvert what it seems to celebrate."[6]

Eighteenth-century novels often represent the conflict spatially. Early realistic fiction often seems to value the organized and stable realm of the bourgeois household; the family or domestic space is typically both the starting point and the end point in eighteenth-century narrative. But plot itself depends on less stable and predictable realms: the Garden, the Road, the City. It is necessary to leave the unchanging, endlessly self-regulating world of the home—to move beyond the boundaries of order and rectitude—in order to precipitate interesting stories. Thus the picaresque tradition, and the eighteenth-century novel's obsession with wayfaring, wandering, journeys to the city, and so on. Narrative begins with the transgressive step, the journey out of the *maison paternelle*, the house of the father.[7]

It should be clear right away how the novel of masquerade fits, loosely, into this picaresque tradition. To get to the masquerade in the first place, one must journey out of ordinary existence, away from the patterns of everyday life, into a world of strangeness, transformation, and mystery. In eighteenth-century fiction the masquerade is literally a topos, or place, somewhere out there, waiting to be discovered. It may be associated with a larger educational confrontation with chaotic urbanity: in several eighteenth-century novels the scene takes its place, in the manner of a set piece, as part of the classic theme of initiation—the hero or heroine's introduction to the "Town." Sometimes it is part of a series of topoi—one (though usually the last) in a number of unusual adventures. In *Tom Jones* and Smollett's *Adventures of Peregrine Pickle*, for example, the masquerade room is one among several urban sites the hero visits in his peregrinations; we see the underlying serial structure quite clearly.*

Yet given the particularly complex part the masquerade played in eighteenth-century life, the scene is never without special ambiguities. It crystallizes the conflicting imperatives at the heart of contemporary fiction.[8] Just as the actual masquerade brought to light certain underlying and problematic impulses in eighteenth-century English society, so the fictional masquerade scene could be said to unleash those transgressive forces present just under the ordinarily decorous surface of eighteenth-century narrative.

One might call the masquerade topos a master trope of destabilization in contemporary fiction. Its role is never merely static or emblematic. True, images of mask and masquerade can always be made to carry fixed emblematic meanings in eighteenth-century literature. As we have seen, contemporary satirists, drawing upon ancient iconographic traditions, reinscribed the masquerade's conventional association with the themes of deception and inauthenticity. Within the fluid world of contemporary prose fiction, however, the occasion has a more dynamic significance. It is associated with the disruption, rather than the

---

*On the thematic affinity between the picaresque and the scenery of masking and carnival, see Babcock, "Liberty's a Whore," pp. 109–10. Granted, the more a work approximates what Babcock calls the "antidevelopmental narrative" of the true picaresque, the less instrumental the impact a masquerade scene may have on plot per se. The scene becomes simply one among many disconnected adventures, as with the first masquerade episode in *Peregrine Pickle*. There, the masquerade in chapter 44 is merely an excuse for obscene comedy, when Peregrine's painter friend, disguised as a woman, is forced to urinate among gentlemen masqueraders. The episode leads nowhere in particular; it is simply followed by other disparate events. In a more structured work such as *Pamela*, though the masquerade initially seems part of a picaresque sequence, it has a narrative importance outweighing other episodes. Here the plot "takes": following B.'s masquerade liaison with the Countess, one thing does lead to another, and a more complex action involving the heroine evolves.

stabilization, of meaning. Befitting its deeper link with the forces of transformation and mutability, the masquerade typically has a catalytic effect on plot. It is often connected with the working out of comic or providential narrative patterns. Yet this plot-engendering function almost invariably undermines whatever emblematic meaning the episode might otherwise be expected to carry. The scene prompts larger ideological and thematic inconsistencies. Almost invariably, the fictional masquerade escapes any kind of moral reducibility, just as the eighteenth-century novel itself moves away from the formulaic didactic content of satire and moral allegory.

Since these subversive effects will be described in more detail in later chapters, I will merely sketch them here. They are often veiled at the start by a certain conventional fictional rhetoric. Aware of readers' moral expectations, English novelists of the period usually preface the masquerade episode with some sort of didactic gloss. Thus even before the masquerade occurs, the heroine may be warned against it; or a character invested with special moral prestige, often a guardian or clergyman, may inveigh against its voluptuousness and excess. Virtuous characters, forced into attending a masquerade by the less pristine, may articulate vague anxieties about what dangers the event will hold—as when Pamela, in Richardson's sequel, wishes she did not have to go to the Haymarket with her husband, or when Harriet Byron, in *Sir Charles Grandison*, fears the masquerade she is to attend will be "the last diversion of this kind I shall ever be at" (Vol. I, p. 116). And sometimes the narrator himself locates the occasion within a larger satiric or moralizing context, as in *Amelia*. As one might expect, the danger the masquerade poses is primarily sexual (and threatens heroines far more than heroes), though the event is associated with all kinds of malignity and vice. In advance of any actual representation of the scene, the contemporary novelist, like the satirist, may attempt to limit the role of the masquerade to that of moral emblem.

We see in this effort a superficial connection with the programmatic didactic literature of the period and the familiar attacks of the anti-masquerade writers. As in those works, the reader is invited to comprehend the masquerade as a transparent epitome of vice, part of the moralized topography of the corrupt Town. The masquerade itself masquerades. Ostensibly the scene of pleasure, it is actually the scene of snares—a region of manipulation, disequilibrium, and sexual threat. This conventional opening critique often coincides, particularly in Fielding's novels, with a larger fictional attack on the deceptive and hypocritical nature of human society in general. Besides being the icon of a debauched world of fashion, or the allegory of urban disorder, the masquerade may intimate a global dysphoria: a universal inauthenticity, obfuscation, and brutality. The embedded moral condemnation of the masquerade scene confirms the fictional work's didactic pretensions and establishes, at least for a time, the quintessentially virtuous persona of the eighteenth-century English novelist, the unmasker of vice.

Yet such transparency is obscured by the scene itself. Despite the moralistic warnings, characters do, as though by a strange narrative compulsion, end up at masquerades. Indeed, one may take it as a rule that if the possibility of attending a masquerade is raised in an eighteenth-century novel, someone—and usually the heroine—will go. This turn toward the carnival world may make little sense in terms of didactic economy; the reader may feel the perniciousness of the occasion has already been sufficiently established. The shift into saturnalia is frequently an irrational-seeming plot development. In *Pamela*, for example, one cannot quite grasp why a reformed B. should force his pregnant wife to attend this scene of riot against her will, but he does. And similarly in *Amelia*, though Booth has strenuously protested his wife's acceptance of masquerade tickets from the sinister Noble Peer, he later insists that she accept a second set of tickets from the equally devious Colonel James. The crucial move from domestic salon to assembly room—from the predictable scenery of everyday life to the estranging realm of the carnivalesque—is almost always accompanied by a logical discontinuity, an incursion of irrationalism into the ordered cosmos of eighteenth-century psychological as well as topographic representation.

How to explain the curious attraction the scene exerts? Like its real prototype, the fictional masquerade must be considered a kind of pleasure-mechanism for author and reader alike. There is first the simple pleasure of local color. Eighteenth-century masquerade episodes generally convey the specular delights of the occasion—the exquisite visual incongruities of the costumed crowd. The fictional diversion conventionally diverts by adding an element of spectacle, in the ancient sense, to the otherwise quotidian landscape of the realistic novel. Thus in Burney's *Cecilia*, for instance, the reader may take vicarious pleasure in the rich and marvelous entertainment depicted there, where men turn into "Spaniards, chimney-sweepers, Turks, watchmen, conjurers, and old women," and women into "shepherdesses, orange girls, Circassians, gipseys, haymakers, and sultanas" (Vol. I, p. 169).

But the masquerade diverts in a second, more important sense. The verbal rendering of this beautiful and various phenomenological realm, the space of endless enchanting metamorphosis, typically coincides with an even more gratifying transformation: the proliferation of intrigue itself. The masquerade episode serves as a point for narrative transformation—the privileged site of plot. Above all, the masquerade is the place where significant events "take place." It is a classic locale in which the requisite mysteries of the story itself may be elaborated. This plot-producing function follows from the nature of the diversion. In life as in fiction, as we have seen, the eighteenth-century masquerade was a cultural locus of intimacy. There persons otherwise rigidly segregated by class and sex distinctions might come together in unprecedented and sometimes disruptive combinations. Masquerading substituted randomness and novelty—prerequisites of imbroglio—for the highly stylized patterns of everyday public and private exchange.

The open-endedness introduced into the system of human relations by the masquerade is perfectly suited to the elaboration of plot, which as Tzvetan Todorov has pointed out, depends on an initial destabilization of the ordinary—a disequilibrium at the heart of things. In his study of the fantastic, Todorov defines the minimum requirement for narrative, that "nucleus without which we cannot say there is any narrative at all," as "a movement between two equilibriums which are similar but not identical." In the genre of the fantastic—including fantastic tales of the eighteenth century like Walpole's *The Castle of Otranto* and Beckford's *Vathek*—that which precipitates movement, the necessary catalyst for narrative, is usually the supernatural intervention, a mysterious or extra-logical incursion that radically disrupts the stable modes of ordinary fictional existence. "Habitually linked to the narrative of an action," the marvelous element, Todorov writes, "proves to be the narrative raw material which best fills this specific function: to afford a modification of the preceding situation, and to break the established equilibrium" of the fantastic text. Social and literary operations here coincide, for "in both cases we are concerned with a transgression of the law."[9]

A comparison might be made between the role of the supernatural in fantastic literature and that of the masquerade in certain putatively realistic or secularized eighteenth-century narratives. The masquerade episode is likewise a transgression of the law, albeit a nontranscendental one; it deranges the orderly system of human relations intimated elsewhere in eighteenth-century English fiction. The masquerade engenders a set of *liaisons dangereuses* by throwing characters into proximity who would never meet if an exhaustive sociological decorum were truly the goal: the high and the low, the virtuous and the vicious, the attached and the unattached. And by the same token, the episode may bring about, for a time at least, the alienation of characters who *should* be together in the fictional world by virtue of established conjugal or familial ties: husbands and wives, parents and children, guardians and wards. Out of the masquerade's surplus of scandalous dialectical transactions, a multitude of intrigues may develop. True to its magical-seeming, transformational nature, the carnivalesque episode characteristically provides the mimetic disequilibrium on which plot itself depends.

This analogy with the supernatural event is not as arbitrary as it might seem. In several masquerade scenes a literal association with marvelous agency is inscribed atavistically in the imagery of costume. Important characters either come under the influence of others disguised as supernatural beings, or disguise themselves as such. Tom Jones meets the "Queen of the Fairies" (Lady Bellaston) and falls as though by magic under her sexual and economic sway; in *Cecilia* the heroine's sinister suitor, Mr. Monckton, appears before her in the shape of Lucifer. In Inchbald's *A Simple Story* Miss Milner dresses as the goddess Diana, transfixing all who see her. Since each of these distinctively costumed characters either perpetrates masquerade intrigue or is instrumental in later plot developments, the sartorial hints of supernatural power might be taken as allegories of narrative power. And just as the actual masquerade gave people in the increasingly secularized eighteenth century a way of acting out memories of the traditional world of magic and folk belief—as witches, conjurers, devils, and the like—so the masquerade set piece gave vestigial fantastic and marvelous literary elements a paradoxical second life in realistic eighteenth-century English fiction.[10]

Characteristically, then, the masquerade episode precipitates plot. More often than not—and this will be a crux in my argument—it precipitates a comic plot in particular. It engenders a rewarding or euphoric pattern of narrative transformation, even for characters, like the beleaguered heroines of contemporary fiction, whom one would not expect to benefit from its disarming travesties. Granted, the beneficent instrumentality of the occasion may not be immediately obvious: the narrative repercussions of the masquerade can seem painful or melodramatic on the surface. But it is important to notice how frequently the episode's ostensibly disastrous "consequences" (to use Fielding's term) turn out to be a necessary prelude to something else: the amelioration of a central character's fortunes, the providential rewarding of the heroine. Like the Fortunate Fall (with which it has strong symbolic resonances), the masquerade stands out in eighteenth-century English narrative as an indispensable event—as that temporary plunge into enigma and difficulty without which the comic destiny of characters could not be realized.

Consider, for example, the situation in *Sir Charles Grandison*. The "cursed masquerade" early in that novel bears all the conventional marks of evil narrative agency: Harriet Byron is abducted from it by the odious Sir Hargrave Pollexfen, and her sexual ruin seems inevitable. After the "fatal news" of her kidnapping, her distraught Uncle Selby exclaims that while he formerly believed public masquerades "more silly than wicked," he now declares them "the most profligate of all diversions" (I, 119). The reader soon learns, however, that Harriet has miraculously escaped the expected fate: in a timely piece of action, the paragon Sir Charles hears muffled screams coming from Sir Hargrave's coach, and liberates her from her abductor.

Such is the happy accidental meeting on which Richardson's romance plot depends, for Harriet and Sir Charles later fall in love and marry. Yet, one could argue, it is Harriet's initial movement into the world of sexual danger, represented by the masked assembly, that diverts her toward her ultimate sexual reward. Without the masquerade she would neither be absorbed, as she is, into the beatific Grandison household (where she is taken after her ordeal) nor come to know her "god-like" benefactor so intimately. The masquerade excursion is paradoxically responsible for all her subsequent happiness and the essential erotic comedy of Richardson's novel. Again, this quasi-magical plot function is obscured on the surface of the fiction: Harriet's relieved relations afterward revile the occasion that has caused such "barbarous" suffering. But it is inscribed subliminally, in comments like those of Mr. Reeves, who suggests that Harriet's experience represents "a common case" heightened into "the marvelous" (I, 137). Harriet too has the sense of wondrous agency: "How shall I bear this goodness!" she exclaims after her adventure. "This is indeed bringing good out of evil! Did I not say, my cousin, that I was fallen into the company of angels?" (I, 145).

One might multiply cases in which the heroine's masquerade venture results in an affirmation or a reconstitution of the comic plot of the heterosexual romance. Roxana meets her most powerful patron, the Duke of M——, at the masquerade, attracting him with her lubricious "Turkish dance." In a somewhat more sedate manner, Burney's Cecilia also attracts a lover at the masquerade, her future husband, Delvile. In Inchbald's *A Simple Story*, though the masquerade episode appears at first to estrange Miss Milner and Dorriforth, it is a necessary preliminary to that ecstatic reconciliation scene during which Dorriforth marries his ward on the spot. And as we shall see shortly, even in Richardson's highly moralistic sequel to *Pamela*, Mr. B.'s masquerade flirtation with the Countess is not the disaster for the heroine it seems to be: it too sets up a transporting moment of "éclaircissement" later, when B. renounces his would-be paramour, begs his wife's forgiveness, and reaffirms his love for her.

Not only is the masquerade episode, then, a dense kernel of relations out of which plot in general develops, but it is specifically implicated in the larger comic patterns of eighteenth-century English fiction. Without it many of the providential-seeming turns of contemporary narrative are difficult to imagine. Yet such instrumentality also undermines the conventional moral significance of the topos, and threatens the didactic coherence of the work in which the masquerade occurs. By its very comic agency, the carnivalesque episode contradicts its superficial negative inscription within the eighteenth-century text, and reveals itself instead as part of the hidden, life-giving machinery of narrative pleasure. It ceases to be merely an emblem—of hypocrisy or anything else—at the moment it facilitates, like a kind of covert deus ex machina, the ultimate reward of characters and readers alike.

This scrambling of emblematic meaning, it turns out, is often paradigmatic; it can signal a general collapse of didactic accountability in the masquerade novel. The scene typically leaves in its wake what I will call, borrowing from the ancient thematics of reversal and chaos, a World-Upside-Down effect.[11] Following the characters' carnivalesque excursion, the ordinary social or metaphysical hierarchies of the fiction may suddenly weaken or show signs of being overthrown altogether. Masquerade scandal is contagious: it spills over into everyday life. The reader experiences a sense of ideological topsy-turvydom, as though the ambiguous transformations on the narrative level had somehow precipitated thematic changes too. In Bakhtin's term, the fictional world itself is carnivalized.

I will offer specific examples of this phenomenon in subsequent chapters—particularly in the discussion of Fielding's *Amelia*, a novel in which the upside-down effect is especially pronounced. Suffice it to say here that the masquerade is typically linked to three kinds of ideological reversal in eighteenth-century English fiction. First, true to its traditional association with the power of women, the masquerade threatens patriarchal structures. Normative sexual relations in the fictional world may be overthrown, and female characters accede here to new kinds of sexual, moral, or strategic control over male associates. At the same time the obscure and the "low" find new kinds of status at the masquerade; servants challenge masters, and complex scenarios involving social mutability and the exchange of public roles may develop. Class as well as sexual arrangements are modified. And finally, somewhat more abstractly, the scene may be linked with patterns of characterological or moral reversal, particularly in novels like Fielding's, in which a highly dichotomized, even allegorical typology of character ordinarily prevails. Otherwise lucid moral types suddenly behave in a fashion conspicuously unlike themselves: ostensibly good characters (such as the reformed B., Tom Jones, and Amelia) act in peculiarly compromising or questionable ways, while stereotypically villainous characters are equally strangely rehabilitated.

The carnivalization of eighteenth-century English fiction is thus a multifaceted phenomenon. If the process begins with a localized or strictly anecdotal representation of the masquerade—the discrete scene or set piece—it does not end there. The invocation of the conventional topos almost always coincides with an elaboration of plot, and in particular the comic plots of sexual consummation and social mobility. At the same time the scene injects an enigmatic and destabilizing energy into the ordinarily polite and reactionary world of eighteenth-century representation. The literary artifact is transformed as a consequence: the masquerade novel seldom retains its claim to didactic purity, following the representation of this least purifying of diversions. It may suddenly seem a contradictory or hybrid imaginative structure—double in potential significance, unrecuperable according to any straightforward didactic logic. With the turn toward the irrational world of carnival, the eighteenth-century English novel becomes unlike itself: it diverges from its putative moral project and reshapes itself as phantasmagoria and dream.

For the novelist the masquerade topos satisfies diverse conscious and unconscious imperatives. In discussing specific works I will consider matters of intentionality, and examine to what degree the subversive effects of individual masquerade scenes may reflect larger, explicitly premeditated authorial designs. Certainly the pervasiveness of the topos in eighteenth-century fiction suggests a general ambivalence on the part of writers regarding the didactic project itself. For contemporary novelists, caught between the contradictory imperatives of the new genre, representing the masquerade may be a way of indulging in the scenery of transgression while seeming to maintain an aspect of moral probity. The occasion can be framed in the conventional negative manner, yet its very representation permits the novelist, like his characters, to differ from himself: to cast off the persona of the moralist and turn instead to the pleasures of "Intrigue." Seductive fantasies quickly take the place of staid instruction. For writers like Richardson and Fielding, in whom the imaginative conflict between moralism and subversion is intense, the masquerade may function as a figure for ambiguous authorial intentions—the textual sign of an inward tension regarding the novelist's conventional role.

Throughout this part of my study I draw upon Bakhtin's notion of the carnivalesque, a concept he developed most memorably in *Rabelais and His World*. Bakhtin used the term mainly to indicate a thematic—that traditional body of festive imagery preserved in European literature in various forms from the Middle Ages through the Romantic period. But it can also suggest a process of generic destabilization. The carnivalized work, he argues, resists formal classification, and instead, like Rabelais's *Pantagruel*, combines a multiplicity of literary modes in an increasingly mixed or "polyphonic" form.[12] It is worth noting finally that eighteenth-century novels containing masquerade scenes often display a notable generic instability. At times the masquerade scene may even prompt a formal shift in the work in which it occurs. In *Amelia* the scene coincides with a general shift from the satiric to the mimetic mode. In Richardson's sequel to *Pamela* there is even more generic instability. After the masquerade scene the text becomes a true hodgepodge of discourses—a mixture of embedded exempla, "table talk" (the symposia of the B. and Darnford households), and miscellaneous non-narrative items, such as Pamela's lengthy commentary on Locke's *Education*. Just as the masquerade episode precipitates narrative transformations, it also prompts generic transformation—instigating, in the classic Bakhtinian mode, lapses in consistency on every literary stratum.

The chapters that follow—on *Pamela*, Part 2, *Amelia*, *Cecilia*, and *A Simple Story*, in that order—flesh out these as well as related theoretical issues. The arrangement is chronological and organic. The opening discussion of Richardson explicates the basic role of the masquerade scene in eighteenth-century fiction: its function as a plot catalyst. Because narrative interest is otherwise curtailed in *Pamela*, Part 2 (the plot sequence involving the masquerade is the only real chain of events in this often-maligned novel), the work provides a clear-cut preliminary specimen— almost a test case—of the scene's transformational power. The chapter on *Amelia* returns to the masquerade's instrumental role, but the main concern here is with its destabilizing thematic effects. In looking at the two masquerade scenes in that interesting work, I identify the imaginative conflict in Fielding, which I also take to be representative of his age, between an "emblematic" and a "transformational" masquerade—between Fielding's desire to present, like the satirist, a static *carnaval moralisé*, and his pleasure, as a novelist, in the more fluid and provocative scenery of comic disorder. The next two chapters turn to two late works, Burney's *Cecilia* and Inchbald's *A Simple Story*. Here my interests are almost entirely thematic: the masquerade's utopian aspects and the special significance of the carnivalesque in women's writing. Burney and Inchbald both delineate the utopian (and particularly feminist) potential of the masquerade, yet differ noticeably in the degree to which they allow its disruptive power to shape their narratives. Their contrasting treatments suggest ways of thinking about the ambiguous ideological role of the topos at the end of the eighteenth century, and the eventual disappearance of the masquerade from English literature and society. The final chapter is a brief coda on the attenuation of the masquerade set piece in nineteenth-century writing.

The discussion of these novels is not intended primarily as advocacy in the traditional critical sense. Several have indeed been unfairly neglected (particularly *Amelia* and *A Simple Story*); yet none is an established classic. Fielding's novel has been the only contender for canonical status, and a somewhat dilatory one at that. *A Simple Story*, as Lytton Strachey and others have noted, is remarkable, but hardly a work of unrivaled formal technique. Each novel here somehow violates the ancient aesthetic criteria—revivified in this century by the New Critics and others—of unity, logic, and thematic consistency. No one could claim these novels as flawless or as always coherent works of art.

Yet for the student of the carnivalesque, their interest is great. They offer compelling variations on a characteristic eighteenth-century theme. It is for this reason above all that I have chosen them. Traditionally grounded aesthetic judgments may not be applicable or even desirable. Indeed, in speaking of masquerades, perhaps the more chimerical the work, the better. The disruptive imagery of the carnivalesque, one might argue, is exactly what makes these novels such paradoxical, even baffling, literary artifacts. The topos is bound up with larger failures of continuity and uniformity: this is its meaning and its fundamental, though often unacknowledged, attraction. Perhaps as critics begin to leave behind the legacy of the New Criticism, interesting themselves more and more in the disunities, as well as the unities, of literature (not to mention its social and ideological contexts), we are at last in a position to appreciate the value of these sometimes perplexing, yet also rewarding, works.

Each of these novels, finally, has a place in eighteenth-century cultural as well as literary history. In what follows the basic homology should always be kept in mind: that the literary fascination with the masquerade, displayed most intricately in fictional works of the period, mirrors the generalized interest the carnivalesque held in English society. It may seem an obvious enough point to make, but the way the masquerade functions in contemporary narrative (as an episode at once diverting and yet threatening to the implicit taxonomies of the fictional world) is roughly analogous to the way it functioned in eighteenth-century culture (as a discontinuous, estranging, even hallucinatory event, yet one that carried with it an intense cognitive and cathartic éclat). Psychologically speaking, little separates writers who exploited the masquerade topos, and readers who cherished it, from those who created the event itself. Whether fictional or actual, the masquerade articulated otherwise unassimilated impulses in the eighteenth-century imagination—toward chaos, parody, and the exquisite transfiguration of the everyday.

For the space of a century the culture of the masquerade institutionalized dreams of disorder. While contemporary satirists complained of too much whirl, too much metamorphosis, in the masquerade—"So many various changes to impart, / Would tire an Ovid's or a Proteus' art," wrote the poet Christopher Pitt—novelists turned with relish to the occasion's exemplary reversals.[13] This "World painted in Miniature" became the emblem of an endless and fascinating mutability.[14] True, the mercurial imagery of the carnivalesque gave shape to a fantasy of change that, in one form or another, always lies at the heart of narrative. But the masquerade novel also had a compelling historical specificity. By embracing the spectacular, secretive figures of the carnival world, eighteenth-century English writers reenacted a larger contemporary flight into irony and illusion. The fiction of the masquerade was an epitome of the imaginative regime in which it flourished—and a mark of the eighteenth century's own ambivalent escape from consistency, transparency, and the claims of a pervasive decorum.

4

The Recarnivalization of Pamela: Richardson's 'Pamela,' Part 2

In some mysterious way it does not altogether surprise us that Pamela, sublime amphibian ("half one, half t'other," with "arms she knows not whether to swim with, or to hold before her"), should go to a midnight masquerade. Indeed, her appearance at the Haymarket, midway through Richardson's otherwise baleful sequel—*Pamela*, Part 2— has an odd, dreamlike rightness about it. This is not to say that Pamela herself feels at home. Mr. B. has brought her, against her inclination, to this most licentious of London "diversions," and paragon that she is, she is properly appalled. "Out upon these nasty masquerades!" she cries; "I can't abide them already!" (p. 264). Later, when B.'s masquerade flirtation with the "bold Nun" (the Countess) has developed into an illicit intrigue, Pamela's anti-masquerade rhetoric intensifies: "O why were ever such things as masquerades permitted in a Christian nation?" (311).

Yet the voice of conventional outrage seems peculiarly misplaced, uncanny, like that of a ventriloquist's dummy. For one feels a shock of familiarity, a kind of déjà vu, seeing Pamela here, in the midst of universal taxonomic chaos. Her body, appropriately enough, is an image of festive contradiction—a walking

130

double entendre. She wears the dress of a "prim Quaker," yet she is visibly, even wildly, pregnant with Mr. B.'s child. She is the visual embodiment of carnival confusion. The spectacle brings to mind, obscurely, something else about her, something the rest of Richardson's untoward, evasive continuation has tried to make us forget: her double history, and its own gorgeous, theatrical violation of distinctions. The phantasmagoric figures pressing in upon her—"one Indian prince, one Chinese Mandarin, several Domino's of both sexes, a Dutch Skipper, a Jewish Rabbi, a Greek Monk, a Harlequin, a Turkish Bashaw, and Capuchin Friar"—seem to recognize her (265) and claim her as one of their own. "I know you!"—the quintessential masquerade insinuation—everywhere greets this "Lady Would-Be." Encircled and fêted, Pamela reigns over the swirling crowd, its unwilling cynosure, a queen of misrule.

To write at all of *Pamela*, Part 2, let alone of a single vignette, is to run a danger—of having no reader. The novel itself has had few; unlike its memorable, convulsive predecessor, Richardson's sequel has evoked little in the way of love or controversy. Literary historians have had only disparaging words for the second *Pamela*: it lacks a unifying plot; nothing "happens" in it; the constant burbling praise Richardson devotes to his faultless heroine is repetitious and charmless, even vaguely squalid. The most sympathetic critics acknowledge the work's shortcomings. Given its dearth of compelling incident, one cannot, writes Margaret Doody, "conscientiously" recommend the sequel to the general reader.[1] For Richardson's biographers T. C. Duncan Eaves and Ben D. Kimpel, the infelicities of *Pamela*, Part 2, beggar critical discourse itself: "It is hard to think of another work by a reputable writer for which there is so little to be said as for the second part of *Pamela*."[2] What then to say, one might wonder, about a work for which little may be said? Where to go with a text that seems to go nowhere?

One possibility is to go to the masquerade. I speak only half-facetiously, for *Pamela*'s critics have done just this—departed, as it were, for a carnival at the heart of the text. Even as they despair of the whole, they gravitate to the part: one scene in the sequel, they allow, does gratify us after all, does stand out (however briefly) as a moment of excitement, color, pleasure. "The masquerade and the affair with the dashing young widow that develops out of it," Mark Kinkead-Weekes observes, is the "central episode" in which Part 2, almost in spite of itself, comes temporarily to life.[3] Doody concurs: the masquerade scene and the resulting complications involving B. and the Countess and Pamela are "more spirited, more dramatic" than anything else in the work.[4] And even the dour Eaves and Kimpel agree that the "elaborately worked up" masquerade episode provides some "faint hints" of a story in a text otherwise devoid of such enjoyments.[5] This is not to say the part redeems the whole; the consensus is that the sequel remains an imaginative failure. But the part is definitely worth remarking. Like eighteenth-century aestheticians, modern critics fetishize the masquerade sequence, extract it and preserve it as the single beauty in a singularly unbeautiful book, a capsule of narrative delight in a narrative of few delights.

The exception is both compelling and provocative. For we do find the "masquerade scene" (and consequent intrigue) more pleasurable than anything else in Part 2. It comes as a relief—oddly discontinuous, perhaps, with the rest of the text, and yet somehow a mysterious, radiant center. Once B. begins his enigmatic flirtation with the masked "Nun," we feel for the first time in the presence of the real story, the one we have been awaiting. But this pleasure is itself enigmatic. Why should this textual diversion be so diverting? What is the relation between this scene of pleasure and the pleasure we, as readers, take in the scene? Most important, what connects the masquerade—the exemplary public site of intrigue—and plot itself? How to relate Pamela's excursion into the topsy-turvy world of carnival and *Pamela*'s (brief) excursion into story?

Such questions have a deceptive simplicity. It is impossible to examine the diverting part of the novel without examining the whole. The masquerade episode in the second *Pamela* is an especially interesting specimen of its type, and suggests much about the complicated antitaxonomic fantasy at work, just under the surface, in classic eighteenth-century fiction. But like the real masquerade, which always reflected back on the world outside, the masquerade scene cannot be treated in isolation. Richardson's sequel as a whole is an extended, if ambiguous, confrontation with carnivalesque possibility; its moment of actual carnival cannot be detached from the surrounding rhetorical and ideological context. The readability of the masquerade sequence (whatever that entails) can be explained only in light of the unreadability of the text in which it is so curiously embedded. To understand the disruptive appeal of the Richardsonian masquerade—to theorize its pleasurable shock—we must consider first our displeasure with all those scenes of "*humdrum* Virtue" preceding it. To appreciate the world of carnival, one might say, one must first endure a world without.

One might begin with a commonplace: sequels are always disappointing. "Few continuations," writes Richardson in the preface to Part 2, have the "good fortune" to be judged "not unworthy the *First* Part" (vii). And in a sense no sequel is as good as its predecessor: sequels inevitably seem to fail us in some obscure yet fundamental way. The circumstances governing the production of sequels suggest why this is so. At least since the early eighteenth century, when the economy of literary production began to take something of its modern capitalist form, the sequel has been an offshoot of the best-seller syndrome. It is an attempt to profit further from a previous work that has had exceptional commercial success: only charismatic texts, those with an unusually powerful effect on a large reading public, typically generate sequels. *Robinson Crusoe* is a classic eighteenth-century example of the sequel-generating fiction; and so too, of course, is the first *Pamela*.[6]

Charismatic fiction draws its power from deep collective sources. It articulates underlying cultural fantasies; it gratifies, in particularly profound or euphoric ways, pervasive cultural wishes. This was certainly the case in the eighteenth century with *Robinson Crusoe* and *Pamela*; as Ian Watt was the first to argue, these books achieved unprecedented popularity because of the talismanic mythic material they encoded.[7] So powerful is the charismatic story that it creates in readers a desire for "more of the same." The readers of sequels, one could say, are motivated by a deep unconscious nostalgia for a past reading pleasure, the original story of dream and fulfillment. Like Job, they want to "receive everything double." The producers of sequels have always recognized and tried to exploit this subliminal desire for repetition.

The problem, obviously, is that the sequel cannot be the same as its originating text.* Though it establishes a connection with its original by invoking the same characters, a sequel must, on the surface at least, tell a different story. Typically the sequel allegorizes its difference from the original by claiming to show its characters at a later period in their careers. A sequel can never fully satisfy its readers' desire for repetition, however; its tragedy is that it cannot literally reconstitute its charismatic original. Readers know this; yet they are disappointed. Unconsciously they persist in demanding the impossible: that the sequel be different, but also *exactly the same.* Their secret mad hope is to find in the sequel a paradoxical kind of textual doubling—a repetition that does not look like one, the old story in a new and unexpected guise. They wish to read the "unforgettable" text once more, yet as if they had forgotten it.

Pamela, Part 2, suffers from the inevitable debility of every sequel: it is not, and can never be, *Pamela*, Part 1. It is not, obviously, the cherished plot of the past: Pamela is not back where

---

*One might make a theoretical distinction between a text that generates a sequel—a single, usually unsuccessful continuation of its characters' adventures—and one that generates a series of new texts, as was the case with Conan Doyle's first Sherlock Holmes story, "A Study in Scarlet." The detective novel is typically prone to spawning an indefinite number of follow-up texts, new mysteries involving the same detective-protagonist. It is not clear, however, that these secondary texts, though composed after the first text, can properly be called sequels, for no internal connection, chronological or otherwise, is usually made between their plots and the plot of the original. Each novel in a detective series is autonomous, even though its characters may appear in a host of works. This seems to reflect the exceptional nature of the mystery genre itself: its subordination of character to plot, its insistent focus on a discrete enigma to be solved, its reliance on certain formulaic elements that may be reworked in an indefinite number of new, ahistorical combinations.

she started, a servant in the household of the dying Lady B. Rather she *is* Lady B., now married to her former master and happily ensconced in "high life." From the start the sequel has no chance of telling the amazing story of her exaltation again, for she is exalted already. But this limitation does not entirely explain the intensely displeasing effect of Part 2. The novel is more than a disappointment. At times it seems almost to insult us, to affront our expectations, including our very desire for repetition. Even for a sequel, it is exceptionally frustrating. Part 2 seems both to tease and to thwart us.

To understand the unusually problematic nature of the work, we must review for a moment Richardson's reasons for composing it. These were demonstrably complex. In the preface to Part 2, he notes cryptically that he has been "provoked" into writing a continuation against his inclination (vii). This is true in part. One provocation, certainly, was a host of spurious sequels—*Pamela's Conduct in High Life* (1741), *The Life of Pamela* (1742), and so on—that attempted to cash in on *Pamela's* success. Richardson's annoyance with them has been well documented.[8] Faced with these "Imitations," Richardson felt obliged to provide readers with a "true" account of his heroine's post-nuptial life.

At the same time, however, Richardson had less transparent motives. Above all he wanted to refute the charge, put forth most damagingly by Fielding, that *Pamela* was a book with revolutionary moral and social implications. Why Richardson should have been upset by this accusation (he never forgave the author of *Shamela*) must remain a psychological mystery. For *Pamela*, Part 1, is of course a revolutionary story.[9] It was the sheer transgressive energy of the novel—the way it so dramatically challenged ordinary social and sexual norms—that gave it, more than anything, its tremendous appeal. And *Pamela* remains, one could argue, one of the great carnivalesque plots in literature. It has to do with the violation of taxonomic boundaries, with the unprecedented (and gratifying) coupling of things that should remain apart: high and low, masters and servants, rakes and virgins. It celebrates a world of fluid human relations;

its impulses are insistently, even convulsively, antihierarchical. Pamela herself is at once the emblem and the beneficiary of this joyfully destabilized fictional world—the ultimate carnivalesque heroine. For her very nature is magically altered. Her "happy turn" is also a turning into—a metamorphosis of low into high, maid into mistress. She is the symbol of euphoric transformation. Her being eludes simple classification; her history is everywhere the history of a double identity, identity in the process of becoming something else. Like the text bearing her name, Pamela is an affront to all that is fixed, uniform, lapidary.

In itself Pamela's story could seem nothing less than revolutionary to eighteenth-century readers, for it demystified supposedly natural distinctions and categories. It suggested that one's place in the world might change, that social identity was not irrevocably fixed by nature, but subject to odd historical alterations. Richardson intensified the charged effect of this story, moreover, by explicitly affirming its repeatability. The sort of transformation undergone by the heroine, Part 1 suggested, might occur again elsewhere: the plot of the "happy turn" might be reenacted by others. The notorious "Virtue Rewarded" subtitle encouraged readers to think of repetition: one who emulated Pamela's behavior, it hinted, might reasonably expect a similar exaltation. "The joy of the chambermaids of all nations," Lady Mary Wortley Montagu called the novel, in part because it hinted that any chambermaid might be transformed.[10] Mr. B.'s inflammatory statement near the end of the novel, that a gentleman "ennobles" the woman he marries, whatever her original status, provided the mechanism: any infatuate lord, the suggestion was, might use his ennobling power (here almost a kind of patriarchal mana) to exalt at will. Granted, Richardson tried to limit the domain of potential metamorphoses—only women could change their natures, and then only at the behest of men— but a certain transformational magic was unleashed in the world all the same. Given one paradigmatic misalliance, an ensuing carnivalization of the social order itself—the spawning of a multiplicity of Pamelas—became a possibility.

Part 1 intimated a World Upside-Down—a world in which serving girls became ladies simply, it seemed at times, by donning ladies' clothes.[11] Contemporaries were right in fearing the novel's saturnalian implications: by suggesting the underlying theatricality of social relations (Pamela learns to "act the part" of a lady), the novel, as we now see clearly, challenged the essentiality of those relations. Part 2 began as an apparent retreat from such topsy-turvydom. However illogically, Richardson (who often enough had an extraordinarily alienated sense of his own creations) was from the start at pains to deny the charge that *Pamela* sanctioned misalliances or social leveling. A sequel offered the obvious opportunity to take the denial even further, to refute once and for all complaints against his fiction's revolutionary message. Part 2 originated as a somewhat paradoxical revisionist gesture—a rearguard attempt to silence disturbing (if justifiable) criticism.

The covert ideological project shaping Part 2 is one, as it were, of decarnivalization. With his second *Pamela* Richardson set out to efface the carnivalesque aspect of the first. The task was to remove from Pamela's story its subversive element—all traces of the transformational and the theatrical. Pamela's dangerously hybrid nature had to be clarified retroactively, and the basic fact of her shocking metamorphosis—the "happy turn" itself—had somehow to be unsaid. Quality had to be defined after all as something more than just a matter of fine clothes. A new and purified *Pamela* would vindicate the old, save it from the critics, and save it, in effect, from itself.

But such a project, of course, was perverse from the outset. The scandalous history the sequel had to revoke was nothing less than the plot of its own original. The problem was to do away with the tale already written, even as one elaborated upon it. The greater part of the second *Pamela* frustrates so profoundly for just this reason. Not only does it fail to repeat for us the story we subliminally desire—the compelling story of its predecessor—but it tries to suggest, in paradoxical and strange ways, that there is no story to repeat. It attempts to erase the memory of its own charismatic original. For the most part, Richardson's sequel is more than just plotless. It is an assault, in every sense problematic, on plot itself—the transformational history of *Pamela*, Part 1.

I emphasize the strangeness of the assault; it is nowhere straightforward. The rhetorical deviousness of the sequel adds to our discomfort. Richardson, after all, could have "decarnivalized" his heroine's story relatively simply, through a single modification. The problematic impact of Part 1 might have been nullified in an instant (and the categories of social existence reaffirmed) by one short yet effective narrative operation: some disclosure in a sequel that Pamela was a lady all along, even before her marriage to Mr. B. A Fieldingesque plot twist involving mistaken parentage and a revelation of the heroine's true gentle birth would have solved at a stroke the taxonomic problem of Part 1, its implication that class boundaries could be magically overthrown. Several of Richardson's imitators had revised Pamela's history in just this way: on the Continent, Carlo Goldoni attributed aristocratic origins to the heroine in his continuation of *Pamela*; likewise, in England, the "High Life Men" made the same decorous "improvement" on the original.[12] The disclosure of hidden genteel origins restored a kind of taxonomic purity to the heroine. No longer the unsettling embodiment of categorical ambiguity, she became proof there was no such thing.

Richardson chose against this easy solution. In the preface to Part 2 he writes that he will avoid "all romantic flights, improbable surprises, and irrational machinery" in his sequel (vii). This statement—ostensibly a simple claim for the verisimilitude of what will follow—is crucial, for it attests to a debilitating ambivalence operating in Part 2. Clearly, despite external pressure, Richardson could not bring himself to do away entirely with that wishful, subversive story he had already written. Given a chance to domesticate Pamela's story by invoking the familiar romantic plot of mistaken identity, he does not. He is unable, at bottom, to substitute the conventional safe plot of disclosure for the more radical plot of metamorphosis.

Hence the paradox: Richardson both wants and does not want his original story. He wants to undo the carnivalesque plot of Part 1, yet he refuses the one uncompromising gesture necessary to undo it. Caught between irreconcilable imperatives, he falls back, finally, on an unhappy half-measure. Recognizing the danger of the plot of metamorphosis, but unable to let go of it altogether, he tries instead to mystify it. *Pamela*, Part 2, is analogous to an act of repression: it attempts to cover over, without ever really revoking, the very story on which it relies for its raison d'être. For its first half at least, the sequel pretends to forget (and tries to make us forget too) the tale we already know— even, paradoxically, as it continues from the point where that tale left off.

The effect is painful indeed, and the logical problem is devastating, for how can we forget *Pamela* by reading a second *Pamela*? The various patterns of mystification at work in the sequel inevitably fail, since it is clearly impossible for Richardson to have and yet not have his original story. Because only repressed— never done away with—the plot of metamorphosis retains a subterranean hold over this supposedly purified text. It breeds contradictions and tensions, disturbing an otherwise becalmed narrative surface. And finally, it behaves as repressed material is wont to do. At the enigmatic heart of the fiction, the forgotten story of Pamela's gratifying transfiguration makes an abrupt reappearance. Disguised yet unmistakable, like a visitation from the past, the plot of the "happy turn" returns.

It comes as no surprise that this uncanny process of repetition, which one might call the recarnivalization of Pamela, begins in a scene of carnival. The plot of metamorphosis returns when the sequel itself turns, atavistically, to a world of metamorphosis. It returns, in short, at a masquerade.

For much of its first half Richardson's sequel resembles nothing more than a bad conjuring trick, a clumsily executed piece of textual sleight-of-hand. The point of the trick is to make the plot of Part 1 disappear: to make the reader believe that despite

Pamela's "blessed change," the manifest alteration in her condition, she has not in fact been changed. "Uniformity," a concept often invoked here, is Richardson's abracadabra-word, connoting more than just spiritual conformity, though it is used at times too in its strictly theological eighteenth-century sense.* Applied to the heroine, it suggests a mysterious, wishful *quidditas*—the state of being perpetually "like" oneself. The uniform Pamela, we are meant to believe, is (and has always been) redundant with herself. She has never been transformed. The vague metaphysical language is typical of the sequel's new sublimated mode. Yet Richardson seems oblivious to the paradox that every assertion of Pamela's uniformity must remind us, abysmally, of her revolutionary history. He keeps up the bustling work, the patter, of mystification.

Some of Richardson's methods are primitive enough. At times the characters of Part 2 simply forget the facts of Part 1. No one remembers where "Mrs. B." came from, or what she was—even though, paradoxically, everyone exclaims over her fitness for high estate. Clearly the reader is meant to participate in the general amnesia. Thus early in the sequel, when Mr. B. retells the story of his courtship of Pamela before a host of rapt relatives and friends (all of whom react as though they had never heard it before), he omits the crucial change he has wrought upon Pamela by marrying her—the "exaltation" of his bride from servant to gentlewoman. The fact of her amazing social movement is obscured. Instead B. stresses Pamela's primordial moral unchangeability: her virtue, he says, was so "uniform and immoveable" that she "half-disarmed" him from the outset (118). This elliptical version of events initiates a pattern of mystification that will recur throughout the first half of the sequel: praise for Pamela's spiritual immutability, her "rigid virtue," becomes a way of not talking about her disturbingly fluid social identity. The em-

---

* Before the London journey, while describing life in the "blessed mansion," Pamela hopes that Mr. B. will soon be "uniform" enough to join her and the rest of the household in their Sunday morning offices: "I hope in time, I shall prevail upon the dear man to give me his company—But, thank God, I am enabled to go thus far already! . . . This is my comfort, that next to being uniform *himself*, is that permission and encouragement he gives *me* to be so" (140).

phasis is on her power to transform others in the moral sense, even as she remains herself "uniformly" virtuous. She "moves" others to regeneration by her own "immoveable" goodness. Thus concludes B., in a fit of uxorious rhapsody, "Since I could not make an innocent heart vicious, I had the happiness to follow so good an example; and by this means, a vicious heart is become virtuous" (121).

Others too seem to have forgotten Pamela's origins. Oddly enough, her own parents appear not to recollect that she is, or ever has been, their daughter. In one of the early letters in the sequel, her father is deferential toward her to the point of aphasia. He writes to the "lady," not to the child: "We hardly know how to address ourselves even to *you*; . . . viewing you as the lady of so fine a gentleman, we cannot forbear having a kind of respect, and—I don't know what to call it—that lays a little restraint upon us" (4). As the sequel proceeds, Pamela's relations with her parents become increasingly estranged and indistinct: it is hard to imagine that this insignificant pair ever were her mother and father. Without going so far as to deny Pamela's parentage outright, Richardson seems to want to achieve the same phenomenological effect: though not a changeling, the heroine might as well be. Like the aged godparents of fable, whose time of guardianship is over, Pamela's parents dwindle into irrelevance. As they cease, so to speak, to recognize their "exalted" daughter, the sequel itself ceases to recognize them.

In place of the troublesomely low Andrewses, Richardson attempts, retroactively, to provide the heroine with a new, more decorous set of kin. Mr. B.'s relations do more than tolerate Pamela: they are shown wishfully incorporating her, after the fact, into the ranks of quality. Through a crude sort of collective statement—cast always in the form of an encomium upon Pamela's excellences—B.'s aristocratic kin discover lost connections between themselves and the heroine. They remember, as it were, a new past for her, and collectively naturalize her unprecedented appearance among them. Again, Pamela's real origins are obscured.

Thus though genteel birth clearly does not figure in Pamela's actual history, Lady Davers and the rest talk as if it did, and indeed, as if they believed it did. Everyone agrees that Mrs. B.'s attributes are "naturally" those of a lady. "Why this," marvels the Countess of C., speaking of Pamela's gracious demeanor, "must be *born* dignity—*born* discretion—Education cannot give it" (136). A primitive hermeneutics operates: since Pamela displays certain conventional tokens of high birth, the relatives exclaim that she must be highborn. By some fluke of Providence, we are invited to believe, her gentility has simply been hidden, and now it translucently reveals itself. As the Countess prettily observes, Mrs. B. is like a "fine flower," exquisite and strange, returned to its rightful place, "transplanted from the field to the garden" (92).

At times the imaginary heritage is even more specific. Lady Davers's elaborately self-conscious addresses to her "Sister" Pamela affirm, with a peculiar retroactive force, the familial bond between them. The address becomes a curious sort of performative utterance, establishing, again after the fact, an archaic tie between the two women. Insistently applied, the terms of kinship become magically absorptive. They have the power to reshape personal history.* Thus at church, when Lady Davers says to the heroine, with ritual imperiousness, "In this solemn place, I take thy hand, and acknowledge with pride, my *sister*" (142), the effect is almost baptismal. In a strange temporal reversal Lady Davers (and Richardson) return to Pamela her "lost" nobility.

Any character who remembers a different Pamela, the serving girl of Part 1, is silenced. Mr. B.'s recalcitrant uncle, Sir Jacob Swynford, is the obvious case in point. The porcine Sir Jacob, a heavy-handed specimen of Richardsonian grotesque (he appears

---

*In *Adultery in the Novel* Tony Tanner comments on a similar process of familialization in *Sir Charles Grandison*: "In the novel, characters are constantly stressing the desire to draw everyone into one big family. Where family ties do not exist, kinship terms are applied to incorporate others. . . . There is no *real* affiliation or consanguinity in the new 'relatives' who result from this endless process of 'familialization.' . . . Strangers become 'fathers,' 'mothers,' 'sisters,' 'brothers' by a sort of benign conspiracy of reappellation" (p. 178). In *Pamela*, however, this "benign conspiracy" is more than just a sentimental ideology of kinship: it is part of a larger rhetorical effort to obviate history, and in particular the scandalous matter of the heroine's low origins.

"more an ostler than a gentleman"), objects to his nephew's marriage on the obvious grounds that it has violated the principle of
distinction (171). Arriving too late for the wedding, he alone
among the relatives excoriates the notion of Pamela's uniformity. His is a voice out of the past—the voice of taxonomic outrage. Thus his satire on her name before he meets her is also
a satire on her disturbingly unclassifiable nature: "Pamela—did
you say?—A *queer* sort of name! . . . Is it a Christian or a Pagan
name?—Linsey-woolsey—half one, half t'other—like thy girl—
Ha, ha, ha" (166).

But the challenge he poses is short-lived. The scene of Pamela's
paradoxical charade as Lady Jenny, a young woman of quality, is
clearly, if clumsily, designed to exorcise vestigial complaints
about her hybrid status. Meeting "Lady Jenny" (while Pamela is
supposedly indisposed), Sir Jacob wishes aloud before the company "that Mr. B. had happily married such a charming creature, who carried tokens of her high birth in her face, and
whose every feature and look shewed her to be nobly descended"
(167). When the charade is dropped, Sir Jacob, functioning as the
stooge of the piece, is humiliated and abashed. Obligingly, he
instantly revises his opinion of his "linsey-woolsey" niece, and
falls, like the rest of the family, into spasms of uncontrolled encomium: "Bless you! said he, and stamped—who can choose
but bless you?" (169). Sir Jacob too claims that genteel birth
must account somehow for Pamela's extraordinary graces: "Why,
Madam, you seem to me born to these things!" (170). And to B.
he adds, "Why, nephew, I believe you have put another trick
upon me. My niece is certainly of quality!" (171).

Compliments cannot undo history, however, and the episode,
like so much in the first half of the sequel, is suffused with
bathos. Richardson seems mostly unaware of it, just as he seems
unaware of the disquieting rhetorical effect of showing Pamela
impersonating a lady. Even as he intends the opposite, the scene
with Sir Jacob enforces our sense of the theatricality of Pamela's
genteel behavior. Had she appeared before him, say, in the dress
of a servant—without the outward trappings of quality—and
had he then still seen in her the "tokens of high birth," the effect

might have been more convincing. Then such tokens might indeed have seemed providential, the indissoluble signs of essence, rather than just the effect of a certain costume and manner. But as it stands, the episode perversely confirms the power of theatricality: Pamela seems to be a lady simply because she looks the part. One might call such a scene an ideological slip by Richardson. As when Lady Davers tells Pamela that no woman in the neighborhood "better keeps up the part of a lady, than you do" (135), one senses a subterranean confusion, as if the author were himself unsure whether the heroine's gentility was a matter of nature or of theater. Such slips accumulate in the first half of the novel, contributing much of its rhetorical tension. They are the preliminary signs of a textual ambivalence that later, in the masquerade sequence, will produce a disruptive, totalizing return of theatricality. Pamela's domestic masquerading accidentally prefigures a more inclusive and extravagant scene of role-playing—one that will have ironic consequences both for the shape of the sequel and for Richardson's revisionary project itself.

For the moment, however, the project continues. What one might call the sequel's screen memory—its wishful projection of a set of false origins in place of Pamela's true history—is not the only mystifying strategy at work. Pamela's uniformity, it turns out, has its active as well as its retroactive dimension. To wit, though her own history has been a model of taxonomic disorderliness, she is here installed, somewhat ludicrously, as the agent of order, its spokeswoman and instrument. Throughout the first half she operates as a sort of taxonomizing angel, bringing metaphysical clarity to the fictional world, or at least to that part of it represented by Mr. B.'s "sweet mansion." Her ordering powers are to be suspended later, when she and B. leave this microcosm for the larger, confused world of London and its dangerous diversions. But until that revelatory journey she exerts an almost magical influence on behalf of purity, boundary, and the status quo.

The heroine of Part 2 is the enemy of change. She polices the fictional world, correcting for changes that have already occurred and thwarting further changes, whether moral or sociological. Her influence is characteristically figured in spatial terms: she returns things (and persons) to their rightful place. Across time, Pamela is the enemy of deviation and diversion—any sort of swerving or turning away from the self. She whose own history might be figured as an ecstatic upward curve is here the preserver of straight lines. Her influence is geometrical: she is the principle of rectitude itself.

In the moral sphere Pamela's actions are mainly of the corrective sort. She rescues those who have sunk "beneath" themselves, or slipped out of themselves, by performing vicious actions. Evil alienates the doer from himself or herself: vice is a mask one adopts, virtue the true self to which one must return. Hence Pamela's acts of reformation are not so much transformations as acts of symbolic reconstitution: she restores uniformity to those whose natures have become chaotic, dramaturgical. Already she has redeemed Mr. B. from the "innumerable meannesses" that alienated him from himself in his youth (120). He is on the way to becoming "uniform *himself*" (140)—that is, morally congruent with himself. Pamela piously hopes that on their trip to London he will not "deviate" again or behave in a way unbefitting his true virtuous nature (121). Mrs. Jewkes, the villainness of Part 1, has been similarly returned to herself. Whereas before, as Pamela's former jailer admits, she "was acting a part that now cuts me to the heart to think of" (47), she has now been shown "the right way," and thanks to Pamela's example, proceeds along "the happy path" of virtue. It is a path without turnings: "Turn not either to the right hand or to the left," the heroine counsels; "the reward is before you" (66).

Pamela's powers of moral reorganization are such that she reforms even those who seem to have slipped out of the category of the human altogether. Sir Jacob Swynford, despite being the spokesman for ontological purity, is a carnivalesque apparition, more swine than human. With his "little and fiery" eyes, "yellow and blackish" teeth, and "rough paw," he is, as Lady Davers says, more "surly brute" than man (160, 165). His mixed-up appearance is the outward sign of an equally confused moral nature. His "haughtiness" has paradoxically lowered him to subhuman status; his manners, everyone agrees, are beastly. Yet again, so moving is the spectacle of Pamela's uniformity that Sir Jacob's disparate being is clarified in her presence. "Confound me for a puppy!" he cries after realizing who Lady Jenny is (171), while his "angel" of a niece lifts him back up, by the force of her goodness, to full humanity: "I am sorry I have acted thus so much like a bear," he exclaims contritely; "and the more I think of it, the more I shall be ashamed of myself" (170). Pamela once again undoes the effects of deviation, rescuing Sir Jacob from categorical ambiguity and moral self-alienation. As she tells Miss Darnford, "It would be discrediting to one's own practice, if one did not appear at one time what one does at another" (138).

Pamela preserves the sociological as well as the moral status quo. Here her reactionary influence is even more absurd, for in the social realm she herself has hardly been the same thing at "one time" and "another." Moreover, her metamorphosis holds exemplary subversive power, since it is eminently susceptible to repetition. As Sir Jacob bluntly states, the problem with Mr. B.'s marriage, despite Pamela's excellences, is the example it sets "*to young gentlemen of family and fortune to marry beneath them*" (171). One might expect Pamela's dramatic ascent into high life to excite, he suggests, rather than to discourage further disturbances of the social order. Again Richardson tries to obscure the problem. B. has an answer for Sir Jacob: Pamela's particular history cannot be repeated because Pamela is exceptional. So rare a creature is Pamela, B. says, so extraordinarily virtuous and accomplished, "no *two* princes in *one age*" are in danger of making misalliances (174). The argument is fatuous, however, and Richardson seems aware that he needs to strengthen his case. His solution is to show the heroine in a compensatory role, actively obstructing repetitions of her own history. As if to make up for her problematic changeability, she now makes sure no one else is likewise changed.

Like a kind of human Panopticon, the heroine scans the fictional world, on guard against events that resemble or bring to mind her own "happy turn." She is a domestic vigilante, abruptly forestalling any potentially carnivalesque violations of the social order. Early in the sequel, for example, when her parents request that certain of her cousins be allowed to work on Mr. B.'s Kentish estate, it is Pamela herself who forbids it, explaining that she "would not wish any one of them to be lifted out of his station, and made independent, at Mr. B.'s expence, if their industry would not do it" (13). Yet it is of course a similar "lifting up" the heroine herself has experienced, and not entirely on account of her industry.

On another occasion—when she bursts in on Mr. H.'s dalliance with her maid, Polly Barlow—Pamela thwarts an almost exact recapitulation of her own history. Just as the sequel threatens to reproduce the socioerotic scandal of Part 1, a liaison between gentleman and maid, Pamela appears, to prevent the dangerous coupling and reassert the inviolability of social boundaries. Catching the would-be lovers in the midst of amorous play, Pamela draws Polly away and berates Mr. H. for "levelling all distinction." She exhorts her maid not to think "that I would envy any other person's preferment, when I have been so much exalted myself," but her private aside to Miss Darnford regarding the possibility of marriage between Mr. H. and Polly bespeaks her real concern: "it behoved me, on many accounts, to examine this matter narrowly; because if Mr. H. should marry her, it would have been laid upon Mr. B.'s example" (192). Repetition is the issue here—repetition of Pamela's own story. She calls her discovery of the guilty couple "Providential," but the reader finds it simply Richardson's artificial means of asserting once more the nonrepeatability of the plot of metamorphosis.

Like a true ideologue Pamela objects to repetition even in the nebulous form of public memory. When B. considers accepting a baronetcy, she is afraid that the world will accuse him of trying to obscure the fact of his misalliance. "They will perhaps say, 'the proud cottager will needs be a lady, in hopes to conceal her descent'; whereas, had I such a vain thought, it would be but making it the more remembered against both Mr. B. and myself" (98). Every time the new title was used, she argues, her problematic history would be revived in collective memory, and hence made even more susceptible to imitation.

At moments when Pamela displays such self-nullifying humility, it becomes difficult to view her as a realistic character in even the most limited sense. And given her enthusiastic forays against "encroachers," she seems either hypocritical or psychotically alienated from her own past. Gone is the bemused, self-mocking adolescent of Part 1. It is easier to treat *this* Pamela as simply a format or code—a function in Richardson's revisionist scheme. The first realistic heroine in English fiction has been, as it were, digitalized. Metaphorically speaking, Pamela leaves the human realm altogether, entering that of angels and automata. Mr. B.'s perfectly run household—itself an image of the machine—is the external fulfillment of Pamela's taxonomizing influence: a "blessed mansion" over which she rules like "an angel, dropped down from heaven . . . to live among men and women, in order to shew what the first of the species was designed to be" (255).

The domestic saturnalia that Sir Jacob Swynford fears upon first arriving at Mr. B.'s estate ("Who's housekeeper now? I suppose all's turned upside down" [161]) has not materialized. The house Pamela oversees is, if anything, even more a world right-side-up. Mr. B. has retained all of his original servants, but each, amazingly, defers to the new mistress, with a kind of surreal enthusiasm. "We all of us long till morning comes," exclaims the housekeeper, Mrs. Jervis, "thus to attend my lady; and after that is past, we long for evening, for the same purpose, for she is so good to us—You cannot think how good she is!" (146). Despite her carnivalesque leap out of their own ranks, Pamela wields authority over the servants, mysteriously, as though she has always possessed it. She has "such a dignity in her manner" that all the servants are "ready to fly at a look, and seem proud to have her commands to execute" (253).

Pamela's new genteel correspondents naturalize her questionable stewardship with a series of wishful, horrific tropes. Her "heaven of a house," Miss Darnford writes, runs "like a good eight-day clock" (255). Pamela has created a system in which fluidity and exchange are impossible—a mechanism for domestic exactitude. "No piece of machinery that ever was made is so regular and uniform as this family is" (255). Lady Davers similarly figures Mr. B.'s "blessed mansion" as a kind of neoclassical Metropolis, and Pamela as that "master-wheel in some beautiful piece of mechanism, whose dignified grave motions . . . set a-going all the under-wheels, with a velocity suitable to their respective parts" (26). The only possible motion in such an environment is an endless turning in place: Pamela's mechanical home preserves hierarchies, fixing every member eternally in position.

The image of the machine gives way at times to even more blatant (and disturbing) visions of hierarchy, as in Lady Davers's advice to Pamela that she consider herself "the task-mistress, and the common herd of female servants as so many negroes directing themselves by your nod" (26). Here the true problem of hierarchy (that is, how is Pamela, originally one of the "common herd" of female servants herself, now to distinguish herself from them?) is occulted through a process of fantastical rhetorical transfiguration. Davers (and Richardson) try to normalize the master/servant relation, not by appealing to class distinctions (which of course have become problematic), but by drawing an altogether fanciful racial distinction. The historical metaphorics of race and slavery is speciously invoked to validate Pamela's otherwise dubious authority over her former associates. Pamela becomes a colonial power and her servants blacks—such the discourse of mystification.

Pamela's management of the "blessed mansion" translates, finally, into control over its actual spaces, so that the house becomes a fixed, even marmoreal allegory for the orderly system of human relations over which she presides. Under Pamela's influence household social relations are figured by a kind of exquisite prophylactic architecture. The boundaries between bodies—representative always of taxonomic boundaries—are preserved through the rigid subdivision of household space. Everyone has his or her place in the house. The most obvious feature of this symbolic architecture is the vertical placement of masters over servants: Mrs. Jervis, the housekeeper, must now come "up" to see Pamela, her former friend, to receive the occasional gifts of noble beneficence (56). Moments of necessary contact between "high" and "low"—always moments of potential danger—are mediated by an elaborate, ritualized moral hygiene. Thus after Polly Barlow's near-indiscretion with Mr. H., the maid is no longer permitted to approach Pamela in her chamber. "So regular and uniform as all our family is, and so good as I thought all the people about me were," Pamela writes, "that I could not suspect that she, the duties of whose place made her nearest to my person, was the farthest from what I wished" (199). Polly is subsequently exiled to the lowest reaches of the house—the realm of inferior female servants.

Contact between the sexes, even between Pamela and her husband, is severely regulated. Pamela is shown maintaining an odd prophylactic distance from Mr. B. himself. She has her closet and withdrawing room, from which he is exempted. Miss Darnford at one point inquires whether B. is in fact as "regular and uniform" in his behavior to Pamela in private as he is in public—or whether he "breaks not into your retirements, in the dress, and with the brutal roughness of a fox-hunter?" (216). Pamela replies that even when he returns from riding and is impatient to see her, he prefaces his approaches with decorous inquiries regarding her whereabouts and accessibility (219). Though B. suggests on one occasion that such "extraordinary civilities and distances" between husband and wife are unnecessary, Pamela corrects him, asserting that "little delicacies and moments of retirement" exist, "in which a modest lady would wish to be indulged by the tenderest husband" (220).*

The effect of such passages is to enforce a sense of the impermeability of Pamela's person itself, not just her "closet." Befitting one whose ideological task is the preservation of proper

---

*The value set on private space in the "blessed mansion" connects the world of the sequel with that of the original *Pamela*: in Part 1 similar hygienic architectural separations are instituted in B.'s household after his marriage to Pamela. See Folkenflik, "A Room of Pamela's Own." On the subject of privacy as a bourgeois value and its institutionalization in the eighteenth century, see Sennett, *The Fall of Public Man*.

moral and sociological boundaries, her own body, in this first half of the sequel, is bounded and impenetrable. Pamela does not seem to mix with anyone, sexually or otherwise. The contrast in this regard with Part 1 is striking. There the energy of the narrative was entirely directed toward the interpenetration of opposites, the socioerotic mingling of high and low. In their first incarnation Pamela and Mr. B. joined on every level; sexual consummation was only the most literal image of rapprochement.* Yet here Pamela and B. seldom join in any physical sense. (It is not unimportant that Pamela's first "motherhood" in Part 2, represented by the adoption of Miss Goodwin, is a motherhood achieved without intercourse.)

At the same time that the heroine's history is decarnivalized, her body is decarnalized. The two processes entail a similar suppression of transformational energy. If the body of the heroine in Part 1 is in some sense fluid—open to exchange and transfiguration—the body of the married Pamela is a kind of rigid, unchanging bastion, hardly a body at all. It exerts a polarizing rather than an attractive force; she seems to repel rather than draw B. to her. Coming into her exalted presence, he swerves off again, as though affected by an antimagnetic field: "I must take a little tour without you, Pamela; for I have had *too much* of your dear company, and must leave you, to descend into myself; for you have raised me to such a height, that it is with pain that I look down from it" (226).

At this point the impatient reader may also feel in need of a "little tour" without Pamela—or at least not this Pamela, the Pamela of stultifying affect. Richardson's attempts to mystify his heroine's past, to decarnivalize the impact of Part 1, are as undelightful as they are unconvincing. Apart from the endless celebration of Pamela's virtues, nothing actually happens in the first half of the sequel, and one feels the lack of incident pro-

---

* As Richardson's detractors noted, the original *Pamela* treats sexual matters far more explicitly than the sequel does. In addition to the notorious "warm scenes" before their marriage, *Pamela*, Part 1, has a scene in which Pamela and B. are caught in bed together after their marriage by Lady Davers, who is outraged by the spectacle (see Part 1, 434–35).

foundly. There is no plot here, only a denial of plot—no change in the heroine's fortunes, only a denial that she ever has changed, or ever will change. "Uniform and immoveable" Pamela is hardly the sort of being to engender narrative, let alone simple human interest, and as the fiction proceeds from one thankless encomium to the next, a vast readerly ennui sets in. One begins to fear what Roland Barthes has called "the tedium of foreseeable discourse."[13] The disavowal of plot, past and present, takes its toll: *Pamela*, Part 2, threatens to become a text that rolls along and yet goes nowhere, like some interminable ceremonial procession. We long for a turning of the narrative line—some diversion of textual energy into something more diverting.

But there are signs that on a certain level Richardson longs for diversion too. One detects a kind of rhetorical exhaustion on Richardson's part, as if he wished for some escape from the tedium of plotlessness and the burdens of his own intractable ideological project. The signs are displaced at first. Characters begin to intimate that they have little to write about, that life in the "blessed mansion" is short on subject matter. Thus Pamela, in a letter to Miss Darnford, apologizes for her "tedious scrawl" (177), and later excuses herself to Lady Davers for "running on" at length "without materials" (232). Clearly Richardson too feels the lack of "materials" at this point. He faces here in exaggerated form what some have seen as the bourgeois novelist's typical problem: what, apart from the celebration of bourgeois life itself, is he or she to take for a subject? For all its pretended glimpses into high life, Richardson's idealization of Pamela's "uniform and regular" household is after all, as many critics have observed, a thinly disguised paean to bourgeois values: stability, structure, moral and spiritual continuity. But this very idealization creates a difficulty: the representation of a perfectly ordered, endlessly self-replicating and self-affirming world becomes, after a certain point, uninteresting.

Tony Tanner has stated the problem epigrammatically: "The rule of law engenders a dream of indistinguishability."[14] Paradise is indeed boring, and the fiction that sets out to depict it, like *Pamela*, Part 2, inevitably ends up doing something else too.

Endless stasis prompts a desire for novelty, above all in the novel itself: hence the mysterious and apparently paradoxical turn the second *Pamela* takes at its midpoint. Suddenly something happens to disrupt Richardson's ideological project, suspending it indefinitely. Pamela and B. simply leave their "heaven of a house." As if the world of unchanging uniformity had become unaccountably insupportable, the couple abandon domestic perfection and abruptly embark on a tour—a turn toward the protean new world of London.

This journey into urbanity can only be rationalized, one suspects, as a reflection of Richardson's desire for a novel discourse. Journeying is the novelistic motif par excellence—an implicit revocation of those values of stasis and complacency embodied in the modern bourgeois household. The fiction itself takes a tour here—away from the deathless domestic space, the world of rectitude and light, and away from its own exhausting and unsatisfactory project of ideological mystification. It is as though Richardson himself were in search of new scenes.

Within the fictional world the journey is curiously unmotivated, except as a pilgrimage after novelty. Richardson here originates a new bourgeois concept, the secular quest of the vacation. Granted, Mr. B. wants to attend Parliament while in London, and Pamela, it is hinted, will have her first lying-in there, but neither of these explanations is given much weight. Rather the heroine seems to be going in order that she (and Richardson) have something new to write about. Everyone eagerly requests written accounts of the trip from Pamela, and in particular her reactions to the notorious London public entertainments. "The advices you can give us of what passes in London," Lady Davers writes, "and of the public entertainments and diversions . . . related in your own artless and natural observations, will be as diverting to us, as if at them ourselves" (23). That Lady Davers and her friends already know what these diversions are like, having been to them many times themselves, makes no difference. Pamela's artless descriptions, Davers claims, will make her correspondents experience them vicariously as if for the first time. "For a young creature of your good understanding, to whom all of these things will be quite new, will give us, perhaps, a better taste of them, their beauties and defects, than we might have before" (23).

I will return later to this strange assertion—that Pamela's London narrative will somehow have the power to make the familiar new. Suffice it to say that when Pamela and B. arrive in the city (Letter 43), a novel discourse does begin. No more the unwavering textual focus on Pamela's immoveable virtue: she has indeed been moved. Yet this new narrative dispensation, though it brings relief, is also complicated, and complicating. For the quest for diversion is never innocent. It implies deeper desires for change, transformation, and the turning of energy, human or textual, into unexpected forms. It betrays, in a word, a desire for plot. The sudden turn Richardson's sequel takes at this point is also a turn toward plot itself, which until now the work has everywhere sought to exclude.

A pattern of transformation, a story in other words, begins when Pamela and B. reach London. Having so obdurately refused the possibility of metamorphosis, the sequel now embraces it, compulsively, as a universal theme. In London everything is shown in the process of changing from one thing to another: taxonomies collapse; the hybrid reigns.[15] The heroine herself is immediately implicated in this general movement into multiformity. With its "vast piles of buildings" and "concourse of people," London is an archetype of confusion—such a "new world" that she knows not what to make of it (227). Likewise the house in which she and Mr. B. take up residence is a confusingly indefinite double structure "with an airy opening to its back part," facing onto fields, "and its front to a square." The lack of closure or clear outline disturbs Pamela, who is not, she writes in one of her first letters, "reconciled to it, so entirely as to the beloved mansion we left" (228).

Uniformity is disappearing on other levels too. Most peculiarly, the sequel suddenly seems to remember a certain hybrid quality about Pamela herself. For the first time characters appear who call attention—without impunity or censoring—to the heroine's humble past. B.'s lawyer friend, Mr. Turner (who will play an important part in the "turn" in Pamela's fortunes on the night of the masquerade), is the most sinister of these. The "*genteel contempts*" he heaps on her after she arrives in town are a rude reminder (even as they masquerade as compliments) of the theatrical aspects of her situation: "I expected to find an awkward country girl, but she tops her part, I'll assure you—Nay for that matter, behaves very tolerably for *what she was*—And is right not to seem desirous to drown the remembrance of her original in her elevation" (247). After this meeting Pamela is afflicted with an uncharacteristic anxiety about her place in the world; she worries that she is "neither gentlewoman nor rustic," but something "linsey-woolsey," suspended between categories, "as Sir Jacob hinted" (246).

Pamela's very body is losing its uniformity. What has only been hinted before becomes explicit once she and B. arrive in London: she is pregnant with his child. As if in response to the curious doubling energy of the city, Pamela's body itself starts to become a double form. Carrying B.'s child, she both is and is not herself: she is herself and also something more, becoming, as it were, two bodies. This revelation works again as a kind of textual memory. For Pamela, we are now allowed to see, cannot have been as monolithic or impenetrable as the first half of the sequel made her appear. It is as though Richardson were letting something previously censored now emerge: a vision of Pamela's doubleness, her implication in a world of interpenetrations and transformations. For the first time we are invited to imagine her as something other than purely uniform. Indeed, her form now begins to alter before our eyes.

Pamela's pregnancy will become most important (and in one sense most visible) later. She will attend the midnight masquerade—where the fantasy of the double body is institutionalized—at the limit of her term, nine months along. Here the intimations of her condition merely signify a preliminary disruption of uniformity. The sequel is both letting go of a falsifying perception of the heroine and hinting at the totalization of doubleness to come. Richardson has begun to turn away from the inhumanly "uniform and regular" Pamela of the first half,

letting someone else take her place—a Pamela subject to accident, change, and history, the Pamela of memory.

The enigmatic changes taking place are as much psychological as physical, for the idealized relations of Pamela and B. also
change abruptly. They have their first contretemps soon after
arriving in London. In this debate, over whether she should
breastfeed her baby, Pamela, the voice of taxonomy, takes an
uncharacteristically antitaxonomic stand. She wants to nurse
her child. The shift here is interesting: like childbearing itself,
breastfeeding is an anti-individualizing gesture. It prolongs the
bodily communion between mother and child, suggesting on
the phantasmic level a merging or confusion of bodies.[16] B. has
to step in and assert the propriety of orderly separations: he demands that a wet nurse be called for when the time comes.
Pamela unhappily defers, but remains "somewhat wavering"
until her irritated spouse accuses her of behaving "not like my
Pamela" (238). Her self-alienation is contagious: B. confesses
after the argument that he too has acted "a little unlike" himself
(238). For a moment Pamela and B. lapse out of themselves, developing new and unaccountable traits. The scene again hints
at what is to come—the imminent collapse, at Heidegger's
"Midnight Masque," of every kind of visible and psychological
uniformity.

It is at just this point, after this vaguely disturbing exchange,
that Pamela's letters shift focus and the real business of the London excursion begins: her initiation into the "round" of public
diversions. As she describes it, the introduction to the metropolis begins quite literally in a circular motion: B. has already carried her "by gentle turns" around the "vast circumference" of
the city in his carriage, pointing out interesting sites and places
of entertainment (229). This swirling movement, so inappropriate to a representative of rectitude, will soon become a vertiginous downward spiral. For Pamela, even as she is becoming ever
more changeable herself, now enters a series of increasingly disorderly realms, culminating in the masquerade, that vortex of
confusion at the dense heart of the city.

The heroine is carried to three diversions—theater, opera, and masquerade. Like the three trials in a folktale, these events represent an intensification of danger and transformational energy: Pamela finds each more upsetting and chaotic than the last. She herself is altered: her taxonomizing powers, already thrown into question by the protean city itself, diminish with each subsequent occasion. She is less and less able to make sense of what she sees. This debilitation reaches its most extreme point at the masquerade, where Pamela actually becomes not just a troubled observer, but part of the disorder she observes.

Of Pamela's experiences at the theater and opera, reported in a series of letters to Lady Davers, little need be said, except that she finds both spectacles aesthetically and morally confused. Watching Ambrose Philips's tragedy of *The Distressed Mother*, for instance, she is offended by the play's "lewd and senseless" double entendres, which render it inconsistent and "unnatural" (258).* At Steele's *Tender Husband* she complains that the farcical subtitle (*or, The Accomplished Fools*) contradicts the "amiable" title, and that the moral is tacked on at the end of the comedy "without much regard to propriety" (260). Only when proper regulations are observed, Pamela concludes—when tragedies are uniformly tragic, comedies are uniformly comic, and "vice is punished, and virtue rewarded"—will the English stage become a profitable rather than a disorderly amusement (257).

The opera is even less susceptible to taxonomic recuperation. Pamela is unable to make any sense at all out of this improper coupling of sound and sense, the melodic and the discursive, English and Italian. It is "incongruous nonsense" to her, a

---

*True to her role as the preserver of taxonomies, Pamela is everywhere in Part 2 the opponent of modes of linguistic confusion such as the double entendre. Thus in a jocular complaint to Mr. B., Sir Simon Darnford, a great maker of puns, accuses Pamela of condemning "the only instances of wit that remain to this generation; that dear polite *double entendre*, which keeps alive the attention, and quickens the apprehension, of the best companies in the world" (73). Pamela's fears of this form of linguistic impurity seem to be well justified. Later B.'s romantic entanglement with the Countess will be shown to be in part the result of a double entendre: by an ambiguous response to one of her questions, he manages to intimate that he is not married (328). The pun is the semantic equivalent of the carnivalized body—a hybrid thing in which two elements are improperly joined.

"hotch-potch" she finds unintelligible (263). B. explains that operas are less confusing in Italy, where libretto and music are required to be consistent with one another. In England, however, the form is nonsensical, because it is the practice "to mutilate, curtail, and patch up a drama in Italian, in order to introduce favorite airs, selected from different authors" (263). The result is a chaotic, hybrid form in which the instruction, Pamela tells Lady Davers, is none at all (262).

Of all London diversions, however, the masquerade is the most violent affront to order, and the most questionable of public gatherings. A reformed theater, Pamela decides, might be permissible in England; operas are perhaps acceptable entertainment for Italians; but it is not clear that masked assemblies should be allowed in any Christian nation (311). Pamela's uneasiness about this third event—the culmination of her movement into institutionalized disorder—begins even before she gets there. She has heard of the many freedoms practiced at masquerades and has "a great indifference, or rather dislike to go" (263). B. has to work hard to persuade her to accompany him, and only by exerting his conjugal authority does he finally win her unenthusiastic submission (263). B. is left to decide on costumes (the cloak of a Spanish don for himself, Quaker dress for Pamela), for she will have none of it.

Yet the heroine's humiliations are only beginning. Richardson takes an almost perverse delight in showing Pamela caught in this amphitheater of taxonomic collapse. It is her most radical departure from uniformity to date—the absolute antithesis, obviously, of the "blessed mansion." And she is everywhere the victim of the occasion, unable to participate with any pleasure, subject on all sides to travesties and excesses of which she can only disapprove. Alienated from B. (who abandons her and Miss Darnford almost as soon as they arrive at the Haymarket), Pamela can only despise the roiling, jovial masquerade crowd, and deplore, even as she herself is embarrassed by them, the coarse jests and bawdy antics of her fellow guests.

Thus in her letter describing the evening, Richardson has his heroine wax moralistic and complain about the grotesque lapses in decorum she has been forced to witness. The scene is one out of Hogarth or Giuseppe Grisoni; the frolicking Haymarket crowd an image of huddle and indiscretion. Pamela is assaulted by a host of shapes familiar from contemporary visual representations: cardinals, Merry Andrews, parsons, and various ladies in "fantastic" costumes (264–65). She is distressed to find that few, including her own husband, preserve even a limited decorum by "acting up" the characters they are meant to represent. The disparity between costume and wearer remains ludicrously transparent. Thus after watching the "handsome Spaniard" (Mr. B.) jest with a "bold Nun" (later revealed as the Countess), Pamela laments that "the dear gentleman no more kept to his Spanish gravity, than she to the requisites of the habit she wore: when I had imagined that all that was tolerable in a masquerade, was the acting up to the character each person assumed" (264). She is convinced, for her own part, that her Quaker disguise is perfectly suited to her real personality: "I thought I was prim enough for that naturally" (264). Herself aside, the disorder is universal: no one remains uniform. Pamela's judgment on this scene of global incongruity: "I dislike [it] more than anything I ever saw" (267).

Pamela's description has many of the characteristics of conventional eighteenth-century anti-masquerade rhetoric, including some of Richardson's own. In a letter to Lady Bradshaigh in 1756, Richardson blamed "Ranelaghs, Vauxhalls, Marybones, assemblies . . . and a rabble of such-like amusements" for carrying women "out of all domestic duty and usefulness into infinite riot and expence."[17] Here he makes his heroine declaim like many a masquerade "spy" in the eighteenth-century popular press—as though her only purpose at the masquerade were to gather material for censure. Pamela's response is of a piece with her role earlier in the fiction: to object to violations of regularity and uniformity. Her participation, however, is a much more complex and compromising matter. It has ironic dimensions of which Richardson himself seems only half aware. For this "moralizer" against masquerades, as she calls herself, is also, inescapably, a conspicuous part of that very scene she deplores.

Whether she likes it or not, Pamela is implicated in the unstructured spectacle surrounding her. She cannot retain a purely specular attitude as at the play or opera. The carnivalesque inclusiveness of the masquerade—its voluptuous, absorptive swirl—prevents anyone from remaining simply an observer.

From the reader's perspective this absorption of the heroine into the world of masquerade makes for some paradoxical effects. We see Pamela engulfed by the occasion; we see her changed by it. Before, she exerted a powerful influence over the spaces around her, ordering every detail in B.'s "blessed mansion." But here is a space that she cannot order, that instead works a chaotic magic upon her.

This magic has a visual correlative; we see Pamela carnivalized, as it were, before our eyes. On the phantasmagoric plane of the image, she achieves a maximum doubleness of form. I mentioned before that Pamela's pregnancy reaches its extreme point on the night of the masquerade: everyone calls attention to it, just as everyone teases her over the palpable incongruity, her own comments notwithstanding, of her "prim" Quaker garb. "I hope, friend," one "egregious beauish appearance" says mockingly, "thou art prepared with a father for the light within thee?" (265). A weird lady in a "parti-coloured" habit deadpans, "Friend, . . . there is something in thy person that attracts every one's notice: but if a sack had not been a profane thing, it would have become thee almost as well" (265).

Pamela has become a walking contradiction. Her costume both belies her sexualized nature and highlights it, creating an effect of visual oxymoron. Her maximally distended body is also a contradiction of sorts—two bodies in one. She literalizes the festive image of the double body. This two-in-one figure, the pregnant woman, is of course a classic carnival motif. In the *Italienische Reise* Goethe describes a typical scene during the Roman carnival in which male masqueraders mimic pregnancy. One "woman" is taken ill. "A chair is brought, and the other women give her aid. She moans like a woman in labor, and the next thing you know, she has brought some misshapen creature into the world, to the great amusement of the onlookers." [18]

(Pamela herself will seem to give birth as a result of her night at the Haymarket: the "severe pang" of her labor is described in the letter following her account of the masquerade.) The double body of carnival pregnancy plays upon antinomies of old and new, life and death. Out of the endless chain of bodily life, observes Bakhtin, carnival imagery "retains the parts in which one link joins the other" and "the life of one body is born from the death of the preceding, older one." [19]

At the same time, then, that Pamela is made to speak as the would-be scourge of the masquerade, she stands out on an iconic or emblematic level as the very image of its transformational energy. And like the members of the fictional masquerade crowd, the reader is invited to regard her—to visualize the difficult, absurd, unclassifiable nature of her person. Before, in the quest for diversion, we have had signs of her potential for change, but here she is transfigured in the most literal way. Her body itself displays a richness of disorderly, metamorphic possibility.

Richardson seems mostly unconscious of the paradoxical effect he has achieved. One might call this carnivalization of Pamela's form yet another accidental-seeming reawakening of textual memory, albeit the most dramatic and compromising to date. Once again the sequel seems to remember something about the heroine. Memory figures itself as image: Pamela's bedecked, ambiguous body is a phantasmagoric trope for her history itself. Her body obviously has had a past—one not so uniform after all, but involving multiplicity, exchange, union with other bodies. She carries the traces of historic interpenetration; she has been joined with someone and altered thereby. Her person, one might say, bears the signs of plot; it has been implicated in processes of transformation.

The masquerade licenses this release of textual memory. What I am calling Pamela's carnivalization depends, not surprisingly, on an episode of actual carnival. This unconscious overlay is not an innovation on Richardson's part: the conventions of fictional saturnalia, well established in the 1720's by Defoe and Haywood, make plausible the heroine's bodying forth here in her atavistic and unmystified state. From the start, eighteenth-century English fiction implicitly coded the masquerade scene as a moment of symbolic revelation. In Defoe's *Roxana*, for example, the heroine achieves a maximum moral transparency during the masquerade, at the same time ironically that she is most disguised in a literal sense. The truth emerges that she is false: her shamming as the Turkish lady "Roxana" merely exposes to the reader the utter duplicity of her nature. The episode, which occurs midway through the work, epitomizes the latent content of Roxana's entire history in all its manifold hypocrisy. Richardson's own scene of demystification (for his heroine has as much to hide, in a way, as Roxana) simply reinscribes the subliminal pattern.[20]

But Richardson's set piece does more than just allow a momentary, impressionistic refiguring of Pamela as a carnivalesque heroine. The occasion signals—indeed may be said to initiate— a re-creation of her history itself. By this I mean it allows for a release of memory on the narrative as well as the emblematic level: it engenders a story. From the moment of her excursion into this topsy-turvy world, Pamela is embroiled in an intrigue, the consequences of which extend out over subsequent letters in the epistolary sequence and shape the sequel for the first time into the semblance of a real narrative. This "masquerade plot" is relatively short (it has the aspect of an embedded tale), but it is a plot nonetheless. The irony is that it is hardly a novel one. For in a curious fashion, as if reflecting its festive point of origin, Pamela's story turns out to double a plot already known, one containing, from the reader's perspective, compelling nostalgic power.

It is not surprising that the masquerade should provide us for the first time with an embryonic story. I noted in the previous chapter the privileged connection the masquerade topos has with intrigue and plot: the way it engenders narrative as well as moral transformation. This instrumentality grows out of the masquerade scene's special power to disrupt the decorum of human relationships. Two processes are characteristic: the estrangement of the familiar and the familiarization of the strange. Ordinary companions (husbands and wives, for instance) become alienated, lost in the crowd, while mysterious strangers assume the ways of familiarity. The masquerade both breaks accepted ties and replaces them with illicit ones.

The scene in *Pamela* inaugurates both sorts of plot movement. Once at the Haymarket, Pamela is abruptly separated from her husband, and his behavior becomes increasingly peculiar. The Spanish don acts like a stranger, introducing himself to Pamela and Miss Darnford "as if he had not known us" (265). Later he comes upon his wife in the crowd, "but we appeared not to know one another" (265). In addition B. speaks only Italian during the evening—a language Pamela cannot understand—adding another layer of estrangement. Both he and Pamela are assaulted (with very different results) by persons unfamiliar to them. Pamela is accosted by various masked strangers, all of whom she angrily rebuffs. A Presbyterian parson warns her to keep an eye on her husband. B. meanwhile is successfully singled out by a "bold Nun," who speaks Italian with him "with such free airs," Pamela notes, "that I did not much like it, though I knew not what she said" (264). In his fatuous Don Juan guise, B. flirts with the nun for the entire evening, until Pamela, "feigning indisposition," at last convinces him to take her home.

The masquerade scene is brief, encapsulated first in a single letter to Lady Davers. (Later it will be repeated two times, with a difference, in retrospective accounts by B. and the Countess.) Pamela hopes at the end of her letter that she will never have to mention the evening again: "And so much," she concludes somewhat wishfully, "for *masquerades*" (267).

Her wish is misplaced, however, for the transformational pattern engendered here immediately spills over into the narrative at large. In the days that follow the masquerade, the familiar continues to seem unfamiliar, and the unfamiliar upsettingly familiar. Pamela has given birth to her first child, yet B. becomes increasingly diffident toward her. He takes unexplained journeys out of the house, leaving her to brood. To add to her anxiety, Pamela hears from the unpleasant Mr. Turner (the Presbyterian parson at the masquerade) that B. is regularly visiting the "bold Nun," now revealed as "the Countess Dowager of——." Distressed by this alienating behavior (B. is no longer "himself"), the heroine likewise is not herself. She is "in disorder," subject to "wretched vapours" and fits of "strange, melancholy airs" (286, 296–97). Her mood has become fluid, unaccountable. B. is annoyed by the change in her, and complains that she is "quite altered." The estrangement between them sets off a chain reaction of further alienations, notably between Pamela and her surrogate family. She is unable to address Lady Davers as her "Sister" anymore because, she says, her "title to that honour arises from the dear, thrice dear Mr. B. And how long I may be permitted to call him mine, I cannot say" (288). Defamiliarization is also defamilialization.

This turn of events, we notice, is also a curious re-turn. Pamela figures her crisis as a fall—a precipitous downward plunge out of felicity. "After all my fortitude, and my recollection, to fall from so much happiness, and so soon, is a trying thing!" (294). And again: "O what a happiness am I sunk from!—And in so few days too! O the wicked masquerades!" (307). It is as though the original "happy turn" of *Pamela*, Part 1, were being reversed. Pamela is falling back, as it were, toward her origins. The sequel here stands the plot of Part 1 on its head: in Part 1 Pamela and B. moved progressively closer to one another, climaxing in a legal and sexual union; now they veer farther and farther apart. Pamela simultaneously begins what appears to be a descent not only into isolation and loneliness, but also back toward the social and psychological state in which B. originally found her.

We see her replaced in various senses. The Countess becomes a kind of double, usurping Pamela's place in Mr. B.'s life. This lady is rumored to have expressed a wish to become "a certain gentleman's second wife" (295), but at times she appears to be B.'s only wife: Pamela simply recedes into the background whenever her rival appears. B.'s new companion accompanies him on trips to Oxford and Portsmouth. After one of these excursions he tells Pamela that the Countess has "represented" her: "I had a partner too, my dear," he says nonchalantly, "to represent you" (292). The most striking moment of usurpation, however, is when the Countess visits Mr. and Mrs. B. at their house in London, ostensibly to see their newborn son. While B. looks on, the Countess demands to hold Billy, and Pamela hands him over. She seems to hand over her very motherhood with the gesture, as well as her claim on the other Billy, B. himself. The moment is murderous: "I *yielded* it to her: I thought she would have stifled it with her warm kisses. 'Sweet boy! charming creature,' and pressed it to her too lovely bosom, with such emotion, looking on the child, and on Mr. B., that I liked it not by any means" (299–300).

Most important, Pamela's phantasmagoric replacement by the Countess is equivalent to an eerie sociological re-placement. Pamela appears to revert, albeit mostly in the realm of her own anxious fantasies, to an earlier place—the place of origins, the place held before her exaltation. During the Countess's visit, for instance, Pamela symbolically humbles herself: she wears a plain white damask gown, like that of a servant, so as not to "vie" with her aristocratic tormentor. The Countess is "dressed as rich as jewels, and a profusion of expense, could make her" (298)—a vision of luxury and power. Again Pamela's claim on high estate seems only a matter of clothes. Confronting a true lady, she divests herself of the garments of gentility, as if to divest herself of a sham gentility itself.

And there are other divestitures. Pamela's formerly "lady-like" gifts mysteriously vanish. When B. asks her to play the harpsichord during the Countess's visit, Pamela uncharacteristically "stumbles over the keys." To her dismay the Countess follows by tripping off an Italian air "very prettily" (301). Faced with the exorbitant charms of her "happy rivaless," Pamela begins to indulge, finally, in elaborate fantasies of self-denial. She dreams of returning, like a prodigal daughter, to her former obscurity. If the "worst come to the worst," she tells Lady Davers, she will go back to her parents' house in Kent, there to live in virtuous seclusion, while the Countess takes her place in public as Mr. B.'s wife. In her most self-abnegating vision of the future, Pamela imagines now and then returning "in some disguised habit" and "stealing the pleasure of seeing him and his happier Countess" (294).

All this from a masquerade. True to its conventional function in eighteenth-century narrative, the masquerade alone prompts these revolutionary complications—or so they seem. For the situation here is not without a certain irony. To be sure, the masquerade lives up to its stereotypical role by precipitating an apparently scandalous sexual configuration: an estrangement between husband and wife, an adulterous affair. From another point of view, however, the masquerade might be thought of as paradoxically restoring, if not in any legal sense, a different sort of order. By bringing together B. and the Countess, the episode has in effect rectified the underlying problem of classification brought on by B.'s marriage with Pamela. On the surface the masquerade has disrupted the sexual order, but at a deeper level it has undone the social transgression represented by the B./ Pamela coupling. The episode belatedly produces precisely the arrangement that should have existed had there been no earlier violation of taxonomic decorum—no illicit coupling in Part 1. Pamela now sinks back into the inferior condition she should have occupied perennially, had she not married Mr. B.; and B. in turn is matched up with exactly the sort of woman, in an ideally ordered world, he should have married, a woman of his own rank. By precipitating B.'s apparent infidelity and Pamela's humiliation, the masquerade scene reinstitutionalizes in a most ironic fashion that very hierarchy of high and low that Pamela and B. (and Richardson) have previously violated.

Richardson flirts here with a disastrous, or at least melancholy, possibility: that B. will divorce Pamela (as she fears), exile her to the country, and take the vivacious Countess as his second wife. Yet such an outcome would solve the very problem the sequel set out to solve: how to nullify the scandalous impact of B.'s misalliance. Whereas the belated revelation of the heroine's high birth, as Richardson correctly foresaw, would have returned *Pamela* to the archaic and dubious realm of romance, a divorce plot (at one level an easily conceivable extension of the masquerade plot of estrangement) might have taken the narrative in quite another direction, more suited perhaps to a would-be proponent of "Nature"—toward the dysphoric realism of the nineteenth- and twentieth-century novel.

But this masquerade tale is not over yet: indeed, it now takes its most compelling, if not entirely unexpected, turn. Unlike his great epigone the Marquis de Sade, Richardson seems unable, finally, to accept any irreversible humiliation for his heroine, however well it might satisfy the demands of an exacting realism. For it soon becomes clear that Pamela's fall out of felicity—like that Fortunate Fall with which it is associated (410)—is only the necessary preliminary to a renewal of narrative euphoria. Having reversed the plot of *Pamela*, Part 1, by projecting its exalted heroine back toward her low origins, the sequel, as if by a kind of textual mania, now reverses its reversal, thrusting Pamela back up to that high estate from which she has fallen and reconfirming—by a symbolic reenactment of her original "happy turn"—her disorderly, festive union with Mr. B.

This reenactment begins with a moment of intense theatricality. Pamela, desperate with anxiety, forces Mr. B. to act out with her a mock trial, in which, she tells him, she will be the criminal and he the judge. B. is to "pronounce sentence" on her, "or if you won't, I will upon myself: a severe one to me, it shall be, but an agreeable one, perhaps, to you." Most peculiarly, she places three chairs in a joined row as props between them, to represent "the bar at which I am to take my trial." B. is perplexed by her "fantastic" behavior, but agrees (310–12).

Crucial here is what Pamela considers to be the crime. It is not what one might expect—B.'s apparent breach of their marriage vows—but the marriage itself. She admits she is guilty of a "change in temper," but what she seems most guilty about is marrying B. in the first place, and thus changing her status in the world. She is an advocate for her own punishment: she wants B. to humiliate her publicly, to divorce her and marry the real lady. "The Countess is a charming lady," she argues. "She excells your poor girl in all those natural graces of form, which your kind fancy . . . had made you attribute to me. And she has all those additional advantages, as nobleness of birth, of alliance, and deportment, which I want" (316). Pamela wishes to rewrite the past and efface the fact of their marriage: "Happy for you, Sir, that you had known her Ladyship some months ago, before you disgraced yourself by the honours you have done me!"

(316). As an ultimate act of taxonomic rectification, she is ready
to return to the country and her "first duties," and devote herself in isolation to praying for Mr. B.'s well-being.

Here Pamela once more is the defender of purity and boundary, only now she seems to recognize the compromising aspects of her own history. She turns the purifying impulse back
on herself. (It is not so farfetched to see the line of chairs she sets
up between B. and herself as an architectural literalization of the
categorical boundary that should exist between them.) But the
effect of her prophylactic discourse is utterly, explosively paradoxical. For if Pamela now acknowledges her historic trespass
against cultural decorum, her creator, who seems himself perversely affected by the scene of self-abasement he has engineered, suddenly will not. Or at least he has ceased to care what
anyone thinks of his "linsey-woolsey" heroine. Thus even as
Pamela lodges her complaint against her own "criminal" history, this history is, through a piece of wild, magnanimous
business, restaged. Afflicted to the utmost by Pamela's confession, a lachrymose, hysterical B. now proceeds to repeat his
own exemplary carnivalesque gesture by "lifting up" the heroine once more. "Exalted creature!" are his first words to the
prostrated Pamela. And abruptly he pushes aside the chairs that
separate them, taking her in his arms: "Noble-minded Pamela!
Let no bar be put between us henceforth!" (320). Pamela still
gravitates downward, but her athletic consort lifts her up for
good: "I should have sunk with joy, had not his kind arms supported me" (320).

With giddy, disorienting physical pleasure, Pamela now relives that same euphoric upward movement she has known before—the "exaltation" of Part 1. After B. intimates that he and
the Countess have not, after all, become lovers, Pamela is raised
to new heights, the equivalent of a saint or martyr shooting upward in a baroque ceiling. "I had a new ecstacy to be blest with,
in a thankfulness so exalted, that it left me all light and pleasant,
as if I had shook off body and trod in air; so much heaviness had
I lost, and so much joy had I received" (321). And through a
kind of bizarre, Saint Theresa–like physiological mimesis, her

body itself reinscribes the signs of rapturous upheaval. (This application of the physical symptoms of spiritual ecstasy to an eminently social situation is a classic instance of *Pamela*'s historic secularizing impulse.) The reader can only sympathize with B.'s concern: "My eyes were in a manner fixed," Pamela tells Lady Davers, "that he was a little startled, seeing nothing but the whites; for the sight was out of its orbits, in a manner lifted up to heaven—in ecstasy for a turn so sudden, and so unexpected!" (321).

_____

Sometime after Mr. and Mrs. B.'s gratifying reunion—which concludes with B. agreeing to break off all relations with the Countess—Pamela is able to reflect on the meaning of the events that have followed the "fatal" masquerade. Afflictions, she decides, are necessary—not only because they "teach one how to subdue one's passions," but because when alleviated they have a paradoxical power to "redouble our joys" (324). And in a sense the sequel has indeed redoubled Pamela's joys. In a microcosmic form she has re-experienced her own ecstatic history. She has, one could say, been recarnivalized.

The pleasure the masquerade sequence gives the reader is the pleasure of repetition. For at this point *Pamela*, Part 2, completes exactly what seemed impossible before: it repeats the saturnalian fantasia of Part 1. To be sure, this reenactment takes a displaced, abbreviated form: in contrast to the drawn-out coupling of Part 1, the reunion of Pamela and B. in Part 2 is achieved relatively swiftly, with little in the way of intervening narrative suspense. One can imagine that a more dramatic and complex story could have developed if the heroine had in fact left Mr. B. and returned to low estate, instead of simply fantasizing about it. The mock trial foreshortens the narrative, bringing about the euphoric repetition with a somewhat banal facility. The main point still stands, however. Thanks to the masquerade, the sequel has reproduced the charismatic plot of its own original—a festive history of exchange and commingling between high and low. This repetition also means a "redoubling of joys" for readers of the sequel, for we find reinscribed here the very story that, hope against hope, we have scanned for, and that indeed the fiction has sought for so long to have us forget.

Granted, Richardson's part in all this is ambiguous. The events during and after the masquerade have an unplanned, accidental quality, as if the author were simply letting his story take him where it would. The scenic representation of carnival inspires him with a certain carnivalesque authorial energy: in a swift, joyful, seemingly unexamined series of textual gestures, Richardson utterly undermines the ideological edifice so laboriously built up earlier around his heroine. The business of mystification is forgotten as he plunges forward with his intoxicating tale of doubling bodies and collapsing boundaries. Like the quintessential carnival-goer, Richardson lets all he has buried emerge— above all, the dream of transgression and transformation that has been *Pamela*, Part 1.

After this atavistic outburst something best described as a sort of textual remorse sets in. As if embarrassed by this diversion of his authorial energies, Richardson returns to the everyday work of mystification, with unprepossessing results. Of the remainder of *Pamela*, Part 2, most is as tedious as what has gone before; Richardson does not trust himself with any more excursions into plot. Following Pamela's theatrical "éclaircissement" with her husband, narrative interest is eclipsed on all levels. The London scenes wind up: B. breaks off his liaison with the Countess (who is dispatched to Italy, the home of the masked balls she so enjoys), and he and Pamela leave the "undelightful town," returning home to the "blessed mansion." Episodes ensue, but these have little coherence and are really nonevents. Pamela has smallpox, but it leaves her miraculously unchanged. She has innumerable children, but none of her later pregnancies figures in any way. She and Mr. B. travel both to the north country and to the Continent, but nothing of these journeys (except that they take place) is mentioned. Instead the remainder of the sequel dissolves into a series of random didactic fragments. Pamela is reinstalled as the voice of order. Her lengthy commentaries on Locke's *Education* (solicited by a newly domesticated B.) contain much in the way of classificatory wisdom: she advocates teach-

ing children politeness to servants so that later their "distinction" will be increased, "and their authority strengthened"
(402). Likewise she believes in the taxonomy of toys: children
are to keep each plaything in its "allotted place" and "keep account of the number and places of them severally" (415). (It is in
keeping with the new sobriety of the sequel at this point that
Pamela, whose own history has been one of ecstatic illegal
turns, should condemn all whirling toys—"tops, gigs, and
battledores"—the mechanical simulacra of transformation and
vertigo.) Pamela finally becomes the neighborhood advocate of
sexual prophylaxis. At the end of the sequel we are given in full
several allegorical tales she tells neighboring young women
about the dangers of sexual impurity, as well as her edifying
counsel to Miss Goodwin to cultivate "discretion and prudence"
and avoid all "pernicious diversions" such as balls and masquerades (477). The sequel itself becomes a carnivalesque hodgepodge of thoughts on education, embedded tales, exempla.*

Ironically, as if to reinforce the general eclipse of story, the tale
of the masquerade itself is retold—yet as though nothing had
happened there after all. Both Mr. B. and the Countess subsequently recount the events during and after the masquerade, but
in such a way as to suggest that what seemed to take place—an
illicit connection between them—never did. True, B. gives a
somewhat compromising description of his flirtatious exchanges
with the nun and subsequent visits to her house, but the purified heart of his story is that nothing ever happened between

*I rely here on Bakhtin's description of carnivalesque discourse—discourse that, like
Rabelais's *Gargantua* and *Pantagruel*, resists generic classification and instead combines a
multiplicity of literary modes in a single polymorphous form. Unlike Swift and Sterne,
whose preservation of the Rabelaisian tradition has often been noted, Richardson is seldom perceived as an author whose works retain vestiges of this carnivalesque literary
tradition. The emphasis on Richardson as one of the inventors of the realistic novel has
drawn our attention away from those moments in his work when a kind of generic promiscuity takes over, as in the latter part of *Pamela*, Part 2, and in much of *Grandison*. In
such moments linear narrative is subordinated to other kinds of discourse—embedded
exempla, "table talk" (the symposia of the B. and Grandison households), the treatise on
education (Pamela's comments on Locke). Richardson has little of the comic scatological
energy one associates with Rabelais, Swift, and Sterne (his might be labeled, highly
paradoxically, a Puritan carnivalesque), but by such lapses out of generic uniformity, he
betrays his connection, however attenuated, with the archaic and festive literary tradition
Bakhtin has so memorably described.

them. Once the Countess discovered he was married (he did, he
admits, mislead her on this point with a double entendre—"out
of gaiety, rather than design"), they entered into a friendly "kind
of Platonic system, in which sex was to have no manner of concern" (334). The rumors regarding a sexual liaison between
them have been entirely the work of the malicious Mr. Turner,
now revealed to have been jilted once by the Countess. Mr. B.
and the Countess sanctimoniously extemporize on the dangers
of masquerading. "Those are least of all to be trusted at these
diversions," a contrite B. acknowledges, "who are most desirous to go to them. Of this I am now fully convinced" (334).
And the Countess, even as she prepares to leave for Italy "for
the sake of her own character," admits that she has loved "balls
and concerts, and public diversions, perhaps, better than I
ought" (374).

These repetitions of the masquerade episode are not really repetitions at all but displacements of Pamela's original incriminating account of the evening. They are anti-narratives, designed to
efface the appearance of a story. They have a rhetorical function
analogous to that of Part 2 itself. They are pieces of revisionist
discourse, intended to convince the reader that no matter what
seems to have happened at the masquerade, no violation of decorum did take place—no breach of uniformity and no illicit
coupling. Nothing has happened; the suggested adultery plot
has gone unfulfilled. The revocation of story here has a generic
aspect, for Richardson's refusal to embrace the story of postmarital infidelity, seen in historical terms, meant a delay in the
fictional evolution of the marriage plot. Loosely speaking,
English narrative through Austen is primarily concerned with
courtship, the events leading up to (or obstructing) marriage.
The sequel to *Pamela* is in more than one sense a dead end. For
any hint of that great structuring theme of the nineteenth-
century novel—adultery—we must await Fielding's *Amelia*.

As with the sequel's own retellings of Pamela's history, we may
question the ultimate impact of these rhetorical returns to the
scene of the masquerade. Even if these sanitized accounts effectively dismiss from our minds any visions of promiscuity between B. and the Countess (and a cynic would say they do not),

they cannot fail to remind us of that other improper coupling—between Pamela and B. themselves. The irony is that in order to undo the surface damage done by the "wicked masquerade"—to renew the marital bond between Mr. and Mrs. B.—Richardson has had to rejoin them symbolically. Thus a trial scene magically becomes a kind of second marriage, and a "criminal" becomes, once more, a "lady." The disorder wrought by the masquerade in the realm of married and unmarried persons is negated, but only at the cost of reintroducing disorder, in a highly conspicuous and theatrical fashion, into the realm of class relations. High and low have to be joined again, in order that high and high be kept apart. Whatever the other intentions of its teller, each embedded retelling of the masquerade affair thus serves ironically to spotlight the B. couple, and to bring to mind again their indecorous, incorrigible, unforgettable history.

As though themselves afflicted by a sort of repetition compulsion, the characters of *Pamela*, Part 2, seem at the end unable to let go of the masquerade plot, even as they try to deny it. Late in the novel, while reviewing for her parents the history of Mr. B.'s progress toward moral and spiritual "uniformity," Pamela is inescapably reminded of the traumatic occasion that seemed for a time to bring him to the brink of relapse: "But in the midst of these comfortable proceedings, and my further charming hopes, a nasty masquerade threw into his way a temptation, which for a time blasted all my prospects, and indeed made me doubt my own head almost" (430). Even the invisible editor of the supposed collection of Pamela's letters cannot forget the masquerade. In the appended conclusion to the sequel, he offers a parenthetical return to that festive scene of confusion at the heart of the narrative: "Mr. B. (after the affair which took date at the masquerade, and concluded so happily) continued to be one of the best and most exemplary of men" (481). The masquerade is here contained, circumscribed by a sort of moralized typography, the parenthesis—but it is present nonetheless. Even as we are invited to imagine Mr. and Mrs. B.'s uniformly blissful and unsullied future, we are reminded of that very affair that has deranged, parodied, and reaffirmed their own transgressive union.

The ideological and formal paradoxes of the masquerade

scene in *Pamela*, Part 2, cannot, finally, be underestimated. The thematic irruption of the carnivalesque is never innocent in classic eighteenth-century texts; Richardson cannot make it so here. He tries of course to domesticate it. The heroine's pious animadversions against its freedoms, the retrospective acknowledgment of the dangers it poses to the sanctity of marriage—each explicit criticism connects Richardson's text to the larger cultural diatribe which from the 1720's on held masquerading to be an expression of the demonic, and the poisonous fruit of a corrupt modernity. At a superficial level *Pamela*, Part 2, bears the features of this conventional complaint; none of Richardson's middle-class readers, clearly, would have found his heroine's position on masquerades incomprehensible or exceptionable.

As I have been suggesting, however, what one might call the subliminal function of the episode (both for author and for readers) is far more important. The scene is not just an authorial exercise in denunciation. It is not just what Pamela, with her scolding ripostes to friars and Merry Andrews, tries to make of it—"a general satire on the assemblée" (266). Rather it represents a crisis of textual memory. The role of the episode is mnemonic. It allows a momentary, euphoric commemoration of everything *Pamela*, Part 2, has elsewhere sought to obliterate: the true story of its carnivalesque heroine; her historic lapses out of uniformity; the presence, in the world of social forms, of a certain transformational magic. It is that moment at which the sequel remembers its own original. The masquerade is at once the symptom of the ideological tension underlying Richardson's sequel and the generator of this narrative release. It allows the author of *Pamela*, who like his characters has half-consciously sought some diversion from his own intractable rhetorical project, to do what seemed compromising and impossible before: to repeat the unrepeatable story of Part 1, to return to Pamela's "happy turn" and turn her around again. The invocation of the set piece is the means by which Richardson's ambivalence finds expression: with the turn toward the carnivalesque, his suppressed impulses toward intrigue, theater, and metamorphosis make an abrupt saturnalian return.

This irruption of textual memory is also a catharsis for the reader. The masquerade gives us something we desire. I mentioned before Lady Davers's odd charge to Pamela—that by her "artless and natural" observations on London entertainments, she make them new for her readers. That which has become too familiar, too much itself, will be altered and estranged by Pamela's novel discourse. Yet Lady Davers here requests descriptions of just those things she has already seen: she does not want true novelty, only the appearance of novelty. She wants identity and difference at one and the same time, a doubling up of the familiar and the unfamiliar.

This paradoxical wish is an allegory for the wish of the sequel reader. We too want the old presented in a new guise, the known in the shape of the unknown. We want a repetition of past pleasures, but one that is also uncanny—the same plot as before, only clothed in strange garments. Yet for a moment this is, after all, just what Richardson's sequel achieves. At the climax of the masquerade story—with Pamela's ecstatic, theatrical embrace by B.—the sequel seems to accomplish the impossible. In a displaced transfigured form, it gives us the charismatic tale again. The heroine's joys are "redoubled" even as her own history repeats—in a new time and place, in a new *Pamela*.

Richardson's sequel stands at this point in a paradoxical relationship of sameness and difference to its original. Even as it remains on many levels a different text—the lexical level being only the most obvious—*Pamela*, Part 2, becomes an uncanny double to its predecessor. The two parts of *Pamela* become for a moment curiously redundant, like two transformations of the same structure, two variations on the same dreamlike theme, two forms of the same fluid body. As Pamela is recarnivalized, so is the text bearing her name. *Pamela* comes to stand for an ambiguous twice-told tale, a story at once itself and something else again, two novels in one, one novel in two, a narrative double entendre.

As much as it revels in secrets, the eighteenth-century masquerade is also the unraveller of secrets, including the difficult, grandiose secrets of the paragon. The world of masks is both

Pamela's undoing and her remaking, for it engages not the uniformity but the hidden paradoxes of her nature. "So *uncommon,* yet so like *yourself,* has been the manner of your acting!" exclaims B. near the end of the novel (321). The masquerade returns Pamela to that which is changeable and theatrical, the carnival of history itself. If it rewards the paragon, it rewards her not so much for her virtue—that startling singularity for which she is lauded elsewhere—as for her festive duplicity. In the end the reward the masquerade offers to Pamela (and to the reader of her story) is pleasure: the pleasure that comes of returning, of letting go of secrets, of seeing desire itself turn to ecstatic fulfillment.

5

Masquerade and Allegory: Fielding's 'Amelia'

One might begin with fear, then a release from fear. Fear—the fear of being fooled—animates *The Masquerade*, the first of Fielding's many seminars on the world of masks. The poet, new to Haymarket pleasures, is exploring Heidegger's assembly room in the company of a mysterious lady in a velvet hood. When, in their perambulations, he and his guide come across a clutch of whores busily working the crowd, he asks a question that makes her laugh aloud. "Madam, how from another woman / Do you strumpet masqu'd distinguish?" (198–99). She responds with brutal gaiety and a universal satire. Virtue itself, she says, is a "masque"—and "it wou'd look extremely queer / In any one, to wear it here" (220–21). Which is not to say there are no fools, at the masquerade as in the real world, ready to find virtue in the smile of an anonymous inamorata. She illustrates her point with an exemplary scene of unmasking:

> The lover, who has now possess'd,
> From unknown Flora, his request;
> (Who with a pretty, modest grace,
> Discover'd all things but her face:)

Pulls off her masque in am'rous fury,
And finds a gentle nymph of Drury,
Curses his lust—laments his fate,
And kicks her out of bed too late.   (375–82)

The face beneath the visor, marked with disease, is a burlesque epiphany. In the aftermath of nocturnal carnival, while the gamester "mourns his losing lot," the lover fears "that he has got" (385–86).

For all its banality the lady's vignette, like Fielding's poem itself, conveys a primitive, paranoiac lesson. This lesson, that corruption wears a mask, that trusting in appearance is folly, is no less telling for being a traditional and obvious one. The world provides no respite from fear, we are warned; one's only defense against treachery is a perpetual radical vigilance. The best epistemology consists in the expectation—a constant unmasking in advance, so to speak—of global deceit.

One may contrast this allegorical scene of unmasking, however, with a scene that is not so transparent. Again a lover seeks the truth—the face under the mask—but with less predictable, less pedantic results. The episode, in *Amelia*, is part of a story the hapless Booth, cast into prison at the start of the novel, tells Miss Matthews—the history of his wooing of Amelia. An unmasking, it turns out, has figured powerfully in the courtship of Fielding's hero and his paragon wife.

Booth recounts that for a long time before his betrothal to Amelia, he was never particularly attracted to her, despite her having as much beauty "as ever fell to the Share of a Woman" (Book II, chap. 1).[1] Only after a "cruel Accident" involving an overturned chaise, in which her "lovely Nose was beat all to pieces," did he find himself suddenly drawn to her. To the fascinated Matthews he reveals that it was the sight of Amelia in a mask after her accident that captivated him. A conspicuous if perverse element in this passion, Booth admits, was a desire to see her disfigured face. That Amelia had lost her "exquisite" beauty was by this time common knowledge; jealous former acquaintances jested that she would never again "turn up her Nose at her Betters." In a kind of flashback Booth describes drinking tea alone with her and announcing his morbid desire: "I begged her to indulge my Curiosity by showing me her Face." Amelia's response is polite but ominous: "She answered me in a most obliging Manner, 'Perhaps, Mr. Booth, you will as little know me when my Mask is off as when it is on'" (II, 1).

Indeed, for all Booth's voyeuristic gravitation to the disfigured woman, one cannot help fearing, for a moment at least, a bouleversement of ardor comparable to that depicted in *The Masquerade*. The reader braces for a scene of shock and recoil. This apprehensiveness is due as much to Fielding's narrative as to Booth's, for in the preceding book of the novel, Fielding has already provided the reader with an unforgettable type, as it were, of physiognomic devastation: "Blear-Eyed Moll," the deformed and frightful-looking prostitute who accosts Booth when he first arrives in the prison yard. Moll too has sustained an injury to her nose, though for different reasons than Amelia. "Nose she had none, for Venus, envious perhaps at her former Charms, had carried off the gristly Part; and some earthly Damsel, perhaps from the same Envy, had levelled the Bone with the rest of her Face: Indeed it was far beneath the Bones of her Cheeks, which rose proportionately higher than usual" (I, 3). Ironically, the net effect is the same as that of Amelia's accident, or so one might imagine. Even as Amelia goes to unmask her own ravaged countenance, one cannot help remembering this earlier face, in all its nightmarish aspect. Moll's Goyaesque visage lingers in the mind like a ghastly souvenir, and one fears the worst: the visible depredation of Amelia's own "former Charms."

The moment of unmasking, however, is a non sequitur. It has nothing to do with precedent, or with any access of fear. The heroine's potentially terrible face produces no terror. Instead it produces a convulsion of desire. "A thousand tender Ideas rushed all at once on my Mind," Booth tells his listener; "I was unable to contain myself and eagerly kissing her Hand, I cried, 'Upon my Soul, Madam, you never appeared to me so lovely as at this Instant.'" Oddly, neither Booth nor Fielding gives any actual description of Amelia's appearance. We are left only with the paradoxical assertion that disfigured, Amelia is not only still beautiful, but somehow more beautiful than before. The moment of exposure is utterly cryptic: loss has become indistinguishable from gain, misfortune from fortune. But it elicits an undeniable catharsis. Booth's morbid curiosity gives way to ecstasy, and the reader's own anxiety to real if puzzled relief.

The paradox of Amelia's insistent beauty makes any traditional allegorical reading of the scene impossible. Unlike the unmasking in *The Masquerade*, this unmasking reinforces no epistemological lesson, promotes no familiar paranoia. The mask itself, the crucial prop in both scenes, is here transvalued. It has become the instrument, not of deception, but of euphoria. Indeed, Amelia's mask cannot be said to "disguise" anything, to hide an underlying deformity, for the deformity it conceals turns out to be identical to beauty. It screens no hidden evil; it marks no discontinuity between devious appearances and a world of truth. It functions instead as the agent of a marvelous dialectical confusion. Unmasking produces ecstasy precisely because it makes no difference. It establishes no distinction, visual or moral, between former charms and present ruin, beauty and its vastation, impeccability and corruption. Antithesis gives way to oxymoron: opposing terms to a mystifying and pleasurable unity. Where no difference exists finally between the tokens of virtue and those of vice, the notion of deceit itself becomes problematic, as well as the classical epistemology in which it figures. In the world where Amelia removes her mask, there is little, after all, to fear.

I do not juxtapose these vignettes innocently, of course: they point up in a striking figurative way the ambivalence that Fielding, perhaps even more than Richardson, characteristically demonstrates toward the imagery of the carnivalesque. Self-alienation, self-transcendence—masquerade and civilization—these, for Fielding, are the themes of paradox. Indeed, Fielding's two "masks"—one composed of conventional negative allegorical meanings, the other emanating strange transformational power—could be taken as symbols of an imaginative tension one finds everywhere in his writing. Tellingly perhaps, two actual masks appear amid the emblems of Fielding's authorship in Hogarth's well-known engraving of his friend, the frontispiece to the *Works* of 1762 (Fig. 28). These are the masks of drama-

28. Frontispiece to Fielding's *Works*, after Hogarth, 1762, showing the masks of comedy and tragedy

turgy, representing the conventional antithesis of comedy and tragedy, and they hint at Fielding's career as a playwright. But they also intimate, however accidentally, something of Fielding's double vision regarding the idea of the mask itself. As a way of indicating the special nature of Fielding's genius, Hogarth foregrounds the comic mask—the mask of metamorphosis and laughter—and shows it overlaying the tragic mask, which is turned away from the viewer in a strangely foreshortened manner, like the face of someone asleep or dead.

Again, it is no surprise that masks in general figure so prominently, if also paradoxically, in Fielding's work. His career coincided almost exactly with the remarkable resurgence of theatricality in eighteenth-century urban English life. Fielding repeatedly acknowledged the contemporary obsession with masks, disguises, and mock saturnalia. The novelist began writing in the 1720's, the decade in which Heidegger's "Midnight Masque" achieved its greatest notoriety. Fielding's first published work was in fact *The Masquerade* of 1728. Like Hogarth's *Masquerade Ticket*, which preceded it by a year, Fielding's poem was heavily topical, making a detailed assault on the disreputable Haymarket assemblies. He followed this work with contemporary references to Heidegger and the masquerade in his plays *The Author's Farce* (1730) and *Miss Lucy in Town* (1742), and in satiric pieces in the *Champion* (see Feb. 19, 1739–40). Even some years later, when Fielding's career was drawing to a close, the masquerade remained a compelling public topic. The year of *Tom Jones*, 1749, was also the year of one of the most spectacular masked balls of the century—the Jubilee Masquerade at Ranelagh, which thousands of people attended. Again in 1751, the year of *Amelia*, the masquerade was subjected to a different kind of public scrutiny when the English bishops pronounced it responsible for the Lisbon earthquake.[2] The masquerade remained a productive topos for Fielding to the end: in his last two novels the masquerade set piece is an important episode. So crucial (and so perplexing) is the role of the masquerade in *Amelia*, indeed, that that novel alone makes Fielding a significant if somewhat incorrigible figure in the literary history of the carnivalesque.[3]

While timely, Fielding's evocation of the carnival world, even in the reduced form of the fashionable eighteenth-century London masquerade, is never merely decorative. His masquerade scenes are never simply local color. He takes the representative tropes of carnival too seriously—much more seriously than twentieth-century readers are inclined to take them. For Fielding, as for his contemporaries generally, mask and masquerade remained charged with ambiguous philosophical and ethical meanings that we, for the most part, have lost sight of. That tension one sometimes detects in Fielding's writing, between a desire to moralize the world of masquerade and a countervailing fascination with its characteristic scandals, is to this extent an exemplary one. His two masks—one deceptive, one liberating—illuminate certain basic contradictions in eighteenth-century sensibility itself, with its odd mixture of rationalism and irrationalism, decorum and revolutionary fantasy.[4]

How to gloss this double conception of the mask? Fielding's ambivalence toward the imagery of the carnivalesque might be said to epitomize a larger pattern of cultural and philosophical transformation. To be sure, the mask has always been a profoundly rich and ambiguous artifact. It has been called the most complex theme of folk culture.[5] One cannot exhaust all of its possible meanings or reduce it to a single historical significance. And yet one can argue that its primary associations have in fact altered in a very distinct way over time. Writers other than Fielding have found discontinuities in its meaning. For example, Bakhtin and Caillois, as we have seen, both speak of an "old" mask and a new, and point to the strange repression, in modern Western society, of the mask's ancient talismanic power. Whereas the old mask, that of shamanistic ritual or medieval carnival, embodied "the joy of change and reincarnation"—the spiritual and organic union of opposites—the mask of modern times is no more than a screen, a disguise or "false front," evoking new and sinister realms of alienation. Instead of working marvelous transformations, the mask now "hides something, keeps a secret, deceives." It has become an ethical rather than a magical object.[6]

Both Bakhtin and Caillois, again, use this phenomenology of

the mask to support a larger, intensely elegiac philosophical hypothesis: that the codification of rationalist thought and the rise of modern individualism in the seventeenth and eighteenth centuries destroyed the organic metaphysics of earlier centuries and the archaic belief in the unity and wholeness of experience. The notion of a deceptive or secularized mask could only emerge after a certain notion of the subject had itself emerged. The ethical themes of deceit and pretense, of masquerading in the negative sense, depend on a prior concept of the separate individual, a quantifiable, unique self, indisputably distinct from other selves.

None of which is irrelevant to Fielding, or to that critique, explicit in so much of his writing, of the mask that deceives. A number of eighteenth-century writers reflected the new dispensation. The author of *A Seasonable Apology for Mr. H----g--r* (1724), for example, castigated the mask as the mere trivial instrument of human chicanery, a mark of "prophane history." A writer for *The Craftsman* (March 23, 1734) connected it with the eminently banal deceptions of the politician. A convocation of masks, the "*Masquerade*" itself, was "no better than a *Screen*"—a veiled reference to Walpolean intrigues. An observation in an anonymous work on the masquerade ("Calculated to amuse and instruct all the good Boys and Girls in the Kingdom"), dated 1780, summed up the new epistemology: "When people mean to make believe they are what in reality they are not, you know a mask must be necessary." [7]

Fielding himself, as we shall see in more detail shortly, often invoked the mask as a prime symbol for the "pernicious Designs of that detestable Fiend, Hypocrisy." [8] The prostitute's mask in *The Masquerade*, icon of betrayal, is the mask of modernity. Quite predictably too, outraged rationalism is the prevailing philosophical mode in that poem. The poet has little sympathy for the masquerade's "mysterious wild meander"—its antic shapes, intimations of mutability, and "heap" of human "incoherencies." The fear of deceit is subordinate always to a more pervasive fear that crucial distinctions—between persons, between rational categories—may, in the moment of travesty, be undone.

But the critique of hypocrisy, as I have already tried to hint with regard to *Amelia's* more equivocal masquerade, is not the whole story. Fielding's position is often inconsistent; at times he seems aware of a different potential altogether in those same tropes that elsewhere elicit his satire and mistrust. An intermittent awareness of the mask's vestigial transformational life complicates the rationalist project of demystification.

These flashes of memory illuminate the ambiguities of an age. Extrapolating from Bakhtin, one may view the eighteenth century itself as the transitional era par excellence in the history of the carnivalesque—precisely because both the old and the new metaphysics coexisted here in an uneasy rivalry. Granted, as traditional intellectual histories have always emphasized, the new rationalist ideology was clearly in the ascendant. The century's classic authors—Swift, Voltaire, Johnson, Diderot, and at times Fielding himself—were among its cultural disseminators. Yet at the same time one finds uncanny reminders of the older popular metaphysics, such as the institution of the masquerade, as I have already argued. Bakhtin himself points to the brittle resilience of carnivalesque themes in baroque and rococo literature, even in writers usually considered the epigones of Descartes and Locke. For all their other disparities, parts of *Gulliver's Travels*, the philosophical tales of Diderot, Sterne's narratives, and the eighteenth-century comic novel in general share, for example, what he calls a "carnival-grotesque" element, the purpose of which is always "to consecrate inventive freedom" and liberate "from conventions and established truth." [9]

The imaginative emblems of the carnivalesque—the images of mask, *sotie*, charivari, and *bal masqué*—retain hints of their traditional charisma. And thus, though the process of its symbolic impoverishment has begun, the mask never entirely loses its ancient noumena. Whether reduced to boudoir toy or fashionable accessory, private erotic fetish or collective accoutrement (as at the masquerade), the mask, in Bakhtin's words, never becomes "just an object among other objects." On occasion it still can be seen in the eighteenth century—and sometimes even today—as "a particle of some other world." [10]

Fielding's writing, and above all his final novel, *Amelia*, contains important traces of this atavistic or antirationalist tradition. As with Richardson, it is the invocation of a carnival landscape, specifically the inverted midnight world of the masquerade, that unleashes a latent imaginative content. For Fielding, as for his predecessor, the masquerade is that charged topos around which forgotten or subversive possibilities cluster. And as in eighteenth-century narrative generally, the masquerade becomes that site in Fielding's fiction, both topographic and textual, real and rhetorical, from which unbidden dreams unfold.

I focus on *Amelia* in part simply because the topos is here so insistent. In few English novels of the eighteenth century does what one might call the ontology of the mask have such centrality. This work contains not just one but two masquerade scenes—a doubling, as it were, of set pieces. The contradictory relationship between these scenes, each of which serves a very different narrative function, is one of the fiction's crucial ironies. Like the disparity between Fielding's two versions of the mask, it invites an explanation.

The topos may also account for more general discontinuities in Fielding's novel. *Amelia* has always been regarded as Fielding's least ingratiating and accountable work of fiction. That it betrays a Janus-like quality—disturbing oscillations in tone, peculiarities of plot and character, general thematic confusion—is undoubtedly true. Unlike *Tom Jones*, *Amelia* resists recuperation as a unified artistic whole; it has never been adduced as a New Critical heterocosm. When commentators on the fiction attempt to explain this confusion, however (other than in the crudest biographical terms), the explanations offered usually turn solely on Fielding's unsuccessful juxtaposition of incompatible generic conventions. Thus Ronald Paulson writes of *Amelia*'s characteristic "mixing of novelistic and Juvenalian conventions." Other critics point to the somewhat awkward overlap of satiric themes with themes of the sentimental domestic epic.[11]

Such observations are helpful as far as they go. *Amelia* may indeed be said to fluctuate between allegory and "History"— between the schematic and highly stylized devices of the "Universal Satire on Mankind" and what we have come to recognize as mimetic narrative. It has features both of the traditional satiric anatomy, as Frye describes it, and of a more fluid, innovative naturalism. But this outward generic fluctuation is symptomatic of inconsistencies at a deeper level. Fielding's carnival theme is an important clue to this deeper level, as well as its most spectacular manifestation. If the masquerade topos seems circumscribed at the start of the novel by a larger pattern of allegorical meaning, appearing at first to be merely the most obvious sort of moral emblem—a banal icon of that deceptive human society Fielding has promised in his preface to expose—it soon loses this symbolic transparency. Like Amelia's unmasking, the subjective effects of the masquerade are unprecedented and ambiguous: the occasion's surprisingly euphoric "consequences" (to use the fiction's own term) ultimately cannot be reconciled with any previously established pattern of rational instruction. As in *Pamela*, the representation of the masquerade subverts the superficial didactic project and effects the metamorphosis of the fiction into something other than pure exemplum. *Amelia* becomes a less familiar, less homogenous, less rational rhetorical structure.

I am less concerned to name what *Amelia* becomes than to describe how the process of transformation occurs. Again, I hope to support a larger theoretical premise: that even as the masquerade makes its appearance in eighteenth-century English fiction as the primary trope of social and moral instability, as a kind of microcosmic World Upside-Down (to be censured and exorcised), it produces a profound rhetorical instability in the very fiction that sets out to contain it. As in *Amelia*, the drastic mystique of the carnival world pervades those works that try to domesticate it, bringing about their own lapse away from the cherished modern paradigms of purity, coherence, and legibility.

Certainly it is hard to say how much the ambiguity informing Fielding's use of the masquerade topos in *Amelia* is intentional and how much it may reveal an underlying desire to escape intentionality, moral seriousness, and the burden of having to say only what one means. It may be, though never acknowledged by the novelists themselves, that the basic function of the masquerade in eighteenth-century narrative is precisely to permit a displaced expression of *what was not intended*—to allow for a kind of authorial fugue away from official ideological positions and from whatever "implied" authorial identity has been consciously established. To borrow Barbara Johnson's phrase, the figure of the masquerade may allow the eighteenth-century narrator to become temporarily "different from himself"—to adopt an unstable, irresponsible persona, even as his characters lapse from integrity and custom.[12] One may allow, though, that it seems unlikely that Fielding entirely preordained the paradoxes of his carnival theme, just as it seems unlikely that contemporary masqueraders were entirely conscious, in the modern psychological sense, of the subliminal wishes their fantastic costumes encoded.

Judging by Fielding's other references to masquerading, in programmatic pieces as well as in the famous interlude in *Tom Jones*, one would expect little conscious ambiguity on the subject. If anything, Fielding's official position on the masquerade remains remarkably, even garrulously, consistent. One cannot ignore the pressure that Fielding, on one level at least, insistently places on his reader to respond to the masquerade only as allegory, only as an emblem of human inauthenticity.

Fielding's opposition takes its most direct and extreme form, as one might expect, in his judicial writings, specifically the *Charge Delivered to the Grand Jury* (1749) and *An Enquiry into the Causes of the Late Increase of Robbers* (1751). These extra-literary pieces are important because they convey his public views in a relatively unmediated way. Fielding's interest in the masquerade was of course professional as well as personal; these legal opinions, written during his tenure as a magistrate on the Westminster bench, are part of that larger battle civil and religious authorities waged against the masquerade throughout the century. Fielding on occasion took an active role in the work of suppression; in June 1751 he was the magistrate who reprimanded a group of masqueraders apprehended when the High Constable of Westminster staged a midnight raid on an illegal assembly near Exeter Exchange.[13] Even so, the severity of some of his strictures may surprise us. In the *Charge to the Grand Jury*, for instance, while commenting on the sources of vice and social ills, Fielding repeatedly denounced those "Places of public Rendezvous"—"Masquerades, Balls and Assemblies"—where modern pleasure-seekers were schooled in the ways of profligacy and luxury. Despite appearing to be "Scenes of innocent Diversion," such places, "where idle Persons of both Sexes meet in a very disorderly Manner," were in fact, he wrote, "Temples of Iniquity." Public "Meetings" like the masquerade were "*contra bonos mores*," and he charged the Jury ("the Hand of Justice") to punish "the Immoralities of the People" and put an end to this growing "Mischief" afoot in the nation.

In *An Enquiry into the Late Increase of Robbers*, Fielding's attack on modern "Voluptuousness" again resolved into a complaint against assemblies, like the masquerade, at which impropriety and excess were the rule: "Now what greater Temptation can there be to Voluptuousness, than a Place where every Sense and Appetite of which it is compounded are fed and delighted; where the Eyes are feasted with Show, and the Ears with Music, where Gluttony and Drunkenness are allowed by every Kind of Dainty; nay, where the finest Women are exposed to View, and where the meanest Person . . . may in some Degree mix with his Betters, and thus perhaps satisfy his Vanity as well as his Love of Pleasure?" These assemblies, lately grown up "in and near the Metropolis," were to be distinguished, Fielding wrote, from the more natural amusements of the country, from which the mind might indeed "spring up the better, and more brisk from Rest." The masquerade served no such therapeutic function; it was a "notorious Nuisance," and particularly among the lower orders, a threat to morality. Fielding reserved his greatest censure for what he called the "inferior" masquerades of the town, where "Men and Women of loose Reputation meet in disguised Habits." These he saw as nothing more than "Temples of Drunkenness, Lewdness, and all Kinds of Debauchery."

In these programmatic writings Fielding aimed mainly to describe how the masquerade engendered larger social ills. In the *Charge to the Grand Jury* he feared such diversions would soon reduce civil society to a "downright State of wild and savage Barbarism," and in the *Enquiry* he asserted that the viciousness of modern public assemblies was "as infectious by Example, as the Plague itself by Contact." The masquerade was to be feared precisely because it threatened to turn society into its own image. Like a cloud of contagion, it had the power to transform the body politic into a similar mass of corruption.

The imagery of contamination becomes superfluous, however, in Fielding's literary treatments of the masquerade. Here, in the satiric pieces and novels, the masked assembly is not so much a foreign growth threatening to corrupt society as a sign that society is already irretrievably corrupt. It is now symptom rather than cause—less a "Nursery" of vice than the mark of a world in which vice is taken for granted, the spectacular epitome of a fallen populace. This for Fielding is the overriding metaphoric significance of the masquerade: it stands as the living emblem of a wider decay, a theater of excess in which modern society enacts its own perversity.

Fielding's masquerade is above all a *carnaval moralisé*. We have seen how the allegorical vision dominates *The Masquerade* of 1728; in that satire, the depraved "little world" of the Haymarket masquerade clearly mirrors the corrupt metropolis that spawns it. Presided over by the grotesque Heidegger, Satan's "first minister," the midnight revel is the microcosm of a post-lapsarian world. It is a realm of dissimulation, folly, lust, and perpetual, exhausting ironies. Human life has become here no more than "an idle, trifling, feverish dream" (332).

The masquerade has its parodies of piety, just as it has its parodies of beauty and honesty.

> Error! (strange goddess!) ruleth here,
> And from her castle in the air,
> Carefully watches o'er our motions,
> Receives our off'rings and devotions.   (308–11)

But as in the actual "beau monde," deception is the privileged vice of the moment. The ubiquitous visor and costume are but the external symbols of a universal human tendency toward self-mystification and chicanery. Disguised as dainty shepherds and shepherdesses, modern masqueraders may recall a Golden Age of natural, unmediated human relations:

> Such the Arcadian shepherds were,
> When love alone could charm the fair:
> Such the Arcadian nymphs, when love
> Beauty alone in men could move.
> How happy did they sport away,
> In fragrant bow'rs, the scorching day;
> Or, to the Nightingale's soft tune,
> Danc'd by the lustre of the moon!   (250–57)

Yet the poet learns not to be fooled:

> How different is now their fate!
> Both equally conspiring to cheat.
> Florus, with lying billet-doux
> The charming Rosalind pursues;
> Follows her to the play—to court,
> Where-ever the beau monde resort. . . .
> At last the pitying fair relents,
> And to his utmost wish consents.
> No sooner is the nymph enjoy'd,
> Than Florus, fickle youth, is cloy'd.
> He leaves her for another toast;
> She laughs, and cries—pray—who has lost?   (262–75)

At times the simulations of the night are unintentionally revealing: masqueraders expose secret desires, carefully veiled in ordinary society, even as they don their would-be disguises: "Known prudes are there, libertines we find, / Who masque the face, t'unmasque the mind" (73–74). But in or out of the masquerade's "frantic" whirl, everyone finally is a hypocrite, as the poet discovers, and sincerity itself but a "masque" to be worn as one chooses.

In *The Masquerade* the central allegory is worked, as it were, from inside to outside, microcosm to macrocosm. Despite the scene's initial strangeness—where

> in one confusion hurl'd,
> Seem all the nations of the world;
> Cardinals, quakers, judges dance;
> Grim Turks are coy, and nuns advance   (67–70)

—it is precisely its resemblance to the larger world that we are meant to recognize. This localized outburst of mystification and inauthenticity, the satirist suggests, is but the expression of a more pervasive, familiar dishonesty: the moral charade that is society itself. The masquerade is the living image of *hypokrisis*— a place where the role playing found in everyday life is simply given a chic, cynical, self-conscious elaboration.

But Fielding sometimes works the allegory in reverse, as in perhaps his best-known piece of purely didactic writing, the "Essay on the Knowledge of the Characters of Men," collected in the *Miscellanies* of 1743. There the moralist's angry assault on the "Art of Thriving" through hypocrisy—this "great Depravity of Human Nature"—resolves into a bleak initial vision of global theatricality. Vice finds its appropriate figure: so prevalent are deceit and falsehood, writes Fielding, that modern life has indeed become nothing more than a "vast Masquerade." The sot, the gamester, or the rake hides behind the assumed character of "the Cardinal, the Friar, or the Judge," while the few who are truly innocent and good are scorned as well as imposed upon. "Thus while the crafty and designing Part of Mankind, consulting only their separate Advantage, endeavour to maintain one constant Imposition on others, the whole World becomes a vast Masquerade, where the greatest Part appear disguised under false Vizors and Habits; a very few only shewing their own Faces, who become, by so doing, the Astonishment and Ridicule of all the rest."[14]

Fielding gives the familiar metaphor a significant extension when he tries to offer some small hope to the virtuous. "However cunning the Disguise be which a Masquerader wears: however foreign to his Age, Degree, or Circumstance, yet if closely attended to, he very rarely escapes the Discovery of an accurate Observer; for Nature, which unwillingly submits to the Imposture, is ever endeavouring to peep forth and shew herself." The remark serves as justification for what is to follow in the rest of the essay: Fielding's lengthy advice to his reader, almost a semiotics of hypocrisy, in which he describes the various physiognomic and behavioral signs through which deceit reveals itself to the "discerning Eye." It is possible to protect oneself from impostures by learning those "Marks in the Countenance," such as a peculiarly "glavering Smile," by which hypocrisy gives itself away. But with this important invocation of Nature, that authentic body "peeping" forth under the disguise, Fielding's remark also reveals the epistemological underpinnings of the masquerade analogy itself. The author of the "Essay" assumes here what one might call a theology of human character. Not only does each human being possess a true, unchanging "Character" (one that is either expressed or masked in the company of others), but this character is itself morally unambiguous. Good natures are distinct from bad in Fielding's moral scheme; he posits a stable typology of human moral possibilities. Thus he writes of the varying natural "Inclinations" individuals display toward good or evil, and of how "like trees bearing different kinds of fruit," human beings carry with them an innate predisposition to perform either good or bad actions. Such a "Difference of Inclination or Character" as may be found from one person to the next, he observes, obliges the theoretician of human nature to acknowledge "some unequivocal, original Distinction, in the Nature or Soul of one Man, from that of another."[15]

Much has been written on this static notion of character: the resemblance of many of Fielding's fictional characters to the staple types of allegory and romance, their representative (as opposed to specific) qualities, and their limited psychological range. The traditional view has much to recommend it: often enough Fielding's characters indeed betray what Angus Fletcher calls the daemonic agency of allegorical figures. They seem to embody a certain moral, social, or psychological idée fixe, and display little of that symbolic variability and emotional ambivalence we connect with the "mimetic" characters of realistic fiction. Often they retain a privileged association with virtue or vice, the traditional poles of allegorical discourse.[16]

One can see how Fielding's allegorical exploitation of the masquerade topos is adapted to this static conception of character. The masquerade of the "Essay," for instance (or for that matter, *The Masquerade*), preserves its allegorical transparency, and fits so lucidly into a larger critique of hypocrisy, precisely because Fielding's view of human nature is here so prejudicial, so lacking in fluidity. The masquerade makes sense as a moral trope—as the emblem of a world in which all appear to be what they are not—only because what the individual really "is" has in some sense already been agreed upon. The *carnaval moralisé* is inextricably linked to a theology of fixed types. Human nature can be disguised because it cannot fundamentally be altered. When Fielding writes that the hypocrite hides his true nature just as the masquerader hides his true form, the underlying epistemological appeal is the same: that there is indeed a truth beneath the disguise, a zone of absolute integrity at once immutable, morally unmysterious, and ultimately visible to the "discerning Eye."

The point is worth remarking, because when we turn to the fiction it is just this appeal that becomes increasingly problematic. The *carnaval moralisé* may be a lucid figure, but it is not necessarily a stable one. It preserves a certain rhetorical integrity within the limited, highly rationalized context of the poetic satire or homiletic essay: one does not question, perhaps, that implicit theology of character on which it rests. But displaced into the expansive and more fluid representational world of prose narrative, such a figure, it seems, cannot survive long. Suppressed aspects of the topos emerge here, including all of its archaic associations with transformation, pleasure, ambiguity, and the enigma of plot.

When such atavistic meanings resurface, a corresponding change is also worked in the realm of human "Nature." Unlike the masquerade of satire and homily, Fielding's fictional masquerades do not ultimately reinforce a monolithic notion of character. They tend instead to subvert the theology of types, even as they subvert, potentially at least, every other kind of moral and metaphysical taxonomy. For example, under the masquerade's mysterious influence Fielding's good and bad moral types may no longer seem so irrevocably distinct. After this scene of collective exchange the fictional world may seem less and less allegorically divided into paragons and hypocrites. Characters suddenly behave in ways contrary to their stereotypical natures, to the point that "Nature" itself becomes a less rational notion, and more of a dialectical paradox. At least for a moment, the Fieldingesque character becomes a kind of epistemological medley—a congeries of antithetical moral and psychological possibilities. Thus one might speak of the basic counterallegorical consequence of the masquerade scene in Fielding's fiction: it transforms the familiar host of types, all of whom become implicated in its exotic badinage, into oxymoronic entities. Even as the masquerade ceases to be recuperable as allegory itself, it undermines the allegorical representation of character, temporarily creating in its wake, as it were, the image of a myriad, carnivalized human psychology.

None of which is to say, still, that Fielding intends us to interpret the masquerade in other than simple didactic terms. Certainly even in *Tom Jones*, where the masquerade already exerts something of its provocative influence on plot and character, one detects an attempt on Fielding's part to preserve the idea of the *carnaval moralisé*. The masquerade episode in that novel, marking one of Tom's first London adventures, retains obvious features of the allegorical set piece. It is relatively brief and highly circumscribed in a formal sense, being contained within a single chapter (Book VIII, chap. 7) purporting to illustrate "the Whole Humours of a Masquerade." Fielding's heading is significant. It suggests at once an authorial will toward rhetorical enclosure— a containment of the topos—and by the reference to humors, the characteristically static psychological taxonomies of satire. Again, we are clearly meant to see the masquerade as the satiric epitome of a corrupt beau monde. And not surprisingly, when the narrator of *Tom Jones* elucidates the basic sham on which the entertainment is founded, he sounds much like the ironic guide of *The Masquerade*. Heidegger, the *"Arbiter Deliciarum"* and sponsor of the masquerade, is nothing more, he explains, than the "great High Priest of Pleasure," who "like other Heathen Priests, imposes on his Votaries by the pretended Presence of the Deity, when in Reality no such Deity is there" (XIII, 7).

Lady Bellaston, that somewhat disingenuous Queen of the Fairies, is made to utter similar conventional sentiments a page or two later. Intent on taking Tom home with her, she reiterates the familiar satiric complaint that the masquerade itself masquerades—that is, while pretending to chic and frivolity, it is actually quite tiresome. "You cannot conceive," she tells him, "any Thing more insipid and childish than a Masquerade to the People of Fashion, who in general know one another as well here, as when they meet in an Assembly or a Drawing-room. . . . In short, the Generality of Persons whom you see here, may more properly be said to kill Time in this Place than in any other; and generally retire from hence more tired than from the longest Sermon." With the allusion here to Hogarth's *Masquerade Ticket*, in which depraved masqueraders are shown "killing" one of their fellows dressed as Father Time (see Fig. 8, p. 23), Fielding invites the reader to visualize his scene too in frozen pictorial terms as the static icon or Hogarthian emblem of immorality. Lady Bellaston's sanctimonious gloss frames the meaning of the masquerade in the conventional manner, even as it serves her own luxurious, rampant purposes.[17]

These attempts at circumscribing our view of the masquerade do not altogether obscure, however, its more paradoxical instrumental function in Fielding's narrative. We cannot completely escape the paradox, for instance, that even here, where the masquerade scene is only a relatively brief interlude in the action—only one among many topoi of the polite world—it is also an indispensable part of Fielding's larger narrative design. The plot of *Tom Jones* unfolds as it does in its latter stages precisely because of that crucial action taking place here: Tom's seduction by Lady Bellaston. True to its role in classic eighteenth-century plots (where it brings together characters who otherwise would not meet), the masquerade in *Tom Jones* generates intrigue by producing this highly problematic liaison. The post-masquerade affair in turn engenders a host of subsidiary plot complications, not least of which is the hero's somewhat disturbing economic dependence on Bellaston. How this sinister entanglement will be undone and Tom's love for Sophia reaffirmed constitutes a major technical difficulty to be resolved in the last part of the fiction. Again one might say that the figure of the masquerade, in emblematic terms the quintessentially useless occasion, is also paradoxically necessary—to narrative itself. Quite apart from its moral redaction, it is part of the machinery of narrative pleasure: by placing a further, seemingly insurmountable obstacle in the way of Tom and Sophia's reconciliation, it both prolongs the comic business of the novel and intensifies our relief at the eventual happy outcome.

The scene has its perverse impact on character too. Of all the many episodes in the novel, it is the Bellaston sequence that has most troubled *Tom Jones*'s moral apologists—mainly because Tom himself, the archetype of uncomplicated good nature, here seems to behave in an uncharacteristically mysterious, even venal way. The "Want of a Shilling," some have felt, hardly explains his precipitate and degrading affair, or the apparent betrayal of his passion for Sophia Western. Such actions indicate an unprecedented if cryptic will toward self-aggrandizement, at odds with that "natural grace" and "generosity of soul" traditionally seen as the hallmark of his highly stylized character. As R. S. Crane was one of the first to point out, Tom seems morally out of sorts in these scenes: "not himself."[18]

The dissonance here may be a minor one, lasting only as long as the Bellaston affair itself, but it is nonetheless suggestive. What we sense as an inconsistency in Tom Jones's nature—and in Fielding's realization of the character—dates, in textual terms, from the night of the masquerade, when Tom so shockingly succumbs to Lady Bellaston's blandishments. When Tom dons the costume supplied by the Queen of the Fairies, he becomes not only physically but morally unrecognizable. On what level the scene might be said to prompt Tom's subsequent puzzling transformation is a vexed epistemological issue; but we cannot help feeling an obscure causality at work. *Tom Jones* reveals in embryo the strange power of the carnival figure: the way it can disrupt the Fieldingesque code of character itself, by allowing the deformation of types into their opposites. The fact that Tom's "good" nature eventually reasserts itself—that he becomes, after this hiatus, the same lucid, even banal moral type he was before—should not distract us from the basic theoretical point that the fictional representation of the masquerade is persistently associated with the destabilization of consistent or coherent character, even as it precipitates, on the level of plot, an embarrassment of rich, scandalous incident. In an Aristotelian sense it conserves nothing. Rather, like a kind of textual vortex, it is that locale through which characters cannot pass without exposing what is *un*characteristic—how they differ, as it were, from themselves.

In *Tom Jones* the threat such destabilization poses to the allegorical coherence of the narrative itself is minimized: the masquerade is part after all of the insidious metropolitan landscape so pointedly abandoned in the last book, when Tom and Sophia return to Squire Allworthy's estate in pastoral Somerset. Though one cannot exactly say that Fielding has succeeded here in moralizing away the masquerade, it is part of a world that can be left behind. Its problematic delirium may still exist at the end of the novel, but it exists somewhere else, in the demonic anti-realm of the city. The situation in *Amelia* is altogether different. There it may seem that the world of the masquerade, with its endless unsettling transformations, is precisely what one can never escape, for it is nothing less than experience itself—an experience devoid of rational content or moral logic. Simultaneously the book itself skirts logic, substituting ambivalence and difficulty for the transparent antinomies of allegory. To this oxymoronic structure—for *Amelia* is surely not entirely what Fielding conceived it to be—we may now turn.

Again one must begin with an irony: that the moralistic impulse—the impulse toward complete rhetorical transparency—is if anything stronger in *Amelia* than anywhere else in Fielding's fiction. It is palpable from the start: in the dedication to Ralph Allen, Fielding baldly announces the purpose of his fiction will be "to promote the Cause of Virtue, and to expose some of the most glaring Evils, as well public as private, which at present infest the Country." The metaphor of exposure is significant.

For Fielding indeed seems to have conceived *Amelia* along the lines of the anatomy or satiric allegory. Already, in the peculiar opening books, one finds he is as much concerned here with "unmasking" and enumerating contemporary vices as with developing a coherent mimetic action. The glaring evils glare indeed. From the start *Amelia* displays an element of hypertrophied didacticism, the artistic effects of which have often been calculated.[19]

The fact raises the interesting possibility that it may indeed be the work in which the conscious allegorizing tendency is strongest, where there is a surplus of didactic intention, that also shows the most revealing counterdidactic impulses. As the will toward didactic control over the reader intensifies, as an author strives more and more to make his or her fiction an entirely accountable ethical paradigm—the perfect allegorical *kosmos*—so an antithetical tendency, a submerged will toward scandal and impertinence, may intensify. The human need to embarrass oneself is most pressing when the embarrassing gesture is out of the question. One result may be a disruptive or uncanny episode. Certainly in the case of Richardson, the strain of writing an unambiguously "good" book in *Pamela*, Part 2, seems to have unleashed a certain subversive (and unintentional) mischief in the central sections of that novel. The fact that the scenery of the carnivalesque—the ultimate sign of moral and metaphysical chaos—is so prominent in these otherwise hidebound fictions suggests, again, the explosive working out of a previously suppressed alternative content.

In any event, at least for its first half *Amelia* displays an intense, seemingly inescapable didacticism. So insistent is this "instruction," the moralist's obsessive revelation of human guile, that one has little sense in the opening books of any real plot or forward narrative momentum—only of a somewhat desultory textual movement, like Booth's perambulations around the prison yard, from one scene of iniquity to another. Virgilian echoes notwithstanding, Fielding's formal procedure here is not so much the elaboration, in the classical sense, of a single unified action, but the satiric projection of a series of discrete moral set pieces. Like those disparate images in the World Upside-Down prints of the seventeenth and eighteenth centuries (donkeys flaying men, fishes in the sky; see Fig. 29), the narrator's cynical anecdotes create an impression of semantic overdetermination, for the ultimate meaning each conveys is the same. Human life is topsy-turvy, and the wise person remains perpetually on guard against its outrages.

Of necessity Fielding establishes his narrative persona early—that of the confidant, or the discloser of secrets. He takes it on himself to explicate the fictional world for his readers, to be our moral watchdog, to uncover what the world hides from view. He will illuminate the dark truth behind appearances. Addressing the reader in the second chapter of Book I, he writes that his "usual Manner" will be to "premise," or disclose in advance, "some things which it may be necessary for thee to know." The reader in turn is cast as the recipient of privy information, one who learns the truth. The process of reading is figured as a privileged movement from exteriority to interiority. The narrator will lead us, he implies, from outside to inside, toward a

29. *The World Upside-Down.* Detail of an anonymous engraving published by Bowles and Carver, ca. 1790.

certain hidden content. Thus those multiple chapter headings early in *Amelia* promising a penetration of surfaces, and entry into a realm of truth: "Containing the Inside of a Prison" (I, 3); "Disclosing Further Secrets of the Prison-House" (I, 4); and the title of the chapter in which Miss Matthews is introduced, "Containing . . . some Endeavours to prove, by Reason and Authority, that it is possible for a Woman to appear to be what she really is not" (I, 6).

The truth of course is disillusioning: a logic of inversion governs the world of appearances. Things are not what they seem; everything masquerades in fact as its opposite. Whatever is, one may be sure, is wrong—the antithesis of what it might be, in an ideally ordered human community. The world of *Amelia*, like that of the "Essay on the Knowledge of the Characters of Men," is indeed a "vast Masquerade," a panorama of deception, the *mundus inversus* itself.

The logic is apparent immediately. Justice Thrasher's court, before which the hapless Booth is brought in Book I, is a cruel, almost Brechtian parody of justice—the allegory of a corrupt society, where evil is rewarded and good maligned. One soon grasps the pattern: a serving girl on an errand for her mistress is charged with soliciting and treated like a common whore; a badly beaten man is imprisoned for supposedly assaulting an unscathed accuser; Booth himself is punished for trying to rescue an innocent man from a gang of street bullies. We learn to expect the inevitable reversal of our expectations, and the fulfillment of a dark, continuous moral irony.

This pattern of reversal is expressed even more strikingly in the prison scenes that follow. Here the overthrow of normal human relations is complete. The prison yard—into which the reader, like Booth, is also, as it were, abruptly thrown—is a scene of nightmarish alienations, a surreal walled garden in which corruption and hysteria flourish. No one in this carnival of misery is what he or she seems: human affect, as in an anxiety dream, is shockingly misleading. Robinson, the Methodist "Philosopher" who befriends Booth in the yard, is really a pickpocket; a pretty girl with "Innocence in her Countenance" turns out to be a streetwalker, and discharges a volley of oaths at the confused captain (I, 4). Ordinary social relations are parodied. Women, Blear-Eyed Moll among them, assail male inmates with sexual overtures, and beat them when they refuse (I, 3). A homosexual prisoner, "committed for certain odious unmanlike Practices, not fit to be named," is given "various Kinds of Discipline" by a group of prostitutes (I, 4). Moral sympathies are consistently violated. While incorrigible malefactors seem to flourish in the prison—Moll, perversely, is one of the "merriest Persons" to be found there—the innocent, falsely incarcerated, waste away. Emblematic vignettes convey the prevailing malignancy: a "little Creature" Booth sees crying in one corner of the yard has been imprisoned by her father-in-law, a grenadier, for allegedly doing him "bodily Harm"; elsewhere, a starving young woman and her father languish, charged with stealing a loaf of bread (I, 4).

The prison scenes, one could say, are a generic cue to the reader. They situate us immediately in the anti-world of satire and condition a certain generic expectation about what is to follow. We learn here what is, in the inverted world of the anatomy or moral allegory, a familiar mode of interpretation: to distrust the appearance, to anticipate the eventual exposure of any simulacrum of goodness. Fielding's narrator trains his reader in the ways of suspicion. The result is that, at least at the outset, we may experience a paradoxical intellectual complacency, even an ennui, in the face of this "Universal Satire on Mankind." Its revelations follow a predictable hermeneutic pattern; its somber didactic message is nothing if not overdetermined.

One irony of the situation, to be sure, is that the reader's moral schooling is in no way matched by that of Booth himself, who is the focus of interest in these sections. He remains the epistemological naïf, perpetually fallible and perpetually surprised by each new example of chicanery he encounters. By the time Miss Matthews appears the disparity is well established: the reader, thanks to Fielding's incriminating clues, cannot help but suspect her; Booth, however, does not. Her odd demeanor, oscillating between she-tragedy posturing and comic coquetry, raises no question in his mind—or not, at least, until it is too late. Polite conversation between them resolves into sexual conversation; and thus begins the emotional entanglement that will produce so much difficulty for Booth in *Amelia*'s remaining books.

Booth's muddled passivity in the face of "snares" may be taken, however, as yet another generic cue, for it resembles in many respects the exemplary naïveté of the allegorical hero. Booth's very vacuousness—his curious lack of presence or of distinct moral personality—connects him with the cipherlike characters of traditional allegory: Everyman, Spenser's Red Cross Knight, Christian of *Pilgrim's Progress*. His "wavering" spiritual condition (I, 3) is symptomatic of a larger indefiniteness in his nature; he represents a kind of unbounded or free-floating textual energy. Such indistinctness conditions in turn the expectation again that *Amelia* itself will be a narrative structure of a certain familiar and highly formulaic type: the *psychomachia*, or battle of vice and virtue. In the first books of *Amelia* Fielding sets the stage for such a battle by suspending his hero between two worlds: that of Miss Matthews, the embodiment of lassitude and corruption; and that of Amelia, representative of moral purity and the domestic virtues. The crucial question at this stage is in fact the classic question of allegory: whether Amelia (whose name itself suggests the possibility of active goodness) will be a sufficiently potent force in the fictional world to draw Booth definitively into the camp of the virtuous, or whether her own virtue will in turn succumb, disastrously, to the schemes of the vicious. She loses her first skirmish in absentia, when Booth copulates with Miss Matthews in the prison. But we still await with some curiosity the outcome of this confrontation between virtue and vice, and the effect Amelia's actual presence will have on Booth's embryonic, imprecise moral nature.[20]

In subsequent books, when Amelia is in fact introduced and we mark the true extent of the troubles, financial and otherwise, besetting the Booths' marriage, the implicit allegorical pattern persists. Again, for approximately the first half of the novel, we

have little sense of any underlying teleological narrative concern, other than this vague battle between the forces of good
and evil. What we might call the basic embedded issues in Fielding's plot—whether, for example, Amelia and Booth will ever
witness a true change in their fortunes and escape poverty—
tend to get lost in a welter of discontinuous, fragmentary episodes: the "exquisite Distresses" the Booths are somewhat bathetically made to undergo. Like hero and heroine, Fielding's
reader is caught up in this world of painful, disarming accident:
we confront incidents with no apparent connection to one another, except that they confirm, in emblematic terms, the intol-
erable hypocrisy of human society and the cruel impostures that
innocence must endure.

Thus the claustrophobic, circumscribed picaresque of Books
III through VI, containing Booth's account of his courtship of
Amelia, and their subsequent postmarital London travails. All
the moral pathology associated with the little world of the
prison recurs in that larger human community through which
Booth and Amelia so guilelessly move. The couple are close
prisoners in a metropolis of evil, the full scale of which they
only intermittently perceive, if they perceive it at all. Most significant is what the reader sees and they cannot: the degree to
which they are deceived and imposed upon by virtually everyone they encounter. Hypocrisy is global: from Amelia's "glavering" sister Betty, who feigns compassion for her disenfranchised
sibling, to Monsieur Bagillard at Montpelier (the first of many
"Friends" of the Booths with designs on Amelia's virtue), to the
sinister London trio made up of Colonel James, Mrs. Ellison,
and the circumspect, nameless "noble Peer." Each of these characters is in varying degree unmasked by Fielding's narrator: that
is, we are apprised of their real natures—or seem to be—well in
advance of the Booths themselves. Thus long before the captain
or his wife becomes suspicious, for instance, of the villainous
peer, the reader has already had a multiplicity of ironic clues
about his character, including the barely veiled secret of his lust
for Amelia. We are subject to continuous moral and emotional
disillusionment, even in excess of that disillusionment suffered

by Amelia and Booth themselves, for we can perceive what they so demoralizingly cannot—that their reverses are part of a larger, insidious syndrome, a consistent absence of authenticity in the realm of human relations. "Friend" and "Enemy," the narrator will observe later, are "often synonymous in the Language of the World" (IX, 2). But even before this piece of bleak commentary, the lesson has been instilled to depressing excess. We come soon enough to scrutinize the fictional landscape with cynicism, even paranoia, as again and again seemingly benevolent characters are exposed as malingers, pimps, and deceivers.

I made an analogy earlier between Fielding's formal method and the World-Upside-Down plate; the technique here, as well as Fielding's theme, could again be described as iconographic. The narrative in these early scenes, already spasmodic, has a tendency to stop altogether whenever Fielding is concerned to frame a particularly egregious instance of moral or ontological chaos. The result is a static, almost pictorial set piece, as in the unnumbered "Additional Chapter" in Book V.[21] Here one of Amelia's children develops a fever, only, it seems, to allow the narrator a satire on doctors and apothecaries. Arsenic and Dosewell are World-Upside-Down figures: the doctor turned poisoner, a satiric inversion of the familiar kind. Fielding admits the episode is not strictly necessary: "some Readers will, perhaps, think this whole Chapter might have been omitted." Yet, he maintains, it justifies itself by its instruction: "though it contains no great Amusement, it may at least serve to inform Posterity concerning the present State of Physic." One senses the satiric topos—"the present State of Physic"—taking precedence over the dynamics of narrative, forcing the fiction again into the characteristic mode of the visual anatomy, complete with caricatured, essentially pictographic illustrations of vice and folly.

At other times the satiric impulse produces simple uncanniness: what one might call a freezing of the freakish or discontinuous image. An example occurs during Booth's visit in Book III to Major Bath at Montpelier, where Booth finds his friend dressed, "whimsically enough," in "a Woman's Bed-Gown and a very dirty Flannel Night-Cap." We already know Major Bath, "a very aukward, thin Man, near seven Feet high," as a kind of *miles gloriosus,* whose discourse "generally turned on matters of no feminine kind, war and martial exploits being the ordinary topics of his conversation" (III, 8). Bath tells Booth that his remarkable costume is due to the fact that he is nursing his ailing sister (and he is indeed warming a posset for her), yet this peculiar explanation hardly seems to account entirely for his strange appearance. One suspects—for the episode is otherwise unmotivated—the scene is meant to bring to mind again the stereotypical imagery of the World Upside-Down. Like the death-dealing doctor, the "warrior in skirts" is a conventional motif in World-Upside-Down engravings, deriving perhaps from ancient stories of Hercules and Omphale, but suggestive in any case of those sexual and social reversals characteristic of the *mundus inversus.*[22] The spectacle of the ordinarily martial Bath in transvestite deshabille likewise has its pictorial aspect: it too tends to stop the narrative flow, almost in the manner of a cinematic freeze-frame. (It is worth noting that the moment was selected for representation by *Amelia's* early illustrators. In the Henley edition, with engravings by Rooker and Corbould dating from 1793, the scene is the frontispiece to Volume I.) But it also points up again the generalized topsy-turvydom of the fictional world. Bath's travesty is a specimen of aberrance—comical enough, yet indicative too perhaps of other even less explicable inversions in *Amelia's* moral landscape.

Among the many similar instances of inversion and bathos in the first half of *Amelia,* one species of reversal is especially worth noting, for as we shall see it has an obvious relevance to the matter of the masquerade. One might call the phenomenon the transvaluation of pleasure. It particularly affects the pleasures of sociability, and it makes sense given the pervasive fictional atmosphere of betrayal and exploitation: in a world where no one may be trusted, one expects little in the way of true human community. But the negativity with which Fielding here treats even the most minor form of collective pleasure—whether it be the shared meal, the game, or more inclusive public entertainment—is unremitting. It is indeed the "Party of

Pleasure," the human grouping or institution designed purely for enjoyment, that seems, in *Amelia*'s dark world, to produce the direst and most ironic consequences. Much of the demoralizing effect of Fielding's novel has undoubtedly to do with this pervasive thematic syndrome: that ordinarily refreshing occasions, the lightest of festivities and amusements, are represented as having nothing but sinister ramifications. For the reader, as for *Amelia*'s characters, there is no apparent escape, even temporary, from what one might call the code of disappointment, the oppression and tawdriness of the quotidian.

Just as the hypocritical individual is a dangerous simulacrum of affection and good will, so in Fielding's novel the pleasures of society are an equally dangerous simulacrum of delight. Their real function here, it seems, is to bring about pain and havoc. Nor does it make any difference whether one seeks one's pleasure in the anonymity of the crowd—at seemingly benign public places—or in a more intimate domestic setting. In a public space, such as the pleasure-garden, one is vulnerable to random, absurdly violent assaults—the meaningless brutality of strangers. When Booth and Amelia, seeking a brief respite from trouble, take a walk with their children in the park in Book IV, their son Billy is inexplicably attacked by a passing foot soldier with a bayonet, and saved only by the timely intervention of Booth's associate Sergeant Atkinson, who happens to be walking by. The episode has an ostensible significance in Fielding's plot—it reintroduces Atkinson, and later establishes the Booths' relationship with Mrs. Ellison, who offers Amelia a "restorative" when they return to their lodgings—but the violence here may nonetheless seem in excess of any narrative demand. Not surprisingly, the scene is almost immediately adduced to illustrate the requisite moral lesson: that the most "trifling adventure," even a stroll in "the green Fields of London," is capable of producing, in the narrator's words, "the most unexpected and dreadful Events" (IV, 7). A similar point will be made later when Amelia, walking in Vauxhall Gardens with Dr. Harrison, is physically assaulted by two rakes and made the butt of lewd jokes, to her pain and vexation (IX, 9).

The private pleasure party, held in the safety of one's own home, turns out to be no less problematic. Indeed, a less than pious reader might well be moved to laughter by the sheer number of times in *Amelia* that the most horrific disasters attend upon a scene of domestic celebration. Everything encompassed by the concept of "Civility" in the novel, all the ordinary pleasures of social existence, seem tainted by ill fortune. The pattern is set from the start, beginning with Miss Matthews's prison account of her history. Here one learns that a series of "musical Evenings" given by Miss Matthews's father prompted her first fatal attraction to Cornet Hebbers, for whose attempted murder she has been imprisoned. She was subsequently seduced and ruined by him, she tells Booth, when she became intoxicated at the festivities held in honor of her sister's wedding (I, 8). Likewise, in Mrs. Bennet's retrospective narrative a few books later (during which she also gives Amelia a crucial warning about the dangers of the masquerade), the same dysphoric syndrome is at work. The death of her own mother, relates Mrs. Bennet, resulted from an innocent family "Festival," Mrs. Bennet's sixteenth birthday party. Not wishing to disturb the servants, her unfortunate parent went by herself to refill a teakettle at a well, and promptly fell in and drowned. Misery everywhere supplants joy: the pathetic discovery once made, Mrs. Bennet tells Amelia, the family's "high degree of Mirth" evaporated, and they fell together into "the most bitter Agonies of Despair" (VII, 2).

The same principle of transvaluation operates, less melodramatically perhaps but still insistently, in those scenes of domestic sociability in which Booth and Amelia themselves engage. Meals taken with acquaintances, visiting one's neighbors, simple attempts at gaiety and friendly intercourse—all seem to produce the most troubling complications. Booth's memorable dinner with Miss Matthews in the prison, with its parody of domestic arrangements, is exemplary in this regard, but it is only the first of many such perverse parties. For Booth, later evenings spent with "Friends"—Captain Trent, for instance—lead to irksome problems: on one occasion, he loses all of his and

Amelia's remaining money gambling with Trent and others, who have of course been set up to entrap him (X, 5).

But even the seemingly most structured forms of social intercourse have their dangers. Of the varieties of domestic civility represented in *Amelia*, none is so insidious finally as that genteel entertainment Booth refers to at one point as the *partie quarrée*, the private pleasure party, usually held in one's own lodgings, consisting of two married (or otherwise related) couples (III, 9). The heterosexual quartet is the characteristic social configuration in the fictional world. Scenes involving actual quartets recur throughout *Amelia*, beginning with that sociable foursome in Montpelier made up of Booth, Amelia, Major Bath, and his sister Miss Bath. But often too one may have the sense of a "latent quartet" structuring the novel's fictional situations, as in the prison scene itself, where Amelia and Cornet Hebbers—the absent sexual partners of Booth and Miss Matthews—are in a sense the missing members of an implicit and highly significant *partie quarrée*.

The most important feature of the *partie quarrée* is its moral instability. This instability is paradoxical, for the figure itself suggests a certain ideal geometry of social relations. It squares, so to speak, the virtues of fidelity and fellowship. Nothing might seem more decorous (as indeed it seems to the Booths) than a neatly symmetrical relation between two legitimate couples. That stylized occasion around which the *partie quarrée* forms— the shared meal, the hand of cards, the evening of conversation—appears to represent an idealized fusion of distance and intimacy, politesse and candor. But such decorum is fragile, as is the shape of the figure itself. For throughout *Amelia*, as one might expect in a fiction where adultery is so prominent a theme, the *partie quarrée* repeatedly dissolves into a problematic, disorderly cluster of transgressive psychological and sexual relations. Rather than affirming licit bonds, it threatens them by providing the opportunity for the formation of new and morally subversive connections between the very members of the couples that compose it. The image in little of civilized exchange, it contains the seeds of its own destruction.

In the Booth/Bath *partie quarrée* the potential for disaster is mostly implicit, yet even here the figure of the quartet is associated with a certain amount of moral chaos. After the Booths and Baths have spent a number of evenings in each others' company, Monsieur Bagillard, who has himself had designs on the heroine, accuses Major Bath of trying to seduce her and cuckold Booth under the guise of friendship. One result—for Bath denies the charge—is a bloody duel between him and Bagillard (III, 9). More important, the reader is apprised of an intrinsic danger in the pattern of sociability itself: the adulteration of legitimate relations is a constant possibility.

Later versions of the configuration confirm the threat. The foursome made up of Booth and Amelia and Colonel and Mrs. James (who is of course the former Miss Bath) contains a doubling of subversive cathexes: Colonel James hopes to seduce Amelia, and Mrs. James harbors a covert passion for Booth. Even more sinister is the *partie quarrée* organized by Mrs. Ellison (the Booths' landlady) and her supposed cousin, the Noble Peer. Pretending friendship (the Peer has claimed he will use his influence to help Booth), they invite the Booths to dine on several occasions. Later, however, in the crucial seventh book of the novel, the reader learns along with Amelia that such hospitality has from the start been a ruse. Some previous tenants in the Ellison house, Mr. and Mrs. Bennet, were treated to similar niceties; but there the *partie quarrée* was simply one step in the Peer's elaborate scheme, abetted by Ellison, to rape Mrs. Bennet. A similar fate has been planned for Amelia. The ritualized exchange of civilities thus is not an end in itself, but part of a malevolent secret plot against virtue. And again, the reader is forced to confront the pervasive moral brutality of the fictional world, where even the most innocent-seeming of domestic pleasures reveals a hidden, maladive, even obscene instrumentality.

The representation of the masquerade—the most expansive and theatrical of social festivities—is linked to the *partie quarrée* on a number of levels. The formation of the sinister foursome at Mrs. Ellison's, midway through the fiction, sets up the first reference to the masquerade: once the requisite number of evenings have been passed in sociability, the Peer proceeds to the next stage in his nefarious scheme, which is to present Amelia with tickets for a masked assembly at Ranelagh (VI, 5). In turn Mrs. Bennet is led to reveal to the heroine her own tragically instructive history. But thematic connections are also palpable. With its tendency to dissolve into a morally unregulated, adulterous human unit, the *partie quarrée* has a proleptic symbolic relation to the masquerade crowd itself, which represents unregulated sociability in its most demonic form. There, of course, the transgressive relationship will be all. In one sense the masquerade is simply the pleasure party universalized. Its characteristic locale, the assembly room, both parodies and magnifies the domestic salon; its systematic travesties but give outward form to the pervasive hypocrisy of everyday life. It summarizes, in effect, the *liaisons dangereuses* implicit in the most ordinary-seeming of human exchanges.

Not surprisingly, the masquerade figures first in *Amelia* as a sort of extenuation of the *partie quarrée*—as yet another example, though perhaps the most diabolical to date, of pleasure transmogrified. We are clearly meant to interpret it as another type—the emblem even—of malevolent sociability. One hardly has a chance to do otherwise, in fact: almost as soon as going to the masquerade becomes a narrative possibility, the Peer's invitation prompts a flood of didactic comment within the fictional world. The masquerade itself is unmasked in the customary way, as an image of false delights.

Indeed, the manner of the masquerade's unmasking might seem to preclude its representation. The point of Mrs. Bennet's crucial masquerade confession, after all, will be to prevent Amelia from making the same mistake she did—to keep the masquerade from being part of Amelia's own history. But even before this interesting intervention, there are other attempts to keep the masquerade from happening. Booth himself is suspicious of the Peer's invitation for once, though mainly because he has had hints from Colonel James regarding the Peer's reputation as a rake. The captain is sufficiently moved to animadvert on the masquerade in the conventional manner. When the devious Mrs. Ellison presses the Peer's tickets on Amelia, exclaiming what a "delicious Place" the masquerade is ("Paradise itself can hardly be equal to it"), Booth forces his wife to refuse the gift. Later he explains that a masquerade ticket is "perhaps the very worst and most dangerous" thing a woman may receive from a man, for "few Men make Presents of those Tickets to Ladies without intending to meet them at the Place." Amelia objects that he has nothing to fear from her virtue, but he continues: "The Snares which might be laid for that Innocence, were alone the Cause of my Apprehension. I feared what a wicked and voluptuous Man, resolved to sacrifice every thing to the Gratification of a sensual Appetite with the most delicious Repast, might attempt" (VI, 6). Though none of the Peer's stratagem has yet been confirmed, Booth (and Fielding) inscribe the masquerade with a familiar ethical significance: it is the preeminent site of "Snares," the place where plots against virtue are inevitably set in motion.

The exchange has an ironic aspect, not only because of Booth's morally problematic status as an adulterous husband, but also because he does in fact later relent and give Amelia permission to go to Ranelagh with Mrs. Ellison. This gesture in turn, however, provokes a new burst of anti-masquerade discourse. Fielding somewhat crudely prepares us for some revelation: when Amelia announces to the landlady that she will be going after all, Mrs. Ellison's mysterious, learned friend Mrs. Bennet (also present) turns unaccountably grave. Later, while Ellison extols "the extreme Beauty of the Place and Elegance of the Diversion," Mrs. Bennet becomes "extremely melancholy" and casts looks "of no very pleasant Kind" on the speaker (VI, 8). One is hardly surprised when she turns out to be the author of that anonymous poem in the next chapter warning Amelia of a "dreadful Snare" laid for her "under a Friend's false Pretence." It is her story, of course, related in Book VII, that will demystify the masquerade once and for all—or at least, for a time, may seem to.

In itself the point of Mrs. Bennet's melodramatic "masquerade tale" is clearly didactic. It is intended to alert Amelia to the danger she is in, and this it does by exposing the masquerade as the culminating event in a preexisting plot against innocence—a plot in which Mrs. Bennet has already to her sorrow been ensnared. The masquerade has been the symbolic end point, the climactic scene, in Mrs. Bennet's own disastrous history: she now relates this history precisely so that Amelia will not have to

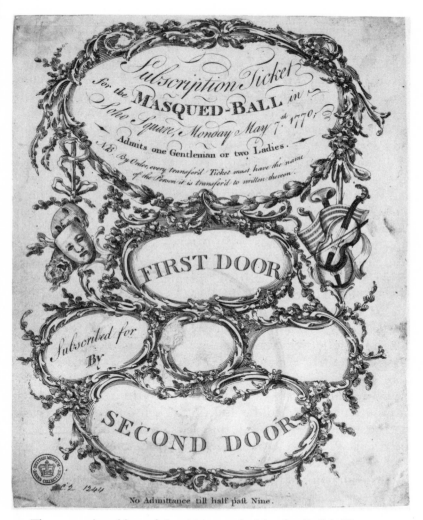

30. The century's emblem of vice. Masquerade ticket for Carlisle House, 1770.

reenact it. Her story, one might say, is paradigmatic, but in a negative sense: it is meant to obviate its own repetition.

For all its subsequent outrageousness, this story is also highly conventional. Certainly Mrs. Bennet's account bears many resemblances to those salacious tales of masquerade disaster popular in eighteenth-century periodicals and in works like Haywood's *The Masqueraders: or, Fatal Curiosity* (1724). Fielding appears to have borrowed many of the standard lurid features of such tales without much modification.[23] Thus the early events of Mrs. Bennet's life—her upbringing, her marriage to the impoverished cleric Mr. Bennet, their move to London and into lodgings at Mrs. Ellison's—are but prologue to her sexual ruin at the hands of the dastardly Peer. Like Amelia, it turns out, Mrs. Bennet was treated to the hospitality of Mrs. Ellison and the Peer; like Amelia too, she was given masquerade tickets. And true to that function stereotypically ascribed to it in the exemplary tales, the masquerade facilitated her downfall. Attending without her husband (who had been sent on a spurious mission by the Peer), she found herself "intoxicated with foolish Desires, and liable to every Temptation." Temptation included the obsequious attentions of the Peer, in whom she was secretly proud to perceive a "Passion." Having given up "the Outwork of her Virtue" by being at the masquerade in the first place, Mrs. Bennet agreed to let the Peer accompany her home. He offered her a glass of drugged punch; she swooned and was raped (VII, 7). As in conventional tales of masquerade seduction, this gothic violation produces a horrific domestic coda: Mrs. Bennet tells Amelia how she was infected with a "Pollution" that she in turn passed to her husband, who thus discovered her (unintentional) lapse from wifely virtue. He reviled her and then succumbed to the infection. Their only child likewise died soon after (VII, 9). All this, Mrs. Bennet concludes, was the result of her single tragic error—the demonic "Residue" of that one "fatal Night."

The main point of Mrs. Bennet's story is that her suffering has been the result of a "long, regular, premeditated Design" against her, and that the same trap is now being laid for Amelia. This scheme, which can be repeated with an unlimited number of victims, is characterized by the strategic manipulation of public as well as private diversions. It is now revealed, for example, that an oratorio Amelia attended earlier with Mrs. Ellison was also part of the Peer's design: a gentleman in a "rag Coat" there who engaged them in polite conversation was the Peer himself, in disguise and hunting (with Mrs. Ellison's help) for new victims (IV, 9). Mrs. Bennet was marked for her own destruction in identical circumstances. But the masquerade, the exemplary scene of delirium and danger, is the public amusement most suited, obviously, to the realization of private schemes; thus it serves as a stage for the worst part of the Peer's plot, the actual entrapment of the victim. As in Richardson's sequel to *Pamela*, one detects an implicit negative hierarchy of diversions here: the masquerade is worse than the oratorio, for its intoxications are active and participatory rather than merely specular (or auditory). As its acolytes give themselves over to the occasion— indeed, are absorbed by it—they become the actors in a larger drama of vice and abandon.

Mrs. Bennet's salutary tale has its intended impact: Amelia listens with horror and immediately sends back the tickets. This unmasking of the Peer's plot likewise has a profound narrative impact: it seems to prevent the plot of sexual ruin from becoming the plot of *Amelia* itself. By this timely exposure Amelia herself is exempted from the role of victim. Her paragon status is preserved and her innocence instructed—all without any direct (and one suspects indelibly compromising) experience of the masquerade and its dangers. She is granted a license *not* to reenact the masquerade's classic scenarios of manipulation, disequilibrium, and degradation. Like a narrative *cordon sanitaire*, Mrs. Bennet's history mediates between Fielding's heroine and disaster, separating her from a melodramatic realm of plot and machination, violence and despair.

Such is also perhaps the ultimate extension of Fielding's allegorical method in *Amelia*. Just as the masquerade represents the most dangerous fictional evil to date—imposture in its most devastating and worldly guise—so Mrs. Bennet's tale represents the allegorical gesture of truth-telling in its most potently altruistic form. Mrs. Bennet is a heroine of knowledge, one who has foresuffered all, precisely that Amelia herself should not suffer. By pointing to the evil hidden behind the facade of delight, she replicates the narrator's own gestures of moral revelation. The logic of reversal holds once more: the ultimate scene of pleasure is in fact the ultimate scene of ruin. Like everything else in the fictional world, the masquerade itself wears a mask. But Mrs. Bennet's history removes the mask; it isolates the masquerade's intrinsic pathology and nullifies its secret destructive power.

Her disclosure carries a special, even exaggerated force not only because the masquerade pretends to a more seductive pleasure than any other form of diversion (paradise itself does not seem equal to it), but because her words prevent the most dire-seeming of possible events in the fictional world: the compromising of the one exemplar of unconditional virtue *Amelia* has provided. By preserving the heroine's unambiguously pure status, Mrs. Bennet's intervention also appears to preserve the shape of Fielding's *psychomachia*. Amelia is free here to remain what she has been—the embodiment of uncomplicated virtue and a moral beacon to Booth. Her symbolic role, essentially that of the type, is unimpugned by incident. Thus Mrs. Bennet's exposition of the *carnaval moralisé* effectively protects the allegorical status quo. It seems to mitigate against plot on every level; it stays any potential unmotivated, unprecedented, or irrational narrative development; and it confirms the fiction's underlying satiric and anatomizing tendency. The reader's function, consequently, also seems to remain the same: to be a passive receptacle for instruction. Like the heroine, Fielding's reader is again made here the recipient of a discourse at once pedagogic and ostensibly therapeutic—the beneficiary of an unmasking that is both specific and universally suggestive.

None of which makes any less bewildering the next (one is tempted to say first) event in Fielding's novel: a masquerade. The discontinuity here is shocking, as though the logical ground on which the fiction were founded had suddenly shifted. From the recollected or mediated representation of the masquerade, *Amelia* makes a startling leap to the thing itself when "Amelia," Booth, and the Jameses together depart for the Haymarket in Book X. And as it does in eighteenth-century fiction generally, this second, more immediate masquerade scene will have its dramatic and disarming effect on virtually every character in the novel. What to make of this perplexing turn of affairs?

Little in the way of new incident occurs before the Booths' strange expedition. Books VIII and IX of *Amelia* are for the most part listless and diffuse, as though the fiction were not entirely sure where it was going, and the episodes here are altogether reminiscent of earlier ones. Booth is arrested again for debt and subsequently released; he and Amelia are forced to remove their things from Mrs. Ellison's; Colonel James is seen brooding again over Amelia, for whom we already know he harbors a secret passion. Likewise there are two perfunctory and predictable satiric set pieces: Booth's encounter with the foolish author at Mr. Bondum's (VIII, 5), and the conversation between Dr. Harrison and the hypocritical clerics (IX, 10). By contrast the abrupt return of the masquerade as a narrative possibility—in the first chapter of Book X, when Colonel James presses tickets on the beguiled Booth—manages both to seem gratuitous and to provide a subtle relief. It makes no sense in didactic terms, for what more does one need to know of masquerades? Such a twist seems to negate the impact of Mrs. Bennet's emblematic history and contradict the implicit allegorical rhythm to which the reader is accustomed. But it also has a cathartic, if irrational, narrative potential. It heralds intrigue of a sort that has so far been missing. We do not entirely regret the disappointment of our expectations, or the implied swerve away from didacticism—baffled though we may be.

Which is not to say that the reader of *Amelia* does not speculate, even here, on the impulses motivating such a surprising narrative development. Fielding's second invocation of the carnival world forces us to look again at his first, including Mrs. Bennet's lugubrious masquerade tale, in a different way. The results are both compelling and unsettling. For reviewed in the light of this subsequent plot turn, *Amelia*'s initial representation of the masquerade no longer seems quite as transparent, allegorically speaking, as it did at first. We notice in retrospect a peculiar quality, even an illogicality or solecism, attaching to Mrs. Bennet's dysphoric revelations, not to mention a vaguely troubling ambiguity in her character itself. That Fielding's narrative should turn back with such apparent perversity toward the compromising world of the masquerade—after giving every indication it would not—may strike us as less completely shocking, if not less odd, when we reflect that an unacknowledged instrumental potential has been associated with the masquerade from the outset. It is implicit in Mrs. Bennet's history, and in the circumstances that succeed her catastrophe. The more we think about it, in fact, the more uncanny Mrs. Bennet's ostensibly lucid disclosures are likely to seem, as indeed she does herself.

The problem has to do with the matter of "Consequences" and the fact that Mrs. Bennet's history seems to admit more of these, paradoxically, than she herself allows. The problem manifests itself first as one of tone. Immediately following Mrs. Bennet's account of her ruin at the hands of the Noble Peer, for instance—a story so horrific that it sends Amelia into a faint at one point and Mrs. Bennet herself into a "violent Convulsion Fit" (VII, 8)—the conversation takes a sudden, puzzling shift to a gossipy and giddy discussion of the virtues of Sergeant Atkinson. (He has made a brief, inexplicable appearance in Mrs. Bennet's apartments during the conversation between the two women.) Mrs. Bennet is soon gaily teasing Amelia with the fact that she has another secret to tell her—that "no Woman" in fact has "so sincere, so passionate a Lover" as Amelia has in the sergeant (VII, 10). This news is succeeded, rather troublingly, by the information that Mrs. Bennet and the sergeant are now married to one another, hence his appearance in her rooms and her knowledge of his secret feelings. Mrs. Bennet (now revealed as Mrs. Atkinson) concludes her disclosures with a bit of sentimental philosophizing: she is not at all bothered by the sergeant's infatuation for Amelia, for "there is no greater vulgar Error than that it is impossible for a Man who loves one Woman ever to love another." Indeed, she continues, "it is certain that a Man who can love one Woman so well at a Distance" (and such passions only reside "in very amorous and very delicate Minds") "will love another better that is nearer to him."

We might be tempted to see Mrs. Bennet's marriage simply as another of those apparently meaningless twists of happenstance with which *Amelia* is filled, were it not that it transforms our sense of her story so ambiguously. For she is revealed here as something more than just the "destined Sacrifice" or exemplary victim of the masquerade. She has moved irresistibly toward a comic transcendence of her own tragedy. Contrary to that unhappy ending seemingly implied in her history, the masquerade has not in fact been fatal to her at all, either in body or in spirit. Rather it has produced, paradoxically, what we can only regard as an amelioration of her fortunes. Through the complex chain of circumstances it initiates (which includes, it must be admitted, the death of her first husband), the masquerade has resulted in Mrs. Bennet's marriage to the one character in *Amelia*, apart from Amelia herself and to a much lesser extent Dr. Harrison, who approaches paragon status. Her "ruin" is thus distinguished by the acquisition of this new and unimpeachable husband, the company of friends, financial comfort, and the freedom to enjoy her scholarly pursuits. Even as she recounts it, then, Mrs. Bennet might be charged with triumphing over her sensational and ghastly history.

The paradox here is implicit: no one calls attention to it within the fictional world, nor does Fielding's narrator. (Indeed, beginning with the scene of Mrs. Bennet's disclosures, the narrator tends to withdraw, and explicit moral commentary, so prevalent before, diminishes.) Yet this presentation of consequences subtly undermines the allegorical logic that until now has shaped the pattern of meaning in Fielding's novel. If in some mysterious way the masquerade is responsible for Mrs. Bennet's present happiness, then the prevailing logic of moral reversal no longer holds: the masquerade can no longer be said simply to represent evil in the guise of pleasure, for it has in fact produced pleasure. It cannot be glossed merely as the quintessential scene of vice, for though it has led Mrs. Bennet into an involuntary union with vice, in the person of the Noble Peer, it has also led her into a union with virtue, in the person of Sergeant Atkinson. The masquerade topos thus begins to lose some of its emblematic lucidity even as it ceases to reproduce a purely negative teleology on the level of plot. Through its association with an enigmatic realm of consequences—all of which belie any wholly malignant agency—the masquerade becomes, allegorically speaking, inscrutable. It can no longer be adduced for the purposes of any truly coherent "Instruction"; it is no longer merely the uncomplicated public image or social reification of the deceitful nature of appearances. Its meaning as moral sign, in short, has been made ambiguous.

This ambiguity has its corollary in the realm of character. If the masquerade becomes, with Mrs. Bennet's subsequent revelations, suddenly undecodable according to the logic with which we are familiar, so too does Mrs. Bennet herself. It is no coincidence perhaps that the character in *Amelia* most profoundly intimate—in every sense—with the world of the masquerade (she will play an uncanny part in the novel's second masquerade scene too, of course) should also be the first major character in the fiction to resist moral recuperation in simple allegorical terms. She is as peculiarly fluid and discontinuous a textual presence as the carnivalesque occasion with which she is associated. Mrs. Bennet's duality is most obvious in the primitive symbolic realm of onomastics: no sooner is she introduced and her history related than her name changes, as it were, when she announces her marriage to the sergeant. The disconcerting effect of her shift in identity is intensified by the narrator's self-conscious manner of handling it. "The Tea being now ready," he writes coyly, "Mrs. Bennet, or, if you please, Mrs. Atkinson, proposed to call in her Husband" (VII, 10). (I shall reinscribe the textual discontinuity by referring hereafter to Mrs. Bennet as Mrs. Atkinson also.) The shift here in the realm of reference replicates the essential irony of her history: that one does not know whether to regard her, in some deeper way, as the "unfortunate" Mrs. Bennet or the "fortunate" Mrs. Atkinson. Just as she is at once the victim of catastrophe and the embodiment of survival, Mrs. Atkinson is at once the same and different from herself: she is, indeed, Mrs. Bennet *and* Mrs. Atkinson.

But Mrs. Atkinson's nature is also morally ambiguous, as the previously noted exchange with Amelia suggests. Here the reader is torn between baffling perceptions of her. On the one hand, she has performed an admirable service for the heroine by saving her from the Peer's salacious scheme. On the other, with her remarks about Sergeant Atkinson and his love for Amelia, she seems to articulate a subversive emotional potential—the possibility that one married person might indeed love another, without moral stigma. In a novel where husbands conspicuously pimp for their wives, and vice versa, such a suggestion is charged and unsettling, even though Mrs. Atkinson may appear to speak only of platonic attachments between persons who are otherwise paragons. That it is her own husband whose affection for Amelia she reveals makes her contention all the more problematic: any potential *partie quarrée* in the fictional world involving the Booths and Atkinsons might seem to be compromised even as it formed. At the same time that Mrs. Atkinson preserves Amelia from coercive adultery at the hands of the Peer, she implicitly raises the possibility of another, subtler form of adultery—one the more dangerous, perhaps, for ostensibly being of the emotions only. Mrs. Atkinson has the curious, fleeting aspect here of the sentimental agent provocateur, even as she retains in other respects all the moral prestige and heroism associated in *Amelia* with the unraveler of secrets and teller of truths.

The narrator, significantly, gives the reader no clue about how to place Mrs. Atkinson in any larger moral or metaphysical scheme—or at least, no clues that are not contradictory. From this point on she will remain a strangely unclassifiable presence. She commits a number of violations of decorum: she drinks too much (as we learn several times); she has an unfeminine interest in learning and the classics (we see her arguing with the insufferable Dr. Harrison); her marriage to the sergeant, for all his virtues, is a kind of *de haut en bas* affair (he is of a lower rank than she), and by it her own social status is made problematic. She seems to represent World-Upside-Down energies, in that she embodies certain kinds of chaos and intractability the narrator has elsewhere castigated. Yet Mrs. Atkinson is never definitively unmasked by the narrator—certainly not in the way, say, that Mrs. Ellison is, or the Noble Peer himself. She is never merely dismissed, either in moral or in narrative terms. The narrator remains mute about her essential character, if indeed she can be said to have one; the reader sees only her contradictory affect in action. True, she is often surrounded by a vaguely suspicious aura. The figure of the sexually compromised bluestocking condenses, after all, two disparate eighteenth-century visions of nightmare femininity. At the same time, despite temporary idio-syncrasies, her good will toward the Booths is indisputable, thus distinguishing her from other, more palpably evil characters in *Amelia*. Likewise she is much loved by the noble sergeant him-self, whose judgment is simultaneously, if somewhat provoca-tively, validated by his affection for Amelia. Mrs. Atkinson's in-creasing prominence in Fielding's fiction (after she tells Amelia her story, her narrative role becomes more significant) is an indication of an intensifying ambiguity in *Amelia* itself. Even here, Mrs. Atkinson personifies a potentially counterallegorical tendency in the work, just as the masquerade might be de-scribed as the tropological manifestation of this same tendency.

When *Amelia* reverts to the world of the masquerade, then, in Book X, however abrupt this narrative turn may otherwise ap-pear, one is not altogether surprised that Mrs. Atkinson should figure so noticeably in the succeeding, highly paradoxical ac-tion. She is an insistent presence; her role in the fiction is so im-portant that she seems temporarily to draw attention away from Amelia herself, whose place she literally takes, in a complex and suggestive piece of substitution, on the night of the masquer-ade. Mrs. Atkinson is the heroine of Fielding's second masquer-ade tale, just as she was of his first. But for a time she is also in a curious way the heroine of *Amelia* itself. For the second mas-querade plot in which she participates is so compelling—and its consequences so crucial in every way to Fielding's novel—as to become indistinguishable, ultimately, from the plot of the fic-tion itself.

That *Amelia*'s second masquerade will be of a different order than its first is obvious from the start. To begin, one notices the utter lack of any didactic preface to the occasion; here, the all-important gift of tickets (which usually seems to evoke in archetypal terms the Edenic gift of the apple) elicits no flood of protective or otherwise inhibiting commentary. True, Amelia, because she already distrusts Colonel James, suspects the motives that lie behind his present to the Booths, and asks Dr. Harrison for advice about how to avoid the occasion. But Dr. Harrison's views are uncharacteristically liberal. Though he admits he thinks the diversion "of too loose and disorderly a Kind for the Recreation of a sober Mind," he also somewhat oddly sees little harm in her going, as long as she goes with her husband (X, 1). Booth too, despite his previous vociferous complaints

31. Anonymous engraving of masqueraders, French, 17th century

223

against masquerading, is here so infatuated with the idea of obliging his friend Colonel James (whose designs on his wife he has no notion of) that he forces Amelia to agree to accompany him. Out of desperation Amelia turns, interestingly enough, to Mrs. Atkinson. All the reader knows at this point is that the latter resolves upon some scheme, for she tells Amelia not to fear: "two Women will surely be too hard for one Man" (X, 1). Indeed, like the heroine herself, the reader can do little here but be swept toward this imminent saturnalia—a saturnalia of narrative, as it were, as well as of persons. For Fielding's masquerade scene is nothing if not a hyperelaboration of incident—an eruption of complicated and enigmatic events, none of which seems contained by any textual gloss or obvious didactic frame.

The movement into complexity begins in the second chapter of Book X, with a mobilization of the *partie quarrée*. As though by convulsion the Booths and Jameses depart in an unexplained haste for the Haymarket. The unstable grouping of the quartet lasts only as long as the journey, however: upon arrival all four are immediately separated from one another and absorbed into the masquerade crowd. The ensuing scene is one of conundrum and chaos. Indeed, the reader of *Amelia*, looking to discover "What Happened at the Masquerade" (Fielding's ironic chapter heading), might well be baffled, for it is by no means clear what is actually happening at all. The representation of the masquerade signals a regression into secrecy: not an unmasking, but a masking of meaning itself.

The effect of mystification is not achieved through any extended description of sartorial phantasmagoria. Unlike comparable scenes in *Pamela*, Burney's *Cecilia*, or even Fielding's own satire *The Masquerade*, there is little here in the way of conventional masquerade *adynata*—few descriptions of specific costumes or of amusing or uncanny characters in the masquerade crowd. Rather the feeling of imbroglio arises almost entirely from the depiction of unaccountable or troubling exchanges between characters who otherwise should not be meeting (again) in the fictional world. Virtually every major character in *Amelia* seems to be here. Besides "Amelia" and Booth and Colonel

James and Mrs. James, the Noble Peer, Miss Matthews, and Colonel Bath are all in the crowd—purely by coincidence, it seems, for their appearances are not otherwise motivated. (Captain Trent will later be revealed to have been at the masquerade also, disguised as a sailor; and one might say that Dr. Harrison is present at least symbolically, for he is the author of a pious letter on the sin of adultery that is circulated and mocked by members of the crowd.) One has the sense of a problematic conclave: a potentially dangerous rencontre of just those characters who, according to all narrative decorum, should have remained apart.

Which is not to say that everyone knows who everyone else is. Some do; some only think they do. A series of puzzling encounters ensues. We see "Amelia" deep in intimate conversation with an unknown domino; Booth is besieged first by a woman in a blue domino, then by a shepherdess. Colonel James searches for his wife (who is wearing a black domino) but cannot find her anywhere in the room; when he approaches the woman he believes to be Amelia (with the intention of seducing her), he is startled when she claims quite bluntly not to know him. That the identities of at least some of these cryptic personages are revealed during the course of the evening only makes matters even more perplexing for the reader; the domino "Amelia" allows to make such "fervent Love" to her is "no other than her old Friend the Peer," while the shepherdess with whom Booth banters (and whom he promises to meet at her lodgings the next day) is of course Miss Matthews. Fielding's characters, half-concealed, half-known to one another, like the mysterious companions of dreams, seem to perform in an inexplicable, scandalous dance—a kaleidoscopic pattern of union and reunion, turn and return.

In the face of this proliferation of perverse couplings, the reader cannot help feeling apprehensive about the future of Fielding's narrative. For all the counterindications in Mrs. Atkinson's history, the allegorical association between carnival and doom may still linger. Several possible catastrophes suggest themselves. Booth seems to hover on the edge of a profound recidivism: his meeting with Miss Matthews bodes nothing but ill for his moral state. The promise she extorts from him to visit her (under the threat of exposing their liaison to the masquerade crowd) is a parody of the classic masquerade assignation, but even so it portends a revival of their intimacies and a renewed threat to his marriage. Still more ominous is the strange meeting between "Amelia" and the hated Peer. Her flirtatious behavior with him is sinister and shocking. We see her greet him with "bewitching Softness" as her "Paramour," as though she were inviting the very violation he once before intended for her. One is forced to confront the possibility that the plot of masquerade rape and humiliation may repeat itself after all in *Amelia*, with the heroine this time the foolish victim.

Particularly striking in this chapter is the phenomenon to which I referred earlier—the disappearance of Fielding's ordinarily intrusive, truth-telling narrator. The familiar voice of the fiction, the perpetrator of exposés, is missing here, even as the reader's desire for information grows. We feel our grasp on *Amelia*'s characters slipping, especially in the heroine's case. She is acting "out of role." Yet we are given no inside view, no explanation for her behavior or anyone else's. We see only externals, the mask and not the face. Fielding's often pedantic narrator, the discloser of secrets, is replaced by one who revels in them: an impervious, sly, purposely mysterious authorial voice, aiming to increase our bafflement rather than alleviate it. In this he succeeds, yet at the cost of a breach of trust; for that estrangement, the reader feels, is a betrayal, in which we are excluded from the realm of truth and cast into one of charade and alienation.

To be sure, Fielding does return to the inside view soon enough, in the next chapter, "Consequences of the Masquerade, Not Uncommon nor Surprising" (X, 3). Yet the unmasking that takes place here is in many ways the most unsettling of any so far. For here one learns of that crucial feminine stratagem played out at the masquerade—Mrs. Atkinson's impersonation of Amelia, who it turns out was not there at all. The ruse is revealed when the Booths and Jameses return home: "Amelia" whimsically rushes indoors ahead of everyone, and has already removed her mask and domino when they come in. Later, when Booth asks his wife to name the person at the masquerade with whom she had been conversing so long, she announces, "I never was at one in my Life." Amelia then reveals that when the party departed for the Haymarket, she pretended to forget her mask, ran briefly back into the house, and handed her costume to her friend. Mrs. Atkinson emerged wearing it, as well as the mask, and deceived everyone thereafter by speaking only in a "mimic Tone." Booth has thus been imposed upon, along with Colonel James and the Noble Peer.

So too in a sense has the reader. Whether or not one has had an inkling of the substitution all along (the physical resemblance between Amelia and Mrs. Atkinson has been pointed out by several characters in the fiction earlier), the fact remains that for the first time Fielding's narrator has seemingly gratuitously withheld a piece of important information in the interest of narrative surprise. Looking back at the first account of the departure for the masquerade in the preceding chapter, one finds no mention there of Amelia's swift return to the house: this is explained only later. Technically speaking, the narrator has not lied, for in retrospect one notices that the description of the masquerade evening contains no direct assertion that the woman who appears to be Amelia is in fact she. Fielding is careful not to have Mrs. Atkinson make any false assertions about her identity during the scene; every statement she makes in response to the Peer's questions applies to her own situation as much as to Amelia's. Yet one might charge the narrator with a certain hypocrisy—an intention to mystify and dupe the reader. Given the narrative persona we are accustomed to, such an imposition cannot help but seem radical and inexplicable. In the most literal way possible, the narrator has abdicated suddenly from the role of unmasker. Much in the manner of the masquerade itself, he leaves the riddle of identity intact, in what may seem a perverse way.

This abdication has further troubling implications. Most important, the reader has no clue how to interpret the moral meaning of Amelia's and Mrs. Atkinson's ruse. Is it not suspiciously like the other examples of deception and role-playing in the fictional world, all of which have been insistently condemned? And what agreement has Mrs. Atkinson reached with the Peer? Granted, Dr. Harrison draws a limited moral lesson from these morning-after revelations: he suggests to Booth that he was foolish to make Amelia go to the masquerade in the first place— it being a scene of "Riot, Disorder, and Intemperance, very improper to be frequented by a chaste and sober Christian Matron" (X, 4)—and approves Amelia's stratagem. (What his opinion of Mrs. Atkinson is, he does not say.) But these remarks do not defuse the sense that the heroine has become, if not the actual perpetrator, the accomplice to an act of hypocrisy of the most theatrical sort. She has had her ostensible reasons, of course, though we notice even here that nothing especially dire seems to have happened as a result of this particular masquerade. She might be forgiven her lapse from integrity on the grounds that she feared worse from the masquerade, even though in this case none of its stereotypical threat has been realized. But for the first time, if only in a muted way, a certain moral ambiguity begins to shade the character of Amelia herself. Like the narrator, she is implicated here in inauthenticity, if not its actual embodiment. Most important, the masquerade has elicited this odd engagement with duplicity—the heroine's first technical lapse from paragon status.

This moment of self-alienation (for one might say Amelia is not herself here) is only one of the masquerade's destabilizing side effects, however. One must look again at the large and curious matter of its consequences, for these the narrator now turns to, rather than any retroactive moral interpretation. Chapters 3 and 4 are both entitled "Consequences of the Masquerade." The repetition is suggestive: it implies a new interest in story over allegory—the place of the masquerade in a larger causal sequence rather than its significance as a topos. Likewise, it suggests the narrator's own new and contradictory role: if he is less and less the elucidator of moral secrets, he is more and more a relator of "Consequences," of a chain of events. He now shows what things follow rather than what things mean. He approximates, in short, the neutral voice of narrative itself. But in that case, one may still wonder, what *are* the consequences of the second and decidedly undisastrous masquerade in *Amelia*?

As in the case earlier of *Tom Jones*, one might speak loosely of two sorts of consequences (though the two are obviously inextricably related on a deeper level): the effect the representation of the masquerade has on *Amelia's* plot, and the effect it has on character. One could make a similar distinction between the narrative consequences of the masquerade scene—its structural function—and what one might call its epistemological or ideological consequences. On a multiplicity of levels, both kinds of consequences turn out to be liberating.

As far as Fielding's plot goes, this masquerade holds out nothing, ironically, but comic ramifications. There is little ambiguity about this, even of the sort seen earlier in the fiction's first masquerade scene. There, to be sure, Mrs. Atkinson derived certain compelling rewards from her masquerade venture, but only at the cost of a powerful and toxic humiliation, her sexual violation. Here, the pattern of loss followed by gain—of a fortunate fall—is for the most part superseded. It is no longer necessary, it seems, to fall in order to gain.

The new dispensation is most vividly apparent, interestingly enough, in the fate of Mrs. Atkinson herself. Fate is perhaps too ominous a term for it, for from this point on her narrative destiny may be visualized even more clearly than before as a steady, elegant upward curve. If her first masquerade was a kind of "exquisite Distress"—productive, in an oxymoronic way, of benefits as well as sufferings—her second is an unalloyed fulfillment of comic possibility. One might call it a rewriting of her first, for Mrs. Atkinson here revises, so to speak, that dysphoric "masquerade tale" written for her the first time around by the Noble Peer. She inverts the fictional pattern of manipulation by entrapping him in a "plot," a scheme of comic revenge.

The reader first learns of this ruse, again, after it has already succeeded, when Sergeant Atkinson inexplicably receives a letter with an officer's commission from the Peer several days after the masquerade. Mrs. Atkinson then explains to Amelia (who is puzzled because she gets a letter from him too) that while pretending to be Amelia at the masquerade, she informed the Peer that if he wished ever to have her "good Opinion," he had first to perform a favor for a certain "worthy Woman" whom he had previously gravely injured (X, 8)—meaning, of course, Mrs. Atkinson herself. The full story of Mrs. Atkinson's conversation with the Peer now comes out: he has agreed to use his influence on behalf of the sergeant in exchange for a renewal of intimacies with the woman he supposes to be Amelia. The letter Amelia receives is a request that she join him at a fashionable assembly.

Granted, the revelation of Mrs. Atkinson's trick creates a minor disturbance in the fictional world—an argument with Amelia, who is embarrassed at having been compromised in the eyes of the Peer (X, 8). This tiff, rendered more as farce than as a serious dispute (Mrs. Atkinson, we learn, has "taken a Sip too much that Evening"), produces a temporary estrangement between the Booths and the Atkinsons, but is subsequently mitigated when Mrs. Atkinson herself meets with the Peer, explains her ruse, and exonerates Amelia.

The force of the stratagem, however, is unaffected by these subsequent developments. The fact of the commission holds: the Peer does nothing to revoke it even after learning how he has been deceived. And the sergeant, like a male Pamela, quickly advances professionally and socially to the rank of captain— Booth's own rank—and the coveted status of gentleman. The change is radical, and best of all, permanent. Mrs. Atkinson's masquerade ruse thus works what one might call a carnivalesque alteration in the fictional world itself. Sergeant Atkinson's transformation is a classically carnivalesque metamorphosis from underling to master, and yet here it takes hold in the realm of ordinary life.

One could say that Mrs. Atkinson rewrites the melodramatic masquerade tale of the past—the tale of female humiliation and abuse—along the redemptive lines of stage comedy. By one scintillating hoax she alters the genre of her own history. No longer the degraded heroine in a trite and pathos-ridden story, she has become the resourceful protagonist in a witty comedy of retribution. The significance of the masquerade itself—the scene of the drama—is likewise utterly changed. No longer is it that clichéd world of sordid abuses and sexual disaster, masculine pathology and female victimization, found in contemporary sentimental fiction. Mrs. Atkinson's second masquerade is more like that represented on the eighteenth-century comic stage: a realm of fortuitous exchanges and ultimately happy metamorphoses. In popular comedies like Griffin's *Masquerade*, for example, Fielding's own *Miss Lucy in Town*, and Cowley's *Belle's Stratagem*, the masquerade is always surreptitiously linked to profitable consequences—marriages between thwarted lovers, the proper transmission of inheritances, the hoodwinking of villains, and so on. Mrs. Atkinson's "belle's stratagem" replays the comic pattern. The treatment she accords the Noble Peer—who is hardly harmed by her ruse, but only exposed as fatuous—notably resembles the light-hearted punishment meted out to foolish or corrupt characters in masquerade farces. If Mrs. Atkinson has here metamorphosed into a different kind of heroine, the Peer has also changed type from the debauched and repulsive ogre of the masquerade tale to the silly, obsessed, yet finally benign comic dupe of the masquerade play. The generic transformation is total.

We will return to the question of whether a generic shift of the kind registered in Mrs. Atkinson's history also occurs at this point in *Amelia* itself, that larger history in which Mrs. Atkinson's revisionist story is embedded. It is enough to say here that the shape of Amelia's narrative destiny repeats that comic curve demonstrated first by her double at the masquerade—as though Mrs. Atkinson's fortuitous experience were in some sense the signal for the imminent happy transformation of Amelia's own prospects.

Though Amelia paradoxically is not even present, the masquerade may again be held responsible for this second, even more dramatic narrative transformation. Prime among the masquerade's consequences, ultimately, is the most compelling comic turn in Fielding's plot: the restitution of the heroine's lost fortune. This is not to say that the masquerade is merely one of those "imperceptible Links in every Chain of Events" mentioned by the narrator in the first chapter of Book XII, "by which all the great Actions of the World are produced." Granted, it is possible to view the occasion in retrospect as simply one link among many leading to the Booths' final happiness, one more element in *Amelia*'s secret comic design. When, in the bailiff's house at the end of the novel, Amelia joyfully learns of her purloined legacy, Dr. Harrison's comment that "Providence hath done you the Justice at last which it will, one Day or other, render to all Men" (XII, 7) invites the reader, along with the heroine, to reflect on the entire chain of ostensible accidents that have produced her good fortune—including the masquerade— and gloss them all as analogous elements in a transcendent providential telos.

The invocation of Providence can be demystified, however. One may treat it in turn as a trope for plot itself—a figure concealing authorial, rather than supernatural, design. When we consider the implicit design of Fielding's narrative, the special role of the masquerade—its particular indispensability in the matter of the heroine's reward—becomes strikingly apparent. Above all it functions as a locus of intimacy, a topographical (and textual) hub, toward which disparate characters are drawn, and out of which is formed a highly motivated, highly influential, yet still minimally plausible human pattern. This preliminary, supposedly accidental convergence of characters is necessary, it turns out, for every subsequent and increasingly charged development in Fielding's plot, which now tends with intensifying purposiveness toward its comic conclusion. After the masquerade, and as a result of its gratuitous-seeming exchanges, *Amelia* begins to lose much of the randomness previously characterizing it (and symbolized always in Booth's hapless peregrinations), and displays for the first time a narrative momentum. The masquerade scene is in fact the crux of Fielding's narrative—a dense, agglutinative kernel of human relations, out of which the heroine's comic destiny is engendered.*

It is impossible to imagine the plot of *Amelia*, and that concluding happy conjunction of characters at the bailiff's house in Book XII, without the prior fateful conjunction of characters at the masquerade. The ironic providentiality of the masquerade is in no way undermined by the fact that the two most significant "accidental" meetings it occasions—between Booth and Miss Matthews and Mrs. Atkinson and the Noble Peer—seem hardly conducive, as we noted earlier, to any good result for the heroine. Neither of these potentially destructive encounters fulfills its negative promise. Booth's masked rencontre with his former paramour, for instance, during which he makes a promise to visit her at home, sets up his subsequent agreement to dine with her when they meet a few days later in the street (XI, 7). He had intended to renege, but on meeting Miss Matthews again, he is forced to honor his word. Yet fortuitously, on his way home from this very assignation (during which, we note, he resists Miss Matthews's attempts at sexual blackmail and decides to confess at last his affair to Amelia) Booth is again arrested, ending up in the same bailiff's house to which Robinson, who knows the secret of Amelia's fortune, will also be brought. In circuitous yet integral fashion, Booth's attendance at the masquerade thus prompts what will turn out to be the most auspicious, as well as the last, of his many incarcerations. When Dr.

---

*An analogous crux in *Tom Jones* is the scene at the inn at Upton, where Fielding first exploits a cultural locale associated with accidental meeting (the lodging place) to strategic narrative advantage. One is tempted to speculate on the way in which certain generative cultural sites often seem necessary to plot in just this way. Inns, hotels, and other places of temporary residence, ballrooms, decks of ships, train carriages, and so on, are all part of a conventional topography of plot—a set of places where actions may indeed "take place." Each is a physically circumscribed yet public realm in which disparate characters may plausibly (and apparently randomly) be thrown together in a way that ultimately produces a significant or patterned result. One thinks of Mann's sanatorium, Elizabeth Bowen's hotel in Paris, or the inn on the river in *The Ambassadors* to which James, in the crucial scene in that novel, fortuitously brings Strether together with Chad and Madame Vionnet. In film iconography, the association between public places and plot is if anything even more insistent than in fiction. Classic examples include the Garbo/Barrymore *Grand Hotel*, the Marx Brothers' *Day at the Races* and *Night at the Opera*, and any of a number of Hitchcock films—*Lifeboat*, *The Lady Vanishes*, *Strangers on a Train*.

Harrison and Amelia subsequently visit him in prison, the clergyman is recognized by the stricken Robinson, who is then moved to confess his part in the cheat practiced on Amelia by her sister and the lawyer Murphy. Not only does Booth's masquerade encounter not lead to the expected renewal of sexual intimacies with Miss Matthews—the opposite in fact—but it is also curiously instrumental in putting Booth in the place he needs to be, in order for the novel's most important moment of disclosure to take place.

An equally fortunate and necessary set of consequences attends upon Mrs. Atkinson's meeting with the Peer—for Amelia. The revelation of the trick played on the Peer, as I mentioned before, precipitates a temporary estrangement between the Booths and the Atkinsons. The result here is that the sergeant, whose emotional reactions earlier have been somewhat histrionic, falls into a melancholy fit, with accompanying fever, and seems to be on his deathbed. He calls for Amelia (who is at this moment reconciling with his wife), reveals his love for her, and presents her with a miniature of herself, which he now confesses he stole from her at the time of her marriage to Booth, purely out of sentimental ardor (XI, 6). This is the very miniature that, after Amelia pawns it to raise money for Booth (XI, 8), is examined by Robinson, who is pawning clothes in the same shop. He recognizes Amelia from her picture, is told of her desperate circumstances, and falls into a state of remorse that will precipitate his confession to Dr. Harrison in Book XII. With Robinson's cathartic utterance (which depends as much on this second sequence of consequences as on the first), the two subplots resulting from the masquerade—the Booth/Matthews and Atkinson/Peer entanglements—merge into a single euphoric story line. Amelia becomes an heiress, Booth is released from prison, and together they return to Amelia's country estate, now revealed as rightfully hers.

Thus the "fatal" masquerade is not merely one of any number of elements in *Amelia* obscurely contributing to the heroine's ultimate reward; it conditions the very plot of reward itself. It permits that initial proliferation of intrigue on which every subsequent link in the novel's chain of circumstance depends. As with the similar episode in Richardson's sequel to *Pamela*, the paradox is that within the fictional world the masquerade itself has the aspect of an insufficiently motivated, even unmotivated occurrence. The fact that Booth and "Amelia" end up at the Haymarket is from one perspective the least plausible, least rational development in Fielding's novel. It is not governed by any prevailing didactic economy; it is not justified by any established allegorical principle. It is not necessary finally, except that it is necessary to the narrative itself. Though seemingly unmotivated, *Amelia*'s masquerade scene nevertheless motivates all that follows. Its fateful couplings both provoke and anticipate the revelatory meetings of the final book; its unstable transactions condition the most significant fictional transaction of all, the transformation of Amelia's own history from one of grief to one of joy.

The rewarding turn of *Amelia's* plot after the masquerade represents a final rebuke to the moral logic that in the novel's early books seems so insistent and at times even oppressive. With the revelation of the masquerade's fortunate consequences, its allegorical legibility (already in question following Mrs. Atkinson's ambiguous story) is permanently obscured; its significance has become paradoxical and indeterminate. The meaning of Fielding's central moral image, the *carnaval moralisé*, is destabilized at the very moment when the masquerade itself becomes a destabilizing instrumental force within *Amelia*'s fictional world.

It is important to define this process of destabilization—here enacted in relation to the image or topos—because it also repeats itself so exactly on the level of character in *Amelia*. One may speak of the transformation in rhetorical terms: the figure controlling meaning in the novel after this point is no longer the antithesis but the oxymoron. The case of the masquerade is paradigmatic. What before was only hinted, now is plain: one can no longer interpret the masquerade simply as the antithesis of what it seems to be, that is, as the scene of vice that masquerades as the scene of pleasure. Its real meaning is no longer derived simply by reversing its apparent meaning, for the two sorts of meaning have become strangely indistinguishable. Of course, the reader of *Amelia* can never forget the reputation of the textual masquerade, just as Fielding's eighteenth-century readers would have been unable to forget the actual masquerade's stereotypical association with danger and licentiousness. One cannot ignore the allegorical weight the topos has previously been made to carry. Rather, its new significance—that of euphoric agency—is superadded upon the old. The masquerade is now somehow both the stereotypical source of evil and a mysterious instrumental force for good. It cannot be made to seem other than paradoxical. Like the oxymoron, it fuses two contradictory sorts of meaning, producing a kind of semantic jamming in Fielding's fiction—a doubling of interpretative possibilities.

One witnesses a similar shift from the antithetical to the oxymoronic mode of signification in the realm of character. It is as though the moral destabilization of the masquerade figure—what one might call its ideological overdetermination—triggers a similar outbreak of ambiguity in the world of Fielding's characters. After the masquerade the moral typology of character on which *Amelia* has been implicitly founded, though never collapsing entirely, becomes distinctly unstable. By the end of the fiction it is maintained only precariously. One sees a breakdown (or near-breakdown) of that hierarchy of types so essential earlier to the underlying fictional pattern of the *psychomachia*. Fielding's cherished dichotomy between knaves and paragons may no longer seem so resolutely preserved; indeed, as though by some extra-logical symbolic process, the best and the worst now appear to merge with one another in curious ways. After the enigmatic, transforming occasion of the masquerade, one might say, character itself is carnivalized.

More and more of Fielding's characters begin to resemble Mrs. Atkinson—to approximate her doubleness and moral ambiguity. I spoke earlier of her indefinite hybrid nature—the ways in which she is repeatedly associated with the World Upside-Down, the adulteration of categories, mediation between opposites. To borrow a phrase from Natalie Davis, she is the "disorderly woman" of Fielding's novel—a mercurial affront to rigid metaphysical and social classifications. From the start she has transcended Fielding's ordinary moral schema, for she acts inconsistently—sometimes purely in her own interest, sometimes in the interest of others, sometimes in an idiosyncratic combination of the two (the masquerade ruse). Contrasted with *Amelia's* other, more clearly defined allegorical types, Mrs. Atkinson seems a more plausible character in many ways; at certain moments she even seems briefly to anticipate the more problematic "mixed" characters of nineteenth- and twentieth-century realistic fiction.

Granted, the reasons why Mrs. Atkinson seems particularly plausible have to do with our own conventions of what constitutes a realistic representation of character. The notion of character as dualistic and contradictory, rather than monolithic and morally uniform, is a particularly modern idea. Though obviously a philosophical theme now and then earlier (one thinks of Pope's *Essay on Man*), the idea of the moral and emotional inconsistency of the individual has drawn special impetus from Freudian theory and the development of psychological concepts of ambivalence and unconscious motivation. We have internalized a model of behavior that incorporates contradiction. Nonetheless it is possible to speak of Mrs. Atkinson, loosely, as a mimetic rather than an allegorical character: she displays what is to us a familiar ambiguity.

It is precisely this kind of ambiguity that now manifests itself in even the most obdurately fixed of *Amelia's* types, as if the fiction itself were lapsing from allegory into a subtler mimetic mode. We have already noted the odd beneficence of the Noble Peer after the night of the masquerade: his apparent willingness to let Sergeant Atkinson keep his officer's commission, and the lack of any vengefulness or hostility directed at Mrs. Atkinson or Amelia. Such complacency, suggesting a mitigation of pure villainy, exemplifies one sort of characterological complication in the latter half of *Amelia*: the unexpected improvement of the knave. After the masquerade scene the novel's vicious characters, its ubiquitous hypocrites and debauchees, are no longer quite so vicious. Besides the Peer there are other examples of sudden, inexplicable benignity. After Colonel James's attempt to seduce Amelia fails (he does not even find her at the masquerade), Colonel James too lapses into stoic, inoffensive calm. He seems to have lost his desire for the heroine entirely. The frighteningly Machiavellian aspect of his character recedes, or at least becomes indistinguishable from a certain jaded savoir faire, and he becomes merely something of a psychological enigma: a cryptic, intelligent, at times strangely attractive presence in the fictional world. (He is infinitely more witty than the tiresome Booth, and alone among Fielding's characters in *Amelia* possesses a certain indefinable chic.) He retains his ambivalent status as Booth's friend until the end.

Most important, however, *Amelia*'s happy denouement itself depends on a crucial suspension of knavery. The thief Robinson is a compelling example of the supposedly incorrigible villain who suddenly performs an unaccountably virtuous act. With his timely prison confession he temporarily exempts himself from the ranks of hypocrites—those who keep their secrets—and assumes the implicit prestige of the truth teller. That Robinson later reverts to crime and is hanged (after the action of the novel ends) does not erase the effect of his noble gesture, or the momentary moral complexity that here attaches to his otherwise repellent character.

If after the crux of the masquerade Fielding's villains seem oddly less villainous—and in some cases remarkably helpful in the working out of the Booths' happy destiny—one sees the opposite change in his ostensibly good characters. If the knave is improved, the paragon, as in *Pamela*, is compromised. The most significant embodiment of this syndrome is of course the heroine herself. I have already described Amelia's disconcerting participation in Mrs. Atkinson's masquerade ruse as an early sign of ambiguity in her character. Amelia allies herself with the secret-keepers here, entering if only for a moment the realm of the charlatan and the opportunist. Granted, as we saw, she has good reasons. But for the sake of preserving her virtue, conceived here only in the limited modern sense of sexual purity, she forgoes virtue in the archaic sense, the sense implied in the ancient concept of *virtus*. She allows her essence, as it were, to be divided: she both is and is not that "Amelia" whom Booth accompanies to the masquerade.

On the phantasmic level the impersonation here is the paradigmatic indication of the underlying tendency toward the destabilization of fixed character. It is an enactment, in the most literal way possible, of the nonuniformity of the individual—the carnivalesque dream of the double body. Amelia's secret is her second "body"—the body of masquerade—with access to privileges and pleasures not available to the first. Yet this secret, though primary, is not her only secret, nor is the masquerade the only time when the paragon displays unsuspected, even aberrant depths to her nature.

If Amelia deceives Booth in the matter of the masquerade, purposely veiling knowledge in the classic manner of the hypocrite, she later deceives him again, though for what at first seem justifiable reasons. She is conspicuously silent, for instance, about Colonel James and his subtle designs upon her (IX, 6). Once more, her putative motive is good: she wishes to preserve Booth from dueling with the Colonel on her behalf. But her action is also vulnerable to the most subversive and cynical of interpretations—that she unconsciously courts Colonel James's adulterous attentions. We need not interpret her action this way—indeed, only the most perverse reader would—but even so, the gesture of secret-keeping inevitably produces complexities that implicate the paragon in a questionable moral realm.

Even when she gives up her secret, the heroine's role playing is unsettling. Witness the revelation in Book XII that Amelia has known of Booth's infidelity with Miss Matthews all along. When he confesses his transgression, she admits that she has had a letter with a "feigned Name" on the subject, but has forborne saying anything about it. "Here, my Dear," she exclaims, "is an Instance that I am likewise capable of keeping a Secret" (XII, 2). The reader is taken aback by this disclosure. It is of course another example of the narrator's hypocrisy, since he has led us to believe that Miss Matthews's letters to Amelia—for Matthews is indeed the author of the betraying letter—have miscarried. More important, Amelia too is suddenly revealed by her own admission as a person who is as able to deceive as any. That such a revelation jars is a testimony to the degree to which the emblematic aspect of her character has been emphasized earlier. On some level we have believed her, like those automatons of virtue in traditional allegory, incapable of disingenuousness.

Perhaps the most striking instance of the compromising of the paragon takes place in the memorable chapter—one of the most interesting in all of Fielding—following the masquerade, when Amelia visits Sergeant Atkinson on his supposed deathbed (XI, 6). Like Colonel James's machinations, the details of their charged exchange will be kept a secret from Booth by the heroine—here with very good reason, for her role in this scene is distinctly problematic. This meeting of paragons begins with a preliminary compromising of Sergeant Atkinson. He confesses that he did in fact steal the miniature of Amelia, set in gold and diamonds, discovered to be missing so long ago. In his wife's conversation with Amelia, the reader has had hints already of his motive: not greed, but a desire to possess "that Face," the image of the woman he loves. "If I had been the Emperor of the World," he passionately begins—until Amelia, in deep embarrassment, stops the outpouring. Not only is the sergeant suddenly exposed as a thief, though of a decidedly sentimental kind; he is also the purveyor of a hidden, disturbing, incorrigibly adulterous passion. Amelia is profoundly affected. When he asks to kiss her hand before she calls his wife, she becomes flustered and engages in hysterical disavowal, "carelessly" reaching out her hand while murmuring in confusion, "I don't know what I am doing." She betrays every sign, albeit in the crudely conventional style of eighteenth-century popular fiction, of inwardly reciprocating his transgressive desire. Following this visit with the sergeant she is in such a state of disorder that she sheds "plentiful" tears and has to drink "a great Glass of Water" to calm herself.

Matters are now further complicated by the shocking commentary made here by *Amelia*'s narrator, who takes it upon himself, paradoxically, to unmask the heroine herself. "To say the Truth," he writes, "without any Injury to her Chastity, that Heart, which stood firm as a Rock to all the Attacks of Title and Equipage, of Finery and Flattery, and which all the Treasures of the Universe could not have purchased, was yet a little softened by the plain, honest, modest, involuntary, delicate, heroic Passion of this poor and humble Swain." Like anyone whose chastity is not "hewn out of Marble," he concludes, Amelia here felt a "momentary Tenderness" in spite of herself—at which Booth, "if he had known it, would perhaps have been displeased."

I say shocking, for despite all its understatement and euphemism (we note the string of hygienic adjectives describing the sergeant's passion), the narrator's gloss on the scene does not entirely avoid its morally subversive implications. Indeed, in a larger literary context we are tempted to admire the passage's uncharacteristic liberality and insight. However stylized, it is probably the most sympathetic, least ironic representation of female desire in all of Fielding's fiction. In a way quite remarkable for Fielding, the scenario here may even bring to mind later highly psychological novelistic depictions of sentimental adulterous passion—Rousseau's *La Nouvelle Héloïse*, for example, or Goethe's *Die Wahlverwandtschaften*. As later eighteenth-century novelists were to realize, it was precisely the exquisite, "modest," most sublimated adulterous passion that carried the most revolutionary implications, both for society and for the shape of narrative itself. In Amelia's subtle, palpitating "Tenderness" for the sergeant, there are foreshadowings both of a more exacting psychological realism and of those transgressive plots of desire and consummation characteristic of the later *roman larmoyant*.[24]

Which is not to say, again, that Fielding represents any actual transgression on Amelia's part, but only to say that such a narrative development now seems possible in the fictional world in a way that it did not before. The sergeant miraculously recovers, of course; he and his wife are reconciled with the Booths, and later, at the very end of the novel after the happy discovery of

Amelia's fortune, the *partie quarrée* is reconstituted. The Atkinsons make a three-month visit to the Booths' country estate—the first visit, the narrator implies, of many more to come (XII, 9). The reader cannot help being left uneasy, however, and not just because of the dubious reinstitution of the novel's primary geometrical figure of adulterous sociability. The secret passion between Amelia and the sergeant is simply left unneutralized (the narrator never refers to it again), and our conception of the heroine has been profoundly altered. Her erotic invulnerability has in fact been the characterological basis on which the logic of *Amelia*'s allegory has depended. Yet as a result of that emotional éclaircissement with the sergeant, she is abruptly revealed to us as one likewise responsive to illicit passion, likewise vulnerable to paradoxical depths of emotional experience. However obliquely, the reader is invited to imagine an alternative future for Fielding's heroine, one characterized not by unwavering fidelity to Booth and the ineffable complacency of the paragon, but by the divisive patterns of erotic discovery.

This, then, is the most radical consequence following upon the masquerade: its exemplary disruptions anticipate a disruption in *Amelia*'s code of character itself. Most important, even the heroine is affected by the tendency toward destabilization. It is she, indeed, who is likely to seem least "like herself" after the event, and most liable, as we have seen, to atypical, amorphous action. If she seems here less the pure creature of allegory, less the representative of a didactic idée fixe, one suspects that this is because the masquerade itself—with which her narrative destiny has been so intimately connected—has already violated the novel's reductive allegorical pattern. Amelia's unprecedented moral fluidity is but a realization of the masquerade's adulterating influence on the fictional world—and the mysterious power of the figure to insinuate, in the place of moral certainty, a tropology of ambiguity and complexity.

Fielding makes faint attempts, to be sure, to restore a kind of didactic legibility to *Amelia* in its final sections—even, paradoxically, as the comic irrationalism of the fictional world is becoming everywhere triumphantly apparent. Like Richardson in similar circumstances (in the sequel to *Pamela*), Fielding seems to be half-aware that a certain allegorical purity has indeed been lost, and tries after the fact to reinstate it. There is a brief effort to reinstall the familiar textual figure of the moralized antithesis. Thus Booth's spiritual conversion in the bailiff's house in Book XII seems intended to remind the reader of the earlier structuring pattern of the *psychomachia* (and bring to it a certain artificial closure), even though that pattern has by this point been utterly superseded by a less didactically constrained and far more seductive comic narrative. After reading Barrow's sermons, Booth is freed from all previous theological "Doubts" and will indeed "be the better Man . . . as long as I live" (XII, 5). The scene of his conversion is not effective, however, and not just because Fielding has in no way prepared the reader for the somewhat improbable image of Booth reading sermons. The idea that for all his previous "wavering" Booth now wholeheartedly rejects vice and embraces virtue is difficult to accept mainly because the allegorical antithesis between virtue and vice has itself by now been so severely undermined. It is hard to see what Booth's announcement entails, given that the masquerade and its ambiguous consequences have thrown entirely into question those logical dichotomies on which the notion of conversion is founded. One cannot be converted so easily from bad to good, one might object, when the categories of good and evil have themselves been so insistently blurred. Fielding's return here to the structure of the *psychomachia* thus seems a wishful attempt to reinstill the reader's faith in precisely those moral polarities that *Amelia*'s manifold travesties have elsewhere confounded.

A similar point can be made about the final journey Booth and Amelia make back to the country—away from London and its attendant distresses—after the recovery of her fortune. Clearly this journey is intended to create for the reader another closure effect, much in the manner of that final remove to Somerset occurring in the last pages of *Tom Jones*. Fielding here invokes the conventional rhetorical antithesis between the city (the archetypal scene of chaos and dissolution) and the country (the

realm of virtuous, cleansed human relations) to impart a specious last-minute impression of moral lucidity to his fiction. Vice
is merely a function of landscape, such a detail implies, and by
escaping the city the Booths have also, once and for all, escaped
vice itself. But again one may question how well the conventional logic holds up. As we have seen, the multiple problems
connected with the interpretation of the masquerade—itself a
physical space, yet one associated paradoxically with both pain
and pleasure—makes difficult any didactic exegesis according to
topography, or the moralizing of locale. Anywhere, the microcosm of the masquerade room suggests, has an equal potential
for disclosing suffering or joy. And once again the reader feels
the strain of Fielding's effort to reinstall an allegorical dimension—here by invoking one of allegory's typical methods of
symbolic resolution, geographical displacement. Indeed, when
one reflects back on the many outrages and abuses the Booths
have suffered in earlier books in the country, as well as the city,
one may wonder whether any coherent archetypal dichotomy
between city and country has ever been established in *Amelia* at
all. One's sense of false or misapplied closure devices is total.*

In the face of the failure of such recuperative gestures in the
last chapters of *Amelia*, the radical impact of Fielding's masquerade scene becomes, if anything, even more palpable. This narrative crux, we realize, is in the most profound sense the turning
point in Fielding's fiction. It is the moment at which the seeds
of a pervasive incoherence are sown. For after its paradigmatic
metamorphoses, nothing in *Amelia* is any longer what it has
seemed to be. Or that is, nothing is any longer only what it has
seemed to be. Everyone and everything now manifest a mysterious, supplemental, oxymoronic dimension—an extra body of
possibility, a contradictory double form.

I have attempted to sketch the different textual levels on
which this transformation from singularity to duality occurs.

*The country is the site of *Amelia*'s first moral outrage: the theft of Amelia's fortune
by her sister. Later, in Book III, Wiltshire is the scene of Booth's foolish attempt to set
up an equipage—resulting in his excoriation by vindictive neighbors and the subsequent
exhaustion of his already depleted financial resources (III, 11).

On the level of pure structure, the simplest narrative level, the masquerade scene marks a turn in *Amelia* away from the relatively under-plotted, static, and disconnected representation of incident toward a far more highly articulated and momentous pattern of circumstance—toward a chain of consequences, and an ironic, providential-seeming comic destiny. Though its instrumentality is veiled in the moment—and we have been led to believe that it will be of an entirely different order—the masquerade is in fact the event without which the amelioration of Amelia's fortunes would not take place. Like the deus ex machina in classical dramaturgy, it is miraculously responsible for a proliferation of significant, ultimately euphoric incident. Despite its initial encoding as the catalyst of disaster, it is also the catalyst of pleasure. As in classic eighteenth-century narrative generally (classic in Frank Kermode's sense), the scene of masking and transformation is both the textual signal for, and the means toward, the comic transformation of the heroine's own destiny.

But the representation of the masquerade precipitates certain changes also in the realm of character. The tropes of character become potentially multifarious, as though Fielding's types were swerving away from themselves into new realms of ambivalence and moral dialectic. Fielding's dramatized narrator is the first character to become, as it were, different from himself. The masquerade chapter, as we have seen, marks the point where he ceases, in a startling manner, to tell his reader the truth— where he forgoes the role of anatomist and indulges instead in that of the playful withholder of secrets. He becomes as teasing as that imaginary and fruitful world he describes. Similar forms of characterological duplicity are evident elsewhere: the repair of the knave and (hinted) embarrassment of the paragon are but the most obvious signs in *Amelia* of a new psychologistic dispensation. However much these hints of transformation remain merely potential rather than actual disfigurements of Fielding's typology of character, they nonetheless intimate the possibility of a more controversial conception of human nature, and provide a momentary escape from the monolithic, inhumane, profoundly unsentimental types of didacticism.

All of *Amelia*'s post-masquerade divagations might be taken together, however, as signs of a shift on a much more expansive level—that of genre. The carnivalesque moment is also the moment at which Fielding's novel becomes different from itself—that is, becomes something more than just the anatomy of "glaring Evils" it has advertised itself to be. The topos of transformation provokes a transformation of the fiction from allegory of a would-be schematic sort, replete with framed souvenirs of a World Upside-Down, to a plot: to a charged, suspenseful confrontation with this very world of disorder, secrets, and pleasure. Chapters in a comic mystery supplant the moralist's anecdotes of the dystopia, while the story of an arbitrary-seeming rewarding (Amelia's recovered inheritance has the moral banality of a sweepstakes win) takes the place of dogged satires on society. We can label the generic change variously as a shift from a satiric to a comic mode, or indeed as the modulation of eminently allegorical discourse into what we are tempted to call novelistic discourse—a shift toward mimetic or proto-realistic narrative.

Angus Fletcher's distinction between allegorical and realistic fiction is suggestive here. "Whenever a literary work is dominated by its theme," he writes, "it is likely to be called an allegory, on the grounds that thematic content is not usually so free of logical control that it could be there by accident. The contrary assumption that mimetic art resists thematic excess follows from the way Aristotle defined mimesis, namely as an 'imitation of an action,' since 'action' (*praxis*) in Aristotle's sense can and does exist without any help from secondary rationalizations, that secondary level which he called 'thought' (*dianoia*)."[25] As *Amelia* loses its thematic lucidity—a loss marked most dramatically in the compromising of the trope of the *carnaval moralisé*—it embodies this same shift from emblematic to mimetic art, substituting obscurity, multivalence, and indeterminacy for the ultimately translatable codes characteristic of the allegorical mode.[26]

246

Whatever label one wishes to apply to *Amelia* finally—allegorical or realistic, emblematic or expressive—the novel remains a hybrid literary structure, one form in the process of becoming another. Its implicit unclassifiability, the mixing of incompatible generic categories, may account for some of the uneasiness with which the work has often been received. *Amelia*'s two masquerades—the masquerade as emblem (the *carnaval moralisé*), the masquerade as action (the masquerade scene)—are but a carnivalesque externalization of its contradictory nature, the overt thematic manifestation of its exquisite yet often disturbing duality.

At this point it may appear that I have skirted an obvious epistemological problem by speaking so elliptically of the manner in which the representation of the masquerade in *Amelia* "conditions" or "precipitates" a host of subsequent textual transformations. I have treated the topos, one might argue, as a kind of ghost-in-the-machine in Fielding's novel—almost a supernatural textual agency that of itself provokes the counterallegorical explosion of ambiguity and fluidity so palpable in the second half of the fiction. To identify the masquerade scene in Book X as the narrative crux of the novel, the mark of a formal chiasmus—the point at which *Amelia*'s carefully woven didactic skein begins to unravel—is to deal only obscurely in the problems of agency, instrumentality, and intention. Indeed, one might ask, what conditions the topos itself?

The question returns us necessarily to the larger topic with which we began—the role of the carnivalesque in Fielding's fiction. I suggested at the outset that Fielding's invocation of the themes of carnival, whether via the single image (the mask) or via the spectacle (the masquerade), is always profoundly ambivalent: those contrasting versions of the mask one may infer from his work, for example, like the two masquerades of *Amelia*, are but a sample of contradiction, the sign of a deeper imaginative paradox.

It is always possible to account for this ambivalent treatment of the carnivalesque strictly in terms of the author's psychology—as the reflection of a private debate on the highly charged issues of order and disorder, restraint and release, purity and impurity, authenticity and theatricality. The masquerade can symbolize any or all of these antinomies. Indeed, there is much to suggest that for Fielding the carnivalesque was above all an especially timely personal imagery—a means of expressing, without necessarily resolving, certain imaginative tensions. If, as Claude Rawson has suggested in *Henry Fielding and the Augustan Ideal Under Stress*, we tend now to see Fielding as a more psychically intricate author than before—as one torn by the philosophical problem of order and decorum, rather than as simply a somewhat crude mouthpiece for conventional Augustan values—his complex invocation of the carnival world might be adduced as the compelling sign of this inward debate. Like his fascination with criminality, low life, and the morally and socially marginal, Fielding's representation of the transgressive realm of the masquerade can indeed be interpreted as symptomatic of a characteristic ambivalence about order itself— and everything encompassed by the concept, so central to his fiction, of "civility." The masquerade topos thus becomes the rhetorical index to an internal paradox.[27]

Which is not to say that Fielding ever consciously elaborated the theme in this way. Had one asked the author to justify his exploitation of carnival forms, one suspects he would have merely pointed, again, to the didactic potential in such figures: their susceptibility to moral gloss, their symbolic aptness within a larger philosophical critique of hypocrisy. One detects in Fielding little of the intentionally heuristic and multivalent use of the carnivalesque that one sees later, say, in Flaubert.[28] Rather, the compromised form the carnivalesque takes in Fielding's fiction suggests unconscious, or at least unintellectualized, conflict. One has to speak always of Fielding's double psychological investment in the masquerade topos—the combination of manifest and latent factors that conditions its multifarious appearances. If the representation of the masquerade is precipitated on the conscious level by the author's will to moralize, it may be seen on another, more subliminal level as the token of an antithetical desire to subvert categories. The figure of the masquerade, one suspects, gave Fielding a gratifying opportunity to dwell on the tropes of disorder and moral inversion while seeming (even to himself) to preserve his orthodox stance as a satirist and disseminator of official viewpoints and values.

It is perhaps more rewarding, however, to treat *Amelia* as an embodiment not only of Fielding's private ambivalence regarding the themes of carnival, but also of a cultural ambivalence. Fielding's masquerade novel is exemplary in this regard: its dual nature intimates something of the dramatic duality of eighteenth-century culture itself. In the simplest historical terms, Fielding's paradoxical treatment of the masquerade topos in his last novel replicates on an aesthetic plane the response of mainstream eighteenth-century English civilization to the actual institution of the masquerade. Fielding's moralistic framing of the topos is reminiscent of the larger masquerade complaint of the eighteenth century, while his barely disguised absorption in the mystifications of the occasion parallels the continuing contemporary fascination with the world of masquerade phantasmagoria.

Amelia's epistemological implications are also exemplary. Despite its initial validation of a theology of types, or world of essences, Fielding's novel surreptitiously encodes the possibility of transformation. Like that of her predecessor Pamela, Amelia's euphoric "masquerade tale" is an implicit affront to notions of stasis, uniformity, the conservation of the ontological (and emotional) status quo. Her history intimates a deeper potential for change in human affairs. It suggests that the individual may be one thing at one time and something else at another. The masquerade is the textual figure for such mutability: the image of plot, the trope of existential possibility. The masquerade provokes a revelation—the unmasking—of hidden potentiality in the fictional world. It is that stage upon which the individual loses his or her incorrigible specificity—and the textual site at which the disparate stories of self and other merge, and become indistinguishable.

In this regard, however, Fielding's carnivalized narrative again suggests an analogy with eighteenth-century culture. If the incursion of the masquerade in *Amelia* results in the collapse of a certain antithetical logic in the fictional world, so the real institution, in its most profound aspect, seems to have been a collective enactment, or bodying forth, of a similar collapse. The masked assembly was both a symbolic suspension of the cognitive principle of binary opposition around which eighteenth-century culture was organized, and a rejection of the concept of the individual, the rationalist subject itself. Like the traditional fantasy of the World Upside-Down, the masquerade was never merely an escapist reversal of the conditions of ordinary life. Its particular éclat always exceeded that of simple inversion, though inversion was of course the symbolic gesture on which the occasion was founded. Its theatrical exchanges inevitably raised the possibility of subversion too—the undermining of supposedly natural, or essential, distinctions between opposites. When the individual was free to take on the body of the other, the very dichotomy between individuality and alterity was thrown into question. The masquerade was a comic rebuke to rational individualism itself in that it dramatized a phantasmic, dialectical unity between self and other. It enacted an overthrow of alienation, and functioned as a collective meditation on the theme of metamorphosis: a sensuous, visionary realization of the oxymoron, the both/and rather than the either/or.

In the realm of spectacle and symbolic theater—a realm at once atavistic and utopian—the masquerade marked the moment at which eighteenth-century culture became different from itself, diverging from its own theorems of decorum and metaphysical probity. Just as the novel of masquerade (of which Fielding's remains perhaps the classic specimen) is finally always the novel of contradiction, so the culture of masquerade was also the culture of contradiction. It contained its own anti-image; it institutionalized this carnivalesque challenge to its own institutions and extra-logical affront to its own logic.

It is an interesting question whether what I have referred to here as the novel of masquerade and the culture of masquerade might be taken as paradigms, respectively, of the novel itself and of culture itself. It may well be, for example, that *Amelia*'s hybrid status—its seemingly perverse shifting between allegorical and mimetic modes—is characteristic, albeit in a somewhat extreme form, of the novel in general. The novel from its beginnings, it has been argued, has been a "transgressive mode"—one that has always seemed "to break, or mix, or adulterate the existing genre-expectations of the time."[29] Ostensibly wedded to the celebration of bourgeois civilization, including the moral sanctity of the bourgeois family, the novel since the eighteenth century has also contained elements antithetical to its self-justifying didactic mission. If, as Tony Tanner suggests, we take adultery as the hidden fantasy of the genre and the key to its formal nature, then the novel of masquerade, which almost always raises the possibility of adultery on many levels, might well seem an epitome of the form.

Likewise, the culture of masquerade may be paradigmatic. In the sense that culture always hesitates, as it were, between the perception of its own institutions as natural, and conversely, as social constructions (*pace* Marx and Weber), it is possible to see in eighteenth-century civilization an exemplary image of human society. The characteristic eighteenth-century oscillation between repressive ideology of various kinds and self-conscious celebration of the principles of "Liberty"—a struggle played out, certainly, on every level of English culture during the period—is only a more extreme example, one suspects, of the conceptual tensions implicit in any form of social organization. If what anthropologists such as Claude Lévi-Strauss and Mary Douglas suggest is true—that culture encodes within its rituals symbols of its own artifactual nature—then one might indeed see in eighteenth-century society, with its complex response to the traditional world of carnival, a prototypical human cosmos. The masquerade was only one way in which eighteenth-century culture studied itself (and it remained always a highly problematic and ambiguous way of knowledge), but it represented nonetheless a revelatory symbolic expression—a form by which contemporaries might recognize not only what they were, but also what they might be.[30]

I began this discussion of *Amelia* with an image of hallucinatory ambivalence: Amelia's mask. Yet the detail here might be

taken by synecdoche to stand for Fielding's masquerade novel itself. *Amelia* is likewise an image of ambivalence, a dream of discontinuities and contradictions. I have tried to show how the fiction's carnivalesque scenery is responsible for the elaboration of
this dream. But such scenery refers us ultimately, of course, to
the realm of culture itself. If *Amelia* makes such remarkable use
of the masquerade topos—a use as strange as it is exemplary—
the novel but refracts the enigmatic perception of the carnival
world that Fielding shared with his contemporaries. To be sure,
the novel of masquerade always articulates on one level what the
culture of masquerade, with its oligarchs, allegorists, and sys-
tematizers, also articulated: that the liquid, seductive world of
masquerade is the world of deception. But at the same time,
however embryonically, works like *Amelia* also hold out a quite
different insight: that experience is more mercurial and many-
colored than it may seem. Said metaphorically, the mask is no
longer simply black, for its blackness has resolved into a world
of ever-changing, chameleon hues.

6

Masquerade and Utopia I:
Burney's 'Cecilia'

In Fanny Burney's *Cecilia: or, Memoirs of an Heiress* (1782) and Elizabeth Inchbald's *A Simple Story* (1791), what has always been secretly known about the masquerade—the insinuation of a century—is at last explicit. This realm of dream, dismay, and laughter is also, par excellence, the realm of women. What one might call the sexuality of the masquerade is the crux of its meaning for these writers— themselves women, and the late inheritors of a now-familiar scenery of the carnivalesque. For the woman novelist of the second half of the eighteenth century, the masquerade topos is at once an imaginative donnée—part of an embellished legacy of modern moral emblems—and an emotional dilemma. What to do with this classically feminine space—the space, implicitly, of her own desire? She may begin by acknowledging it, simply, as such.

To be sure, eighteenth-century writers before Burney and Inchbald had intimated the gender of the masquerade. The critic in 1724 who satirized the occasion as "a kind of Festival, dedicated to the Goddess of Wantonness . . . *Venus Libatrix*," rendered it, metonymically, as a female domain: part of a phantasmic matriarchy, the territory of Eros. Others, describing it as a voluptuous midnight country of "Whores," ruled over by sinister beldam figures like Mother Needham, did much the same, though in a somewhat less rhetorical manner. Novelists of the first half of the century reinscribed the gynocentric association and made it more ambiguous. In *Roxana* Defoe rewrote popular fantasia when he placed his heroine's greatest triumph, the seduction of the King, at the masquerade, transforming the occasion into the morally problematic yet glamorous theater of female power. And as we have just seen, Richardson and Fielding also preserve a subliminal connection between the masquerade and euphoric female destiny. In both *Pamela* and *Amelia* the masquerade episode covertly prompts the social and erotic victory of the heroine, even as it disguises itself, at first, as an embarrassment or threat to her hopes. It is linked to the story of the heroine's gratification; it is the occasion from which her pleasure itself derives. The heroine's sexual and economic reward bespeaks the subterranean influence of carnivalesque values on an otherwise polite and reactionary fictional world.

The World Upside-Down is a feminocracy; the magisterial, dominant, or disorderly woman its most potent emblem.[1] It should not surprise us that when eighteenth-century writers wish to embody the anti-world of the masquerade, they inevitably figure a gynesium—a realm pervaded by female desire, authority, and influence. Historical reasons for the association are not hard to seek. I have already described in Chapter I the revolutionary behavioral privileges the masquerade granted women in matters of discourse, gesture, and sexuality. For respectable women masquerade anonymity meant freedom from social constraint; the mask guaranteed entry into a world of unprecedented moral and sensuous liberty. Purely in light of its physical arrangements—the premium on enigma—one might describe the masked assembly as a kind of machine for feminine pleasure.

Anonymity had its philosophical implications as well. For eighteenth-century women masquerade disguise represented a political as well as existential release. By divesting her of her name—a name inevitably associated with the power of husband

or father—anonymity obscured a woman's place within patriarchy. Under patriarchy a woman's name is never her own but
merely inscribes her secondary status. If we accept Lévi-Strauss's
description of culture as a symbolic system of exchange in
which women function as objects of exchange circulated between men, then a woman's name, one could say, encodes the
history of her circulation within the patriarchal economy.[2] In
the eighteenth century her name defined her as daughter or
wife, indeed as the "natural property" (in *Cecilia*'s telling phrase)
of the man whose name she bore.

With the anonymity of the mask, however, the eighteenth-
century woman made an abrupt exit from the system of sexual
domination. For a brief, charged moment, the masquerade suspended the archaic pattern of Western gender relations. In the
exquisite round of the assembly room, a woman was free to cir-
culate—not as a commodity placed in circulation by men, but
according to her own pleasure. Those critics who claimed the
masquerade engendered an "Amazonian race," a society based
on female sovereignty, had a point: the masquerade was indeed a
microcosm in which the external forms of sexual subordination
had ceased to exist. The masquerade symbolized a realm of
women unmarked by patriarchy, unmarked by the signs of exchange and domination, and independent of the prevailing sexual economy of eighteenth-century culture.[3]

Depending on one's stake in the matter, such an occasion
might seem demonic or exhilarating. For Burney and Inchbald,
not surprisingly, the gynesium of masquerade is an entirely provocative domain—a charismatic part of the landscape of the
imagination. But then the obvious question presents itself: does
the scenery of the carnivalesque mean something other, or
something more, for the eighteenth-century woman writer than
for her male counterpart? That such should be the case makes
intuitive sense, given the charged sexual meaning of the occasion. I have already speculated on the subliminal role of the carnivalesque for male novelists like Richardson and Fielding, and
on how the masquerade set piece may express a desire for a temporary escape from the burdens of moral seriousness. In *Pamela*

and *Amelia* the masquerade episode has the quality of a hiatus or fugue—an authorial flight out of didactic consistency. For the male moralist the scene marks a holiday lapse in decorum, and a return to the atavistic pleasures of intrigue and mystification. He may suddenly appear to relinquish ideological control over the direction of his narrative. Indeed, the scene intimates a deep wish to forgo control—to abandon masculine authorial prestige and dispense with the problematic cachet of moralism itself.

The female novelist's use of the same episode, however, may suggest wishes at once more scandalous and more pragmatic. The desire here may be for more control than less—revolutionary rather than languid. For the woman writer, one suspects, the carnivalesque is not so much a festive hiatus as a way of articulating a subterranean will to power. An analogy might be made with contemporary transvestism. When the eighteenth-century man adopted female dress as his masquerade costume, his gesture represented a form of self-burlesque: a cathartic (and comic) release from the exertions of masculinity. He agreed to give up the external signs of his own power and relax in the guise of frivolous femininity. But the woman sporting male attire was a symbolic figure of a different sort, one inevitably projecting more radical aspirations after power, sexual prestige, and masculine authority. The woman novelist invoking the carnivalesque re-created these aspirations in the literary realm. In the topos of the masquerade she invoked the imagery of power. For her the masquerade may have been less a dream of relinquishing control than a dream of unprecedented autonomy.

This latent content can be described more precisely. In psychoanalytic terms the female representation of the masquerade ineluctably seems to embody narcissistic fantasies. It is not surprising that both *Cecilia* and *A Simple Story* are archetypal dramas of female narcissism—that each tells the story of a marvelous Heiress, whose beauty, wealth, and charm exceed those of any rival and elicit constant homage. In the case of Cecilia the homage is general (she has a sea of admirers); in the case of Miss Milner in *A Simple Story*, it comes from a single man, Dorriforth, who passionately combines a multiplicity of masculine roles (father, brother, guardian, and lover) in his relationship with his ward. In each novel the narrative problem is the same: how to contain this extraordinary female presence within the conventional plot of female *Bildung*? How will the heroine be absorbed into the world of sexual and economic subordination? The masquerade scene is an emblematic moment in her history; it is the point at which her affective power is greatest and the problem of her socialization is least resolved.

In using the term female narcissism I do not mean to suggest that the fictions of Burney and Inchbald are motivated either by what in simpler days was called vanity or by unusual yearnings after infantile satisfactions. Rather, I invoke the term in the transvalued sense of modern psychoanalysis, as a code for adaptive psychological adjustment. Popular misconceptions notwithstanding, modern psychoanalysis has never defined narcissistic disorder as excessive or debilitating self-love, but rather as the opposite of self-love: the primacy of a false self characterized by self-denial and self-contempt, lack of spontaneity, and a constant deference to internalized parental dictates. Healthy or adaptive narcissism, by contrast, might be properly defined as uncorrupted self-love; it is a state marked by respect for one's own desires and needs.[4] I take it for granted that within patriarchal society, with its asymmetrical power relations and insistence on pathological feminine self-sacrifice—what Mary Wollstonecraft called woman's "State of Degradation"—the female fantasy of economic and sexual autonomy constitutes narcissism in this rehabilitated sense. It is a trope for essentially progressive or liberating emotional directives. For the woman writing in patriarchal society, the fantasy of the gynesium—the world of the Heiress—may in fact transcribe psychically valuable aspirations.

Seen in a collective or political context, such aspirations resemble utopianism. One might argue that the collective transformation of female narcissism is indeed female utopianism—or more simply, feminism. For the eighteenth-century woman writer the masquerade is a utopian domain: this "second world" of carnival (in Bakhtin's phrase) must always be for her, at the deepest level, an ideal space, a mode of freedom.[5] In a very literal sense it is the antithesis of the repressive domestic salon: an actual site of unprecedented pleasures. But it is also part of an imaginary architecture of gratification. The woman writer, one suspects, must at some point part company with the eighteenth-century satirist—with the masculine representation of the masquerade as a corrupt dystopia, and indeed with the entire contemporary satiric language of masquerade "Whores," dominatrixes, and "Goddesses" of wanton. The masquerade is not finally, for her, the image of a disordered cosmos (for how can that world be disordered in which one finds oneself at the center?), but a subliminal image of possibility.

Women novelists of the eighteenth century do not necessarily render this feminine utopia in an unconflicted way. The masquerade remains problematic precisely because it is the gynesium. It cannot, in the end, be reconciled with any patriarchal geography; it threatens that real world of masculine domination with which, to uphold its mimetic and didactic pretensions, eighteenth-century narrative must always negotiate. However much the woman writer may be drawn to the scenery of female power, she must also contend with a world right-side-up, the prevailing symbolic order, in which women are given names, guarded and cherished, and exchanged as objects by men.

How she chooses to treat the carnivalesque episode—and whether it carries any transformational potential in her fictional world—will suggest much about the plausibility of her narrative. Burney and Inchbald, we shall find, differ drastically in this regard. Burney presents her utopian scenery only to renounce it in the interests of verisimilitude: though *Cecilia* begins as a fantastical projection of female narcissism, it reverts to a more dysphoric realism in the painful working out of its heroine's story. The compromised narrative role of the masquerade suggests Burney's reluctant commitment to the conventional plot of female *Bildung*, and her standard if reactionary inscription of gender relations. Inchbald's fiction, by contrast, insistently parodies the traditional female plot. The Heiress is never successfully contained within the everyday world of domesticity and repression. The incursion of the carnivalesque, midway through the novel, epitomizes the utopian direction of the work as a whole. Of course, one may ask whether the novel does not enter the world of romance at this point, and whether its claims are not finally more visionary than realistic. Certainly, to the extent that *A Simple Story* projects a final triumph of female narcissism—and hints at a corresponding carnivalization of gender relations in the fictional world—it dispenses with traditional plausibility. The simple story turns out to be an extraordinary one—a utopian discourse, violating utterly the conventional grammar of the eighteenth-century female plot.[6]

I will return to matters of genre and plausibility. What is most important here is the philosophic and political content of the female carnivalesque. One cannot escape the conclusion that utopia itself may be a metamorphosis of gender: that the ideal *kosmos* may have a sex. The eighteenth-century masquerade, in its departure from patriarchy, had a sex. It is not surprising that this incorrigibly feminine topos should prompt utopian designs in the work of the woman novelist.

Like *Pamela*, Part 2, Burney's *Cecilia* may be said to begin, in a theoretical sense, with a masquerade. The episode takes place early in the novel—in the first volume of the five-volume 1782 edition—just after the heroine has come to London to take up residence and fortune. Burney wastes no time setting the stage. No sooner has Cecilia joined her guardians, the Harrels, at their house in Portman Square, than she is swept up in their frenzied preparations for an "at home" masquerade. These consist, ironically, of making home itself unrecognizable. Like Hogarth's feckless couple in *Marriage à la Mode*, the spendthrift Harrels turn their house into a trashy monument to improvidence: a vast, kitschy pleasure-mansion, complete with fairy-tale ramparts, "elegant awnings," dessert-tables "ornamented with various devices of cut glass," and a multitude of colored lamps fixed "in fantastic forms" (Vol. I, pp. 158, 164).[7] Cecilia observes the domestic upheaval with the Burney heroine's typical mixture of expectation and unease: "The whole house was then in commotion, from various arrangements and improvements which were planned for almost every apartment that was to be opened for the reception of masks. Cecilia herself, however little pleased with the attendant circumstances of wantonly accumulating unnecessary debts, was not the least animated of the party; she was a stranger to every diversion of this sort, and from the novelty of the scene, hoped for uncommon satisfaction" (I, 163–64).

By now one recognizes, of course, the intensely literary nature of the moment. In that the heroine both desires and hesitates over it, the masquerade has from the start its familiar and paradoxical subjective aura: she awaits the Harrels' party in the curious, ambivalent way the neophyte awaits the initiatory ritual. Yet the primal scene has, as it were, become familiar. The reader of Burney's other fiction immediately recognizes the conventional situation: a novice-heroine is about to undergo her "entrance into the world," an initiation into social life itself. Urban amusement—the unfamiliar realm of theater, opera, Vauxhall, and the like—plays a charismatic part in this process of female *Bildung*. *Evelina*, we recall, is structured by the heroine's progress through a series of popular London entertainments, each of which becomes an anagram for civilization itself. Confrontation with fashionable metropolitan life is Burney's primary metaphor for learning one's place in the symbolic order. One anticipates something similar here—the masquerade as a rite of passage in a larger process of socialization.

But the hint of danger associated with the masquerade is also conventional. Cecilia is "little pleased" with certain "attendant circumstances." The masquerade retains its obliquity, its vaguely sinister ambience. There is a suggestion of the now-familiar anticipatory moral bracketing. Burney modifies the traditional critique of the masquerade, however, in one important respect: Cecilia is worried, not that the party to come will be a scene of wantonness, but that it represents a "wanton" accumulation of debts. For the Burney heroine the masquerade is no longer primarily a sexual threat; it has become almost exclusively an emblem of luxury and the improper use of riches. Will the Heiress be ensnared by the sheer lavishness of the fashionable life the masquerade exemplifies?

Such a shift in emphasis from the erotic to the fiscal makes sense, given the profound financial theme of Burney's fiction. *Cecilia* turns on money matters, above all on how the heroine will dispose of her fortune. Even before the Harrels begin their elaborate preparations for the masquerade, Cecilia has been warned against extravagance by the mysterious misanthrope, Albany, who exhorts her with Biblical fervor to "discard the sycophants that surround you, seek the virtuous, relieve the poor, and save yourself from the impending destruction of unfeeling prosperity!" (I, 109). The Harrels themselves are on the brink of financial ruin: endless household renovations, parties, and (in the case of Mr. Harrel) surreptitious nightly gambling bouts have left them, like denizens in some rococo Jazz Age, at the mercy of creditors. The masquerade is but another frivolous expense. The reader awaits Cecilia's own exemplary confrontation with this world of beautiful waste.

This decarnalization of the masquerade also reflects Burney's distinctive manner—her shift away from conventional hysteria and her attempt to make the carnivalesque episode less melodramatic. By turning her attention from sexual to economic dangers, Burney makes the masquerade less interesting to the reader in a sense: she depathologizes it. It is less a region of taboo—a place where sacred objects are defiled—than a specimen of vulgar consumerism. The occasion is still morally outré, but its dangers have become quotidian, indeed bourgeois.* The major sin it represents is one against the pocketbook.

Burney's understated tone suggests a pervasive desire to rationalize the carnivalesque—to make it less discontinuous with the mundane, the life of polite society. It reflects her characteristically sophisticated perspective; she approaches her fictional situation with a studied calm. Borrowing a term from the the-

---

*Compare Fielding's attack on masquerades in his *Enquiry into the Causes of the Late Increase of Robbers*. Fielding tells the story of "an honest Gentleman who carried his Wife and two Daughters to a Masquerade, being told that he could have four Tickets for four Guineas; but found afterwards, that in Dresses, Masques, Chairs, &c., the Night's Entertainment cost him about twelve" (p. 6). Fielding exaggerates the fiscal pathos: not all public masquerades were this expensive. The *Weekly Journal* for April 19, 1718, describes "lesser Masquerades" of the town, open to the public at "five and three shillings a piece." Fielding himself speaks of "inferior Masquerades," modeled after those at the Haymarket but catering to a less fashionable clientele (p. 12).

ory of communication, one might describe the style of the first part of *Cecilia* as a cool medium: the characteristics of the narrative voice are detachment, a faint world-weariness, and complete intellectual control over all the affective aspects of story.

The point is worth remarking because a similar impulse toward control—toward a nonmelodramatic containment of the carnivalesque—informs many features of Burney's masquerade scene itself. Much in her rendering of the familiar set piece suggests the conscious *exercice du style*. At least at first glance, this is a masquerade scene heavily mediated by literary precedent and imaginative restraint.

The conventionality manifests itself in several ways. Many descriptive details, first of all, are more or less generic. Of the masquerade crowd itself, the "general herd of the company," Cecilia finds, are dressed in dominos; "for the rest, the men were Spaniards, chimney-sweepers, Turks, watch-men, conjurers, and old women; and the ladies, shepherdesses, orange girls, Circassians, gipseys, haymakers, and sultanas" (I, 169). The reader of eighteenth-century masquerade literature will immediately recognize the conventional reference to sartorial *adynata*. Likewise the crowd's behavior, though Cecilia finds "incitements to surprise and diversion without end," is presented in formulaic terms. Everyone is determined to be bad, though being bad, at this point, has its requisite forms. Thus the heroine, like many before her, is jostled and teased, and suffers from the "freedoms" all around her. She is unfamiliar with the droll lingua franca of the masquerade, but the reader recognizes the recycled nature of the verbal tags and facetious gestures: "Even the local cant of, *Do you know me? Who are you?* and *I know you*; with the sly pointing of the finger, the arch nod of the head, and the pert squeak of the voice, though wearisome to those who frequent such assemblies, were, to her unhackneyed observation, additional subjects of amusement" (I, 168). This is a controlled, literary delirium—saturnalia by rote.

On a more abstract level Burney's use of individual sartorial symbols contributes to the overall stylization of the scene. Individuals already known to Cecilia—the dramatis personae of her new London life—one by one reveal themselves by their costumes, which function here like signs in a gorgeous, yet eminently legible characterological code. Burney quite explicitly uses masquerade costume in the familiar eighteenth-century comic mode, as a paradoxical transparency of the self. In 1777, a few years before the publication of *Cecilia*, one would-be satirist had written: "Everyone [at the masquerade] divests himself of his borrowed feathers, and following his natural propensity, assumes the character which suits him best. In short, everyone humours his own genius so exactly that whoever are well-acquainted with the temper and disposition of our nobility in public life will have no difficulty tracing them out."[8]

True, there are a few minor characters here whose disguises diverge so radically from what they really are that the effect is one of simple burlesque discontinuity: Miss Larolles, a vacuous town "Voluble," appears as Minerva; the Cicero in the crowd turns out to be an illiterate rake. But in the case of major characters—and most of the important characters of the novel are present in this scene—Burney plays out the conventional paradox. Each betrays himself (to the reader if not always to the heroine) by the oddly lucid form of self-estrangement each has chosen. Costume becomes the somewhat banal sign of the role each character will play in Cecilia's subsequent history. Sir Robert Floyer, the lascivious suitor whom Cecilia will later reject, is a Turk; Belfield, the dilettante poet, is a hapless, *raffiné* Don Quixote. Mr. Gosport, the bemused, vaguely Proustian figure who becomes Cecilia's instructor in social etiquette, is a schoolteacher. Other characters' costumes are even more blatantly allegorical. True to the villainous part he will play (he secretly lusts after both Cecilia's person and her fortune), the hypocritical Monckton is garbed as a "black Lucifer," while Delvile, soon to emerge as the romantic hero of the piece, is clad in a chic (and morally impeccable) white domino. Delvile at one point spells out what is already obvious to the reader: "You will find me as inoffensive as the hue of the domino I wear" (I, 184). At moments such as these one cannot help sensing the author's behind-the-scenes presence. Through this eminently rational code of costume, Burney seems to make the carnivalesque over into a closed system—a suave, unambiguous, entirely rhetorical operation.

Burney's mediated approach to the carnivalesque is manifest, finally, in one more important way: she shows from the start a highly self-conscious understanding of the narrative as well as the emblematic uses of the masquerade scene. Burney's plot, we recall, will ultimately turn on the idea of *amor impossibilia*: the thwarted and crisis-ridden love of Cecilia and Delvile, who meet here for the first time. The terms of Cecilia's legacy will prove the great stumbling block to their happiness: Delvile's haughty father forbids their marriage when he learns that his son will have to humiliate himself by taking the nonaristocratic name of Beverley in place of "the ancient name of Delvile." Burney's is thus the time-honored plot of erotic misalliance in a new, middle-class guise.

More forthrightly than either Richardson or Fielding in similar circumstances, Burney uses the masquerade to set this plot in motion. From the start she seems quite consciously aware of the occasion's hidden instrumental connection with transgressive desire and is able to exploit the topos far more purposively than either of her predecessors. Burney's premeditation is reflected in that of her characters: Delvile, we find, has crashed the Harrels' masquerade precisely with the intention of seeing the heroine, even though the Delviles and the Harrels are not on visiting terms. True, Delvile's father is one of Cecilia's three legal guardians, but Delvile senior considers Cecilia too "low"—and the Harrels too parvenu—for social connection. Young Delvile, however, has been told of Cecilia's charm and beauty by his friend Mr. Biddulph (who is also enamored of her), and secretly attends in hopes of seeing her.

Not surprisingly, the fantastic scene provides the perfect stage for the acting out of powerful illicit desire. Amid the revelry and hubbub Delvile's passion, already mediated by Biddulph's, is further intensified by a host of masked rivals—among them Sir Robert, Mr. Arnott, and Mr. Monckton—all vying for Cecilia's attention. She in turn is fascinated by the discreet approaches of the mysterious white domino; subjected all evening to the "pointed and singular" attacks of uncivil admirers (I, 169), she finds him a relief. As she and Delvile perform their polite duet of cohesion, the reader recognizes the familiar topoi of romantic convention, including "love at first sight," and wonders what difficulties will beset this attractive yet obviously fated pair.

A single, highly specific literary reference to *Romeo and Juliet* confirms Burney's self-conscious exploitation of the carnivalesque. Echoes from the Shakespearean play will later pervade Burney's text, "What's in a name?" being the unstated question on which the heroine's destiny turns. Will Delvile defy his father and take Cecilia's name in place of the "proud" name of Delvile? The implications of the question constitute the feminist drama of Burney's novel. Once the theme of *amor impossibilia* has sufficiently developed, roughly midway through the novel, explicit references to the Shakespearean drama multiply. Thus in Volume III, when the full impropriety of Cecilia's and Delvile's attachment is first made clear, Lady Honoria Pemberton, a *ficelle*-like character staying with the heroine at Delvile Castle, jokes that she is going to tell "Mortimer," the younger Delvile (who is about to renounce Cecilia and leave for Bath), "to look up at your window before he goes off, for if he will play Romeo, you, I dare say, will play Juliet, and this old castle is quite the thing for the musty family of Capulets: I dare say Shakespear thought of it when he wrote of them" (III, 230). Delvile senior, she continues, "may serve for all the Capulets and all the Montagues at once, for he has pride enough for both their houses, and twenty more besides." In the following departure scene Delvile himself misquotes Romeo (*"he jests at scars who never felt a wound!"*), as though telepathically privy to Lady Honoria's remarks. Later there will be other moments reminiscent of Shakespeare's drama—notably in the lovers' plan for a secret marriage (IV, 102–19), which like that of Romeo and Juliet ends in disaster.

Such explicit parallels have a recursive effect, lending new significance to earlier scenes in the novel. One sees retrospectively that Burney's opening episode, with Delvile's anonymous appearance at the "forbidden" masquerade of the Harrels, is like-

wise motivated by Shakespearean precedent. It is the equivalent
of Romeo's surreptitious visit to that masked revel—Capulet's
"old accustomed feast"—at which he first meets Juliet (I, ii, 20).
Burney's carnivalesque episode, like Shakespeare's, incorporates
the fateful meeting on which all else in her story hinges. Obviously Burney lends the transgressive moment a novel class dimension: the masquerade marks the spot where aristocracy and
bourgeoisie come together in problematic union. But the basic
parallel remains. We are invited to analyze the masquerade as an
event that imitates another on two counts—as both cultural and
literary repetition. The occasion itself is an eighteenth-century
redaction of Renaissance festivity, but its function in Burney's
plot also replicates that of the paradigmatic masking scene in
Shakespeare. So carefully is the repetition premeditated that one
cannot posit for Burney, as one might for Richardson or Fielding, any accidental or unconscious artistic exploitation of the
carnivalesque sequence. She is utterly aware of its critical role in
her plot, for this plot is intentionally fashioned to resemble
another.

Obviously Burney sentimentalizes Shakespearean precedent:
Cecilia does not end, after all, with the death of its heroine and
her lover, but with their marriage. Conceivably one might describe Burney's novel as a typically eighteenth-century rewriting
of Shakespeare, akin to those "improved" versions of *King Lear*
and the like, complete with happy endings, that proliferated on
the contemporary London stage. Even in otherwise analogous
scenes, Burney makes subtle modifications in the direction of
comedy. In the masquerade episode itself, for example, when
Delvile arrives at the Harrels' house, he has no qualms comparable to Romeo's premonition of tragic doom before Capulet's
party—

> Some consequence, yet hanging in the stars,
> Shall bitterly begin his fearful date
> With this night's revels. (I, iv, 107–9)

This occasion in Burney's rendering, even down to the meeting
with Cecilia, contains nothing in the way of mortal danger.
Similarly, Lady Honoria's facetious roulade on the Capulet-like

behavior of old Delvile suggests Burney's work of ironic comic transmutation: it places the reader in a realm, not of trauma and bloodshed, but of drawing-room banter.

To be sure, *Cecilia* also allows for a "comic" reading—in Northrop Frye's sense—in that it depicts the final integration of a problematic individual, a potential scapegoat or *pharmakos*, into an established social community.[9] At the outset of the novel, Cecilia is a problem, not least on account of the remarkable cultural threat implicit in her very situation as an heiress. The terms of her legacy, which is the source of her power, are a direct affront to masculine hegemony; the startling requirement that her husband take her name in place of his own is a gratuitous challenge to the legal and moral theorems of patriarchy. Unwittingly enough (she seems an unlikely psychological candidate for sexual rebellion), Cecilia represents an unprecedented and potentially disruptive kind of female autonomy. Within the fictional world her inheritance is almost universally perceived as a scandalous violation of patriarchal decorum. One character laments in her presence that such "a fine fortune, got as a man may say, out of the bowels of one's mother country," should "in default of male issue, [be] obliged to come to a female, the law making no proviso to the contrary" (V, 221). By voluntarily divesting herself of her fortune late in the novel in order to marry Delvile, Cecilia makes the name clause moot, obviates the disturbing prospect of a female lineage, and belatedly establishes her claim to conventional female status. Members of her London circle regard this step as a necessary compromise with social forms—as an example of the wisdom expressed by Mr. Monckton early on, "that experience shews that the opposition of an individual to a community is always dangerous in the operation, and seldom successful in the event" (I, 22). The heroine's self-denial, one might argue, rectifies a defect in the Law; it restores order to a temporarily disordered world, and marks out, via symbolic theater, the return of the status quo. Her marriage to Delvile brings her story to a point of conventional closure, and confirms her now-respectable position within the patriarchal fictional world.

Given such a reading, Burney's intensely literary masquerade episode might be seen, almost ornamentally, as an embedded allegory of a familiar comic story. From one angle the little plot it traces out—in which the heroine is surrounded (literally) by a number of unwanted suitors, only to accept, finally, the attentions of the white domino—is a symbolic epitome of the romance plot of the novel as a whole. The men who besiege Cecilia in the assembly room—Monckton, Sir Robert Floyer, Mr. Arnott, and the rest—are also her pursuers in reality. For reasons of sex, avarice, or both, each seeks, unsuitably, to engage her. Only Delvile, after a series of dance-like maneuvers, ends up at her side. The episode is thus a kind of miniature or insignia of the plot of heterosexual romance: like a shadow play, it forecasts the final union of Cecilia and her aristocratic lover, and intimates a larger comic movement in the fiction as a whole.

Such a recuperation of the masquerade scene is temporarily satisfying. The indecorous episode is rhetoricized: it becomes a form of prolepsis. The disturbing feminine power of the carnivalesque is contained within a larger structure of intention. To read the scene in this way is to be true to one critical stereotype of Burney herself as a proponent of the thoughtful, chic, highly finished comedy of manners—a kind of proto-Austen. The masquerade, from this perspective, is finally only an aesthetic event, not a political or psychological one. It takes place in the ideal space of literature; it is part of a comforting, abstract world of precedent. The episode itself is shaped by precedent—Shakespeare—but it also functions as an embedded precedent within the history in which it occurs. It is a comic blazon of *Cecilia*'s romance plot itself.

The only problem with such a characterization of Burney's carnivalesque—and indeed with the view of *Cecilia* as a comedy—is that it is insufficient, finally, to explain the psychic complexities of Burney's often painfully articulated fictional world. Despite the use of precedent *Cecilia* has much to do with what is unprecedented; despite the final valorization of convention, it is also, paradoxically, about the failure of conventional gestures to console. The emotional tone of the work is unpredictable: Burney's attempt at comic control of her material, like Fielding's in *Amelia*, repeatedly fails. Any comic précis of *Cecilia* must necessarily exclude much, notably the current of uneasiness and melancholia that eddies through the book. The novel often lapses into bizarre and hectic melodrama. The shocking suicide of Mr. Harrel amid the fairy lights of Vauxhall, the story of Albany's confinement in a madhouse, Mrs. Delvile's hemorrhage and illness, the several duels (including one between Delvile and Monckton), and Cecilia's own sufferings—her depression after Delvile renounces her, the humiliation of her abortive secret marriage, her penultimate bout of temporary madness, in which she wanders hysterically through hallucinatory London streets—these do not so much suggest the comic world of Austen's drawing rooms as the lurid mise-en-scène of nineteenth-century opera. An unintegrated gothic strain runs through *Cecilia*: an element of arabesque and excess that becomes more pronounced even as Burney brings her narrative to its ostensibly happy conclusion.

One can state the problem as one of plot as well as tone. For *Cecilia*, paradoxically, is as much a story of loss as a story of comic rewards. Granted, the novel ends with the heroine's marriage, the talisman of conventional socioerotic success; but at the same time it is also, strangely, a story of deprivation and panic, and of the heroine's inexorable alienation from power. Cecilia's masochistic bargain with the Delviles, an arrangement that robs her simultaneously of name and fortune (and symbolically of her autonomy), is the climactic moment in this plot of loss, though it is not by any means the only humiliation she suffers. Burney seems not to have consciously anticipated this darkening of her heroine's story, for its details come as successive shocks to the reader. Set against *Evelina*, *Cecilia* has a discontinuous, confused narrative structure. Its ending—with its intimations of anguish barely surmounted—seems profoundly at odds with its bright beginnings and the essentially hopeful narrative topos of the heroine's "entrance into the world." Structurally, the novel is a kind of anacoluthon, its emotional grammar conflicted.

Not surprisingly, Burney's masquerade scene takes on special significance when the novel is seen in this light—not as a sentimental patriarchal comedy, but as a more diffident, even poignant account of female co-optation. Burney does everything she can to disguise the episode as a technical flourish, but its charisma, again, exceeds that of the ornament or literary fancy. Though stylish, the masquerade is never merely style. It carries a supplementary emotional power—a residue of what Bakhtin would call "theoretical pathos."[10]

The masquerade scene draws its force, one suspects, from the woman novelist's own ambivalent desires. In phantasmic terms the scene is indeed a point of origin: an image of that paradisal realm of power and self-gratification out of which the Heiress (and her female creator) can only fall. It is a paradigmatic moment of wish-fulfillment, the scene of a success already achieved, the token of a utopia that already exists. The masquerade occurs at the beginning of Cecilia's history, one might argue, because it serves an inaugural emblematic function. It externalizes that fantasy of autonomy with which Burney's novel itself begins—the transgressive female aspiration after an unlimited power, the dream of the Heiress itself. In the end, of course, it is precisely this dream that will be given up, just as the Heiress leaves behind her claim on grandeur in favor of the bathetic pleasures of renunciation.

Before this act of self-divestiture, however, nothing but delight—as a return to the masquerade must show. The utopian aspect of the scene is revealed most strikingly in its obsessive spectacles of homage. For Cecilia the Harrels' party is a festival of celebration, in which she is at the center of an effusive and ever-growing throng of sycophants. Her affect is at once imperial and adhesive; she fuses the roles of ingenue and matriarch in a seductive and paradoxical manner. All are drawn to her. Her admirers "encircle" and "besiege" her with their desire, yet their very assault is stylized, a mode of adoration. They are fans, in the modern sense, and all are men. The scene is a classic projection of the heroine's heterosexual charm. Other women tend to drop out of sight, leaving Cecilia the beloved object, even at the outset, of an exclusively male pack.*

Cecilia's singularity, this talismanic relation to the crowd, has something to do with her unconventional mode of presenting herself at the masquerade. She is inappropriately dressed for the occasion, since she is not in costume or mask. From the start she finds herself "far more conspicuous in being almost the only female in a common dress, than any masquerade habit could have made her" (I, 168). The reader is given a perfunctory explanation for her "lack of a dress": Mrs. Harrel (who is also without a costume) has informed her that "it was not necessary for ladies to be masked at home, and said she should receive her company herself in a dress which she might wear upon any other occasion" (I, 167). The advice does not seem entirely well judged, for the heroine's lack of disguise immediately causes her embarrassment. Cecilia soon wishes she "had herself made one of the number" of incogniti (I, 167).

One wonders, however, whether Cecilia's conspicuousness is so unpleasing on a deeper level, and whether Burney has not engineered this moment of exposure for her heroine. Though Cecilia feels self-conscious, her situation is unmistakably similar to that of narcissistic fantasy. True, her lack of a costume challenges the spirit of the occasion; in sociological terms she stands in relation to the masked crowd rather as a naked person, in the ordinary world, would to a group of clothed persons. She has broken the collective sartorial contract, and by extension, the implicit decorum of the group. Contrary to what one might

---

*Elias Canetti's description of crowd behavior in *Crowds and Power* is suggestive here. Cecilia's role resembles that of the crowd crystal—Canetti's term for the special individual or group of individuals around whom a larger crowd forms: "The clarity, isolation and constancy of the crystal form an uncanny contrast with the excited flux of the surrounding crowd. The process of rapid, uncontrollable growth, and the threat of disintegration, which together give the crowd its peculiar restlessness, do not operate within the crystal. Even in the midst of the greatest excitement the crystal stands out against it" (p. 74). The masquerade crowd combines aspects of several crowd types Canetti distinguishes in his book, notably the reversal and feast crowds.

expect, however, other masqueraders neither taunt her nor laugh at her lack of costume. Instead, each seems transfixed by the sight of her unadorned beauty.

One might connect this odd situation with Freud's famous account of dreams of nakedness in *The Interpretation of Dreams*. Such embarrassment dreams, according to Freud, typically allude to the exhibitionistic pleasures of childhood and express latent narcissistic desires. The detail indicating this underlying fantasy content invariably turns out to be the surprising and somewhat implausible reaction of spectators to the dreamer's appearance: "The dreamer's embarrassment and the spectator's indifference constitute a contradiction such as often occurs in dreams. It would be more in keeping with the dreamer's feelings if the strangers were to look at him in astonishment, or were to laugh at him, or be outraged. I think, however, that this obnoxious feature has been displaced by wish-fulfillment." The wish in question is for a return to an earlier time: "Only in our childhood was there a time when we were seen by our relatives, as well as by strange nurses, servants, and visitors, in a state of insufficient clothing, and at that time we were not ashamed of our nakedness. . . . This age of childhood, in which the sense of shame is unknown, seems a paradise when we look back upon it later, and paradise itself is nothing but the mass-phantasy of the childhood of the individual." Dreams of nakedness, he concludes, are *"exhibition-dreams."*[11]

Cecilia's lack of disguise can of course be recuperated other than as a displaced version of physical nakedness. We might see the heroine in more conventional allegorical terms simply as someone exempted by her moral nature from the prevailing deceptions of the masquerade—an exemplar of integrity in a world of dissimulation. Such a reading would accord with the characterization of Cecilia as a young woman of "intuitive" virtue, a theme to which Burney frequently returns. But one senses that Burney wants her heroine to be conspicuous for deeper reasons too—to be known by the masquerade crowd in a most pleasurable way—in order to reward her, as it were, with a moment of purely narcissistic delight. Cecilia's ostensibly acciden-

tal exhibitionism allows her to triumph, and in a manner structurally akin to the classic wish fulfillment.

Certainly the fantasy of singularity eliciting homage is present in other details of the scene. The heroine's admirers perform
a kind of ritual theater of submission in her presence. Thus the
"black devil" (the sinister Monckton) pays her wordless, feral
devoirs, complete with a bestial mummery of obeisance: "he
cleared a semi-circular space before her chair, thrice with the
most profound reverence bowed to her, thrice turned himself
around with sundry grimaces, and then fiercely planted himself
at her side" (I, 169–70). There he remains for much of the evening, an odd, Ubu-like figure, "growling" and gyrating ob-
scenely like a consort from another, more primitive realm. By a
kind of metonymy of bodies, his very attentions seem to speak
of Cecilia's own strangely "diabolical" charm, to which several
masqueraders jokingly call attention. When, for example, she
attempts to escape her ubiquitous "*black guard*," Mr. Gosport
laughingly chides her: "and pray, madam, after playing the devil
with all mankind, what right have you to complain that one man
plays the devil with you?" (I, 184). In the judgment of the crowd
Cecilia out-lucifers Lucifer, who kneels to her here in a parody
of self-abasement.

Others mimic the devil's acts of homage. "Don Quixote"
(Belfield) makes a series of unabashedly subservient gestures in
Cecilia's presence, kissing his spear in chivalrous "token of alle-
giance," and genuflecting before his "most incomparable Prin-
cess" (I, 172). The effete Gosport, dressed as a pedant, wants to
cast his rod, "this emblem of my authority," at her feet and "forget, in the softness of your conversation, all the roughness of
discipline." Such an act, he allows, would be "a confusion to all
order," and yet he takes perverse delight in the humiliating image of the schoolteacher enslaved by the charms of his lovely
pupil: "Should I examine you in the dead languages, would not
your living accents charm from me all power of reproof? . . .
Were your fair hand spread out to me for correction, should I
help applying my lips to it, instead of my rat-tan? If I ordered
you to be *called up*, should I ever remember to have you sent

back? And if I commanded you to stand in a corner, how should I forbear following you thither myself?" (I, 181).

The white domino, who now gravitates to Cecilia's side, takes up the theme of goddess worship. He, the schoolteacher, and the devil, he observes, are like a "three-headed Cerberus" guarding her—as though, somewhat surreally, Cecilia were the infernal cavity itself. Her feminine power is so great, he argues, that she has transformed ordinary relations of dominance and submission, power and bondage. She seems passive, "imprisoned" by her admirers, but they are in fact her slaves: "You have doubtless been the aggressor, and played this game yourself without mercy, for I have read in your face the captivity of thousands" (I, 178). Delvile fears that once he has freed her from the attentions of the black devil, her first use of her "liberty" will be "to doom your deliverer to bondage" (I, 180).

Cecilia's night at the masquerade concludes on a note of primitive narcissistic fantasia—an orgy of ovation. Sir Robert Floyer, the Turk, exclaims he has seen "nothing handsome" in the assembly room besides her. Mr. Briggs, the most eccentric of her guardians, who has materialized (owing to his avarice) in the bedraggled homemade guise of a chimney sweep, rallies her about her "sweethearts" and jokes that she may soon have any husband she wishes. The white domino, taking his leave, charges Cecilia with hypnotizing him, and addresses her in the lover's language of paradox and reversal: "Instead of growing weary by the length of my stay, my reluctance to shorten it encreases with its duration; and all the methods I take, whether by speaking to you or looking at you, with a view to be satiated, only double my eagerness for looking and listening again! I must go, however; and if I am happy, I may perhaps meet with you again,— though if I am wise, I shall never seek you more!" (I, 202–3).

The reader has little access to Cecilia's sentiments during all of this, apart from learning that she feels a "manifest preference" for the attentions of the white domino (I, 197). Burney does not present the heroine's experience in subjective terms; we see her instead from the outside, as the central figure in a kind of magic theater. Her masquerade debut is a bravura performance, though one, paradoxically, unintended by the performer. She appears baffled by the acclaim, achieving her succès d'estime through no will of her own, it seems, but entirely through the indulgence of her creator.

One cannot help noticing too how much the situation here dramatizes the heroine's status in the fictional world, which likewise seems a work of authorial wish fulfillment. True, one might interpret Cecilia's masquerade success cynically, just as one might interpret her prominence in London society cynically. Cecilia is beautiful and charming, but she is also the object of a collective economic fixation. As an heiress, she is that rich "natural property" over which fortune hunters understandably contend (I, 19). She is surrounded by suitors at the masquerade just as she is surrounded in everyday life by those seeking wealth without tears.

But it is important to remember how much real power Cecilia has. With the crucial exception of a husband, Burney has given her heroine everything at the outset of the novel. The twinkling attentions of the fortune hunter seem a small price to pay for the pleasure of standing outside the usual system of sexual subordination, which is exactly what Cecilia does. Her masquerade triumph is but an externalization of Burney's fictional premise— the fact that, in Delvile's words, the heroine is profoundly "at liberty." Economic and sexual liberty seem ultimately indistinguishable in this euphoric pattern. The Heiress does not (unless she is one of Inchbald's fearlessly intelligent heroines) articulate it as such, but financial independence permits her, as one of its perquisites, the classically masculine prerogative of erotic object-choice.[12] To put it bluntly, Cecilia is free to buy any sexual companion she desires: in Burney's inverted vision, she is a consumer and not the consumed. Even the patriarchal institution of marriage does not appear to threaten her freedom. She will mark her husband in the accepted masculine manner—will make him into a wife, in fact—by imposing on him her own name, that of the "charming Miss *Beverley*." Fortune hunters or no, her suitors, like the prospective consorts of a queen, must adopt the feminine posture of waiting to be chosen.

The masquerade is thus an exemplary event for the Heiress, akin to a court masque dramatizing the authority of a monarch. She is sovereign here; the carnival world belongs to her. But in a sense the rest of the fictional world belongs to her too. At the start of *Cecilia* there is no discontinuity between microcosm and macrocosm, inside and outside. The World Upside-Down is in fact everywhere. For Burney's heroine the fictional world is a gynesium, as utopian in its arrangements as the masquerade itself. The dream of female narcissism, one might say, can go no farther.

Yet Burney's narrative must go farther, and wish fulfillment give way to the literary equivalent of the reality principle. What *Cecilia*'s narrator refers to, in a telling oxymoron, as "the accumulated misery of being young, fair, and affluent" (I, 28) is shown to be just that, in a curious, even neurotic process of literary and ideological transvaluation. The process is by no means a necessary one, unless we consider the return to a conventional pattern of female *Bildung* in some sense psychologically necessary to the author herself. *Cecilia* begins as romance; one can imagine it continuing as such. Burney, however, perhaps cannot.

Reading through the remaining four volumes of *Cecilia*, one indeed senses Burney's ideological retreat from her initial vision of female authority. The retreat is total—and mortifying. Long though it is (even by eighteenth-century standards), the rest of the novel can in fact be reduced to a series of anecdotes of loss. Each is worse than the last: once Burney establishes the pattern of masochistic recoil, her fiction becomes increasingly compulsive in structure and morbid in its effects. It is as though Cecilia were slowly being killed off by her own creator: she is made to endure a process of degradation so intense that it culminates, in the penultimate mad scene, in a mock dissolution. Cecilia does not die in the literal sense, but she does in an imaginative one. The Heiress, if not the woman, must die. Likewise the masquerade world, with its feminocentric values, is negated. A conventional female destiny overtakes the heroine in a way that is at once inexorable and gothically alienating, for in a final horrific touch Burney makes her heroine's mock death indistinguishable from her marriage.

The collapse of the Harrels' fortune in Volume III is the first anecdote of loss, even though initially it seems to bear only an ironic relation to the heroine's story. Burney has, after all, carefully distinguished Cecilia's moral and economic values from those of her improvident guardians. How, one might ask, could her fate ever come to resemble theirs? But in one sense their disaster does have a proleptic relation to Cecilia's own history. In symbolic terms it foreshadows the infolding, or implosion, of that world of unpaid-for pleasures in which she herself has been implicated. Literally speaking, the Harrels are impresarios of the carnivalesque: the masquerade has taken place in their house. At the start of the novel their Portman Square lodging is a utopian residence where luxury and delight proliferate at no cost. Harrel simply shuts the door on creditors. This economic utopia falls apart, however, when an execution for debt is placed on their house and possessions. In a piece of baroque Grand Guignol, Harrel kills himself soon after amid the phantasmagoria of Vauxhall.

The morbid pun implicit in the concept of the execution is significant, for it intimates the demise of what might be called carnival space—the space of the feminine. The implications for the Heiress are twofold. The scene of her triumph disappears; the actual house associated with the masquerade ceases to be part of the habitable world of the fiction. Utopia, or at least this particular version of it, is now indeed nowhere. Cecilia cannot enter it again. But the Harrels' fate also introduces the profound psychological theme of repayment. Cecilia will pay, with her fortune, for the dubious privilege of enacting a merely conventional plot of heterosexual romance. But she is also paying back, as it were, for those gifts initially bestowed on her by her own creator: components of the narcissistic fantasy itself. Repayment, in the sense of compensation for the guilty wish, will become the imaginative compulsion shaping her history from this point on.

The Harrels' ruin affects Cecilia directly at one point, when she attempts to save them by lending Harrel what is in effect all of her paternal fortune. (Her legacy comes in two parts, the separate bequests of father and uncle.) After Harrel's suicide Cecilia realizes that this part of her fortune will never return to her. This loss is her first major financial reverse: she too, ironically, has begun the process of paying back. The Harrels' losses anticipate her own, and her history will grotesquely parody their economic catastrophe.

Burney soon begins to make her heroine pay in other, less obvious ways. The loan to Harrel, after all, is extorted (he has threatened suicide earlier); Cecilia's charitable donations to poor families (made under the guidance of her mysterious mentor, the semilunatic Albany) seem not to be. She engages in these benevolent projects throughout the first half of the novel. They have the status of voluntary acts: she takes "exquisite satisfaction" in relieving others from penury (III, 28). Yet in light of displaced *authorial* intentions, Cecilia's charities might be seen as enforced: they represent the theme of repayment in its morally sentimentalized form. The heroine's loss here is relative, of course, since she is still a wealthy woman, easily able to afford the luxury of good works. Only Albany, that strangely Blakean figure, thinks she should give away her entire legacy as charity. She rejects his fantastic proposal. Nevertheless, to the extent that Cecilia does begin here to divest herself of wealth, she prefigures her later act of voluntary self-impoverishment—her capitulation to the Delviles and the patriarchal economy they represent. The plot of loss disguises itself as philanthropy; a virtuous Heiress, Burney shows us, wants to give her money away.

With Cecilia's move to Delvile Castle after the death of Harrel (III, 154), the motifs of impoverishment, entrapment, and despair—signs of the morbidification of the world of the Heiress—become ubiquitous. Cecilia's worsening situation is again intimated by the spaces she must inhabit. In contrast with the Harrels' carnival mansion, Delvile Castle is a "Gothic ugly old place," a "gaol" from which "festivity, joy, and pleasure" are utterly absent (III, 155). The dilapidated and tomb-like atmosphere is perfectly suited to the familial necrophilia practiced by the prideful Delvile senior. (Burney characterizes Delvile senior's ancestor worship at one point as a fixation on "dead carcases" and "mere clay and dirt"; III, 149). It is here, fittingly enough, that Cecilia faces for the first time the devastating fact that marriage with Mortimer Delvile is impossible as long as the terms of her legacy stand. She is trapped by the "house of Delvile" both literally and emotionally.

The heroine's inevitable confrontation with the Delvile family is rendered in a series of increasingly excruciating vignettes. Delvile senior, incensed by Cecilia's love for his son—the "chief idol of his pride" (III, 162)—repeatedly humiliates and rebuffs her. Delvile himself responds histrionically to the situation, convincing himself that he must renounce Cecilia forever. Significantly, he never blames his father for making them miserable with his insufferable pretensions, but attacks Cecilia by railing against the source of her power, the legacy: "O cruel clause! barbarous and repulsive clause! that forbids my aspiring to the first of women, but by an action that with my own family could degrade me forever" (III, 244). Even Mrs. Delvile, an emotional ally earlier in the novel, sacrifices Cecilia in the face of Delvile senior's outrage. This beautiful and defeated woman sympathizes with the heroine and her son but feels psychologically compelled to reiterate her husband's inflexible opinions. She thus becomes an apologist for patriarchal principle, and in urging Cecilia to forget Delvile, merely demonstrates her own lack of power within the family group. "I come to you, then," she tells the heroine, "in the name of Mr. Delvile, and in the name of our whole family; a family as ancient as it is honourable, as honourable as it is ancient. Consider me as its representative, and hear in me its common voice, common opinion, and common address" (IV, 127). Trapped herself in a loveless marriage, Mrs. Delvile represents feminine subordination in its most poignant form, and stands as a disturbing embodiment of Cecilia's own possible future.

The interrupted marriage in Volume IV (102–19) is an example of pure gothicism, dramatizing once more the themes of denial and female anguish. It dismisses any lingering hope that

Cecilia will succeed in possessing both her lover and her inheritance. She reluctantly agrees to marry Delvile clandestinely, we recall, after he decides to break with his family: "That he should love her with so much fondness as to relinquish for her the ambitious schemes of his family, and even that darling name which so lately seemed annexed to his existence, were circumstances to which she was not insensible" (III, 321). The scene in the church that follows is melodramatic to a degree. (Which is not to say that it is unmemorable: Charlotte Brontë rewrote it in *Jane Eyre*.) A mysterious woman, later revealed as a tool of Monckton's, inexplicably calls off the marriage in the middle of the service. Cecilia is carried off in a state of shock and mortification (IV, 107). The moment is a critical one in the destiny of the Heiress: it marks the final point at which she might reconcile, however subversively, the claims of love and autonomy. Burney briefly teases us with the hope of such a reconciliation. But the symbolic impact of the scene is clear: no such subversion is possible. One cannot, in the phrase used by Roland Barthes, outplay the Father. The last utopian stratagem is doomed to fail.

Following this turn Burney's denouement has a certain bleak logic. With Mrs. Delvile's permission (though not Mr. Delvile's), Cecilia and her lover do marry in a second secret ceremony (V, 148–49). But the event is in no way joyous: indeed, it barely seems to alter the mood of the fiction at all, which remains one of claustrophobic oppressiveness. The union is apparently unconsummated, for Delvile almost immediately flees the country after wounding Monckton in a duel (V, 177). Cecilia's marriage is thus made to seem a nonmarriage, and no erotic gain counterbalances the overwhelming pattern of her losses. Even at the end of the novel, Burney gives no hint of any sexual reward for the heroine in marriage: that the union is seemingly platonic only intensifies one's sense of the painful bargain Cecilia has made. Likewise Cecilia is now officially dispossessed, for she has given up all—name and legacy—in exchange for Mrs. Delvile's consent. She immediately faces poverty; the house in which she has been living since leaving Delvile Castle is seized by the distant relation to whom her fortune now reverts, and she is cast out on the streets (V, 204). After this "ejectment" Delvile senior discovers the marriage, berates her, and refuses to help her. The work of degradation is almost complete.

She was suddenly, from being an object of envy and admiration, sunk into distress, and threatened with disgrace; from being everywhere caressed, and by every voice praised, she blushed to be seen, and expected to be censured; and from being generally regarded as an example of happiness and a model of virtue, she was now in one moment to appear to the world, an outcast from her own house, yet received into no other? a bride, unclaimed by a husband! an HEIRESS, dispossessed of all wealth! (V, 205–6)

Only the final ordeal of madness remains. Burney's narrative itself becomes somewhat unhinged at this point. The plotting in the last volume of *Cecilia* is garish and hysterical, and comes more and more to resemble sheer paranoid fantasy. Events conspire to plunge Cecilia into a state of operatic extremity. Returning from France, Delvile discovers her in conversation with their mutual friend Belfield, immediately suspects she has been unfaithful, and in a murderous rage abandons her without waiting for an explanation. She pursues him into the London streets and in a nightmarish sequence becomes lost in the labyrinth of the city. At this point she succumbs to a lunatic fit. Strangers take her into an inn, and believing her an escapee from Bedlam, confine her in a tiny room. She has amnesia; phantasms and horrors besiege her. Like Clarissa in her madness, Cecilia fantasizes her own death, imagining that her remains will "moulder" in the same coffin with those of Mr. Monckton, whom she believes killed in the duel with Delvile (V, 256). She thinks Delvile too is "massacred," and reviles her marriage to him as "a work of darkness, unacceptable, and offensive!" (V, 260). The landscape of madness modulates into that of terror and guilt—the anti-fête, the rupture, the theater of death itself.

Cecilia's madness suggests unconscious protest, and her violent outbursts read like signs of inner rage. When the distraught Delvile finally tracks her down, she regards him "with mingled terror and anger," even while appearing not to recognize him, and demands that he leave. Significantly, she cannot remember his name; she fears he will "mangle and destroy" her (V, 265). Somewhere Cecilia seems to recognize her losses, and she reacts with hatred to the man with whom they are associated. In her madness she is not a compliant victim: for the first and only time, she despises her fate.[13]

Burney does not allow this speaking delirium to last, however. The Heiress's symbolic resistance to her destiny is over almost as soon as it begins. Cecilia lapses into a comatose state resembling death. In this "insensible" condition her body is inspected by other characters. Delvile and the doctor, Lyster, obsessively watch over her; they are later joined by Henrietta Belfield and Albany, who brings a group of poor children to view the "hand-maid of charity" on her deathbed (V, 282). Cecilia is displayed as if she were already a corpse. Most important, Delvile senior, who now arrives at the inn, is transfixed at the pathetic sight of her "pale image." Stricken with remorse, he belatedly reconciles himself to his son's marriage.

This scene of perverse specularity is a parody of the Heiress's masquerade triumph earlier. Cecilia is again the object of attention, gazed at and admired by a crowd. The sickroom, as in a dream, fills with ever more observers: she has "nurses and attendants even more than sufficient, for Delvile had not relief but from calling in more help" (V, 270). But the tribute she exacts is that of a corpse. She has become an "exquisite cadaver"—the sacrificial victim, the object of an uneasily disguised collective necrophilia. Delvile senior's change of heart is particularly in keeping with the pervasive aura of morbid fixation: as a corpse, Cecilia attracts him in a way she has never attracted him before. Stilled, silent, she draws him in, and he in turn is prepared at last to admit her into his phantasmic family of the dead.[14]

To be sure, Burney does not leave her heroine in this state of pseudo-death forever. Cecilia returns to the daylight world in a chapter ambiguously titled "A Termination." She and Delvile are reunited and later reconciled with his father (V, 286). But someone, of course, has "died." Cecilia's bout of madness—the saturnalia of the psyche—is over, but so too is the rebellious, intractable reign of the Heiress. With this figurative demise,

Burney brings her retrograde plot of female disenfranchisement to its tortuous conclusion. In the moment of ambivalent recovery Cecilia is reborn—as the docile, impoverished female, stripped of power and plenitude, a sacrifice to the traditional script of female *Bildung*.

That Cecilia's mock death is also the final stage in a larger allegory of female socialization is suggested, finally, by the concluding comments of Lyster, the physician presiding over her reawakening. His is a kind of mock-therapeutic voice at the end of Burney's novel, the voice of ideology disguising itself as psychoanalysis. He offers the heroine a soothing, subtly revisionist interpretation of her own history: female lack is part of a higher natural order. The real source of her suffering, he insists, has not been Delvile arrogance—or the implacably patriarchal order it represents—but the primitive folly of her uncle, who left her an "unnaturally" encumbered legacy in the first place. In seeking to perpetuate the Beverley name in a female heir, he committed the original sin of "PRIDE AND PREJUDICE." His "arbitrary will" was an attempt to "correct the course of nature" and is itself now justly corrected (V, 303).

Burney seems to recognize briefly how appalling such mystification is. In the last pages of the novel—as though conscious her happy ending has in fact become more like a nightmare—she attempts an artificial work of reparation. An old aunt of Delvile's, previously unmentioned, is "dazzled" by Cecilia's "extraordinary sacrifice" and leaves her a fortune. The event is a blatant afterthought; we have been told throughout the novel that the Delviles have no money left, and that Delvile must marry an heiress to rebuild the family wealth. Nonetheless, Delvile is now overjoyed to "restore to her through his own family, any part of that power and independence of which her generous and pure regard for himself had deprived her" (V, 317).

The reader feels little relief. The turn is too arbitrary and false—too numbingly a piece of literature—to alter the note of despair on which *Cecilia* concludes. The heroine's final reverie is an abrupt return, without quarter, to the theme of loss. No "happiness" without "some misery," Cecilia muses at the end of her story; no "general felicity" without "partial evil." But one senses too a deep disorder of the spirit, and mourning that will never end. "She knew that, at times, the whole family must murmur at her loss of fortune, and at times she murmured herself to be thus portionless, though an HEIRESS." The utopian fantasy of the self is preserved typographically. Cecilia retains a buried sense of herself, indeed, as an HEIRESS, but the word is all she has. The last "memoir" of the Heiress, paradoxically, is the memory of having been an Heiress. The knowledge must go underground. In the novel's final sentence, Cecilia opts for the one remaining comfort of the slave—"chearfullest resignation" in the face of suffering (V, 320–21).

Suppressed in this moment of dissociation is any souvenir of the carnivalesque. I use the word here first in its most expansive sense—as the moral and philosophical topos of liberty.[15] It is difficult to connect the end of Burney's fiction with its beginning. The masquerade itself seems impossibly distant—recessed in time as well as in space—by the time we reach *Cecilia*'s last page. The zone of freedom that the masquerade represented has vanished. Instead Burney offers a scenery of constriction and imprisonment. The reader too feels confined, though in the ideological sense. For *Cecilia* is ultimately an antilibertarian fable suggesting the impossibility of individual transcendence. The symbolic order—William Godwin's "things as they are"—takes revenge on the revolutionary individual. She must accept the degrading structures of everyday life or be destroyed. Joy, liberty, the dream of being remarkable must be given up.

But Burney's story has too its compelling specificity, for the dreamer is a woman. Despite the fact that Burney's pessimism has general cultural implications (*Cecilia* could be called, in the largest sense, an anti-Jacobin fiction), one must not lose sight of this specificity. Female experience is the paradigmatic antiromance; the heroine's "entry into the world," or into the social order, the exemplary impoverishment. And therefore in the end, for all the surface excesses of the narrative, *Cecilia* tells a familiar tale. It reiterates cultural commonplace; it is a kind of dilated maxim on women's destiny. It is mythology in Barthes's sense—the "proverbial" speech that transforms history into nature, and replaces complexity and contingency with the "simplicity of essences" and an "unalterable hierarchy of the world."[16]

To be sure, the utterance remains a profoundly ambivalent one. If *Cecilia* is a proverb on Woman, it is one pronounced, oddly enough, in female accents. Patricia Meyer Spacks, one of the best modern commentators on Burney, writes of the novel's "increasingly impenetrable rhetoric"—the manner in which Burney's conflicting fantasies of self-assertion and self-deprecation drain the work of emotional and artistic coherence.[17] From the twentieth-century perspective Burney's strangest achievement in *Cecilia* is the way she seems half to endorse, half to regret, the cultural situation she represents—the implacable investment of the "world" in the plot of female subjugation.

Certainly no eighteenth-century woman novelist before Burney had uncovered so starkly the ideological contradiction in fictional marriage—that it might be represented as a punishment as much as a reward, an algebra of loss as well as gain. Later, in *Maria; or, The Wrongs of Woman* (1798), Wollstonecraft would theorize the contradiction specifically in the light of eighteenth-century women's political and economic oppression, but her novel in a sense merely adapts themes already implicit in *Cecilia*. The special poignancy of Burney's fiction is that she half-recognizes how much women give up in marriage, yet feels obliged to preserve the traditional plot of female destiny. She remains trapped in a conventional literary inscription of female experience. Marriage retains its closural narrative force: the heroine's story can have no other ending, it seems, apart from death itself. But whether marriage is really a reward, a euphoric compensation for female sufferings, has become an emotional crux. In this imaginative ambiguity one senses, paradoxically, the incipient realism—the grim embryonic verismo—of Burney's vision.

The imaginative conflict appears most strikingly, I have tried to suggest, in the ambiguous handling of the carnivalesque. Of course, one might argue that the carnivalesque generally evokes ambivalence in eighteenth-century novelists of whatever gender, and that the contradictions in Burney's treatment of the masquerade do not differ so drastically from those we have already encountered in Richardson and Fielding. True, Burney tries to circumscribe the masquerade scene in more artful ways than her male precursors: we recall the highly self-conscious Shakespearean allusion, the effort at a literary rather than simply moral or allegorical containment of the topos. But just as in *Pamela* and *Amelia*, the masquerade scene in *Cecilia* betrays a supplementary, seemingly unpremeditated function: it triggers a release of latent content. Like similar episodes in the novels of her predecessors, Burney's masquerade is a moment of discontinuity and breakthrough—the point where buried impulses erupt into expression.

Likewise this latent content can itself be characterized in universal terms. As I argued earlier, one can always generalize the unconscious appeal of the carnivalesque and see in the imagery of festivity a nostalgic collective projection of a return to infancy. A fitting emblem for this projection might be Addison's description in *Guardian* 154 of Haymarket masqueraders in the costumes of babyhood—of men "in leading-strings, seven foot high."[18] With its theoretically limitless supply of delights, masquerade license alluded to a state of primal well-being, a Golden Age of bodily satisfactions. *Et in Arcadia ego.* For men and women alike the eighteenth-century masquerade gave to certain primal sensations (which Freud would later associate with the narcissistic pleasures of infancy) a stylized kinesthetic repetition: dreams of sensuality and surfeit, of power and homage, of being massaged, as it were, by the world itself.[19]

At the same time, however, to treat the carnivalesque only as a sexually undifferentiated phenomenon is to miss an important part of its meaning. Narcissistic fantasies have a different fate in the lives of men and women; though part of the birthright of both sexes, such dreams are expressed diversely, and have a different cultural significance for men and women. The social order validates male narcissism at the expense of the female; patriarchy in fact might be described as the cultural externalization of male narcissism. It maximizes masculine political, intellectual, social, and sexual gratification; it represents a macro-economy of masculine pleasure. Within such an economy female narcissism plays an entirely peripheral part. It is typically repressed or channeled into trivialized forms such as the culturally sanctioned female arts of physical adornment and self-beautification, or it joins those lost "utopian dreams" of which Wollstonecraft speaks so movingly in the *Vindication of the Rights of Women*.[20] Culture itself, one might say, is based on a fundamental asymmetry in the realm of desire—in the degree of fulfillment accorded male and female narcissistic impulses.[21]

It is not enough, then, to characterize Burney's masquerade

32. An all-female group of masqueraders. *Dressing for a Masquerade*, by Thomas Rowlandson, 1790.

simply as a theater of desire, for it is also specifically a theater of female desire. It has a political content. It dramatizes the unfulfilled wishes for power and authority lying just under the surface of this otherwise intensely well-behaved feminine narrative. These wishes have a gender: they express the deep structure of women's fantasy life within patriarchy. What is fantasied is the derangement of the status quo—becoming captor instead of captive, Heiress instead of Woman. In Burney's revolutionary projection, one is oneself the girl of one's dreams.

Psychic recoil, however, seems inevitable. Thus the men and women in Burney's world remain trapped finally in ostensibly natural categories—an eternal, lapidary structure of dominance and submission. Utopia is nowhere, and narcissism depoliticized. The narcissism of the masquerading woman is shown to be narcissism of the familiar negative and limited kind—a mere momentary delusion, a *folie des grandeurs*. The carnivalesque, and all that it signifies, is suppressed, and its dream of liberty denied.

The recoil pattern in Burney's fiction raises interesting issues for the sociologist of literature. Might one detect signs here of a larger cultural pathology of female authorship? In *Reinventing Womanhood* Carolyn Heilbrun has suggested that female novelists of the eighteenth and nineteenth centuries are particularly likely to punish their heroines in odd ways—to cut them off from some original hope or promise—precisely as a way of compensating for their own transgressive authorial accomplishment in the traditionally masculine realm of literature. Women writers seem unwilling to grant to their heroines the same sexual or professional success they have achieved themselves; George Eliot is a striking example. The heroine's symbolic emasculation, Heilbrun suggests, may be an anagram for suppressed authorial guilt, and her dysphoric fate the mark of the woman writer's own inward, vestigial crisis of authorship.[22]

Certainly Burney—who in the preface to *Evelina* implored "Gentlemen" critics to regard her authorial "sins" with justice, if not mercy—fits the model of anxious female authorship. (Inchbald will violate the same paradigm.) What is striking in

288

Burney's work is the severity of the recoil. The pattern of her narrative contrasts profoundly with that of previous eighteenth-century masquerade novels. Richardson and Fielding begin with irony and revert to romance; the elementary structure of the wish fulfillment still has a shaping power in *Pamela* and *Amelia*. The carnivalesque retains its traditional ameliorative instrumental power, providing the mechanism by which loss gives way to gain. But Burney inverts the wish-fulfillment structure and transforms romance into irony. Granted, Cecilia meets her future husband at the masquerade, but this meeting, as we have seen, brings with it a myriad of painful consequences. For Burney the thematic and instrumental functions of the carnivalesque are thus profoundly and irrevocably at odds. The masquerade episode at once marks out the symbolic domain of the Heiress—the extent of her triumph—and instigates her fall. After this crucial, perverse turning point, the pattern of ironic metamorphosis takes over: richness turns to vacuity, pleasure to pain, life to death.

How to describe *Cecilia* finally? Like the masquerade itself, the work mediates between the psychological and the political, between private and collective meanings. One might venture a double characterization. In one sense, the novel allegorizes individual authorial conflict: its structure resembles that of the narcissistic disorder. It suggests the recoil of the self upon the self—a haunting incapacity to free oneself from the scenarios of loss, deprivation, and mourning. Yet this very syndrome might be redescribed in political terms: Burney's novel is a dystopia, the projection of failed revolutionary hopes. To borrow Wollstonecraft's phrase, it depicts that "state of degradation to which Woman is reduced." Rejecting the utopian scenes of the carnivalesque, Burney wistfully accepts this specificity; she is ultimately at home in dystopia. In the depths of her disorder Burney simultaneously reveals herself as that most painful case, the female apologist for the ancien régime.

7

Masquerade and Utopia II: Inchbald's 'A Simple Story'

Moving from Burney's novel to Elizabeth Inchbald's *A Simple Story*, one travels a great distance. Inchbald offers the reader a new terrain, a fictional world that has been utterly transformed. The difference is in part aesthetic. *Cecilia*, for all its interest, can scarcely be called an artistic success. The work is at once constricted and over-elaborate, hesitant and diffuse. Five volumes extenuate the underlying imaginative dilemma: Burney's language manages to seem both dilated and emotionally imprecise. The style of *Cecilia* is the linguistic equivalent of anomie: clichéd, bleached out, the rhetoric of enervation. Despair speaks here in the borrowed phrases of sentimental fiction; repetition has become a verbal as well as psychological syndrome. Burney's familiar plot takes shape, fittingly, in a language of ennui, replete with tics and backtracking.

Inchbald's novel, by contrast, is a tour de force—a small masterpiece neglected far too long. Without exaggeration the case might be made for *A Simple Story* as the most elegant English fiction of the century. (And one need not exclude any of Sterne here.) The emotional exactitude, the subtlety of imaginative statement, make it one of the finest novels of any period. Inchbald shares the profound interiority of Jane Austen and Henry James; hers is also a world of the utmost intelligence and wit. Yet here too, paradoxically, is the same freedom—the exquisite extremism—one associates with Emily Brontë. *Wuthering Heights* may be the work *A Simple Story* most anticipates, not only because of the similar double narrative structure (each fiction takes place over two generations), but because of the way Inchbald succeeds in communicating, with startling economy, reserves of the most intense feeling. Inchbald's modern editor, J. M. S. Tompkins, matches the spare, beautiful idiom of her subject when she notes that *A Simple Story* "had . . . for its generation, and still has for readers who can learn its language, an overpowering sense of reality."[1]

The differences between Burney and Inchbald are biographical as well as aesthetic. In contrast with Burney's polite fiction-making, sudden fame, and entry into literary and court circles, Inchbald's somewhat raffish theatrical career, as well as her Catholicism and her Jacobin sympathies, set her apart from many contemporaries. James Boaden's *Memoirs of Mrs. Inchbald* (1833) attractively summarizes her exploits, which included associations with Godwin's circle, theatrical love affairs, and at a masquerade in 1781, a notorious appearance dressed as a man. Boaden asserts that many of the "frolics" of Inchbald's heroine, Miss Milner, including the masquerade that figures so subtly in *A Simple Story*, had their origin in Inchbald's own sometimes daredevil career.[2]

The contrast extends to the two novelists' reputations. In comparison with Burney, Inchbald is usually treated as a strictly minor literary figure; she has received none of that moderate yet continuous critical scrutiny accorded the author of *Evelina*. Readers are more likely to recall that one of Inchbald's plays, *Lovers' Vows* (1798), is featured discreditably in *Mansfield Park* than they are to have read either her drama or her fiction. *A Simple Story* itself has had an obscure literary half-life; though it has always had admirers (from Mrs. Edgeworth to Lytton Strachey), it has never been a part of the canon of indispensable eighteenth-century texts. Like its witty, intractable protagonist, the novel has preserved a certain renegade status, but has hardly been well known.[3]

It is tempting to speculate that some of this neglect may be due to Inchbald's sardonic rendering, verging on parody, of a conventional world of eighteenth-century literary representation. Hers is not a vision that flatters the symbolic order. This impatience with "things as they are" lends her fiction, even now, a certain ideological illegibility. We do not yet know, perhaps, how to read her fully, for *A Simple Story* is a restlessly anti-authoritarian, even avant-garde work. It insistently satirizes conventionality, self-restriction, physical and psychic inhibition—the morbid state, in Freudian terms, of civilization itself. Much of the power of the novel lies in its dramatization of liberation from the restraints imposed by culture. Inchbald's is a world in which impulses toward contact—starting with those of the body itself—triumph over taboo. Ordinary gestures have a marvelous affective power here; they dismantle internalized structures of alienation. Human longings find an answer; human needs confound and circumvent sclerotic patterns of decorum and politesse. It is debatable whether the twentieth century, the most frightening epoch of alienation to date, is any better equipped than the eighteenth to confront Inchbald's radical vision of consummation.

But the libertarian impulse has too its specifically feminist dimension, for this is a world, above all, of female gratification. What Burney can only intimate, in a disjunctive episode of pleasure later abjured, is at the heart of Inchbald's fiction. *Cecilia* remains legible in an ideological sense; for all its impacted moral anguish, it validates the familiar cultural and literary themes of female *Bildung*. But *A Simple Story* offers an unfamiliar image of female plot. Here the heroine's desires repeatedly triumph over masculine prerogative; familial, religious, and psychic patterns of male domination collapse in the face of her persistent will to liberty. In both a social and a literary sense, Miss Milner (the first and most potent of *A Simple Story*'s two heroines) could be said to embody an unprecedented feminine destiny. She is never, to borrow a word from *Clarissa*, successfully "enwomaned."

She escapes that symbolic emasculation Simone de Beauvoir has identified with the process of being made female in patriarchal society.[4]

The mysterious last words of Inchbald's fiction sum it up. There, as though by way of explanation for her remarkable tale, Inchbald acknowledges that Miss Milner never received

A PROPER EDUCATION

The words are set off in the text like a strange, incomprehensible charm. They call attention to precisely what has been absent from the start—any prescriptive rendering of female socialization. One is not surprised to learn of Inchbald's associations with Mary Wollstonecraft, for *A Simple Story* sometimes reads like a fantastic, exuberant transformation of the *Vindication*. Even the traces of Wollstonecraft's occasional self-pity have been removed. This story of failed "education" is also a lyrical assault, a rhapsody of transgression, in which masculine authority is insistently demystified, female aspiration rewarded, and the conventional world of eighteenth-century representation transformed in consequence.

If I seem to describe a carnivalized fictional landscape, that is precisely my intention. Inchbald's novel has, indeed, its requisite masquerade scene: like her contemporaries Inchbald turns at a compelling moment in her fiction to the conventional topos of liberty. Given her political sympathies, one might anticipate this gravitation toward the imagery of reversal. What is perhaps unexpected, however, is the transformation she works upon it, for in one important sense—the instrumental—the episode seems no longer strictly necessary. Literally speaking, Inchbald's masquerade scene is barely a scene at all. She presents nothing in the way of conventional masquerade spectacle—indeed, her "set piece" is over in a sentence or two. Likewise, in contrast with Fielding's or even Burney's use of the topos, the masquerade in *A Simple Story* generates little intrigue to speak of—no theatrical structure of enigma and revelation—though it will prompt the final ethical and psychological confrontation between Miss Milner and her fiancé, Dorriforth.

Inchbald has a less pressing need for the externalized scenery of transgression because the pattern of her narrative is already powerfully transgressive. The fictional world itself globalizes carnivalesque impulses. One of the paradoxes of *A Simple Story* is that it shows us the traditional imagery of scandal on its way toward obsolescence: a minimalist carnivalesque. Inchbald does not turn to the set piece for instrumental purposes, for she no longer needs its hidden mediation. The subversive technical functions served by such scenes in Richardson, Fielding, and Burney are in Inchbald's novel implicit in the narrative as a whole. She renders transgression directly; it is the very essence of her plot. Likewise, ordinary life, rather than the colored crystal of the masquerade, has become the supercharged site of pathos, liberty, and delight.

What, then, is the meaning of the scene? Inchbald invokes the masquerade quite explicitly as an emblem of liberation. This, for the first time in eighteenth-century English fiction, is a politicized carnivalesque, a consciously utopian image—the signature, if not the instrument, of an incorrigibly feminist plot. Like the rape of Clarissa (though bearing an entirely different emotional weight), Inchbald's masquerade could be called an abstract vignette: it pervades the text in which it is not, strictly speaking, represented. Like an object in a dream one cannot quite see yet knows is there, it condenses the radical concerns of Inchbald's fiction.

I have already intimated the nature of these concerns: *A Simple Story* is a story of law and its violation. It is about the breaking of vows, the crossing of boundaries, the reversal of prohibitions. The rhythm of the fiction is repetitive without seeming repetitious. Each half of the novel is structured as a chain of violations. The pattern of rebellion is linked to the struggle for power between men and women: the law is masculine, the will that opposes feminine. In the first half of the novel, Dorriforth, the somber guardian and priest, gradually gives way to the ardor and yearning for intimacy of his ward, Miss Milner; in the second half, in his new incarnation as Lord Elmwood, the embittered widower and father, he yields again, this time to the poignant emotional pleas of his daughter Matilda, whom he has earlier banished from his sight.* Patriarchal injunctions—against passion, connection, presence—are repeatedly overturned.

Female energy, in Inchbald's vision, has the power to transform space. Her fictional landscape is always initially organized according to a repressive masculine logic of permitted and proscribed zones. The reader of *A Simple Story* cannot help recalling, for example, the Bluebeard-like manner in which Dorriforth, in both sections of the novel, subdivides the physical world and forbids his female ward entry into certain tabooed spaces. To penetrate the proscribed realm, for the woman, is to risk separation from the beloved other—a physical and existential alienation of the most extreme kind. In the first half of the novel, the masquerade is the primary forbidden zone. Dorriforth will threaten to leave Miss Milner "forever" if she attends this event against his will. In the second half the forbidden zone shifts indoors and becomes part of the domestic scene. Matilda cannot enter the rooms in her father's country house, which he inhabits himself, or come into his sight; if she does, she will forfeit his invisible protection and be "debarred" from him forever (p. 213).

The irony, however, is that threatened punishments are never executed—or at least never completely executed—in Inchbald's imaginative world. Transgressions take place, for whether by accident or design, the heroine always goes where she is not supposed to. But the violation of masculine law results, not in the expected separation, but in the collapse, the voiding, of proscription itself. Banishment is transformed, at the last minute, into ecstatic, extra-logical union. The system of safe and forbidden zones, the symbolic articulation of space (which one might take as Inchbald's paradigmatic externalization of patriarchal oppression) falls away in the face of female passion and will. The result is utopian—a physical order without negativity, a realm of ideal freedom.

*The February 1791 edition of *A Simple Story* appeared in four volumes. Throughout this chapter I speak loosely of the first and second halves of the novel: the story of Miss Milner occupied the first two volumes in the original edition; the story of Matilda the second two. The page citations in this chapter, however, refer to the Oxford edition (1967), which was based on the 1791 edition but published in a single volume.

Granted, this structure of taboo and violation, masculine proscription and feminine transgression, could conceivably coexist
with a more conventional treatment of the carnivalesque if Inchbald's heroine were a different sort of character. The reification
of the masquerade as a forbidden zone is after all nothing new in
eighteenth-century fiction, and Dorriforth's injunction against
the event is entirely in keeping with conventional moral pro-
nouncements on the subject. Ordinary eighteenth-century heroines guarantee their integrity by what might be called their
nonvolitional relationship to their masquerade adventures. Pamela and Amelia are forced to go to masquerades by indiscreet
husbands, though Amelia escapes with a ruse; Cecilia is swept
up in the occasion, but again not exactly of her own free will.
Cecilia does not go to the masquerade; it comes to her, when
her guardians transform their house into an assembly room.
Technically speaking, the virtuous heroine avoids the taboo zone
of the carnivalesque, though she does, as though by accident,
end up in it.

The result of such passive trespass, as we have seen, is almost
always comic and almost always linked to the plot of heterosexual romance. One may find a lover (*Cecilia, Sir Charles Grandison*); or an earlier erotic union may be repeated in displaced
form (*Pamela, Amelia*). Whatever difficulties emerge from the
unwilled violation of masculine norms also create a core of narrative interest and carry the novel toward its conclusion. The
naturalization of the heroine's carnivalesque union with her
lover—her *amor impossibilia*—is typically the essential problem
masquerade fiction seeks to resolve.*

The first point to be made about Inchbald's masquerade, however, is that not only is the heroine's relation to it not passive,

---

*Parodic forms of the masquerade *amor impossibilia* appear in *Roxana* (Roxana's
briefly scandalous liaison with the "Duke of M——"), *Tom Jones* (the relationship of
Lady Bellaston and Jones), and *Memoirs of a Woman of Pleasure* (the sexual encounter between the prostitute Emily and a homosexual). Each of these sets of relations mimics the
improper coupling motif found elsewhere in eighteenth-century masquerade fiction yet
avoids the conventional sentimental pathos and lengthy extenuation associated with it in
a work like *Cecilia*. The social, economic, and libidinal incongruities represented in
these three episodes are only cynically and temporarily resolved, and narrative closure
comes by other means.

but the episode seems to play no catalytic part in the romance plot of the novel at all. This plot—an extremely indecorous one—has already arrived at a point of apparent closure before the masquerade takes place, near the end of the first half. We recollect the situation. Miss Milner, the beautiful, vivacious heiress, has fallen in love with her guardian, the dignified and austere young Jesuit priest Dorriforth, in whose household she has been residing since the death of her father. After a period of secret infatuation Miss Milner reveals her love to Miss Woodley, her spinster companion, who at first opposes the scandalous attachment. But the fortuitous death of Dorriforth's cousin, Lord Elmwood, suddenly makes Dorriforth the new heir, and necessitates that he give up his priestly vows and marry. After a series of complications (including a period of separation during which Miss Milner attempts to let go of her desire), Miss Woodley informs Dorriforth of Miss Milner's love for him. In a scene of remarkable, restrained emotional intensity, he discovers his own suppressed passion for Miss Milner and is subsequently swiftly and rapturously engaged to her.

What such a summary (which accounts, roughly, for only the first third of the novel) leaves out is the sustained erotic tension, the frisson at the heart of Inchbald's psychological drama. (A similar tension is present in the second half of the novel, though in perhaps even more elemental form, deriving as it does from the charged Oedipal attachment between Dorriforth/Elmwood and his daughter.) Much of this tension grows out of the reader's persistent sense of obstacle—of the overwhelming ethical and psychic obstructions impeding the union of Miss Milner and her guardian. The heroine's passion thrives on, indeed at times seems indistinguishable from, the barriers she faces: hers is a transgressive liaison par excellence.

Yet it is precisely this tension that Inchbald establishes without the mediation of the conventional turn into the carnivalesque. She needs no episode, no moment of fugue or phantasmagoria, to prompt the plot of subversive desire. Instead, she takes this plot as a given, identifying Miss Milner from the start—the moment of her arrival in Dorriforth's house—with the impulses of inappropriate longing. In Inchbald's most radical break with fictional convention, character itself provides the impetus for the *amor impossibilia*. Thus we learn that Miss Milner is beautiful and self-indulgent, possessed of a "quick sensibility," yet prone to "vanity" and "an inordinate desire of admiration." She has "acquired the dangerous character of a wit" and revels in insouciance (15). Yet she possesses too a capacity for deeper response, an imaginative connection with the world that coexists, in the words of one character, in a kind of "intricate incoherence" with her love of the merely delightful. Despite an "immoderate enjoyment of the art of pleasing, for her own individual happiness, and not for the happiness of others," Miss Milner has too a kind of problematic, heartbreaking sweetness: "Still had she a heart inclined, and oftentimes affected by tendencies less unworthy; but those approaches to what was estimable, were generally arrested in their first impulse by some darling folly" (19). This devastating combination of attributes makes her a disruptive force from the beginning—the "stranger in the house" (in Tony Tanner's evocative phrase) who will bring both ecstasy and chaos into the lives of her hosts. After meeting Miss Milner for the first time, Sandford, the irascible older priest who is Dorriforth's spiritual adviser and tutor, instantly condemns her as "incorrigible" and advises that a "proper match" be found for her immediately and "the care of so dangerous a person given into other hands" (42).

By psychologizing the transgressive impulse, turning it inward and rendering it part of her heroine's passionate nature, Inchbald makes it part of the scenery of everyday life. It ceases to be the function of any discontinuous or dreamlike "Evening's Intrigue." Everything follows, instead, from Miss Milner herself. She embodies sexual energy in a house of celibates, disturbing—sometimes farcically—that polite *ménage à quatre* composed of the two sober priests, Dorriforth and Sandford, and two pious "unseductive innocent females," the landlady (Mrs. Horton) and Miss Woodley (7). But Miss Milner also embodies an inchoate political energy—a spirit of anti-authoritarianism. She is no respecter of petty tyrants; her supper-table skirmishes with the blimpish Sandford (who baits her sadistically while at the same time pretending to ignore her presence) are models of particular daring:

> "There are very different kinds of women," (answered Sandford, directing his discourse to Mrs. Horton,) "there is as much difference between some women, as between good and evil spirits."
> Lord Elmwood asked Miss Milner again—if she took an airing?
> She replied, "No."
> "And beauty," continued Sandford, "when endowed upon spirits that are evil, is a mark of their greater, their more extreme wickedness.—Lucifer was the most beautiful of all the angels in paradise—"
> "How do you know?" said Miss Milner. (117)

But by far and away the most important aspect of Miss Milner's character is her yearning, intractable and unerring, for that which is taboo. She longs, as though by reflex, for that which is denied her, banned by convention, edict, or scruple. She is undoubtedly capricious and often desires what is forbidden precisely because it is forbidden. She exemplifies what Georges Bataille calls the "absurd proposition" at the heart of desire— that "the forbidden is there to be violated."[5] "Monastic vows, like those of marriage," Miss Milner overhears someone remark early in the novel, "were made to be broken" (21).

Miss Milner's passion for Dorriforth is illicit on several counts. He is a Catholic priest, bound to vows of chastity, and thus in social terms an obviously unsuitable love object. But her attachment also could be said to violate literary convention. The attraction she feels for the man who is also her legal guardian represents one of Inchbald's characteristic breaks with ordinary novelistic decorum. The guardian/ward relationship is typically a sacrosanct one in English fiction of the period—sentimental in form and nonsexual in nature. The exclusively noneroticized nature of this particular male/female bond is usually marked symbolically by an age difference or the marital status of the guardian. No one expects, for example, the aged Mr. Villars in Burney's *Evelina* to fall in love with the heroine, or she with him; theirs is a purely familial attachment. Likewise, in *Cecilia*, none of Cecilia's three guardians, Harrel, Delvile senior, and Briggs, represents a sexual possibility; each is married or elderly, or both. To imagine an eroticization of the guardian/ward bond, in English literature at least, is to diverge abruptly into the realms of pornography and burlesque; one thinks of certain perverse situations in Cleland, or that obscene relationship depicted, in the next century, in the anonymous pornographic novel *Rosa Fielding: A Victim of Lust* (1876). The guardian/ward relationship of the Lord Chancellor and Phyllis in Gilbert and Sullivan's *Iolanthe* is merely ludicrous. On the rare occasion when such a relationship does become a serious possibility, as in *Bleak House*, between Esther and Jarndyce, it is invariably neutralized as soon as possible.[6]

The situation is different in French writing. There the guardian/ward bond has always been treated more ambiguously, and its subversive narrative possibilities explored. The eroticized relation between M. de Climal and the heroine in Marivaux's *La Vie de Marianne* (1731) set a precedent for eighteenth-century French literature; Laclos and Rousseau offered variations on the theme later in the period. The point is worth making because it suggests something about Inchbald's characteristically "un-English" imaginative concerns. What Lytton Strachey referred to as her "French" manner might indeed be traced to her interest in the transgressive erotic pattern per se. She is far more at home in a tradition that includes Prévost, Rousseau, Stendhal, Flaubert, and Proust, finally, than that of English sentimental fiction, with its heavily didactic emphasis and more indirect representations of sexual desire.

The influence of Rousseau is particularly striking. The charged guardian/ward relationship in *A Simple Story* at times resembles the teacher/pupil dyad of Saint-Preux and Julie in *La Nouvelle Héloïse*; Abelard and Heloise provide the larger intertextual link. One is not surprised to find Inchbald invoking these exemplary French lovers early on in her novel. During a conversation with the heroine and her guardian, after Miss Milner laughs at a pleasantry made by Dorriforth, the jealous rake Lord Frederick Lawnley interjects a sneering Popean reference:

> From Abelard it came,
> And Heloisa still must love the name. (22)

Miss Milner instantly recognizes the hidden aptness of the quotation and has to hold her head out a window "to conceal the embarrassment these lines had occasioned." In his oblivion Dorriforth, however, is untouched. "Whether from inattention to the quotation, or from a consciousness it was wholly inapplicable, [he] heard it without one emotion of shame or of anger" (22).

If Miss Milner is aware, in some sense, of the Frenchness of her passion, no one else in the fictional world is—not at first. She is indeed like a character from a French novel who has strayed by accident into an English one. Without her, Dorriforth's placid household might seem to foreshadow a host of comic vicarages in later English fiction, from Trollope to Barbara Pym. (The Catholic element is unusual, but Inchbald gives even this a distinctly unsensational cast.) Miss Milner disturbs the familiar microcosm. She embodies literary as well as social discontinuity, from which Inchbald draws a range of comic and pathetic effects.

No one knows how to read Miss Milner. Dorriforth certainly cannot, nor can he imagine any way of apprehending their relationship other than as a version of the familiar guardian/ward bond. He comports himself toward her at first as though he too were a character in a novel—the personification of the good paternal guardian. He sees his own role in purely conventional terms: to arrange a marriage for her with some suitable person. Yet she remains an oddly disturbing charge. Dorriforth is distressed by those aspects of her character that violate the literary paradigm he knows—her propensity for the frivolous, her inability to commit herself to any serious ties (she unaccountably breaks off an engagement to Lord Frederick Lawnley), her disquieting erotic power. She is hardly a self-effacing Burney heroine. In the first part of the novel, he is repeatedly oppressed by feelings of responsibility for her that he does not yet recognize—and has no way of interpreting—as desire.

Miss Woodley likewise misreads her wildly, but as the heroine in a sentimental romance. Thus when Miss Milner becomes melancholy, Miss Woodley immediately assumes that she must be in love with Lord Frederick, the feckless peer who has fought a duel on her behalf. Miss Woodley's misdirected diagnosis of Miss Milner's case is an epitome of vulgarity: "'Her senses have been captivated by the person and accomplishments of Lord Frederick,' said Miss Woodley to herself, 'while her understanding beholds his faults, and reproaches her passion—and, oh!' cried she, 'could her guardian and Mr. Sandford know of this conflict, how much more would they have to admire than condemn!'" (46).

Of course, Miss Woodley's banal fantasy of troubled passion in no way matches the scandal of Miss Milner's real attachment. Miss Milner's ringing confession, proffered "with a degree of madness in her looks," that she loves her guardian—"with all the passion of a mistress, and with all the tenderness of a wife"—leaves Miss Woodley aghast, as though witness to an act of sacrilege. For Miss Woodley, "the violation of oaths, persons, or things consecrated to Heaven, was, in her opinion, if not the most enormous, the most horrid of crimes" (73). She attributes her friend's monstrous passion to the failings of her Protestant education: "Had she been early taught what were the sacred functions of a Roman ecclesiastic, though all her esteem, all her admiration, had been attracted by the qualities and accomplishments of her guardian; yet education would have given such a prohibition to her love, that she had been precluded from it, as by that barrier which divides brother and sister" (74). Miss Milner lacks a sense of taboo; her love for Dorriforth is equivalent, in Miss Woodley's eyes, to incest.

Miss Woodley prescribes drastic measures, installing herself as a belated voice of moral decorum. Miss Milner will go to Bath and purge herself of her passion. The necessary "barrier" between Miss Milner and Dorriforth will be restored geographically if not emotionally. "You *shall part*," Miss Woodley admonishes, frightening her friend with dreadful images of Dorriforth's reaction, should he discover her love: "What astonishment! what confusion! what remorse, do I foresee painted on his face!—I hear him call you by the harshest names, and behold him fly from your sight forever, as an object of his detestation" (88–89). One way or another, banishment and loss, she argues, represent the life of the future.

Just at this point, however, the point of maximum difficulty and estrangement (for Miss Milner does go to Bath, and falls abruptly into an agony of despair), Inchbald's narrative turns inside out and moves toward an unexpected, temporarily euphoric closure. The news of Dorriforth's inheritance and release from priestly vows comes to Miss Milner at Bath, and instantly provides her with a sense of enthralling, even sublime anticipation: "she felt, while every word was speaking, a chill through all her veins—it was a pleasure too exquisite, not to bear along with it the sensation of exquisite pain" (102).

One last obstacle obtrudes, however. The new Lord Elmwood, still unapprised of his ward's love, seems likely to marry Miss Fenton, a neighborhood heiress. Miss Woodley—now, like an ambiguous character in a folktale, on the side of Miss Milner and vicariously caught up in her friend's passion—wonders briefly if Miss Milner should not just marry Lord Frederick, to save herself needless suffering. This final crisis, soon resolved, is nonetheless significant because it prompts the heroine to articulate her most compelling manifesto of passion to date— a theory, in fact, of transgressive desire. Miss Milner's unselfconscious celebration of the forbidden object is unprecedented in polite English fiction: "What, love a rake," she exclaims, "a man of professed gallantry? impossible.—To me, a common rake is as odious, as a common prostitute is to a man of the nicest feelings.—Where can be the pride of inspiring a passion, fifty others can equally inspire? Or the transport of bestowing favours, where the appetite is already cloyed by fruition of the self-same enjoyments?" (120). When Miss Woodley is shocked, Miss Milner, in a grandiloquent flurry, offers a thrilling credo: "My dear Miss Woodley . . . put in competition the languid love of a debauchee, with the vivid affection of a sober man, and judge which has the dominion? Oh! in my calendar of love, a solemn lord chief justice, or a devout archbishop ranks before a licentious king" (120).

We detect again the Rousseauian note: like Rousseau, Inchbald offers an aestheticization of instinct, a civilization of eros, that seems inescapably modern.[7] We might agree with Miss Woodley's tactful observation later, when she finally discloses her friend's love to Lord Elmwood, that "Miss Milner's taste is not a depraved one; it is but too much refined" (129). But Miss Milner's remarkable declaration may also bring to mind the characteristic formulations of an even more notorious contemporary. It might seem odd at first glance to juxtapose Inchbald with the Marquis de Sade, but her conceptualization of the erotic has a strange kinship with the subversive projections of the consummate *encyclopédiste* of the perverse. (*A Simple Story* appeared in the same year as *Justine*.) In Inchbald too, the forbidden is sought—and found—over and over again. Desire constructs itself in relation to an endlessly self-extending set of prohibitions; there is always another "sober man," another proscribed object or activity to spur passion. With its intimations of a repetitive, continuously renewable desire, Miss Milner's "calendar of love" bears more than a passing likeness to pornographic almanacs like *The 120 Days of Sodom* (1785). We are in a realm of potentially infinite gratification, a Fibonacci series of pleasurable violations.

Inchbald's heroine dreams of carnivalesque ends—metamorphosis, scandal, euphoria—without the carnival. And paradoxically enough, she achieves them. After Miss Woodley's timely hints (125–31), the new Lord Elmwood recognizes that he himself is the unknown lover for whom the heroine yearns: "Again he searched his own thoughts, nor ineffectually as before.—At the first glance the object was presented, and he beheld *himself*" (130). The *amor impossibilia* is miraculously redeemed: in a transport of passion, the former priest becomes Miss Milner's "profest lover." The house of celibacy is likewise transformed: after the lovers' betrothal (a scene that Inchbald with typically Jamesian delicacy omits), "every thing and every person wore a new face" (136). _____

As Inchbald's last image suggests, this could indeed be called a masquerade story without the masquerade. The narrative situation bears a displaced resemblance to the popular eighteenth-

century masquerade fantasy of the *parodia sacra*, in which priests
and cardinals turned out to be libertines in disguise, and "Sweet
Devotees" the harlots of Drury Lane. The comic idea implicit in
ecclesiastical travesty was that repression could transform itself,
in an instant, into concupiscence, and sacred personages behave
as licentiously as anyone else. Dorriforth's transformation from
priest to lover is at least metaphorically analogous. Granted,
Dorriforth hardly fits the stereotype of the secretly lustful
cleric; he has only the most attenuated kinship with a wholly
parodic character, say, like Ambrosio in Lewis's *The Monk*. For a
long time Dorriforth's sexual desire is entirely unconscious; he
has no hidden designs upon his ward. But he does undergo a
gradual transformation of sensibility—a kind of sentimental
education—that one might take as the psychological equivalent
of carnivalesque transformation. Perhaps it is not surprising, in
this novel of failed female education, that Inchbald's male characters should be insistently reeducated in just this way: that they
learn to forgo austerity and emotional detachment for a new life
of passion and adhesiveness. Dorriforth must yield, as it were,
to the impure power of eros. Thus he enacts the familiar story of
metamorphosis—from chastity to sexuality, from celibate to
lover. He becomes a kind of carnivalesque icon in the novel, a
mediator between socioerotic categories.[8]

Yet it is right here, after the carnivalesque union of Miss
Milner and Dorriforth has apparently already been accomplished, that Inchbald invokes the masquerade topos: the very
point at which such a turn must seem most irrelevant and threatening. Still "lost in the maze of happiness that surrounded her,"
Miss Milner receives a masquerade invitation from "Mrs.
G——" (151). Everything seems back to front; the pattern of
normal eighteenth-century narrative development seems inverted. We seem to move into dangerously uncharted psychological
waters. Given Miss Milner's intractable mixture of love and
wildness, one cannot help fearing the worst. Indeed, the episode
promises at first to be the most damaging revelation to date of
the heroine's idiosyncratic character—an epitome of the "intricate incoherence" that defines her nature.

Inchbald prepares us for just such a limited, almost clinical psychological demonstration. We learn, for example, that Miss Milner's pride, incorrigibility, and love of the taboo have not vanished as a result of her engagement; rather, the very complacency of her happy new condition seems to have intensified her restiveness. Even before the chance to go to a masquerade presents itself, she is building up to new heights of perversity. Disregarding Dorriforth's commands, she renews her "fashionable levities," begins keeping late hours, and runs up bills for "toys that were out of fashion before they were paid for" (139). Like a child she insistently tests the limits of her lover's patience. Dorriforth, it must be said, at first finds something fascinating in the situation. "Blinded by his passion," he is intrigued by the novelty of finding his ward, who had "ever been gentle," transformed into "a mistress, sometimes haughty; and to opposition, always insolent." Miss Milner is "charmed to see his love struggling with his censure—his politeness with his anxiety" (139). Yet the reader has a sense of escalating emotional danger. In an aside to Sandford (who remains resolute in his dislike of the heroine), Dorriforth articulates the basic threat of the narrative—that should Miss Milner continue to challenge his authority over her, he will decide whether to marry her after all "or—*banish me from her forever*" (142).

On some level it is just such a threat, and the renewal of obstacles to passion, that Miss Milner courts. Bored with satisfaction, she interrogates her "flattering" heart in ever more provocative ways: "Are not my charms" she muses, "even more invincible than I ever believed them to be? Dorriforth, the grave, the sanctified, the anchorite Dorriforth, by their force is animated to all the ardour of the most impassioned lover—while the proud priest, the austere guardian, is humbled, if I but frown, into the veriest slave of love" (138). Miss Milner wonders if her lover's devotion would survive "ill treatment." "If it would not," she concludes, "he still does not love me as I wish to be loved" (138).

Inchbald does not sentimentalize this desire at all; indeed, she takes the risk that some of her readers will, like Sandford, lose all patience with the heroine and condemn her yearnings as simply obnoxious. Certainly Miss Milner might be viewed in conventional moral terms as an example of unprincipled hedonism: she wishes for an "enhanced" erotic pleasure, founded upon the domination of her lover (138). While affirming that her heroine's fantasies of power remain "mere phantoms of the brain," never "by system put into action," the narrator also allows that "repeatedly indulged, they were practised by casual occurrences; and the dear-bought experiment of being beloved in spite of her faults, (a glory proud women ever aspire to) was, at present, the ambition of Miss Milner" (138).

At the same time, however, one cannot escape a sense of the deeper sexual and ideological struggle here shaping itself between Inchbald's characters. For all her faults, Miss Milner never loses the reader's sympathy. Her sensitivity invariably redeems her, while her spirit animates an otherwise intensely repressive domestic scene. Inchbald herself seems to understand her heroine's narcissism and how it compensates for a lack of any real power within the fictional world. For Miss Milner is invariably treated as a child by those around her. Seen objectively, her frivolity can be described as understandable frustration in the face of unjust social restraint, while her need for independence is simply that of any psychologically viable adult. It is not clear that the wish to be "beloved in spite of her faults" is a sin—or, the ironic aside on "proud women" notwithstanding, that her creator means us to see it so. Dorriforth is in every respect a far more prideful character: rigid in opinion, priggish, and self-absorbed; his portrait verges everywhere on the satiric. He, just as much as his fiancée, seeks power and dominance; the only difference is that his narcissism is veiled by a mantle of patriarchal prestige. He assumes obedience as his unquestioned right, and like a threatened despot, grimly contemplates his future with an unpacified Miss Milner: "the horror of domestic wrangles—a family without subordination—a house without oeconomy—in a word, a wife without discretion, had been perpetually present to his mind" (142). In this paradigm of patriarchal analysis, order depends, quite baldly, on the subordination of female subjects.

Such passages remind us that the conflict between the heroine and her lover is, after all, a political as well as psychological one. Inchbald seems to intuit the historic implications of the sexual antagonism she delineates here. Indeed, from the twentieth-century perspective her characters resemble nothing less than exemplary figures—representative opponents in a new and unprecedented cultural struggle. Their dispute anticipates that moral, legal, and psychic conflict, repeatedly enacted in Western civilization from the late eighteenth century on, between entrenched masculine authority and aggressive female aspiration.*

Of course, Inchbald does not make it clear at the start how this ideological conflict will work itself out, or indeed on which side—Dorriforth's or Miss Milner's—her own imaginative investment will ultimately be made. The turn toward the carnival-esque, as usual in eighteenth-century fiction, seems merely ominous at first, particularly when the narrator offers the following peculiar and seemingly proleptic warning: "In the various, though delicate, struggles for power between Miss Milner and her guardian, there was not one person witness to these incidents, who did not suppose, all would at last end in wedlock—for the most common observer perceived, ardent love was the foundation of every discontent, as well as of every joy they experienced.—One great incident, however, totally reversed the prospect of all future accommodation" (151).

The fiction seems to promise nothing but reversal—the catastrophic undoing of the plot of heterosexual romance. Miss Milner has received her tickets for the masked ball at the house of "the fashionable Mrs. G——" with "ecstasy" and set her mind to go (151). Dorriforth predictably forbids her to attend. The emotional stakes are instantly raised. Miss Milner says flatly, "she should certainly go," while Dorriforth retreats into a state of incommunicative sorrow and anger, outraged that she should "persist, coolly and deliberately in so direct a contradic-

---

*That Inchbald's imagination tends toward the kind of dichotomizing or emblematic oppositions I mention here—a sort of binary patterning—is borne out by the title and narrative structure of her subsequent novel *Nature and Art* (1796), the story of the contrasting sensibilities of two brothers and their equally dissimilar sons.

tion to his will" (155). His previous threat to end their engagement hangs implicitly in the air. Yet he also holds on to the belief that she will not really go, and as though to test her, absents himself from the house on the evening of the masquerade. Immediately Miss Milner leaves for Mrs. G——'s, in the company of the excited Miss Woodley (156).

The moment is without parallel in serious eighteenth-century fiction. This is hardly passive trespass. No other contemporary heroine, not even Defoe's Roxana, chooses her masquerade adventure in quite this way, with such premeditation and daring. Here is the great "proof" Miss Milner has hoped for—the critical event that will clarify the extent of her power. As she tells Miss Woodley, "As my guardian, I certainly did obey him; and I could obey him as a husband; but as a lover, I will not" (154). The "old sentiments"—her odd, strangely heroic love of liberty and risk—inexorably impel her toward the world of the masquerade, despite the tragic alienation it threatens to produce. The occasion has become a casus belli. "If he will not submit to be my lover," she exclaims proudly, "I will not submit to be his wife— nor has he the affection I require in a husband" (154).

The scene stands out as the most self-consciously politicized invocation of the carnivalesque in eighteenth-century literature. As a narrative event Inchbald's masquerade has only one real purpose: to disclose relations of power, of dominance and submission. More than in any previous work it emerges as an explicitly symbolic domain, a ground of power over which masculine will and feminine desire contend. Dorriforth is the first to encode the event in this manner; by defining the masquerade as a forbidden zone, he makes it over into a rhetorical occasion. Significantly, he gives no reason why the masquerade should be off-limits to the heroine; unlike, say, Dr. Harrison in *Amelia*, he has no moral rationale, no didactic gloss upon the occasion to justify his injunction. Its sole importance for him, it seems, is as an abstract topic upon which he can express his authority. He is in love with the basic gesture of power—what Elias Canetti has called the gratifying, irrational "sting of command."[9]

In turn Miss Milner apprehends that the masquerade somehow embodies her freedom. In one sense it does not matter what
the occasion is, in and of itself. Simply to go there has meaning
enough. The masquerade has in a sense become pure gesture. It
signifies the reassertion of autonomy, the countermanding of
patriarchal whim. For the rebellious heroine, it is the way she
takes charge of her destiny, however dire the consequences.

Paradoxically, this thematic transparency seems to render any
conventional depiction of the masquerade unnecessary. For the
first time Inchbald puts its ideological content uncompromis-
ingly on view. But the spectacle itself becomes peculiarly irrelevant after such a demonstration; indeed it seems hardly to need
narrating at all. Freed of its traditional moral ambiguities and
contradictions, the enacted masquerade loses something of its
mystique. It has become a recognizably feminist enterprise.

With the exception of one important detail, Inchbald's masquerade is thus the least visual, the least present to the reader, of
any contemporary fictional episode. We learn only, somewhat
ironically, that Miss Milner does not really enjoy Mrs. G——'s
ball: "the crowd and bustle" fatigue her, and she is afflicted by
an unexpected and touching tristesse. The delicate ambivalence
suggested here is typical of Inchbald's rendering of her character. Thus "though she perceived she was the first object of admiration in the place," the narrator observes, "yet there was one
person still wanting to admire; and the remorse at having transgressed his injunctions for so trivial an entertainment, weighed
upon her spirits, and added to its weariness" (161). Returning
home at daybreak, Miss Milner is wistful and pensive—a lost
Watteau figure—embodying the spirit of post-saturnalia, its
ashes and ennui.

The heroine's fleeting urge here to be seen and "admired" by
Dorriforth is an important one; I shall return to it in a moment.
It is connected with Inchbald's one concession to conventional
iconography: the description of Miss Milner's masquerade costume, representing the goddess Diana (see Fig. 33). This "elegant habit," which the heroine complements with a pair of
"buskins" and by curling her hair "in falling ringlets," is sug-

33. The costume of Diana was popular at masquerades throughout the 18th century. *Catherine Paggen as Diana*, by Allan Ramsay, ca. 1739.

gestive in several ways. It is literally suggestive, "for although it was the representative of the goddess of Chastity, yet from the buskins, and the petticoat made to festoon above the ankle, it had, on the first glance, the appearance of a female much less virtuous" (155). But at the same time the gender of the costume seems curiously indeterminate. Several characters are not sure whether Miss Milner's disguise is meant to represent a man or a woman. When Sandford, waiting with the angry Dorriforth for her to return from the masquerade, interrogates the servants about what sort of costume she left the house in, the footman describes her wearing "men's cloaths" (including boots), but the maid swears she saw her in "a woman's dress" (160). Like that "Hermaphroditical mixture" of garments worn by the heroine Harriet in Griffin's farce *The Masquerade; or, An Evening's Intrigue* (1717), Miss Milner's costume is at once ambiguously sexual and sexually ambiguous.

The ambiguity here is related to the fact that the heroine impersonates Diana, the most androgynous and sexually elusive of classical goddesses. It makes sense in an obvious way that Miss Milner, enamored of the dramas of control, should choose to represent her. For Artemis/Diana, huntress and amazon, protector of virgins and wild animals, has always had associations with ancient matriarchy and cults of the mother-goddess; in the eighteenth century she was often seen as a profoundly disturbing embodiment of female power.* But more important, Diana also symbolizes autonomous female sexuality—a sexuality without reference to men or male authority. More than Aphrodite, whose charm across the epochs depends upon a world of masculine desire, the "Goddess of Chastity" personifies utopian femininity. Diana is free of ordinary structures of sexual subordination, her erotic inaccessibility a form of mastery. Thus her most famous encounter with a man, the unwitting voyeur Actaeon, is a parable of supernatural female integrity: to see (and desire) the goddess is to metamorphose and die.

The associations with celibacy and power linger, perversely at first, in subsequent scenes. To be sure, when Dorriforth sees Miss Milner, still in costume, on the morning after the masquerade, the power of the goddess seems in abeyance. Unlike Actaeon and his response to Diana, Dorriforth seems oblivious to Miss Milner's beauty, and remains implacable in his will to

---

*Artemis/Diana was originally a fertility goddess similar to the Minoan "Lady of the Wild Things" and the Phrygian Cybele. On her putative connection with matriarchal religion, see J. J. Bachofen, *Myth, Religion, and Mother Right*; and Robert Graves, *The White Goddess*. Given her embodiment of militant female chastity, Diana's eighteenth-century associations are complex. Taking a cue perhaps from Ovid's unsympathetic account of Diana's transformation of Actaeon (*Metamorphoses*, Book III, ll. 138–252), eighteenth-century male artists and composers often treat her as the representative of unnatural denial, erotic self-preoccupation, or female homoeroticism. See Jean Hagstrum's comments on Joseph Bodin de Boismortier's cantata *Diane et Actéon* (1732) and Watteau's *Diana at Her Bath* in *Sex and Sensibility*, p. 288. Diana may have held a less prejudicial place in the contemporary female imagination, however, as Inchbald's treatment suggests. Aileen Ribeiro comments on the popularity of the Diana costume in eighteenth-century English fancy dress portraits in *Dress Worn at Masquerades in England*, pp. 261–64. In Volume III of her *Memoirs*, the notorious Irish courtesan Margaret Leeson describes her appearance at a masquerade as the "Goddes of Chastity, Diana, huntress of the woods."

punish. The long-threatened order of banishment is given. He vows that "in a few days we shall part"—forever (163).

Dorriforth charges his lover with making herself unrecognizable, as it were, to patriarchy. Ruling that he will not see her, he also implies that he cannot; he cannot see her now in the existential sense, and cannot acknowledge either their history or their love. With her act of rebellion she has made herself unknown to him. When in her grief at his injunction, she calls out that her dead father would regret Dorriforth's severity, the former priest declares that she should "'appeal to your father in some other form, in that' (pointing to her dress) 'he will not know you'" (164–65). Her masquerade adventure has made all men blind to her. In the most profound sense the Father no longer knows who she is.*

In this crucial moment, "divided between grief and anger," Miss Milner rallies and accepts the fate she has brought upon herself. "Lord Elmwood," she cries, "you think to frighten me by your menaces, but I can part with you; heaven knows I can—your late behavior has reconciled me to a separation" (164). The symbolism of her costume (which she is of course still wearing) is most potent here: in one sense she has indeed chosen Diana-like chastity in preference to enslavement to another's will. She is reconciled to alienation—to moral and psychic invisibility—if only to preserve her liberty.

Inchbald here temporarily reconstructs a familiar and cruel dichotomy: female independence seems incompatible with sexual rewards; the heroine cannot have both power and the love of her fiancé. The masquerade hints at freedom, but its consequences,

---

*The interplay, in this passage and elsewhere, between fathers, father surrogates, and daughters is Shakespearean in resonance. Boaden notes that Inchbald may have modeled *A Simple Story* in part on *The Winter's Tale*. The complex relations between Miss Milner, Matilda, and Dorriforth certainly resemble those of Hermione, Perdita, and Leontes in several respects (*Memoirs of Mrs. Inchbald*, I, 277). But *King Lear* also comes to mind, particularly in the painful image here of the father's blindness to his daughter. In the second half Elmwood will literally refuse to see or be seen by his daughter. This projection of terrifying emotional themes through the imagery of blindness is very similar to the process Stanley Cavell describes in his classic essay "The Avoidance of Love: A Reading of *King Lear*."

in the real world of men, are dystopian. Freedom in one realm entails loss in another; carnivalesque pleasures cannot be imported into the patriarchal household. To wear the signs of utopia in everyday life—to bring the masquerade home—is to provoke estrangement and hatred, and a devastating end to "engagements."

We recognize the emotional logic; it was painfully at work in Burney. But even here, at the nadir of her heroine's fortunes, Inchbald begins to work a subversive change on this logic and thus alters its dehumanizing force. Her heroine refuses to capitulate and in so doing challenges literary as well as domestic decorum. This refusal alone gives an intoxicating twist to the clichéd plot of female destiny, for whatever happens, Miss Milner has demonstrated an essential imperturbable strength. The masquerade has indeed been her test—an agon—but unlike Cecilia she chooses liberty over ease, and the rigors of self-determination over the comforts of the disenfranchised.

Granted, despite Inchbald's subtle revisionism the narrative threatens to give itself over to the conventional dysphoria. The masquerade, "scene of pleasure" (161), now seems, after all, to have brought about a very real punishment—the imminent loss of Dorriforth's love. But one senses the instability in Inchbald's version of this crudely retributive structure. Dorriforth presents his decision to leave Miss Milner with ceremonial violence, as though it were incontrovertible; yet given the psychic economy at work elsewhere in the fiction, we may wonder if it really is. In a sense he simply re-creates the earlier, eminently unstable time in their history when they were officially unavailable to each other as lovers. The vow to separate reproduces the conditions of the monastic vow: it imitates taboo, sets up a boundary, and makes him once more inaccessible. Yet it also sets up, as before, the possibility of violation. As we have seen, vows have little ultimate force in *A Simple Story*; they are "made to be broken" (21). And this vow seems especially to invite violation. For not only Miss Milner but Dorriforth himself must now contend with the transgressive desire that prohibitions, by their very nature, seem to entail. Given what has gone before—and Dorriforth's own metamorphosis from "proud priest" to "profest lover"—he is now as conscious as she of the potential for transformation and transgression. Swearing to part, yet caught up still in a passionate, complicated interest in one another, Dorriforth and Miss Milner are the perfect candidates for carnivalesque reunion.

And this, of course, is what Inchbald provides. She approaches her remarkable climax with some of her most beautifully understated narrative effects. In a painfully formal letter to the heroine, Dorriforth reveals his intention to leave for Italy "for a few years." This Goethe-like journey, he hopes, will reconcile him "to the change of state I am enjoined; a change, I now most fervently wish could be entirely dispensed with" (175). But during the week of his travel preparations, which he exhorts Miss Milner not to disturb with "further trial" of his feelings, the tension grows steadily between them. They avoid speaking but remain agonizingly aware of one another's presence—conversing, as it were, through the silences of metonymy. Mute objects take on intensely communicative power. When dinner guests, for example, ask Dorriforth if he indeed plans to leave the following Tuesday, Miss Milner's "knife and fork," the narrator observes, give "a sudden spring in her hand," though "no other emotion witnessed what she felt" (178). Later, when she stumbles upon Dorriforth's trunks, "nailed and corded, ready to be sent off to meet him at Venice," she runs to a far corner of the house to sob in despair (180). Dorriforth discovers her and they communicate silently:

> She instantly stifled her tears, and looked at him earnestly, as if to imply, "What now, my Lord?"
> He only answered with a bow, which expressed these words alone: "I beg your pardon." And immediately withdrew.
> Thus each understood the other's language, without either uttering a word. (180–81)

The tension reaches a breaking point on the evening before Dorriforth's departure. Dorriforth himself gives no sign of any change of heart, but nonetheless one senses odd, inexplicable intimations of reversal. Most strikingly, Sandford, formerly the heroine's nemesis, becomes suddenly and unaccountably affectionate toward her, as though sympathizing with her for the first time. His gestures of concern seem authentic: Inchbald does not present them, as she easily might have, as mere senile flourishes or marks of hypocritical triumph. At dinner the old cleric offers the distraught Miss Milner a biscuit, "the first civility he had ever in his life offered her" (182), and when he invites her to breakfast with them the next day (a request in which Dorriforth silently concurs), he addresses her softly as "my dear." However bafflingly inconsistent his kindness, his expression seems to her "most precious" (186).

In the "wondrous" scene of resolution the next morning, Sandford plays the part of deus ex machina. Barely suppressed hysteria is the order of the day here. Miss Milner spills her coffee at the jingling sound of carriage wheels in the drive; Dorriforth jerks himself up from the breakfast table "as if it was necessary to go in haste" (190). He grips Miss Milner's hand in farewell; she responds with a sudden storm of grief. Then Sandford miraculously intervenes. As though by sorcery, the lovers stand "petrified" by his stark, tolling admonition: "'Separate this moment,'—cried Sandford—'or resolve never to be separated but by death'" (190). Without pause the old priest seizes a Bible, and after hearing their mutual declarations of love, tendered in "wonder" by Dorriforth and in "a trembling kind of ecstasy" by Miss Milner, marries them on the spot (191).

Such is not the point of ultimate closure: Miss Milner and Dorriforth have a second legal ceremony a few days later, at which point the narrator educes, without explanation, the strange detail on which the first half of *A Simple Story* suspends—the discovery that the ring that Dorriforth, in haste, places on the heroine's finger is a "mourning ring" (193). I will return briefly to this ambiguous coda (with which Inchbald apparently intended to link the two originally disparate halves of her fiction) in my concluding remarks on the second part of the novel and the relationship between Dorriforth/Elmwood and his daughter Matilda.

But in another sense one may treat the heroine's marriage as

definitive, in that it completes the narrative sequence initiated by
the masquerade episode and places the earlier incident in its
most comprehensive light to date. Granted, reflecting back on
the masquerade from the vantage point of the marriage scene,
one may be conscious at first only of the now-familiar pattern of
teleological reversal—the fact that, as in Richardson and Fielding, the "fatal masquerade" is here not so fatal after all. The ball
at Mrs. G——'s seems in retrospect a Fortunate Fall, promoting
repetition of the most pleasurable kind. For without the post-
masquerade alienation between Miss Milner and Dorriforth,
obviously, there can be no euphoric reconciliation: the heroine's
temporary loss of her lover makes it possible, as it were, for her
to have him all over again. The situation is on the surface much
like that in *Pamela*. With Miss Milner's impromptu marriage, as
in the scene of Pamela's "éclaircissement" with B., "every joy
was doubled by the expected sorrow" (193). Like that "fairer
Paradise" mentioned by Milton in *Paradise Regained*—the reno-
vated paradise of comedy—Miss Milner's is an improved state of
ecstasy, carrying all the surplus delights of secondariness, its
pathos and relief.

Here too, in this new version of the Richardsonian "happy
turn," one senses profound affinities with the psychological
world of romance. Like Richardson, Inchbald allegorizes comic
mutability in a way that has struck some readers as un-
novelistic—too abrupt, fantastic, and implausible according to
strictly realistic canons. "The sustained portraiture of coherent
but changing character over a long period," Inchbald's editor
J. M. S. Tompkins argues, is not the novelist's strong point.[10]
While granting the point, one might describe the seeming incoherence another way—not as the author's failing but as a
manifestation of that generic ambiguity we have already noted
in a number of eighteenth-century masquerade novels. The
movement toward romance, toward an antinaturalistic wish-
fulfillment structure, may be, as I hypothesized earlier, a formal
side effect of the carnivalesque—the generic equivalent of those
processes of transformation it initiates elsewhere in eighteenth-
century narrative. Certainly, after the masquerade in *A Simple*

Story, as in *Pamela*, phantasmic imperatives seem at least as strong as impulses toward conventional verisimilitude. Characters do metamorphose wildly here. Sandford is only the most obvious example of what could be called Inchbald's proto-romantic nonconservation of character. Dorriforth himself has unmistakable affinities with the shape-shifting, psychologically ambivalent beings of romance.[11] But Miss Milner's marriage too, like that of Pamela and B., has a quality of general uncanniness, reminiscent of both magical quest-narrative and wish-fulfillment dream. One detects, in the narrator's summing-up, the complacent, anonymous euphoria of fairy tale: "Never was there a more rapid change from despair to happiness—to happiness most supreme—than was that, which Miss Milner and Lord Elmwood experienced within one single hour" (193).

At the same time, however, Inchbald makes an important and arguably self-conscious modification of the Richardsonian romance precedent. If the marriage scene represents a kind of fairy-tale repetition—Inchbald's return to the carnivalesque plot of union—it is also, to borrow Kermode's phrase, repetition with a difference. For the marriage in no way compromises Miss Milner's central gesture of defiance, the provocative trip to the masquerade. This symbolic assertion of autonomy goes unpunished. Significantly, in the amazing love scene itself, no mention is made of the masquerade excursion. The heroine neither begs forgiveness for her transgression nor promises her fiancé any kind of future subservience. Inchbald instead treats Miss Milner's role in the rapprochement highly ambiguously. When Dorriforth plaintively asks Miss Milner if she will "in marriage, show me that tender love you have not shown me yet?" she responds only in the equivocal, nonbinding, feminine language of gesture: "She raised him from her feet, and by the expression of her face, the tears with which she bathed his hands, gave him confidence" (192). She gives little away, and makes no vows, even in this ostensibly conventional moment of erotic surrender.

Far more than *Pamela*, Inchbald's fiction politicizes the repetition-compulsion at the heart of the romance. Twice in the nar-

318

rative Dorriforth is changed—from severity to softness, from icon of inaccessibility to enraptured lover. But his second transformation differs subtly from the first, confirming, like an experimental datum, Miss Milner's now-complete moral and psychic ascendancy. Via the great intervening "proof" of the masquerade, she has challenged his authority—and won. And precisely because of this crucial episode, the process of repetition modulates into one of supplementation. In *Pamela* the shock of socioerotic reversal symbolized in Pamela's marriage is mitigated by her ultimately slavish deference to her new husband's will. Hers in the end is the traditionally reactionary euphoria of the romance, a euphoria of the erotic alone, signified by the palpable inequalities of her married condition. But Inchbald alters the ideological force of the marriage plot itself. Her iconoclasm shows up most plainly in this work of embedded revisionism: Miss Milner's second union with Dorriforth is better than the first, not just because it redeems her status as a heroine of the erotic, but because, most remarkably, it has also become the sign of her control over her own destiny.*

With this fortunate termination, the utopian promise of the masquerade episode is realized. Miss Milner has, as it were, brought the masquerade home after all. Like the goddess, she has in fact metamorphosed Dorriforth—for the second time— and carnivalized his household. No longer the precinct of authoritarianism, the patriarchal realm metamorphoses into a

---

*The situation may recall those masquerade comedies known to Inchbald from her work on the London stage. Hannah Cowley's *The Belle's Stratagem* (1781) seems in particular to have a bearing on *A Simple Story*. The hero's name, Doricourt, resembles Dorriforth's; the masquerade at Lady Brilliant's suggests the type of affair held by Mrs. G—— in Inchbald's novel. Inchbald edited the play for the *British Theatre* series (London, 1808), and in prefatory remarks admired its "charm" and "humour." Of the central masquerade episode she wrote, "who does not scorn that romantic passion, which is inflamed to the highest ardour, by a few hours conversation with a woman whose face is concealed? And yet, who does not here sympathize with the lover, and feel a strong agitation, when Letitia, going to take off her mask, exclaims, in a tremulous voice,—'This is the most awful moment of my life'?" Nostalgia is a keynote in her summation: "the mention of powder worn by the ladies, their silk gowns, and other long exploded fashions, together with the hero's having in Paris 'danced with the Queen of France at a masquerade,' gives a certain sensation to the reader, which seems to place the work on the honourable list of ancient dramas." ("Remarks," *The British Theatre*, XIX, 4–5.)

space of compassion, sensuality, and delight. Inchbald's imagery of relief still carries the power it held for contemporaries: "Cold indeed must be the bosom," wrote her biographer, Boaden, "that does not sympathise with the bride, when she sees the carriage that was to bear her lover for ever from her arms drive away empty from the door."[12]

And this remains the preeminent meaning of the carnivalesque in Inchbald's fiction: it spills over into the real world of the characters. Inchbald does not really need to dwell on masquerade scenery, or even on the controversial pattern of human relations the masquerade temporarily engenders, for she is interested in these relations only so far as they re-create themselves—after rewarding delay—permanently, in the fictional world itself. She uses the topos to write the first feminist romance. The masquerade, finally, is both the token of utopian aspirations and the lyrical mechanism through which Inchbald grants her heroine everything—the double euphoria of carnival, love and power, in the shape of the everyday.

It may seem that I have exaggerated the revolutionary aspects of Inchbald's conclusion, particularly since it is not, after all, the final conclusion. *A Simple Story* continues into the next generation, with the history of Lord Elmwood (formerly Dorriforth) and his daughter Matilda. What to make of Inchbald's curious joining section, in which we learn in a cursory paragraph or two that the former Miss Milner, after her marriage, has a brief adulterous affair and is exiled for life, along with her baby daughter, to a "dreary" seat in Scotland by her now-embittered husband? Fifteen years have passed when the second half of Inchbald's fiction commences, and the grief-stricken Lady Elmwood, still in exile, is on her deathbed. She dies a few pages later, and the story of her adolescent daughter comes abruptly to the fore. Do these dismaying developments qualify our sense of euphoric patterning in Inchbald's narrative?

Certainly if we insist that *A Simple Story* is somehow all of a piece—a plausible, logically consistent work of art—the vagaries of the second half may force us to modify our notions regarding Inchbald's formal sense of her fiction. With her odd ligature she dispenses with a number of conventional novel-istic desiderata at one blow: temporal continuity, the single recognizable point of closure, overriding organic unity. What follows does not lack power; indeed, readers may disagree with Tompkins, who finds Matilda's story inferior to Miss Milner's. For Matilda's story combines folk motif and family romance in ways prefiguring the starkly supercharged structures of Romantic poetry and fiction. Here, certainly, is Inchbald at her most self-consciously sublime. In the figure of the now-terrible Lord Elmwood, a man paralyzed by compressed love and rage, in Matilda's Oedipal absorption with this invisible tyrant-father, we see the outlines of classic Romantic psychodrama, from *Prometheus Unbound* to *Wuthering Heights*.

Still the fate of Miss Milner remains perplexing. But it does not, I think, undermine the argument I have been making regarding Inchbald's use of the carnivalesque and her ultimate commitment to the utopian structures of the romance. In fact, the problem may illuminate a final important feature of the masquerade theme in *A Simple Story*—one with literary and cultural repercussions in the history of the carnivalesque generally.

To be sure, one might dispense with the problem of continuity by a simple appeal to textual history: the two halves of the 1791 edition may originally have been unrelated. The "mourning ring" omen at the end of the first part seems an afterthought, stuck in to make a rather awkward link to an altogether separate tale. Boaden asserted that the first version of the novel ended with Miss Milner's marriage, and her modern editor Tompkins concurs, suggesting that the novelist "fused" two disparate works that she had on hand in order to "extend a tale that was slender and brief beside the growing bulk and complexity of the novel at the end of the century." As for the alarmingly swift demise of Miss Milner / Lady Elmwood in the second half, Tompkins argues that Inchbald was "reluctant to enter into the collapse of the marriage she had imagined," and was therefore quickly "thrown on the next generation" and Matilda's story.[13]

Such comments make sense, though one objects to the genetic fallacy that because Inchbald's novel was originally an amalgam, we need not treat Lady Elmwood's.death as any more than a belated connective device—as part of a secondary fiction, as opposed to a primary fiction. Tompkins's remark that Inchbald was unable to imagine a tragic end for Miss Milner and turned instead to her daughter suggests a more provocative way of relating the two halves. Matilda is indeed in many respects a surrogate for the novel's original heroine and takes her mother's place, in the reader's mind as well as in the narrator's, with remarkable celerity.

Onomastics play a subtle affective part here. Subliminally, perhaps, it is difficult to recognize the heroine of the first part— "the once gay, volatile Miss Milner" (199)—in the shadowy and evanescent figure of Lady Elmwood. The substitution in the realm of reference suggests an actual substitution of persons. So strong at times is the effect of discontinuity that we seem to be reading about a different woman altogether—someone, as the narrator puts it, "no longer beautiful—no longer beloved— no longer—tremble while you read it!—virtuous" (194). Similar pseudo-erasures occur elsewhere. In the same linking passage, we find that "Dorriforth, the pious, the good, the tender Dorriforth," is lost in Lord Elmwood, "an example of implacable rigour and injustice" (195).

By contrast, Matilda (whose name, on a primitive phonic level, seems consonant with her mother's) seems strangely familiar—continuous with "the first female object of this story" (194). (The reader never learns Miss Milner's first name, yet one would not be surprised to find it the same as her daughter's, given the hints of characterological blending elsewhere. Later, at the first sight of his grown daughter, Lord Elmwood will refer to her by mistake as "Miss Milner.") When Matilda is introduced, the reader has the sense of a return to origins, to the beginning of Miss Milner's story. Matilda is seventeen, the narrator observes, "of the same age, within a year and a few months, of her mother when she became the ward of Dorriforth" (220). Miss Woodley (who is now Matilda's confidante, just as she was her mother's) sees the young woman as Lady Elmwood "risen from the grave in her former youth, health, and exquisite beauty" (221). Perhaps it is less disturbing to read of the demise of a charismatic character when she is so quickly replaced—by herself. We are prepared for an *apophrades*, a return of the dead.

This hint of phantasmic substitution clues the reader in to what is surely the most important fact, critically speaking, about the second half: that its underlying narrative structure, or what one might call its symbolic plot, is almost identical to that of the first half. Matilda's story not only resembles her mother's, it is a displaced recapitulation. For Matilda too transgresses against patriarchal dictate, and she too is threatened with emotional banishment. Yet she too forms, at the last gasp, an eminently gratifying union, and with the same man, no less, who figures so prominently in Miss Milner's history—Dorriforth/Elmwood, her own father.

The repetition clarifies Inchbald's emotional idée fixe, the obsessive pattern of proscription/violation/reward. The second half condenses the wish-fulfillment structures of the first. Like her mother's story, Matilda's story is predicated on the official inaccessibility of Dorriforth/Elmwood. Elmwood has agreed to let his daughter live at Elmwood Castle after her mother's death on condition that she never enter the rooms he himself occupies, or come into his sight while he is in residence. Any transgression will result once again in instant banishment. "If," he tells Sandford, "whether by design or accident, I ever see or hear from her; that moment my compliance to her mother's supplication ceases, and I abandon her once more" (213). The pronouncement is structurally analogous to his priestly vow in the first half, for it crystallizes his physical and emotional distance. With this highly neurotic psychic blackmail, the stricken Elmwood legislates against love itself, armoring himself against human contact even as he claims to protect his unfortunate daughter.

Also embedded in the same prohibition is the "forbidden zone" motif of the first half. Her father's quarters in Elmwood Castle function for Matilda in the same way the masquerade room did earlier for her mother—as a locale into which she must not pass. One recognizes too Inchbald's proto-Romantic negotiation with folk material; Bluebeard is only the most notorious popular example of the pathological controller of space.[14] And like his former injunction, Elmwood's second prohibition seems to invite violation. Matilda tests her father's command in subtle, obsessive ways, haunting his library in his absence, gazing at portraits of him, listening for the sounds of his carriage. And in the end, we recall, she does indeed transgress, by walking into him on a stairway. Of course, she does not premeditate this meeting; it seems accidental, though the narrator gives powerful indications that it has resulted from her unconscious search. Seeing him, Matilda swoons into his arms with an involuntary cry of "Save me!" while Elmwood, likewise by reflex, calls out the name of his dead wife and in a terrible state of unlocking grief presses his daughter convulsively "to his bosom" (274).

Here the underlying narrative pattern of the first half repeats itself almost exactly. The violation of patriarchal taboo brings on its requisite punishment—banishment—yet this punishment is immediately undone by a further unexpected reversal. Inchbald's narrative spins giddily through the turns. Elmwood, despite his emotional response, swiftly exiles Matilda to yet another remote cottage, thus reinstitutionalizing the distance between them. As before, the order of separation is but the necessary prelude to reunion. Matilda is abducted by a minor character, Lord Margrave; Elmwood is stricken with remorse and rescues her. Reconciled to his love for her, he joyfully carries her back to Elmwood Castle. Matilda, seeing her father changed from a repressive tyrant into an affectionate companion from whom she receives "a thousand proofs of . . . love," experiences a vision of natural rebirth: the snowy November fields appear green to her, "the trees in their bloom," and every bird seems to sing "the sweetest music" (331).

With this characteristic gesture, as though reversing an electromagnetic field, Inchbald brings about the romance solution, transforming polarization into attraction, drawing her characters together just as their separation seems imminent. The burgeoning November of the last pages is indeed the green world of romance, the beautiful image of Inchbald's permanent World Upside-Down. For the second time in *A Simple Story*, patriarchal violence is quelled, and feminine delight made paramount. We sense again, compellingly, that for this author the romance conclusion is the only conclusion: she seems unable to tolerate any restriction on her heroine's happiness. In this charmed recapitulation Inchbald undoes the problematic "death" of Miss Milner, relives her own charismatic story, and achieves, like Richardson, a sequel that is also the spectral reenactment of its utopian original.

Yet as this rapid summary shows, the second half of the novel does without one important element present in the first—any reference to the carnivalesque. In Inchbald's second version of the romance, the forbidden zone is no longer externalized. Unlike her mother, Matilda does not go anywhere in order to transgress—anywhere, that is, outside Elmwood Castle. She seeks out no "promiscuous" occasion, no suspect public diversion. Rather, the realm of transgression is inside: it is within the house of the father, part of domesticity itself. A simple meeting on a staircase serves all the functions of the masquerade episode in the first half. Saturnalia has moved inward.

How to account for the interesting absence of the carnivalesque? Some naïve explanations come to mind: one could argue that Inchbald did not wish to repeat the plot of the first half so exactly; one may see traces here of a vestigial didacticism. Several commentators have suggested that Inchbald wished to present Matilda as an improved Miss Milner, guilty of no melodramatic acts of self-assertion, and as one whose "proper education" in virtue surpasses her mother's. The compromising scenery of the carnivalesque might be deemed inappropriate to this new Eve.[15]

But such responses (besides foreshortening numerous ambiguities in Matilda's character) underrate the historical shift taking place here. Matilda's story represents not a disavowal but an internalization of the carnivalesque. The transformational energy of the masquerade in the second half moves into the private world of the bourgeois household, and on a subjective level, into the realm of individual psychology. From the beginning the transgressive space is within—part of home itself—rather than a scene one visits, the *theatrum mundi* "out there."

Theoretically speaking, the change is remarkable. Inchbald turns from the mediating figure of the masquerade to the direct expression of primary content. The movement is characteristic of her imagination. The second half of *A Simple Story* shows a general tendency toward increasingly unmediated representation, in the psychological as well as the formal sense. The psychoanalytic reading illustrates this well. Though both halves of the novel are structured by the Oedipal romance, there is a striking difference in degree of symbolic mediation. In the first half the heroine's Oedipal attachment is mediated by Dorriforth, the "most beloved friend" of her dead father. She promises, on their first meeting, "ever to obey him as her father" (13), and he fulfills all the legal and emotional functions of the paternal surrogate. By contrast, the object of Matilda's desire is in fact her father: there is no displacement of Oedipal interest onto a secondary figure. One senses Inchbald moving closer and closer, in the second half, to an unmediated presentation of a basic wish fulfillment.[16]

Inchbald's internalization of utopian desire also has larger literary and cultural dimensions. The tendency of her fiction to do away with external agents—to psychologize transformational or transgressive impulses and locate their expression within the familial setting—anticipates formal and thematic developments in nineteenth-century fiction. There too, the carnival topos will gradually become obsolete; that is, novelists will rely on it less and less as the outside mediator of controversial psychosexual or political content. The masquerade episode loses importance as the objective correlative of scandal at the moment the novel gains in interiority and self-consciousness. Transgressive longings are centralized, so to speak, in the novels of Eliot, Flaubert, Tolstoy, and James; they haunt the ordinary, complacent realms of bourgeois domesticity, becoming part of the psychopathology of everyday life. In particular, as in Inchbald, the hidden dreams of women come poignantly, and sometimes sensationally, to the fore.[17]

I will return to nineteenth-century adaptations of the carnivalesque in the Epilogue; it is enough here to note Inchbald's typical radicalism. Granted, what I have been calling her internalization of the carnivalesque may reflect too the more obvious historical fact that the masquerade was a dying institution in the 1790's, and had already lost much of its éclat for the writers and readers of realistic fiction. Even in the first half of *A Simple Story*, the representational interest the masquerade holds for Inchbald is slight, as though she were already on her way to dispensing with the iconography of the event even as she transvalues its moral and sexual meanings. Though Inchbald makes the masquerade in some sense the crucial episode in Miss Milner's history, she does so more by allusion, paradoxically, than by representation. In the second half even the allusion is gone.

As I noted in Chapters 1 and 2, the attenuation of the carnivalesque in English life in the last decades of the eighteenth century represents an interesting and perhaps insoluble historical puzzle. Did the gradual disappearance of the masquerade reflect new repressive impulses at work in English society? Or was it simply that the rebellious urges the occasion embodied were channeled into more self-conscious and explicitly political forms?

Burney's and Inchbald's strikingly dissimilar novels of the carnivalesque might be said, in the end, to allegorize this historical problem. *Cecilia*, we saw, transposed the carnivalesque backward in symbolic time and space, making it, by the end of its heroine's story, part of the landscape of nostalgia and unreality. Dreams of female sensuality and power evaporate, the gynesium is destroyed, the house of the Mother (for that, finally, is what the masquerade embodies) is replaced by that of the Father. The collapse marks the return of the status quo—of seriousness, masculinity, and law—yet also leaves behind a strange undertow of yearning in Burney's narrative, an unutterable psychic malaise.

The process in *Cecilia* resembles repression, in its transfer of longing into mourning and its denial and camouflage of hope. Considered as an allegory of the fate of the carnivalesque, Burney's novel anticipates the first historical paradigm I mentioned. The masquerade is obsolete at the end of the fiction because the aspirations it signifies have been hidden from view, distanced and estranged. The novel's programmatic attacks on luxury and excess—on fashion, freedom, and the desires of women—correlate with this underlying symbolic process. They institutionalize repression in the same way that the attacks of eighteenth-century writers on the masquerade articulated a deeper cultural will toward moral censure and the themes of sexual and emotional denial. Implicit in Burney's resolution is a presentiment of Blake's "Jerusalem bound in chains"—fear and false consciousness, the myriad refusals of the dystopia.

Inchbald, by contrast, counters repression with acceptance, denial with transformation. *A Simple Story* also leaves the masquerade behind, not because its imagery of liberation now offends, but because liberation has become the currency of everyday life. The carnivalesque takes a new shape in the realm of emotion. Here indeed, Inchbald revivifies every aspect of the masquerade's utopian theater of freedom: its moral and sensual fluidity, its anti-patriarchalism and celebration of female pleasure, the cathartic escape from mourning and melancholia, the return of *temps perdu*.

Inchbald's transvaluation is analogous to the progressivism of our second historical myth and the argument that the carnivalesque lost its cultural importance because it was replaced in the classic Enlightenment manner by new forms of self-consciousness. Revolutionary political thought, the economic analysis of society, the investigation of women's oppression— these incipient intellectual developments, the radical legacy of the late eighteenth century, may have rendered the subversive appeals of the masquerade unnecessary. Stylized reversals of class and gender may have seemed less suggestive once such reversals became a possibility in everyday life. Inchbald's Jacobinism and her ties with Wollstonecraft's circle (paradoxically combined with Catholic devotionalism) make such a historical allegory persuasive. In the romance formulations of *A Simple Story*, as in

34. *An Incident in the Grounds of Ranelagh During a Bal Masqué*, by Arthur Devis, 1757

the writings of the reformers and revolutionaries of the period, the no-place of utopia indeed becomes this place, the world even now coming into being—the palpable fabrication of human desire.

The contrast between Burney and Inchbald and the contradictory historical narratives they represent is one, finally, between stories of defeat and stories of triumph, between tragic and comic interpretations of experience. The masquerade topos is bound to elicit such extraordinarily contradictory myths, for like all images of an ideal world, its meaning is at once rich and ambiguous. I spoke at the start of one fundamental ambiguity— that the psychological and philosophical appeal of the masquerade may be different for men and women, and its ideality most fully articulated in the eighteenth century in works written by women. The narcissistic projections of the carnivalesque held a charged existential and political meaning for contemporary women precisely because they challenged so powerfully the ordinary structures of female experience in patriarchal society. It was the special achievement of Burney and Inchbald to isolate the utopian power of the masquerade in this new light—to make clear the ancient relation between the carnivalesque and sexuality, the masquerade and women. But it was also their fate to reinscribe in fascinating and conflicting ways the mystery of the masquerade's cultural death. It is perhaps ironic that just at the moment when the imagery of the carnivalesque receives its most refined fictional treatment—for both Burney and Inchbald bring new self-consciousness to the classic topos—this morbidification should set in. What remains at issue in Burney's and Inchbald's work is whether this is a death to be mourned as an inconsolable loss, or whether it is something less catastrophic, the death that brings new life.

8

Epilogue: The Masquerade Topos
After the Eighteenth Century

Whatever this masquerading is, you find yourself dissatisfied when 'tis
over, and though you don't like it perhaps at the beginning, you are sure
to be sorry for the loss of it when it ends. —Joseph Spence (1732)

wo especially revealing
vignettes occur in Harriette Wilson's 1825 memoir of a Regency
masquerade. One is her meeting with a Colonel Armstrong,
dressed after the fashion of an "old, stiff, maiden-lady of high
rank in the reign of Queen Anne. . . . Curiously patched and
painted," he sits on a bench, "with his hoops and ruffles and
high powdered head, his pointed laced lappets, &c., fanning
himself, and talking to his young maids of honour, who sat, one
on each side of him." The other is an equally memorable encounter, in a darkened room, with a fascinating stranger. This
one wears no mask, only a simple brown robe and leather belt.
Caught in silent reverie, he is so astonishingly handsome that
Harriette imagines herself in the presence of a supernatural
being. She fancies him looking "beyond this gay scene into
some other world, which is hidden from the rest of mankind."
Then she has her epiphany: "You must be Lord Byron." Her
companion bows.[1]

Each of these meetings is in its way a sign of the end. The
wigged and powdered Colonel Armstrong, a veritable icon of
decayed grandeur and camp, embodies in a very literal way the

new spirit of anachronism typical of the nineteenth-century diversion. His costume, dating from "the reign of Queen Anne," recalls the period of the masquerade's first appearances in England, yet is already nostalgic and even elegiac, a symbol of exploded fashions. It comments ironically on the masquerade itself, now too an emblem of the past. As for the remarkable apparition of Lord Byron, he also signifies an attenuation of the carnivalesque, though in a different manner. Byron represents the revolutionary individual who transcends disguise. His identity cannot be masked, for he is unmistakable. He reduces the "gay scene" around him to nothingness by the sheer force of his personality. In his presence the masquerade becomes trivial, a mere tinsel backdrop.

What happens to the masquerade in an era of intensified subjectivity and increasingly private phantasmagoria? Certainly as the anecdotes of the memoirist suggest, public travesty became an etiolated phenomenon after the late eighteenth century. Throughout Europe in this period carnival forms were gradually shedding their significance: "On the one hand the state encroached upon festive life and turned it into a parade; on the other hand these festivities were brought into the home and became part of the family's private life. The privileges which were formerly allowed the marketplace were more and more restricted. The carnival spirit, with its freedom, its utopian character oriented toward the future, was gradually transformed into a mere holiday mood."[2]

England was no exception. I have already described the deinstitutionalization of the masquerade in English society during the late eighteenth and early nineteenth centuries: the closing of the public masquerade rooms, the disappearance of entrepreneurs like Heidegger and Mrs. Cornelys, the gradual relegation of the costume party to the periphery of social life. And I have hinted too at some of the historical and philosophical issues surrounding this ebbing of carnivalesque activity. For better or worse, English public life in this period exemplified a larger historical process—the gradual extinction of the "carnival fires" of European culture.[3]

The process had important literary repercussions. Carnival

forms in literature, like those of society, became increasingly marginal and reduced in scope. Commenting on the attenuated role of grotesque imagery in early-nineteenth-century European Romanticism, for example, Bakhtin finds a severely impoverished reflection of the rich traditions of the carnivalesque. Such imagery merely expresses "an individual carnival, marked by a vivid sense of isolation. The carnival spirit was transposed into a subjective, idealistic philosophy. It ceased to be the concrete (one might say bodily) experience of the one, inexhaustible being, as it was in the Middle Ages and Renaissance." There was a falling away from the festive literary themes of laughter and communion, he argues, and a growing fascination with the "interior infinite" of a solitary, increasingly alienated individual.[4] Only Goethe perhaps, whose *Faust* contains an intriguing allusion to the masquerade in Part 2 (I, iii), preserves something of the earlier vision.

To describe all the philosophical and artistic transformations of the carnivalesque in nineteenth- and twentieth-century literature is a task beyond the scope of this book. Such a study, however, would undoubtedly be illuminating. We need a linkage, for example, between the ancient and pervasive tradition of the carnivalesque and its strangely reduced embodiment in the sensuous strategies of nineteenth-century aestheticism, the disorienting synaesthesia of the Symbolists, the motley, heterodox impulses of surrealism and modernism. This postscript, however, will only sketch the specific fate of the masquerade topos to show that the subsequent history of the set piece is in many ways typical of larger developments.

In the previous chapter I suggested that in England, at least, the masquerade set piece loses its attraction for the writers of realistic fiction by the end of the eighteenth century. Granted, there are a few now-obscure late scenes: in Edgeworth's *Belinda* (1801), for example, and in Pierce Egan's farcical Regency travelogue, *Life in London* (1821). But it is difficult to find an extended masquerade episode of the classic sort in the works of the great nineteenth-century English novelists. Austen, interestingly, burlesqued the masquerade topos at the age of twelve in *Jack and Alice* (1787), but dispensed with it in her mature works.[5]

Likewise Thackeray has no masquerade scene in *Vanity Fair* (1847–48), despite numerous references to late-eighteenth-century and Regency high life. The closest thing there to a masquerade is a game of charades in chapter 51, in which Becky and friends dress up as Oriental potentates and houris. In Charlotte Brontë's *Villette* (1853), the heroine masquerades as a man, but again as part of a theatrical entertainment.

Certainly in Dickens's *Pickwick Papers* (1837) one may recall the fancy dress breakfast to which the Pickwickians are invited by the literary "lioness" of Eatanswill, Mrs. Leo Hunter. This splendiferous fête champêtre outdoes "the fabled gorgeousness of Eastern Fairy-land itself."[6] Yet one sees immediately the effects of comic reduction. The hostess is a parody of the classic masquerade doyenne; she presides over the occasion in the guise of Minerva, but recites her "Ode to an Expiring Frog." Sexual danger is utterly absent: the episode is set in daylight; Pickwick attends in ordinary dress; no one wears masks; squalling infants and their parents pervade the scene. The presence of children alone betrays the altered nature of the occasion. Throughout the nineteenth century the costume party, in fiction and out of it,

35. Detail from *After the Children's Ball*, by Albert Ludovici, Sr., mid-19th century

increasingly takes on juvenile associations, becoming more and more part of the symbolic domain of children. A charming mid-Victorian painting, *After the Children's Ball* by Albert Ludovici, Sr., is evocative of the change (see Fig. 35).

Again, one may conclude that the absence of large-scale fictional set pieces reflects the disappearance of the public masquerade in England and the radical transformation of the urban world in which it flourished. In France, by contrast, where carnival tradition had deeper roots and a much longer life, the masked ball or dinner is an occasional topos in the realistic novel through the mid-nineteenth century. Notable scenes occur in Balzac's *Peau de chagrin* (1831) and *Splendeurs et misères des courtisanes* (1843), and in Flaubert's *L'Education sentimentale* (1869). There is even a brief though ultimately insignificant reference to a masquerade near the end of *Madame Bovary* (1857).*

If the topos is preserved at all in later English or American writing, it is only in relatively idiosyncratic or anachronistic contexts, almost as a kind of folkloric survival. To be sure, as in the stories of Hoffmann and Kleist, in much nineteenth-century European literature masquerade scenes tend to migrate out of realistic fiction altogether and into the more circumscribed and stylized realms of the romance and the fantastic tale. Hoffmann's *Prinzessin Brambilla* (1821) is a notable example of the new, self-consciously fantastical mode.[7] The same development is present in nineteenth-century English and American fiction, where the topos is revived almost exclusively in dreamlike, exotic, or morbid settings. Its traditional narrative functions are submerged

---

*The reference is in chapter 6 of the third part. Emma, entering the period of her most frenetic debaucheries, attends a masked ball with Léon: "She wore velvet trousers and red stockings, a wig and a cocked hat over one ear. She danced all night to the wild sound of the trombones. People formed a circle around her, and she found herself in the morning in front of the theater entrance with five or six figures dressed like longshoremen and sailors—friends of Léon who were talking about getting something to eat" (*Madame Bovary*, p. 273). The episode is a strangely vestigial element, however, in Flaubert's novel. The adultery plot develops entirely without its mediation, for Emma by this point has already had two adulterous affairs. The masquerade comes late, produces no chain of incident, and merely documents the penultimate constriction of Emma's hopes. The "phantom" man of whom she continues to dream, a new lover paradoxically fashioned out of "ardent memories," fails here to materialize. The episode itself seems a gratuitous element in Flaubert's anatomy of erotic degradation—the narrative equivalent of the spleen or appendix.

36. After the French Revolution, artists increasingly connected the masquerade with exoticism, morbidity, and death. *Nadie se conoce* (No One Knows Himself), plate 6 of *Los Caprichos*, by Francisco Goya, 1799.

or lost, though the scene may retain a certain suggestive, if limited, symbolic power.

The American Romantics Hawthorne and Poe offer striking examples. Near the end of Hawthorne's *Blithedale Romance* (1852), for instance, the hero, Coverdale, returning to the failing utopian community of Blithedale, stumbles upon an al fresco masquerade put on by the residents (chapter 24). It strikes him as a hallucination or waking dream. This confused scene of Arcadian shepherds, Kentucky woodsmen, necromancers, "gay Cavaliers," and "grim Puritans" mingling in the sunlight is at once an emblem of the residents' visionary aspirations and an emblem of their barren and disturbing alienation from actual life. The disillusioned Coverdale flees from "the fantastic rabble" like "a mad poet hunted by chimeras."[8] The scene itself gives way to the macabre: the marvelous Xenobia, the masquerade's organizer and "Queen" (also the woman behind Blithedale itself), is soon after found drowned. Like the community it represents, the masquerade is perverse—a fantastic omen of estrangement and death.

Poe's *Tales of the Grotesque and Arabesque* (1840) makes masquerading even more sinister and otherworldly. The well-known "Cask of Amontillado" is set in Italy at carnival time; the murderous narrator meets his victim, Fortunato, in a mask of black silk and roquelaure. In "Hop-Frog" a malicious court jester devises a masquerade diversion in which he disguises his master, the king, as an orangutan, chains him to several courtiers in similar costume, and arranges for them all to be burned alive. Finally, the great short story "The Masque of the Red Death" takes place at the frightful masked ball of the hapless Prince Prospero, who walls off his palace against the plague and holds a masquerade, yet is still visited by Death, who appears in the midst of the festivities in the guise of a masked stranger. This gothic conceit is not original with Poe: as early as 1741, Edward Young personified Death as a masquerader in a brooding passage in *Night Thoughts*.[9] And later, somewhat more sardonically, Thomas Rowlandson, in his satirical engraving on the masquerade in the *Dance of Death* series (1814–16), depicted cavorting Regency masqueraders unpleasantly surprised by the

37. *The Masquerade* (*Dance of Death* series), by Thomas Rowlandson, 1814–16

figure of a skeleton dancing in their midst (Fig. 37). But Poe gives the allegory its most terrifying artistic embodiment.

Supernatural, exotic, and morbid elements continue to dominate the minor masquerade fiction of subsequent decades. Sheridan Le Fanu's vampire tale, *Carmilla* (1871), has a crucial Poe-like scene, charged with perverse eroticism, in which a blood-thirsty female vampire selects her victim, the nubile daughter of a general, at a masquerade. In "A Venetian Night's Entertainment" (published by *Scribner's* in 1903, with an interesting frontispiece by Maxfield Parrish), Edith Wharton exploits the carnival world of eighteenth-century Venice to dramatize a moral confrontation between the Old World and the New.[10] The late-nineteenth-century Southern writers George Washington Cable and Col. William C. Faulkner (the great-grandfather of William Faulkner) invoke the set piece as local color. Cable's *The Grandissimes* (1880), set at Mardi Gras in New Orleans in 1803, and Faulkner's *The White Rose of Memphis* (1880), which opens with a riverboat masquerade, reflect the continuing though increas-

ingly circumscribed life of carnival tradition in the American
South. Indeed, a small yet fascinating study might be made of
the persistence of the carnival/masquerade theme in Southern
writing from Poe to James Purdy.[11]

Both sinister and romantic connotations carry over into the
last survival of the set piece in the nineteenth century—its vestigial life in opera. We recall the masquerade's traditional historical association with the opera: the first public masquerades in
England took place at the Haymarket, the site of the first Handel
productions, and the two entertainments were often symbolically
linked by satirists. Later eighteenth-century operas, notably
Mozart's *Le Nozze di Figaro* (1786) and *Don Giovanni* (1787),
dramatized the familiar themes of travesty and the mask. The
association resurfaced when nineteenth-century librettists, in
search of melodramatic and spectacular plot possibilities, turned
again to the masquerade to supply them. In this case, as in
others, the conservative institution of the opera preserved a literary topos that had become in effect obsolete in literature itself.[12] Verdi's *Un Ballo in maschera* (1859), based on the story of

38. *The Duel After the Masquerade*, by Jean-Léon Gérôme, after 1857

Gustavus III of Sweden's assassination at a masquerade in 1792, is the best-known masquerade opera. The mode is tragic, and reinscribes the typically Romantic link between masquerading and death.[13] Other works make a nostalgic return to the lighter eighteenth-century comic themes of flirtation and intrigue: Johann Strauss's *Der Carneval in Rom* (1873), *Die Fledermaus* (1874), and *Eine Nacht in Venedig* (1883), Richard Heuberger's *Der Opernball* (1898), and Carl Nielsen's *Maskarade* (1906). Though not a masquerade opera in the strict sense, Richard Strauss's *Der Rosenkavalier* (1911)—with its neo-rococo ambience and its seductive hero who is actually a woman in boy's clothes—nonetheless alludes to the characteristic imagery and situations of the eighteenth-century masquerade.

Interestingly enough, the operatic exploitation of the masquerade mediates several of the handful of masquerade scenes in twentieth-century literature. Again, the set piece occurs only in the most self-consciously exotic and nostalgic contexts. In Lawrence Durrell's *Alexandria Quartet* (1962), for example, a fantastic costume ball in Egypt is the scene of a Verdi-esque assassination, following which the murder weapon is discovered in a pile of black dominos. Brigid Brophy's *The Snow Ball* (1964) takes place on the night of a 1960's costume party in London, at which guests are disguised as characters in Mozart's operas. Perhaps inevitably the heroine, dressed as Donna Anna, meets an unknown Don Giovanni and begins an affair with him. And in Isak Dinesen's "Carnival," published posthumously (1977), a group of modern masqueraders meets for philosophical badinage and sexual intrigue following the Copenhagen Opera Ball.*

---

* Among twentieth-century writers Dinesen is perhaps the most fond of the imagery of the masquerade, which she makes part of her highly fantastical, aristocratic, imaginative mythos. The words of a character in her story "Carnival" sum up her perception of the almost mystical power of the masquerade theme and its metaphoric relation to the artist: "Your own mask would give you at least that release from self toward which all religions strive. A little piece of night, rightly placed for giving you its freedom without renunciation. Your center of gravity is moved from the ego to the object; through the true humility of self-denial you arrive at an all-comprehending unity with life, and only thus can great works of art be accomplished." (Dinesen, *Carnival: Entertainments and Posthumous Tales*, pp. 67–68.)

One last sign, finally, of the masquerade scene's marginalization is its movement into minor twentieth-century subgenres such as the detective novel or the Harlequin romance type of pulp fiction. Dorothy Sayers's *Murder Must Advertise* (1933) and Ngaio Marsh's *Tied Up in Tinsel* (1972) exploit the topos, as does Susanna Howe's pulp gothic *Masquerade* (1984), a somewhat outré foray into nineteenth-century international high society.

In all these late appearances of the masquerade topos, one has the sense of anachronism. These are miniatures and ornaments, and though they may be delightful, they hardly have great importance. But by their very inconsequentiality, they suggest several rewarding final questions. If, generally speaking, the masquerade scene is obsolete in the major traditions of nineteenth- and twentieth-century writing, one may rightly wonder what takes its place. How, for example, do transgressive fictional scenarios develop without it? What, if any, are the new imaginative tropes of metamorphosis and disorder?

I have already hinted that the impulses embodied in the carnivalesque, for one reason or another, are increasingly internalized in fiction of the late eighteenth and nineteenth centuries. The scene of transformation moves inward, in both a literal and a figurative sense, and transgression is figured in more psychological ways. In part this situation mirrored an actual shift in behavior—what Bakhtin, in the passage cited earlier, referred to as the historic movement of carnival forms into "private life." The multiplicity of scenes in nineteenth-century fiction depicting domestic theatricals, private games of charades and the like, are a literalized manifestation of this change. We think of the Crawfords' group theatricals in *Mansfield Park*, the school play in *Villette*, the charades and tableaux vivants in *Vanity Fair* and *Die Wahlverwandtschaften*. Cases of individualized travesty also play a part in the households of nineteenth-century fiction: Lydia, in a fit of whimsy, dresses up one of her officer friends as a woman in *Pride and Prejudice*; Rochester, in *Jane Eyre*, impersonates a gypsy fortune-teller and visits his own home in disguise.

The shift can also be seen as part of a larger imaginative development: the general movement, often described, away from the traditional narrative structures of the picaresque, and toward the representation of an increasingly subjective, even solipsistic world of spiritual and moral adventure. In topographic terms the family or domestic setting typically takes over as the preeminent site of transformation and mystery in nineteenth-century realistic fiction. No longer is an actual journey outside the house strictly necessary for the elaboration of plots of rebellion or moral and psychological discovery. This anti-picaresque tendency had its roots in experimental eighteenth-century fiction, Sterne's *Tristram Shandy* being an obvious case in point. Ronald Paulson notes the distinctive shift in eighteenth-century narrative away from a pilgrimage or "progress" structure toward the representation of a single locale, the bourgeois household, with its corresponding emphasis on the intricacies of private relationships and the reveries of the individual. By the nineteenth century, and the triumph of a "post-picaresque world of communal integration," the centralization process is essentially complete.[14] In Austen, Eliot, Tolstoy, Flaubert, and James, for example, the psychological intensities of family or married life—the new landscapes of daydream and revolt—have replaced the diffuse scenery of the road. As Milan Kundera writes of Flaubert's Emma Bovary, "The lost infinitude of the outside world is replaced by the infinite expansion of the soul." In the hothouses of private desire, the "great illusion of the irreplaceable uniqueness of the individual—one of the sweetest of European illusions—blossoms forth."*

The masquerade was a part, of course, of an earlier public sphere in which the "irreplaceable uniqueness of the individual" was hardly of primary concern. Indeed, the opposite was the

---

*"The Novel and Europe," p. 15. This is not to say that picaresque elements are altogether excluded in nineteenth-century fiction; one thinks obviously of Dickens, Melville, and Conrad. Likewise, one can find interesting vestiges of an overtly picaresque mode even in the midst of otherwise psychologized landscapes, as in Emma Bovary's trips to Rouen. But in general emphasis shifts away from the externalized journey to the inner journey—the moral or psychological odysseys of the individual, within a more or less restricted or centralized physical landscape.

case: the masked assembly parodied such notions. Byronic singularity, as I suggested earlier, was not at a premium in a world of fluid and ever-changing identities. In the most general sense, then, interest in the fictional masquerade wanes when the fate of the individual, rather than the representation of a shared public landscape, becomes the overriding subject of realistic writing. The shift reflects the pervasive "fall of public man" that, as Richard Sennett, among others, argues, characterizes European culture starting in the eighteenth century. For most of its life the eighteenth-century masquerade remained part of a traditional domain of collective drama and social ritual—however much it also meditated on new themes of secrecy and anonymity. As the public domain changed its nature, however, becoming more fragmented and bureaucratic, so too its once-unifying institutions, the masquerade among them, gradually disappeared from the world of literary representation.[15]

The topographic shift toward the private sphere coincided, finally, with a less mediated and increasingly self-conscious presentation of subversive desire—that charismatic hidden theme in European fiction since the eighteenth century. The masquerade topos suited the novel in its infancy, when proponents of the genre were concerned most intensely with establishing the novel's claim to didactic authority. So intense is the overt moralistic imperative in early English fiction, for example, that transgressive elements appear as it were by accident—either naïvely reported or else smuggled in under the guise of didacticism. The particular appeal of the masquerade scene, as we have seen in the case of Richardson and Fielding, was that it allowed the elaboration of a transgressive narrative and thematic structure, while permitting the novelist to maintain the superficial appearance of moral orthodoxy. However logically discontinuous and morally suspect, the episode could be justified by prefacing it with an explicitly didactic negative commentary.

By contrast, in fiction of the late eighteenth and nineteenth centuries, as the impulse toward crude didacticism weakens and the novelist's absorption in transgressive modes becomes more integrated and self-conscious, the need for an ambiguously me-

343

diating figure such as the masquerade topos diminishes. Scandal—whether sexual, social, or political—can be represented directly. Tony Tanner has argued, for example, that themes of erotic transgression, particularly adultery, have a new moral neutrality and imaginative centrality in the novels of Rousseau, Goethe, and Flaubert. Unlike Richardson and Fielding, these writers rely less and less on devices of ideological or psychological mediation such as carnivalesque intrigue to set plots of sexual rebellion in motion. In England the change is already at work in Inchbald.

As for other dreams of cultural reversal, these too migrate into more self-conscious forms. Many of the utopian impulses previously represented by carnival topoi begin to move out of literature altogether, into political and philosophical writing. The great nineteenth-century tracts on political economy, the writings of socialism, feminism, and other new forms of libertarian thought, embody what one might call carnivalesque wishes in a new discursive and rationalized imaginative form. But even in fiction (and I speak obviously of those works that do not completely exclude the public dimension in favor of private life) provocative social and political elements are depicted, again, in an increasingly unmediated way: sometimes, as in Balzac, Dickens, and Stendhal, in potentially subversive stories of social climbing and class mutability, or later, anecdotally, through the representation of the politicized divagations of the crowd or mob. It is perhaps significant that as the masquerade episode loses its currency in fiction as a primary topos of collective disorder, fictional scenes of the revolutionary crowd become more prominent. Novels by Hugo, Eliot, Flaubert, and Zola offer many examples. Nineteenth-century crowd scenes serve many of the same thematic functions as masquerade scenes did earlier, but they are also usually far more integrated in imaginative terms into the mimetic structure in which they occur. For the nineteenth-century novelist, unlike his or her eighteenth-century counterpart, transgression no longer has the shape of a discontinuous or naïve diversion. It has become in some sense the central, self-conscious concern of the fictional enterprise itself.[16]

The classic masquerade scene, then, is a temporary phenomenon in literary history—and for modern readers, trained to value the sophisticated formal and thematic strategies of nineteenth-century realism, perhaps a somewhat primitive-seeming one at that. In much pre-Romantic writing the episode has the aspect of a piece of unconscious or unintegrated textual machinery. But this is not to malign it or limit its ultimate significance. Indeed, the masquerade scene draws its critical power precisely from the ways it focuses our conceptions of literary history, and raises once again perennial issues having to do with literary form and plot structure, theme and ideology, the role of topoi, the working of tropes.

In thinking about eighteenth-century fiction, as I have tried to show, the representation of the masquerade is profoundly heuristic. Though typically an isolated set piece or detail, the masquerade also bears a significance that might be called synechdochic: it dramatizes the very nature of that text in which it occurs. Like the Freudian dream image, the outburst of phantasmagoria, it illuminates by its very otherworldliness, by the seeming discontinuity with which it masks its deeper connectedness. It is never trivial, though the eighteenth-century novelist is often at pains to make it seem so. It unleashes both contradiction and delight. In so doing, it epitomizes the seductive appeal of narrative itself. It is at once singular and ever-changing, veiled and transparent, part of the half-seen, hidden life of the text. It is what Angus Fletcher has called a *kosmos*—the mysterious, brilliantly faceted jewel that refracts the world around it, inverts its shape, yet somehow conveys the very secrets of its nature.[17]

At the same time, wherever it is invoked the masquerade must always remain a powerful if fantastic historical image—the glittering lozenge, the signature, of past time. It will always be part of the eighteenth century of the imagination, which in the end is the only one we have. It is not possible, perhaps, to escape the exquisitely nostalgic afterimage the idea of the masquerade leaves—or its hints, so ephemerally registered, of a human experience replete at once with beauty and grotesquerie, seriousness and frivolity. But it is not clear that anyone, even the most resolute academician, should wish to. The masquerade's ornamental surface is rich with meaning—indeed, is its meaning. Sometimes enigmatically, the masquerade summarized an epoch of European civilization in a way that both embraced the decorative and moved beyond it.

In *The Invention of Liberty*, the great scholar of eighteenth-century culture Jean Starobinski has written, "From the revels of the *fêtes galantes* to the revelry of the French Revolution the internal transformations of the century can be seen in the changes which took place in the manifold ceremonial of pleasure."[18] The notion that the "ceremonial of pleasure," in all its historical diversity, can unveil the truth has a distinctly modern air, yet its roots lie, as Starobinski himself points out, in the eighteenth-century vision. The paradox of the masquerade—whether in its cultural or literary manifestation—was that it presented truth in the shape of deception, the aspirations of an era in a theater of disguise. The erotics of evasion, of obliquity and laughter, were ironically also those, ultimately, of revelation. The familiarity of the paradox should not make us forget its source. It comes to us from the past—from those, now dead, once part of the swirling game—the masked illuminati of evenings gone by.

Notes

Notes

Full authors' names, titles, and publication data for works cited in short form will be found in the Works Cited section, pp. 371–81. All quotations in the text and notes are drawn from the editions listed there.

CHAPTER I

1. Bakhtin, *Rabelais*, especially chap. 1, "Rabelais in the History of Laughter."

2. Goethe, p. 469.

3. Attendance at Heidegger's public masquerades averaged, according to contemporary accounts, about 700 persons. *Town and Country Magazine*, May 1770, reports that 1,200 persons participated in a masquerade at Carlisle House on May 7, 1770; the same issue describes another assembly at the Pantheon the month before at which "near two thousand persons" were in attendance.

4. See Walpole to Horace Mann, Feb. 25, 1742, and March 10, 1755, in Walpole, *Correspondence*, I (17), 343, 469.

5. Miss Chudleigh's exploit provided the inspiration for the scheme for a "naked Masquerade" described in *Connoisseur*, May 1, 1755.

6. Novak, pp. 1–3.

7. *Universal Spectator*, April 5, 1729.

8. Addison, *Guardian* 154, in Chalmers, XV.

9. Gibson, *Sermon Preached to the Societies for the Reformation of Manners*. A substantial portion of the Bishop's sermon is cited in *An Essay on Plays and Masquerades* (1724), as well as in *Gentleman's Magazine*, Sept. 1771.

10. Centlivre, *The Masquerade: A Poem* (1713). See also Bowyer, pp. 63, 150–52.

11. "John James Heidegger," *Dictionary of National Biography*.

12. Walpole to Horace Mann, Feb. 22, 1771, in Walpole, *Correspondence* VII (23), 271. On Theresa Cornelys, see the *Dictionary of National Biography*; and Ribeiro, "Mrs. Cornelys."

13. See, among others, *A Seasonable Apology; The Masquerade: A Poem*; and Fielding, *Masquerade* (1728, with "Dedication" to Heidegger added in 1731), in Fielding, *Female Husband*. Typical of attacks on Mrs. Cornelys is a caricature in *Oxford Magazine*, Feb. 1771, "Sovereign Empress of the Vast Regions of Taste."

14. See J. H. Plumb's essay on the commercialization of leisure in Brewer, McKendrick & Plumb; and P. Burke, pp. 248–49.

15. Frazer's comments on saturnalia, periodic license, and the Feast of Fools appear in part 7 of *The Golden Bough*, "Between Old and New," pp. 641–59. The historical and critical literature on European and American festivals of misrule has been rapidly growing since 1970. Two essays by E. P. Thompson have been very influential: "The Moral Economy of the English Crowd in the Eighteenth Century" and "Rough Music: 'Le Charivari Anglais.'" Other important recent works are Peter Burke, *Popular Culture in Early Modern Europe*; Natalie Z. Davis, *Society and Culture in Early Modern France*; Emmanuel Le Roy Ladurie, *Carnival in Romans*; and Peter Shaw, *American Patriots and the Rituals of Revolution*. For a long time the most significant literary study of popular tradition written in English was C. L. Barber, *Shakespeare's Festive Comedy*. Barber's work on the drama was subsequently supplemented by Ian Donaldson, in *The World Upside-Down*. The influence of Bakhtin's *Rabelais and His World* began to be felt among English-speaking literary critics in the mid-1970's. An interesting post-Bakhtinian essay from that time is Barbara A. Babcock's "The Novel and the Carnival World" (1974). Ronald Paulson's *Popular and Polite Art in the Age of Hogarth and Fielding* (1979) is a major study of relations between elite and popular traditions in eighteenth-century literature and art, as is Jackson Cope's *Dramaturgy of the Demonic* (1984), which traces historical connections between the Italian commedia and English pantomime. Representative of a burgeoning new wave of post-Bakhtinian English studies is Michael D. Bristol's *Carnival and Theatre* (1985).

16. P. Burke, p. 249.

17. Addison, *Remarks on Italy*, in *Works*, II, 39.

18. Spence, p. 95. See also Horace Mann to Walpole, July 30, 1741: "Oh the charming nights! I am told the bridge is crowded every night"; Walpole, *Correspondence*, I (17), 97. Somewhat less restrained descriptions appear in Casanova's *Memoirs*, a work that stands as a veritable archaeology of the eighteenth-century carnivalesque.

19. See Halsband, p. 185.

20. Walpole, *Correspondence*, IV (20), 46.

21. Barber, p. 5.

22. See P. Burke, chap. 8, "The Triumph of Lent," on the Puritan reformers.

23. A number of such studies are collected in Hay et al. See also Howson; and Brewer & Styles.

24. Barber, pp. 24–35. On the development of the masque, see Orgel.

25. E. Walford, VI, 166.

26. Boulton, I, 86.

27. Walpole, May 3, 1749, in *Correspondence*, IV (20), 47.

28. P. Burke, p. 192.

29. Lady, Maid Marian, Margaret, and Mollie were all female parts traditionally taken by men in the hobby-horse games of rural England. For an account of the she-male, see Cawte, pp. 71, 86.

30. See *ibid.*, chap. 3, "The Hobby-Horse in England from 1590 to 1800."

31. See Paulson, *Hogarth's Graphic Works*, II, 133; and Cawte, pp. 65–79.

32. Cawte, p. 38.

33. *Gentleman's Magazine*, Feb. 1771.

34. *Ibid.*, Jan. 1773.

35. Bakhtin, *Rabelais*, pp. 278–79.

36. Ribeiro, *Dress Worn at Masquerades*, p. 16, cites a lengthy puff in *Lloyd's Evening Post* for one of Mrs. Cornelys's entertainments.

37. Sydney, *England*, I, 145.

38. Fielding, *Enquiry*, p. 6; Richardson, *Grandison*, I, 428. On the price of admittance to Heidegger's masquerades in the second and third decades of the century, the evidence is contradictory. According to a letter quoted in Deutsch, p. 77, Heidegger made between 300 and 400 guineas from each event. Assuming an attendance of 800, this figure puts the ticket price somewhat higher than the "five shillings or three shillings a piece" mentioned by the *Weekly Journal* writer in 1718. Milhous, p. 580, quotes a price of a guinea and a half in 1717. Yet this figure again seems far too high for the date. By the second half of the century, ticket prices undoubtedly had reached this level; Mrs. Cornelys charged two guineas a ticket in the 1760's.

39. Pitt's verse is reprinted in Vol. XLVII of *The Poets of Great Britain* (London, 1807).

40. Singleton, p. 66.

41. Compare Fielding's question in *The Masquerade*: "Madam, how from another woman / Do you strumpet masqu'd distinguish?" (198–99). His Muse's reply is a laughing excoriation of the notion that *any* woman might be virtuous:

> as in the different ages,
> So virtue in the different stages
> Of female life, its station alters:
> In the widow's jointure shelters;
> In wives, 'tis not so plain where laid;
> But in the virgin's maidenhead.
> A maidenhead now never dies,
> 'Till, like a true phoenix, it supplies
> Its loss, by leaving us another;
> For she's a maid, who is no mother.
> And she may be—we see in life,
> A mother, who is not a wife. (224–35)

42. Wright, p. 68, observes that "the masquerade soon became more than a figurative leveller of society; for sharpers, and women of ill-repute and others, gained admission, and the consequence was nightly scenes of robbery and quarrels, and scandalous licentiousness." On the comparison with eighteenth-century fairs, see C. Walford; Jarrett, pp. 157–61; and Paulson's comments on Hogarth's *Southwark Fair* in *Hogarth: Life, Art, Times*.

43. On the psychological effects of wearing costume in public places, see Goffman, p. 126.

44. Walpole, *Correspondence*, I (17), 359.

45. See Fielding, *The Masquerade*, ll. 80ff, and *Tom Jones*, Book XIII, chap. 7, "Containing the whole Humours of a Masquerade."

46. The mock catechism "I know you / Do you know me?" seems to have been established relatively early on. See the reference to such exchanges in Dryden's *Marriage à la Mode* (IV, i, 130ff).

47. On Hogarth's comic indictment of Heidegger in the *Masquerade Ticket*, see Paulson, *Hogarth: Life, Art, Times*, I, chap. 7, "The Bad Taste of the Town," and his commentary on this print in *Hogarth's Graphic Works*, I, 133–34. The "lecherometer" was a favorite eighteenth-century joke. Compare the essay in the *Connoisseur*, Sept. 11, 1756, on the "Female Thermometer"—a device that "being acted upon by the circulation of the blood and animal spirits, would rise and fall according to the desires and affections of the wearer," and could measure "the exact temperature of a lady's passion." The calibrations here range from Inviolable Modesty to Abandoned Impudence. The

author claims he has experimented successfully with this thermometer at "*Play-houses—Operas—Masquerades—Public Gardens*—and other Places."

48. *Weekly Journal*, April 19, 1718.

49. Goffman, p. 39.

50. The figures of Mendacity and Deceit in Ripa's *Iconologia* (1593) both carry conspicuous masks; Deceit's cloak is covered with masks (see Maser).

51. See Climenson, I, 264.

52. Ribeiro, *Dress Worn at Masquerades*, p. 32.

53. Haywood, I, 32–33.

54. Several important historical studies on female sexuality and the role of women in eighteenth-century England appeared in the 1970's. See, in particular, Stone, *Family, Sex and Marriage*; and Trumbach, *Rise of the Egalitarian Family*. Also of interest are the essays in Kanner, *Women of England*, and Boucé, *Sexuality in Eighteenth-Century Britain*. On literary representations of female sexuality, see Staves; Eagleton; and Goldberg. On the eighteenth-century valorization of feminine virtue, Watt's comments in *Rise of the Novel*, pp. 135–73, have yet to be superseded.

55. Wilson, II, 616.

56. Haywood, I, 50.

57. See Trumbach, "London's Sodomites," pp. 12–13.

58. See, for example, Foucault's observation in *History of Sexuality*, pp. 42–43, that it was "the discursive explosion of the eighteenth and nineteenth centuries" that created "the homosexual" as a medical and juridical concept, and "entailed an *incorporation of perversions* and a new *specification of* individuals. . . . As defined by the ancient civil and canonical codes, sodomy was a category of forbidden acts; their perpetrator was nothing more than the juridical subject of them. The nineteenth-century homosexual became a personage, a past, a case history, and a childhood, in addition to being a type of life, a life form, and a morphology, with an indiscreet anatomy and possibly a mysterious physiology."

59. See Castle, "Matters Not Fit to Be Mentioned." On the general association of female transvestism with lesbian behavior in the eighteenth century, see Faderman, pp. 47–61.

60. Boaden, I, 140.

61. Trumbach, "London's Sodomites," p. 15.

62. Ralph, p. 191.

CHAPTER 2

1. Haywood, I, 32. On Fanny Burney's attendance at a 1770 masquerade, see Burney, *Early Diary*, I, 64–65.

2. Caillois, pp. 23–26. The phrase "whirl is King" is cited in Paulson, *Popular and Polite Art*, p. 97.

3. E. Burke, p. 62.

4. *Ibid.*, p. 64.

5. Compare Barthes, *Fashion System*.

6. See Isaiah 3:16–24 for a typical Scriptural attack on dress. Bell, pp. 20–23, discusses the Western mistrust of clothes. Hollander, p. 448, comments: "Clothes stand for knowledge and language, art and love, time and death—the creative, struggling state of man. While they conceal only his unapplied, unrealized body they reveal all of his and its possibilities. But to do this, they (like language) are condemned to contingency, and consequently the idea of them is something of a thorn and a goad. As a concept, clothing resists clarity. . . . As art, dress lacks the possibility of purity. As a straightforward medium for social communication, it is too liable to the unaccountable pretensions of art."

7. Ribeiro, *Dress Worn at Masquerades*. See also Ribeiro's recent summary of eighteenth-century fancy dress styles in *Dress in Eighteenth-Century Europe*.

8. The *Magazine à la Mode; or, Fashionable Miscellany* (London, 1777) distinguished two types of domino and described the bahoo thus: "The difference between [the Venetian and French dominos] is that the Venetian have hanging sleeves and large capes, whereas the French have only close sleeves and small capes; both of them at times are worn for the greater disguise with a Bahoo, a kind of hood which incloses the hair or wig forward over the mask." Cited in Ribeiro, *Dress Worn at Masquerades*, p. 29.

9. Caillois, p. 130.

10. Jefferys's *Collection of the Dresses of Different Nations* contains engravings of Henry VIII and Mary, Queen of Scots, as well as the Four Seasons, Virtue, Peace, Curiosity, and the like.

11. See *ibid.*, III, 11.

12. *Gentleman's Magazine*, June 1769.

13. See Walpole to Horace Mann, March 3, 1742: "I was last week at the masquerade dressed like an old woman, and passed for a good mask"; Walpole, *Correspondence*, I (17), 359.

14. Malcolm, II, 273.

15. *Gentleman's Magazine*, Feb. 1771.

16. *Lady's Magazine*, Feb. 1773.

17. Compare the description of the Duke of Bolton's masquerade in *Gentleman's Magazine*, June 1769, which lists "Capt Pye as Tancred, and his lady as Reuben's wife [*sic*]." A number of portraits of eighteenth-century women dressed as "Rubens's wife" exist; see, for example, John Singleton Copley's *Mrs. Samuel Quincy* (ca. 1761).

18. See Richardson, *Clarissa*, II, 170; and Goldsmith, *The Vicar of Wakefield*, pp. 82–83.

19. Contemporary representations of Somebody and Nobody, Punch, and others appear in *Catchpenny Prints*.

20. Burney, *Cecilia*, I, 169.

21. Walpole, *Correspondence*, I (17), 359.

22. On Boswell's love of self-concealment, see Byrd, pp. 96–97.

23. Bakhtin, *Rabelais*, pp. 39–40.

24. *Ibid.*, p. 26.

25. Lévi-Strauss's assertion that the mythical thought of preindustrial societies is no less complex than the scientific thought of technologically advanced cultures is predicated on the assumption that transcendental structures of mind exist that are themselves binary. See his *The Savage Mind*, and *Structural Anthropology*, especially the section "The Structural Study of Myth."

26. Barthes, *Roland Barthes*, p. 133.

27. See Barish.

28. Singleton, p. 66.

29. *Conduct of the Stage Consider'd*.

30. See *Gentleman's Magazine*, May 1750, on the abolition of "mock-Carnivals" following the 1742 Leghorn earthquake; and Walpole's comments on the English prohibition of masquerades following the Lisbon quake, in Walpole, *Correspondence*, IV (20), 539–40, 548.

31. Fielding, *Enquiry*, p. 4.

32. Haywood, I, 31.

33. Fielding, "Essay," p. 155.

34. Chalmers, XVII, 92. Unlike his more rabid contemporaries, Johnson opposed masquerades less for moralistic reasons than for socially pragmatic ones. After reading of Boswell's appearance as a "dumb conjuror" at the Countess Dowager of Fife's Scottish masquerade in 1773, Johnson wrote to him, "I have heard of your masquerade. What says your synod to such innovations? I am not studiously scrupulous, nor do I think a masquerade either evil in itself, or very likely to be the occasion of evil; yet as the world thinks it a very licentious relaxation of manners, I would not have been one of the *first* masqueraders in a country where no masquerade had ever been before." (Boswell, II, 205, 497.) Nevertheless, Johnson was not beyond making conventional complaints against the masquerade in his published works, as in *London*:

> In pleasing dreams the blissful age renew,
> And call Britannia's glories back to view;
> Behold her cross triumphant on the main,
> The guard of commerce, and the dread of Spain,

Ere masquerades debauch'd, excise oppress'd,
Or English honour grew a standing jest.   (25–30)

35. Goldsmith, *Works*, I, 153.
36. Douglas, pp. 104, 113.
37. Freud, *Civilization*, p. 40.
38. Babcock, introduction to *Reversible World*, p. 14.
39. See Geertz, *Person, Time, and Conduct*; Geertz, "Deep Play"; Turner, *Forest of Symbols*; and Turner, *Ritual Process*.
40. Freud, "Negation," p. 214.
41. Babcock, "The Novel," p. 920.
42. Douglas, pp. 169–70.
43. Compare Marx, pp. 9–11.
44. See P. Burke, pp. 199–204, for a summary of this debate. See also Babcock, introduction to *Reversible World*, pp. 22–23.
45. Gluckman, p. 109.
46. See, in particular, Le Roy Ladurie; and Shaw. The Stonewall riots, considered the beginning of the modern homosexual liberation movement in the United States, began when male transvestites fought back a police assault on the Stonewall bar in 1969. The history of modern subcultural institutions, of which the gay bar is certainly one, casts an interesting light back on the masquerade and its contemporary function. The "safe zone" or secret society may in fact do more than simply provide a haven for alienated social groups; it may also ultimately prompt the formation of a new political consciousness. (See Katz, pp. 337, 427.)
47. Barthes, *Mythologies*, p. 150.
48. Charles Lamb, *The Works of Charles and Mary Lamb*, ed. E. V. Lucas (London, 1912), II, 161; cited in Donaldson, p. 21.
49. Malcolm, II, 274.
50. Walpole, *Correspondence*, VII (23), 192–93.
51. For a general account of sumptuary laws, see Roach & Eicher. On the Black Act, see E. P. Thompson, *Whigs*, pp. 270–77. A number of writers in the 1720's commented on the apparent injustice of the Black Act: while fashionable persons were free to wear disguise at public masquerades, common people could be arrested for the very same action under the new ruling. Interestingly, the point was typically raised as a criticism of masquerades, and not of the law itself. Thus a writer in the *Weekly Journal*, April 10, 1725, mentioned the Black Act only in order to attack masquerades: "by the late Act made against the *Blacks of Waltham*, it is no less than a Felony to go in any sort of Disguise, and so I think it was explained and adjudged in the case of *Towers*, lately try'd and convicted upon the said Act . . . and it is well known he was executed for the same, not without making some Re-

flections and Complaints, that he suffered Death for the same Thing, which some Hundreds of People practised at the Hay-Market, without being call'd to an Account for, whereby he would insinuate as if those lewd Assemblies were conniv'd at." On the Towers case, see Thompson, *Whigs*, pp. 247–49.

52. Wilson, II, 616.

53. *Weekly Journal*, April 10, 1725.

54. Walpole, *Correspondence*, IV (20), 539. See also *Gentleman's Magazine*, May 1750, on the suppression of "mock-Carnivals" at Ranelagh by the Westminster bench.

55. See Leeson, II, 55.

56. *Mrs. Cornelys' Entertainments*, p. 16.

57. Masquerades turn up of course in early-nineteenth-century literature, but they already have an anachronistic air about them. See, for example, the masked assemblies in Maria Edgeworth's *Belinda* (London, 1801), Vol. I, chap. 2, and Pierce Egan's *Life in London* (London, 1821), Book II, chap. 3.

58. Roche, p. 279.

59. "Theresa Cornelys," *Dictionary of National Biography*.

60. For characteristic nineteenth-century accounts of the masquerade, see Boulton, I, 81–128; Malcolm, II, 128–29, 255–56, 272–75; Sydney, *England*, I, 144–50; and Ashton, pp. 215–24.

61. Jarrett, pp. 32, 102. 62. *Ibid.*, p. 102.

63. Plumb, p. 162. 64. Bakhtin, *Rabelais*, pp. 23, 26.

65. *Ibid.*, pp. 321–22. 66. *Ibid.*, p. 24.

67. *Ibid.*, p. 119. 68. *Ibid.*, p. 40.

69. Caillois, pp. 97, 107. 70. See Thomas, pp. 641–68.

71. See Ribeiro, *Dress Worn at Masquerades*, p. 19. This is not to say, of course, that public masking has entirely disappeared in Western Europe and the United States. Mardi Gras and Fasching come to mind as examples of vestigial public carnivals; and Halloween is also an occasion (in the United States) for disguises, though it is perceived primarily as a children's holiday. It is interesting to speculate, however, whether such festivities would persist if they lost their capitalist aspects. Mardi Gras continues to be celebrated in New Orleans, one suspects, mainly because the city's economy depends substantially on tourists. Halloween is an even more severely compromised form of carnival, promoted in large part by candy companies and the sugar industry, and the manufacturers of cheap costumes and toys.

72. Douglas, p. 169.

73. Levey, pp. 62–63. Obviously I am convinced by Levey's controversial interpretation that Watteau's figures leave, rather than embark for, the Island of Love.

CHAPTER 3

1. Other masquerade plays are Aphra Behn's *The Emperour of the Moon* (1687), Susannah Centlivre's *The Perjur'd Husband; or, The Adventures of Venice* (1700), Benjamin Griffin's *The Masquerade; or, An Evening's Intrigue* (1717), Charles Johnson's *The Masquerade* (1719), the anonymous *The Masquerade; or, The Devil's Nursery* (1732), Fielding's *Miss Lucy in Town* (1742), Francis Gentleman's *The Pantheonites* (1773), and Hugh Kelly's *School for Wives* (1773). The masquerade scene gradually lost its appeal for English playwrights in the late eighteenth century, though it was preserved for a time on the Continent in the works of the Sturm und Drang writers, and among later Romantic dramatists and opera librettists. Archibald MacLaren's *The Masquerade; or, Folly Exposed!* (1820) and Thomas Egerton Wilks's *The Black Domino; or, The Masqued Ball* (1838) are among the few self-consciously Romantic English masquerade dramas. A more memorable treatment is Schiller's *Die Verschwörung des Fiesco zu Genua* (1783). There is also an interesting masquerade reference in Act I of *Don Carlos* (1787). Lermontov's *The Masquerade* (1842) is another Romantic adaptation of the eighteenth-century theme. On the treatment of the masquerade in nineteenth-century opera, see chap. 8 below. In twentieth-century drama the masquerade topos has had an ironic reworking in the plays of Pirandello and Frisch.

2. For descriptions of masquerading at the court of Charles II, see Burnet, I, 292. Burnet is cited by the anonymous author of a "Historical Account of Masquerades" in *Lady's Magazine*, May 1775. The nineteenth-century chronicler William Connor Sydney provides additional information on Restoration masquerades in *Social Life in England*, pp. 367–72. On the fêtes of the French court, see the memoirs of Saint-Simon; and Pilon & Saisset.

3. On this commercialization of public entertainment, see Brewer, McKendrick & Plumb.

4. Addison, *Remarks on Italy*, in Addison, *Works*, II, 39.

5. See, for example, Davys's *The Accomplished Rake*; the anonymous epistolary novel *The Masquerade; or, The History of Lord Avon and Miss Tameworth*; or Lee, "The Two Emilys." In the last work, the female protagonist woos her lover at a masquerade while dressed as an Italian peasant. For a Continental example, see Sophie von La Roche's *Geschichte des Fräuleins von Sternheim* (1771).

6. Tanner, pp. 3–4.

7. *Ibid.*, p. 120.

8. Only two critics have looked in detail at particular masquerade scenes: David Blewett, in his chapter on *Roxana*, and Robert Folkenflik, in his article on *Tom Jones*. Both take a somewhat limited ap-

proach, however, confining themselves to speaking of the masquerade's emblematic significance. Taylor uses the concept of masquerading metaphorically, to discuss authorial personae in Defoe and Richardson, but is not concerned with actual masquerades.

9. Todorov, pp. 163, 165–66. For a related discussion of narrative turning points and their association with *aporia*, or disorientation, see M. Brown.

10. See Kalpakgian for a discussion of supernatural elements in Fielding's fiction. On the general waning of folk belief and magic practices in eighteenth-century England, see Thomas.

11. On the history of the World-Upside-Down topos, see Curtius, pp. 94–98.

12. The important concept of polyphony, or heteroglossia, occurs throughout Bakhtin's writings in various contexts too numerous and rich to summarize here. But see in particular *Rabelais*, introduction, and chap. 3, "Popular-Festive Forms and Images in Rabelais." The stylistic implications of heteroglossia are drawn out in the essay "Discourse in the Novel" in *Dialogic Imagination*, pp. 259–422.

13. Pitt, *On the Masquerades* (1727; ll. 19–21).

14. The phrase is from an anonymous essay on masquerades in *Universal Spectator*, April 5, 1729.

CHAPTER 4

1. Doody, p. 90. 2. Eaves & Kimpel, p. 149.
3. Kinkead-Weekes, p. 78. 4. Doody, p. 90.
5. Eaves & Kimpel, p. 150.

6. See, for instance, Defoe's *Farther Adventures of Robinson Crusoe* (1719) and *Serious Reflections during the Life and Surprising Adventures of Robinson Crusoe* (1720). Often the same work that generates sequels also inspires parodies, as was the case with *Pamela*. On the various burlesques of Richardson's novel (including *Shamela*), see Kreissman; and Doody, chap. 4, "*Pamela* Continued: Or, The Sequel That Failed."

7. See Watt, chaps. 3 and 5, for a classic account of the mythic aspects of *Robinson Crusoe* and *Pamela*.

8. See Eaves & Kimpel, pp. 118–53.

9. In her introduction to the Penguin edition of *Pamela*, Doody stresses the revolutionary nature of Part 1, noting the contributions of the nonauthoritarian epistolary form itself: "It is not just the occasional phrase which gives the reader . . . contact with revolt, with the questioning of hierarchy. The novel itself lacks (ostensibly) the controlling, authoritative and soothing presence of the monarchical author" (p. 9).

10. Montagu, II, 200.

11. In the first edition of *Pamela* the heroine's father is at first unable to recognize his daughter in her new gentlewoman's clothes, so much like a lady does she now appear. Richardson later amended the text on this point (see the Penguin edition, n. 250, p. 532), but other hints of clothes-magic were retained (see McIntosh).

12. Eaves & Kimpel, pp. 136–39.

13. Barthes, *Roland Barthes*, p. 149.

14. Tanner, p. 148.

15. Like Pope's in *The Dunciad*, Richardson's representation of London as a protean scene of chaos reflects an eighteenth-century commonplace. See Byrd, pp. 64–65.

16. Bakhtin sees in the motif of breastfeeding a relic of the ancient carnivalesque theme of the duality of the body, and calls attention to Goethe's attraction to this image in Correggio's *The Weaning of a Child* (*Rabelais*, p. 322).

17. Richardson, *Correspondence*, VI, 25.

18. Goethe, p. 461.

19. Bakhtin, *Rabelais*, p. 318.

20. A case can be made for Roxana as another version of the double heroine of carnival. Not only is she, like Pamela, utterly implicated in the world of masquerade, but she engenders a literal "alternative self" in the figure of her maidservant, Amy. I comment on the complexity of their relations in "Amy, Who Knew My Disease."

CHAPTER 5

1. Amelia's problematic injury inspired much contemporary comment, some of it risible. Rothstein, p. 174, n. 11, cites early readers' responses to her disfigurement. One must concur with his observation that "Fielding would hardly have chosen to give Amelia a damaged nose instead of a scarred chin or missing molar if he had not intended the semblance, belying the reality, of lewdness."

2. See chap. 2, n. 30, above.

3. Few twentieth-century critics have dealt specifically with Fielding's writings on the masquerade. Two who have are L. P. Goggins ("Fielding's *The Masquerade*") and Robert Folkenflik ("Tom Jones, the Gypsies, and the Masquerade").

4. Recent commentary on Fielding's work has begun to examine its ideological discontinuities and ambiguities at least as much as its much-vaunted formal achievement. The result has been a long-overdue recognition of Fielding as a more complicated and paradoxical author, certainly, than nineteenth-century commentators realized, or indeed than many of his twentieth-century explicators, the New Critics among them, have been willing to grant. Claude Rawson's *Henry Fielding and*

the Augustan Ideal Under Stress is exemplary in this regard—perhaps the most eloquent version of a non-monolithic or "complex" Fielding—and so too are J. Paul Hunter's *Occasional Form*, Ian Donaldson's chapter on Fielding in *The World Upside-Down*, and Pat Rogers's recent short biography, *Henry Fielding*. Also indicative of the revisionist tendency are Homer O. Brown, "*Tom Jones*: The 'Bastard' of History," and Susan P. McNamara, "Mirrors of Fiction Within *Tom Jones*," both of which question, in different ways, traditional critical notions regarding the legibility of Fielding's most famous work. Jean-Claude Dupas has applied Bakhtinian concepts in an exploratory way to Fielding in "*Joseph Andrews*: L'Excentricité d'un discours carnavalisé."

5. Bakhtin, *Rabelais*, pp. 39–40. Caillois, pp. 130–32, likewise distinguishes the mask of modern society, that of erotic fête and conspiracy, from the traditional sorcerer's mask, the instrument of transformation and magic.

6. Bakhtin, *Rabelais*, p. 39.

7. *The Masquerade, containing a Variety of Merry Characters*.

8. Fielding, "Essay," p. 156.

9. Bakhtin, *Rabelais*, p. 34.

10. *Ibid.*, p. 40.

11. See Paulson, *Satire*, p. 164. Comments on the mixed generic conventions in *Amelia* have been numerous. In many ways Sherburn's famous 1936 article set the stage for such commentary by calling attention to the embedded "epic" or Virgilian plot in *Amelia* and the way it is joined to a satiric attack on the aristocracy. Other critics have also noted *Amelia's* generic uncertainty. Baker points to its uneasy shifting between realistic and romance modes, and Hassall describes the novel's "schizophrenic" split between novelistic and satiric devices. Braudy connects *Amelia* with eighteenth-century historical discourse. Alter offers perhaps the most exhaustive account of *Amelia's* artistic discontinuities.

Two readings of Fielding's novel have been particularly helpful to me in formulating my own. The first is Eric Rothstein's in *Systems of Order and Inquiry*. His comments on what he calls "the epistemology of a veiled world" in the novel have an essential bearing on the implications of the mask. The second is John Bender's excellent chapter on *Amelia* in *The Novel and the Rise of the Penitentiary*. Like the masquerade, the prison is a topos—both a historical site and a part of Fielding's fictional rhetoric. As Bender shows, the representation of social practice is also a key to narrative: prison and masquerade are linked figures in the genesis of Fielding's plot itself.

12. See B. Johnson, pp. ix–xii.

13. An account of Fielding's intervention appears in the *General Advertiser* for June 5, 1751. On his zeal in suppressing other forms of

popular entertainment, such as gaming houses, see the introduction to the Battestin edition of *Amelia*, pp. xxiv–xxv.

14. Fielding, "Essay," p. 155.

15. *Ibid.*, p. 154.

16. On the characterological modes associated with allegory, see Fletcher, chap. 1, "The Daemonic Agent." Fielding's tendency toward stereotypical characterization—the polarized type figures of allegory and romance—has been a popular critical theme for some time. Sacks's chapters on Fielding's "fallible paragons" and "walking concepts" are perhaps the fullest statement on the matter, though one can find helpful statements also in Watt, pp. 260–68, and Frye, pp. 167, 172–73. In "Fielding's Definition of Wisdom," Battestin interprets *Tom Jones* according to what he calls Fielding's emblematic typology of character. See also Coolidge.

17. Fletcher, chap. 2, "The Cosmic Image," comments on the tendency of allegory to present static or emblematic images to the reader— "isolated mosaic imagery"—in place of mimetically realized actions. The "general allegorical transmutation of agency into imagery" reproduces the pictorial quality, the sense of frozen image or tableau, that one so often comes across in explicitly allegorical works. Folkenflik, in "Tom Jones," likewise makes a case for Fielding's iconographic method. Comparing the "false" pastoral of the masquerade room with the "true" pastoral of the gypsy community, Folkenflik argues that the two scenes function as contrasting halves of an allegorical diptych, similar to those found in Spenser and Ariosto.

18. In his classic essay "The Plot of *Tom Jones*" (1950), Crane says it is impossible not to be "shocked" by Tom's entanglement with Lady Bellaston and by the palpable inconsistency in his characterization: "It is necessary, no doubt, that [Tom] should now fall lower than ever before, but surely not so low as to make it hard to infer his act from our previous knowledge of his character; . . . for the moment at least, a different Tom is before our eyes" (p. 127).

19. Few modern readers have agreed with Cleland's judgment (in the *Monthly Review*, Dec. 1751) that *Amelia* delightfully "puts Morality into action," insinuating "its greatest truths into the mind, under the colours of amusement and fiction." Hunter, chap. 9, comments on the impoverishing artistic effect of *Amelia*'s hypertrophied didactic impulse.

20. On the *psychomachia* as a fundamental pattern of symbolic action in allegory, and the paratactic nature of allegorical narrative structure, see Fletcher, pp. 151–61.

21. This extra chapter appears in the Henley edition of *Amelia* only.

22. On the "warrior in skirts," see Kunzle. On the relevance of the Hercules/Omphale story to Tom Jones's sojourn with Lady Bellaston, see Ek.

23. Other examples of the subgenre are Haywood's story of Erminia, *Female Spectator*, I, 32–33; and the anonymous article "Affecting Masquerade Adventure" in *Gentleman's Magazine*, Dec. 1754.

24. Calling attention to this scene, Hagstrum writes of Amelia's response: "Such is the way to a *coeur sensible.*" Hagstrum sees *Amelia* as being ultimately more coherent than I do—"an important novel of controlled sensibility"—yet also takes into account the revolutionary and potentially disruptive elements in Fielding's treatment of love and desire (pp. 180–85). Though the influence of Richardson on the *roman larmoyant* tradition has been much discussed, this very fact, one suspects, may have obscured to some extent those few yet potent fictional moments when Fielding also somewhat paradoxically prefigures this same tradition.

25. Fletcher, p. 220.

26. One might make an analogy also with the shifting between emblematic and expressive modes that Paulson sees as characteristic of much eighteenth-century art. Like the Hogarthian progresses, *Amelia* might be adduced as a paradigm for a transitional aesthetic halfway between the older emblematic forms and a new concept of an ambiguous, multivalent art. See Paulson, *Emblem.*

27. See Rawson, part I ("Nature's Dance of Death").

28. See Babcock, "The Novel."

29. Tanner, p. 3.

30. On the potential for contradiction in cultural conceptualization, see Douglas, especially chap. 9, "The System at War with Itself."

CHAPTER 6

1. On the female iconography of popular insurgency, see Davis, chap. 5, "Women on Top."

2. Lévi-Strauss, *Elementary Structures*, pp. 481ff.

3. Suggestive in this connection is the association made by anti-masquerade writers between female promiscuity and accidental incest. According to the *pensée sauvage* of such writers, the uncontrolled circulation of women at the masquerade made it possible for the defining taboo of culture itself to be violated. Lurid stories of unintentional masquerade incest proliferated. See *The Conduct of the Stage Consider'd*; *A Seasonable Apology*; and *The Masquerade; or, The Devil's Nursery.*

4. In his essay "On Narcissism" (1914), before turning to the relation between narcissism and schizophrenic disorders, Freud briefly discusses the concept of a "primary and normal narcissism." On modern psychoanalysts' return to this less prejudicial characterization of narcissistic impulses, see A. Miller.

5. A limitation of Bakhtin's otherwise profound analysis is the relatively little attention he gives to the privileged status and novel free-

doms carnival granted to female participants. This is not to say that he does not discuss woman in the abstract. At one point in *Rabelais and His World*, for instance, he sharply contrasts the "popular" treatment of women by Rabelais—the representation in *Pantagruel* of their special connection with the positive transformational and carnivalesque forces of "the material bodily stratum"—with the virulently antifeminist formulations of medieval Christianity (pp. 240–41). Yet Bakhtin's comments on medieval and Renaissance carnival are not gender-specific. Carnival represents simply the utopian second life of the "people"— that generalized folk collectivity whose ideals Bakhtin so eloquently champions (p. 33). Despite the exemplary symbolic meaning of their bodies, women do not exist for Bakhtin as a separate political or philosophical contingent in the carnival crowd; he accords them no distinctive euphoria. Davis, chap. 5, offers a more complete analysis, suggesting that antipatriarchal impulses held a central place in the carnival traditions of early modern Europe, and may have represented for the women who witnessed and participated "a resource for feminist reflection on women's capacities" (p. 144). Booth, in "Freedom of Interpretation," addresses a similar issue.

6. On the grammar of the eighteenth- and nineteenth-century "feminocentric" plot, see Nancy K. Miller's *The Heroine's Text* and her discussion of plausibility and genre in women's writing in "Emphasis Added."

7. All references are to the fourth edition (1784).

8. *Lady's Magazine*, Dec. 1777.

9. Frye, pp. 41–43.

10. Bakhtin, *Rabelais*, p. 54.

11. Freud, *Interpretation of Dreams*, pp. 293–94.

12. See Freud, "A Special Type of Object Choice Made by Men" (1910). An interesting feature of this essay is its asymmetry. Whereas Freud implies at the start that both men and women make erotic object-choices—and must reconcile "the demands expressed in their phantasy with the exigencies of real life"—the exclusive presentation, in the body of the essay, of men as choosers and women as the objects they choose severely undermines any active notion of erotic object-choice by women. Later Freud would return to the disparity between male and female object-love ("On Narcissism"; 1914), but here he ignores the important issue of whether the concept of female object-choice has any deep validity within a patriarchal sexual economy. That it does not—at least so far as heterosexual relations go (the ideology of romantic love notwithstanding)—has been the conclusion of a number of feminist theorists. (See Rich.)

13. On madness as female protest, see Castle, *Clarissa's Ciphers*, pp. 119–23; and the introduction to Gilbert & Gubar.

14. Compare N. Miller, "Exquisite Cadavers."

15. That for Bakhtin the carnivalesque is associated with freedom, in both the populist and the literary sense, is implicit throughout *Rabelais and His World*, but particularly in his descriptions of the "frank and free" behavior of the marketplace during carnival time (pp. 10–11), the transgressive nature of popular festive forms (p. 23), and the "disobedient" and "unofficial" quality of carnivalesque imagery (pp. 30–35). See also Starobinski, p. 90.

16. Barthes, *Mythologies*, pp. 143, 154.

17. Spacks, pp. 181, 188–89.

18. Addison, *Guardian 154*, in Chalmers, XV.

19. Freud, "On Narcissism," pp. 56–59.

20. Wollstonecraft, p. 121.

21. Compare de Beauvoir's description of male and female socialization processes, pp. 249–306.

22. See Heilbrun, chap. 3, "Women Writers and Female Characters: The Failure of Imagination."

CHAPTER 7

1. See the introduction to the Tompkins edition of Inchbald, p. vii.

2. Boaden, I, 140–41. On Inchbald's political affiliations with Godwin, Thomas Holcroft, and the other English Jacobins, see Kelly. See Zall for a brief summary of Inchbald's career.

3. On Jan. 14, 1810, Mrs. Edgeworth wrote to Inchbald, "I never read a novel that . . . so completely possessed me with the belief in the real existence of all the people it represents. . . . I am of the opinion that it is by leaving more than most other writers do to the imagination, that you succeed so eminently in affecting it. By the force that is necessary to repress feeling, we judge of the intensity of the feeling, and you always contrive to give us by intelligible but simple signs the measure of this force" (cited by Tompkins, introduction to Inchbald, pp. vii–viii). Lytton Strachey edited *A Simple Story* in 1908 for the *Oxford Miscellany*.

4. de Beauvoir, p. 249.

5. Bataille, p. 71.

6. On *Rosa Fielding* (1876), see Marcus, chap. 5. Conscious of the irregularity of eroticized guardian/ward bonds, Dickens does not allow the projected marriage of Esther and her aged guardian, Jarndyce, to take place; at the end of the novel Jarndyce unselfishly gives his ward over to her real love, Woodcourt. The moment marks a return to normative, desexualized guardian/ward relations. "I clasped him round the neck," writes Esther, "and hung my head upon his breast, and wept. 'Lie lightly, confidently, here, my child,' said he, pressing

me gently to him. 'I am your guardian and your father now. Rest confidently here.'" (*Bleak House*, p. 649.)

7. According to Boaden, I, 287, Inchbald began a translation of the *Confessions* in 1790; but there are many affinities. Boaden himself compares Miss Milner's story to that of Sophia in *Émile*.

8. Dorriforth's sentimental education at the hands of Miss Milner may be seen as a fruitful reversal of the conventional pattern in earlier eighteenth-century fiction in which women characters are educated into sexual passion by male tutors. The early part of *Moll Flanders* (the story of Moll and the Elder Brother), *Pamela*, and *Memoirs of a Woman of Pleasure* offer variations on the theme; *Clarissa* treats it ironically, through Lovelace's frustrated attempts to animate his "charming frostpiece." Inchbald's novel initiates a new tradition in which these implicit tutor/student roles between men and women are reversed. Later Charlotte Brontë would play upon similar reversals in *Villette*. The hero's education into sexual desire at the hands of an older woman is a mainstay, obviously, in nineteenth-century French fiction; one thinks of Benjamin Constant, Stendhal, and Flaubert.

9. See Canetti, sec. 8 ("The Command. Flight and Sting").

10. Tompkins, introduction to Inchbald, p. xvi.

11. Heathcliff comes to mind as the obvious nineteenth-century example. See Frye's comments on Brontë and the romance tradition, pp. 304–7. Boaden repeatedly refers to Inchbald's production as a romance (see, for example, *Memoirs*, I, 288, 290).

12. Boaden, I, 276.

13. *Ibid.*, p. 264; Inchbald, p. 344 (Tompkins note).

14. The tale of Bluebeard, which here lends a sinister shading to Elmwood's character, was well known in the eighteenth century thanks to many contemporary editions and translations of Perrault's *Contes du temps* (1696). Inchbald's theatrical associate George Colman the Younger wrote a play called *Blue Beard* in 1798, a few years after *A Simple Story*. The folk motif of the forbidden chamber, classified under the general heading "Tabu" and the secondary heading "Unique prohibitions and compulsions: The one forbidden thing," is no. C611 in Stith Thompson's *Motif-Index*.

15. Readers have disagreed profoundly about Miss Milner's moral status. Boaden scoffed at any didactic reading of *A Simple Story* and cherished its heroine's vivacity and charm. More recently, however, Kelly has attacked Miss Milner's "lack of moral discipline" and described Matilda's story as an attempt "to atone for her mother's error" (pp. 73–74). Such splits may reflect deeper ideological differences: in Kelly's case, pervasive antifeminism (he speaks of the "excessive and rebellious" heroines of Wollstonecraft and the "hysterical incoherence"

afflicting the work of women Jacobin novelists) seems in part to inform his highly judgmental interpretation of Miss Milner's character.

16. One's sense of Oedipal drama in *A Simple Story* is intensified by the knowledge that Inchbald's father died when she was seven. During the composition of her novel Inchbald was simultaneously involved in writing an autobiography, which she later burned (in 1819) on the advice of her Catholic confessor. See Boaden, II, 231; and Tompkins, introduction to Inchbald, p. xxx.

17. Tanner discusses this centralization and domestication of transgressive impulses. See, in particular, his remarks on the symbolic functions of "la maison paternelle" in Rousseau's *La Nouvelle Héloïse*, pp. 120–33, and his analysis of Flaubert's *Madame Bovary*, pp. 233–367.

CHAPTER 8

EPIGRAPH: Spence, *Letters from the Grand Tour*, p. 96.
1. Wilson, II, 606–19.   2. Bakhtin, *Rabelais*, p. 33.
3. *Ibid.*, p. 119.   4. *Ibid.*, pp. 37, 44.
5. A sample of the twelve-year-old Austen's burlesque, from *Jack and Alice*, chap. 1: "No one could imagine who was the Sultana! Till at length on her addressing a beautifull Flora who was reclining in a studied attitude on a couch, with 'Oh Cecilia, I wish I was really what I pretend to be,' she was discovered by the never failing genius of Charles Adams, to be the elegant but ambitious Caroline Simpson, & the person to whom she addressed herself, he rightly imagined to be her lovely but affected sister Cecilia." (*Minor Works*, p. 14.)
6. Dickens, *Pickwick Papers*, p. 204.
7. Other Romantic reworkings of carnivalesque material are Kleist's "Der Findling" (1811) and De Quincey's *Klosterheim; or, The Masque* (1832).
8. Hawthorne, p. 218.
9. The passage reads in part (Night V: "The Relapse," ll. 870–75, in Young, I, 103):

> The dreadful masquerader, thus equipp'd,
> Out-sallies on adventures. Ask you where?
> Where is he not? For his peculiar haunts,
> Let this suffice; sure as night follows day,
> Death treads in pleasure's footsteps round the world,
> When pleasure treads the paths which reason shuns.

10. Wharton's story is collected in *The Descent of Man and Other Stories* (London, 1904). Parrish's painting is catalogued and reproduced in Lovell, p. 74.

11. The disturbing central episode in Purdy's *Mourners Below* (1984) is a masquerade at which the adolescent hero is seduced by the hostess, and afterward stripped of his costume, beaten, and sexually humiliated.

12. Lindenberger discusses the survival in nineteenth-century opera of the "high style" and similarly outmoded and anti-naturalistic literary fashions.

13. Important visual renderings of the masquerade/death idea are Goya's sinister engraving "Nadie se conoce" (Nobody knows himself)—plate 6 of *Los Caprichos* (1799)—and Jean-Léon Gérôme's painting *The Duel After the Masquerade* (1857), depicting a dying Pierrot collapsing on a snowy wasteland after a post-masquerade duel. See Figs. 36 and 38, above.

14. Paulson, *Emblem*, p. 130.

15. See Sennett.

16. On the nineteenth-century crowd scene in French literature, see Schor. An eccentric return to an earlier, less rationalized conception of the crowd can be found in Raymond Roussel's surrealistic novel in verse, *La Doublure* (1897), which contains lengthy descriptions of masquerade crowds at Nice.

17. Fletcher, pp. 110–13.

18. Starobinski, p. 85.

Works Cited

Works Cited

Addison, Joseph. *The Guardian.* Vols. XIII–XV of *British Essayists.* Ed. A. Chalmers. Boston, 1856.

———. *Works.* 6 vols. Ed. Richard Hurd. London, 1811.

Addison, Joseph, and Richard Steele. *The Spectator.* 5 vols. Ed. Donald F. Bond. Oxford, Eng., 1965.

Alter, Robert. *Fielding and the Nature of the Novel.* Cambridge, Mass., 1968.

Ashton, John. *Old Times.* New York, 1885.

Austen, Jane. *Minor Works.* Vol. VI of *The Works of Jane Austen.* Ed. R. W. Chapman. London, 1954.

Babcock, Barbara A. "'Liberty's a Whore': Inversions, Marginalia, and Picaresque Narrative." In *The Reversible World.* Ed. Barbara A. Babcock. Ithaca, N.Y., 1978, pp. 95–116.

———. "The Novel and the Carnival World." *MLN,* 89 (1974), 911–37.

———, ed. *The Reversible World: Symbolic Inversion in Art and Society.* Ithaca, N.Y., 1978.

Bachofen, J. J. *Myth, Religion, and Mother Right.* Trans. Ralph Manheim. Princeton, N.J., 1967.

Baker, Sheridan. "Fielding's *Amelia* and the Materials of Romance." *Philological Quarterly,* 45 (1962), 437–49.

Bakhtin, Mikhail. *The Dialogic Imagination.* Trans. Caryl Emerson and Michael Holquist. Ed. Michael Holquist. Austin, Tex., 1981.

————. *Rabelais and His World*. Trans. Hélène Iswolsky. Cambridge, Mass., 1968.

Barber, C. L. *Shakespeare's Festive Comedy: A Study of Dramatic Form and Its Relation to Social Custom*. Princeton, N.J., 1959.

Barish, Jonas. *The Anti-Theatrical Prejudice*. Berkeley, Calif., 1981.

Barthes, Roland. *The Fashion System*. Trans. Richard Howard and Matthew Ward. New York, 1983.

————. *Mythologies*. Trans. Annette Lavers. London, 1972.

————. *Roland Barthes*. Trans. Richard Howard. New York, 1977.

Bataille, Georges. *L'Erotisme*. Paris, 1965.

Battestin, Martin C. "Fielding's Definition of Wisdom: Some Functions of Ambiguity and Emblem in *Tom Jones*." *ELH*, 35 (1968), 188–217.

Beauvoir, Simone de. *The Second Sex*. Trans. H. M. Parshley. New York, 1961.

Bell, Quentin. *On Human Finery*. 2d ed. New York, 1976.

Bender, John. *The Novel and the Rise of the Penitentiary*. Chicago, forthcoming.

Blewett, David. *Defoe's Art of Fiction*. Toronto, 1979.

Boaden, James. *Memoirs of Mrs. Inchbald*. 2 vols. London, 1833.

Booth, Wayne. "Freedom of Interpretation: Bakhtin and the Challenge of Feminist Criticism." *Critical Inquiry*, 9 (1982), 45–76.

Boswell, James. *Life of Johnson*. 6 vols. Ed. G. B. Hill; rev. L. F. Powell. Oxford, Eng., 1934–50.

Boucé, P. G., ed. *Sexuality in Eighteenth-Century Britain*. Totowa, N.J., 1982.

Boulton, William B. *The Amusements of Old London*. 2 vols. London, 1901.

Bowyer, John Wilson. *The Celebrated Mrs. Centlivre*. Durham, N.C., 1952.

Braudy, Leo. *Narrative Form in History and Fiction: Hume, Fielding, and Gibbon*. Princeton, N.J., 1970.

Brewer, John, Neil McKendrick, and J. H. Plumb. *The Birth of a Consumer Society: The Commercialization of Eighteenth-Century England*. London, 1982.

Brewer, John, and John Styles, eds. *An Ungovernable People: The English and Their Law in the Seventeenth and Eighteenth Centuries*. New Brunswick, N.J., 1980.

Bristol, Michael D. *Carnival and Theater: Plebeian Culture and the Structure of Authority in Renaissance England*. London, 1985.

Brown, Homer O. "*Tom Jones*: The 'Bastard' of History." *boundary 2*, 7 (1979), 201–33.

Brown, Marshall. "'Errours Endlesse Traine': On Turning Points and the Dialectical Imagination." *PMLA*, 99 (1984), 9–25.

Burke, Edmund. *A Philosophical Enquiry into the Origin of Our Ideas of the Sublime and Beautiful.* Ed. J. T. Boulton. Notre Dame, Ind., 1968.

Burke, Peter. *Popular Culture in Early Modern Europe.* New York, 1978.

Burnet, Gilbert. *History of His Own Times.* 4 vols. Ed. Thomas Burnet. London, 1818.

Burney, Frances. *Cecilia; or, Memoirs of an Heiress.* 4th ed. 5 vols. London, 1784. [Cited by volume and page numbers.]

———. *The Early Diary of Frances Burney, 1768–1778.* 2 vols. Ed. A. R. Ellis. London, 1889.

Byrd, Max. *London Transformed: Images of the City in the Eighteenth Century.* New Haven, Conn., 1978.

Caillois, Roger. *Man, Play and Games.* Trans. Meyer Barash. New York, 1958.

Canetti, Elias. *Crowds and Power.* Trans. Carol Stewart. New York, 1962.

Casanova de Seingalt, Jacques. *Memoirs.* 6 vols. Trans. Arthur Machen. New York, 1959.

Castle, Terry. "'Amy, Who Knew My Disease': A Psychosexual Pattern in Defoe's *Roxana.*" *ELH,* 46 (1979), 81–96.

———. *Clarissa's Ciphers: Meaning and Disruption in Richardson's 'Clarissa.'* Ithaca, N.Y., 1982.

———. "Matters Not Fit to Be Mentioned: Fielding's *The Female Husband.*" *ELH,* 49 (1982), 602–22.

Catchpenny Prints: 163 Popular Engravings from the Eighteenth Century. New York, 1970.

Cavell, Stanley. "The Avoidance of Love: A Reading of *King Lear.*" In *Must We Mean What We Say?* Cambridge, Eng., 1976, pp. 267–353.

Cawte, E. J. *Ritual Animal Disguise.* Cambridge, Eng., 1978.

Centlivre, Susannah. *The Masquerade: A Poem.* London, 1713.

Chalmers, Alexander, ed. *British Essayists.* 38 vols. Boston, 1856.

Cleland, John. *Memoirs of a Woman of Pleasure.* Ed. Peter Sabor. Oxford, Eng., 1985.

Climenson, E. J., ed. *Elizabeth Montagu, the Queen of the Bluestockings: Her Correspondence, 1720–61.* 2 vols. London, 1906.

The Conduct of the Stage Consider'd, with Short Remarks upon the Original and Pernicious Consequences of Masquerades. London, 1721.

Coolidge, John S. "Fielding and 'Conservation of Character.'" *Modern Philology,* 62 (1960), 245–59. Reprinted in *Fielding: A Collection of Critical Essays.* Ed. Ronald Paulson. Englewood Cliffs, N.J., 1962, pp. 158–76.

Cope, Jackson I. *Dramaturgy of the Demonic: Studies in Antigeneric Theater from Ruzante to Grimaldi.* Baltimore, 1984.

Cowley, Hannah. *The Belle's Stratagem.* London, 1781.

Crane, Ronald S. "The Plot of *Tom Jones.*" *Journal of General Education,*

4 (1950), 112–30. Reprinted in *Tom Jones*. Ed. Sheridan Baker. New York, 1973, pp. 844–69.

Curll, Edmund. *Venus in the Cloyster; or, The Nun in Her Smock*. London, 1725.

Curtius, Ernst Robert. *European Literature and the Latin Middle Ages*. Trans. Willard R. Trask. New York, 1953.

The Danger of Masquerades and Raree-Shows. London, 1718.

Davis, Natalie Zemon. *Society and Culture in Early Modern France*. Stanford, Calif., 1975.

Davys, Mary. *The Accomplished Rake; or, Modern Fine Gentleman*. London, 1727.

Defoe, Daniel. *The Political History of the Devil*. London, 1726.

———. *Roxana: The Fortunate Mistress*. Ed. Jane Jack. Oxford, Eng., 1981.

———. *A System of Magick; or, A History of the Black Art*. London, 1727.

Deutsch, Otto Erich. *Handel: A Documentary Biography*. London, 1955.

Dickens, Charles. *Bleak House*. Ed. Morton Dauwen Zabel. Boston, 1956.

———. *The Posthumous Papers of the Pickwick Club*. New York: Modern Library, n.d.

Dinesen, Isak. "Carnival." In *Carnival: Entertainments and Posthumous Tales*. Chicago, 1977, pp. 57–121.

Donaldson, Ian. *The World Upside-Down: Comedy from Jonson to Fielding*. Oxford, Eng., 1970.

Doody, Margaret Anne. *A Natural Passion: A Study of the Novels of Samuel Richardson*. Oxford, Eng., 1974.

Douglas, Mary. *Purity and Danger: Analysis of the Concepts of Pollution and Taboo*. London, 1966.

Dryden, John. *Marriage à la Mode*. Ed. Mark S. Auburn. Regents Restoration Drama Series. Lincoln, Neb., 1981.

Dupas, Jean-Claude. "*Joseph Andrews*: L'Excentricité d'un discours carnavalisé." In *L'Excentricité en Grand Bretagne au XVIIIe siècle*. Ed. Michèle Plaisant. Lille, 1976, pp. 59–79.

Eagleton, Terry. *The Rape of Clarissa*. Minneapolis, 1982.

Eaves, T. C. Duncan, and Ben D. Kimpel. *Samuel Richardson: A Biography*. Oxford, Eng., 1971.

Edgeworth, Maria. *Belinda*. 3 vols. London, 1801.

Ek, Grete. "Glory, Jest and Riddle: The Masque of Tom Jones in London." *English Studies*, 60 (1979), 148–58.

An Epistle to John James H--d--g-r on the Report of Signior F-r-n-lli's being with Child. London, 1736.

An Essay on Plays and Masquerades. London, 1724.

Faderman, Lillian. *Surpassing the Love of Men: Romantic Friendship and Love Between Women from the Renaissance to the Present.* New York, 1981.

Fielding, Henry. *Amelia.* Ed. Martin C. Battestin. Middletown, Conn., 1983. [Cited by book and chapter numbers.]

———. *Amelia.* 2 vols. Ed. William Ernest Henley. New York, 1967.

———. *Charge Delivered to the Grand Jury.* London, 1749.

———. *An Enquiry into the Causes of the Late Increase of Robbers.* London, 1751.

———. "An Essay on the Knowledge of the Characters of Men." In Vol. I of *Miscellanies.* Ed. Henry Knight Miller. Oxford, Eng., 1972.

———. *The Female Husband and Other Writings.* Ed. Claude E. Jones. English Reprints Series. Liverpool, 1960.

———. *The Masquerade.* London, 1728. Reprinted in Fielding, *The Female Husband and Other Writings.*

———. *Tom Jones.* Ed. Sheridan Baker. New York, 1973. [Cited by book and chapter numbers.]

Flaubert, Gustave. *Madame Bovary.* Trans. Mildred Marmur. New York, 1964.

Fletcher, Angus. *Allegory: Theory of a Symbolic Mode.* Ithaca, N.Y., 1964.

Folkenflik, Robert. "A Room of Pamela's Own." *ELH,* 39 (1972), 585–96.

———. "Tom Jones, the Gypsies, and the Masquerade." *University of Toronto Quarterly,* 44 (1975), 224–37.

Foucault, Michel. *The History of Sexuality: An Introduction.* Trans. Robert Hurley. New York, 1978.

Frazer, James George. *The Golden Bough.* Ed. Theodor H. Gaster. New York, 1959.

Freud, Sigmund. *Civilization and Its Discontents.* Trans. James Strachey. New York, 1961.

———. *The Interpretation of Dreams.* In *The Basic Writings of Sigmund Freud.* Trans. and ed. A. A. Brill. New York, 1938.

———. "Negation." Trans. Joan Riviere. In *General Psychological Theory.* Ed. Philip Rieff. New York, 1963, pp. 213–17.

———. "On Narcissism: An Introduction." Trans. Cecil M. Baines. In *General Psychological Theory.* Ed. Philip Rieff. New York, 1963, pp. 56–82.

———. "A Special Type of Object Choice Made by Men." Trans. Joan Riviere. In *Sexuality and the Psychology of Love.* Ed. Philip Rieff. New York, 1963, pp. 49–58.

Frye, Northrop. *Anatomy of Criticism*. Princeton, N.J., 1957.

Geertz, Clifford. "Deep Play: Notes on a Balinese Cockfight." *Daedalus*, 101 (1972), 1–38.

———. *Person, Time, and Conduct in Bali: An Essay in Cultural Analysis*. New Haven, Conn., 1966.

Gibson, Edmund. *A Sermon Preached to the Societies for the Reformation of Manners*. London, 1724.

Gilbert, Sandra M., and Susan Gubar. *The Madwoman in the Attic: The Woman Writer and the Nineteenth-Century Literary Imagination*. New Haven, Conn., 1979.

Gluckman, Max. *Custom and Conflict in Africa*. Glencoe, Ill., 1965.

Goethe, Johann Wolfgang von. *The Italian Journey* [Die Italienische Reise]. Trans. W. H. Auden and Elizabeth Mayer. New York, 1962.

Goffman, Erving. *Behavior in Public Places: Notes on the Social Organization of Gatherings*. New York, 1963.

Goggins, L. P. "Fielding's *The Masquerade*." *Philological Quarterly*, 36 (1957), 475–87.

Goldberg, Rita. *Sex and Enlightenment: Women in Richardson and Diderot*. Cambridge, Eng., 1984.

Goldsmith, Oliver. *The Vicar of Wakefield*. New York, 1964.

———. *Works*. 4 vols. Ed. Peter Cunningham. New York, 1908.

Graves, Robert. *The White Goddess*. New York, 1948.

Griffin, Benjamin. *The Masquerade; or, An Evening's Intrigue*. London, 1717.

Hagstrum, Jean H. *Sex and Sensibility: Ideal and Erotic Love from Milton to Mozart*. Chicago, 1980.

Halsband, Robert. *The Life of Lady Mary Wortley Montagu*. Oxford, Eng., 1956.

Hassall, Anthony J. "Fielding's *Amelia*: Dramatic and Authorial Narration." *Novel*, 5 (1971–72), 225–33.

Hawthorne, Nathaniel. *The Blithedale Romance*. New York, 1958.

Hay, Douglas, et al. *Albion's Fatal Tree: Crime and Society in Eighteenth-Century England*. New York, 1975.

Haywood, Eliza. *The Female Spectator*. 4 vols. 3d ed. London, 1750.

———. *The Masqueraders; or, Fatal Curiosity*. London, 1724.

Heilbrun, Carolyn. *Reinventing Womanhood*. New York, 1979.

Hollander, Anne. *Seeing Through Clothes*. New York, 1975.

Howson, Gerald. *Thief-Taker General: The Rise and Fall of Jonathan Wild*. London, 1970.

Hunter, J. Paul. *Occasional Form: Henry Fielding and the Chains of Circumstance*. Baltimore, 1975.

Inchbald, Elizabeth. *A Simple Story*. Ed. J. M. S. Tompkins. London, 1967. [Cited by page number.]

Ireland, J., and John Nichols. *Hogarth's Complete Works.* 3d ser. Edinburgh, 1883.

Jarrett, Derek. *England in the Age of Hogarth.* London, 1976.

Jefferys, Thomas. *A Collection of the Dresses of Different Nations, Ancient and Modern.* 4 vols. London, 1757.

Johnson, Barbara. *The Critical Difference.* Baltimore, 1981.

Johnson, Charles. *The Masquerade: A Comedy.* London, 1719.

Kalpakgian, Mitchell. *The Marvellous in Fielding's Novels.* Washington, D.C., 1981.

Kanner, Barbara, ed. *The Women of England.* Hamden, Conn., 1979.

Katz, Jonathan. *Gay American History.* New York, 1976.

Kelly, Gary. *The English Jacobin Novel, 1780–1805.* Oxford, Eng., 1976.

Kinkead-Weekes, Mark. *Samuel Richardson: Dramatic Novelist.* Ithaca, N.Y., 1973.

Kreissman, Bernard. *Pamela-Shamela.* Lincoln, Neb., 1960.

Kundera, Milan. "The Novel and Europe." Trans. David Bellos. *New York Review of Books,* July 19, 1984, pp. 15–19.

Kunzle, David. "World Upside Down: The Iconography of a European Broadsheet Type." In *The Reversible World.* Ed. Barbara A. Babcock. Ithaca, N.Y., 1978, pp. 39–94.

Lee, Sophia. "The Two Emilys." In Sophia and Harriet Lee, *Canterbury Tales,* 5 vols. London, 1799–1805, Vol. II.

Leeson, Margaret. *The Memoirs of Margaret Leeson, Written by Herself.* 3 vols. Dublin, 1797.

Le Roy Ladurie, Emmanuel. *Carnival in Romans.* Trans. Mary Feeney. New York, 1979.

Levey, Michael. *Rococo to Revolution: Major Trends in Eighteenth-Century Painting.* New York, 1966.

Lévi-Strauss, Claude. *The Elementary Structures of Kinship.* Rev. ed. Trans. James Harle Bell, John Richard von Sturmer, and Rodney Needham. Ed. Rodney Needham. Boston, 1969.

———. *The Savage Mind.* Chicago, 1966.

———. *Structural Anthropology.* Trans. Claire Jacobson and Brooke Grundfest Schoepf. New York, 1963.

Lindenberger, Herbert. *Opera: The Extravagant Art.* Ithaca, N.Y., 1984.

Lovell, M. M. *Venice: The American View, 1860–1920.* San Francisco, 1984.

McIntosh, Carey. "Pamela's Clothes." *ELH,* 35 (1968), 75–83.

McNamara, Susan P. "Mirrors of Fiction within *Tom Jones*: The Paradox of Self-Reference." *Eighteenth-Century Studies,* 12 (1979), 372–90.

Malcolm, James Peller. *Anecdotes of the Manners and Customs of London* during the Eighteenth Century; including the Charities, Depravities, Dresses and Amusements of the Citizens of London during that Period. London, 1811.

Marcus, Steven. *The Other Victorians: A Study of Sexuality and Pornography in Mid-Nineteenth-Century England.* New York, 1964.

Marx, Karl. "To Make the World Philosophical." In *The Marx-Engels Reader.* Ed. Robert C. Tucker. New York, 1978, pp. 9–11.

Maser, Edward A., ed. *Baroque and Rococo Pictorial Imagery: The 1758–60 Hertel Edition of Ripa's 'Iconologia.'* New York, 1971.

The Masquerade: A Poem. London, 1724.

The Masquerade, containing a Variety of Merry Characters of All Sorts, properly Dressed for the Occasion, Calculated to amuse and instruct all the good Boys and Girls in the Kingdom. London, 1780.

The Masquerade; or, The Devil's Nursery. Dublin, 1732.

The Masquerade; or, The History of Lord Avon and Miss Tameworth. London, 1769.

Milhous, Judith. "Opera Finances in London, 1674–1738." *Journal of the American Musicological Society,* 37 (1984), 567–92.

Miller, Alice. *Prisoners of Childhood: The Drama of the Gifted Child.* Trans. Ruth Ward. New York, 1981.

Miller, Nancy K. "Emphasis Added: Plots and Plausibilities in Women's Fiction." *PMLA,* 96 (1981), 36–47.

———. "The Exquisite Cadavers: Women in Eighteenth-Century Fiction." *Diacritics,* 5 (1975), 37–43.

———. *The Heroine's Text: Readings in the French and English Novel, 1722–1792.* New York, 1980.

Montagu, Mary Wortley. *Letters and Works.* 2 vols. Ed. Lord Wharncliffe and W. Moy Thomas. London, 1861.

Mrs. Cornelys' Entertainments at Carlisle House, Soho Square. London, 1840.

Novak, Maximillian E., ed. *English Literature in the Age of Disguise.* Berkeley, Calif., 1977.

Orgel, Stephen. *The Jonsonian Masque.* Cambridge, Mass., 1965.

Paulson, Ronald. *Emblem and Expression: Meaning in English Art of the Eighteenth Century.* Cambridge, Mass., 1975.

———. *Hogarth: His Life, Art, and Times.* 2 vols. New Haven, Conn., 1971.

———. *Hogarth's Graphic Works.* 2 vols. New Haven, Conn., 1965.

———. *Popular and Polite Art in the Age of Hogarth and Fielding.* Notre Dame, Ind., 1979.

———. *Satire and the Novel in Eighteenth-Century England.* New Haven, Conn., 1967.

———. ed., *Fielding: A Collection of Critical Essays.* Englewood Cliffs, N.J., 1962.

Pilon, E., and F. Saisset. *Les Fêtes en Europe au XVIIIe siècle*. Saint-Gratien, 1943.

Pitt, Christopher. "On the Masquerades." London, 1727. Reprinted in *The Poets of Great Britain*. Ed. Samuel Johnson. London, 1807.

Plumb, J. H. *England in the Eighteenth Century, 1714–1815*. Baltimore, 1950.

Ralph, James. *The Touchstone; or, A Guide to All the Reigning Diversions*. London, 1728.

Rawson, Claude. *Henry Fielding and the Augustan Ideal Under Stress*. London, 1972.

Ribeiro, Aileen. *Dress in Eighteenth-Century Europe, 1715–1789*. London, 1985.

———. *The Dress Worn at Masquerades in England, 1730–1790, and Its Relation to Fancy Dress in Portraiture*. New York, 1984.

———. "Mrs. Cornelys and Carlisle House." *History Today*, 28 (Jan. 1978), 47–52.

Rich, Adrienne. "Compulsory Heterosexuality and Lesbian Existence." *Signs*, 5 (1980), 631–60.

Richardson, Samuel. *Clarissa; or, The History of a Young Lady*. 4 vols. London, 1932.

———. *Correspondence*. 6 vols. Ed. A. Barbauld. London, 1804.

———. *Pamela; or, Virtue Rewarded*. Ed. Peter Sabor. New York, 1979. Penguin ed.

———. *Pamela*. Part 2. Ed. George Saintsbury. London, 1914. [Cited by page number.]

———. *Sir Charles Grandison*. 3 vols. Ed. Jocelyn Harris. London, 1972. [Cited by volume and page numbers.]

Roach, Mary Ellen, and Joanne Eicher, eds. *Dress, Adornment and the Social Order*. New York, 1965.

Roche, Sophie von la. *Sophie in London—1786, being the Diary of Sophie von la Roche*. Ed. Clare Williams. London, 1933.

Rogers, Pat. *Henry Fielding*. London, 1979.

Rothstein, Eric. *Systems of Order and Inquiry in Later Eighteenth-Century Fiction*. Berkeley, Calif., 1975.

Rudrum, Alan, and Peter Dixon, eds. *Selected Poems of Samuel Johnson and Oliver Goldsmith*. Columbia, S.C., 1965.

Sacks, Sheldon. *Fiction and the Shape of Belief: A Study of Henry Fielding*. Berkeley, Calif., 1966.

Schor, Naomi. *Zola's Crowds*. Baltimore, 1978.

A Seasonable Apology for Mr. H----g--r. London, 1724.

Sedgewick, Owen. *The Universal Masquerade; or, The World Turn'd Inside Out*. London, 1742.

Sennett, Richard. *The Fall of Public Man: On the Social Psychology of Capitalism*. New York, 1974.

Shaw, Peter. *American Patriots and the Rituals of Revolution*. Cambridge, Mass., 1980.

Sherburn, George. "Fielding's *Amelia*: An Interpretation." *ELH*, 3 (1936), 1–14. Reprinted in *Fielding: A Collection of Critical Essays*. Ed. Ronald Paulson. Englewood Cliffs, N.J., 1962, pp. 146–57.

Short Remarks upon the Original and Pernicious Consequences of Masquerades. In *The Conduct of the Stage Consider'd, with Short Remarks. . . .* London, 1721.

Singleton, Mary [Frances Moore Brooke]. *The Old Maid*. London, 1764.

Smollett, Tobias. *The Adventures of Peregrine Pickle*. Oxford, Eng., 1983.

Spacks, Patricia M. *Imagining a Self: Autobiography and Novel in Eighteenth-Century England*. Cambridge, Mass., 1976.

Spence, Joseph. *Letters from the Grand Tour*. Ed. Slava Klima. Montreal, 1975.

Starobinski, Jean. *The Invention of Liberty, 1700–1789*. Trans. Bernard C. Swift. Geneva, 1964.

Staves, Susan. "British Seduced Maidens." *Eighteenth-Century Studies*, 14 (1980–81), 109–34.

Stone, Lawrence. *The Family, Sex and Marriage in England, 1500 to 1800*. New York, 1977.

Sydney, William Connor. *England and the English in the Eighteenth Century*. 2 vols. Edinburgh, 1891.

———. *Social Life in England from the Restoration to the Revolution*. New York, 1892.

Tanner, Tony. *Adultery in the Novel: Contract and Transgression*. Baltimore, 1979.

Taylor, Anne Robinson. *Male Novelists and Their Female Voices: Literary Masquerades*. Troy, N.Y., 1981.

Thomas, Keith. *Religion and the Decline of Magic*. New York, 1971.

Thompson, Edward P. "The Moral Economy of the English Crowd in the Eighteenth Century." *Past and Present*, 50 (1971), 76–136.

———. "Rough Music: 'Le Charivari Anglais.'" *Annales: Economies, Sociétés, Civilisations*, 27 (1972), 285–312.

———. *Whigs and Hunters: The Origin of the Black Act*. New York, 1975.

Thompson, Stith. *Motif-Index of Folk Literature*. 6 vols. Bloomington, Ind., 1955.

Tinney, John. *A Collection of Eastern and Foreign Dresses*. London, 1750.

Todorov, Tzvetan. *The Fantastic: A Structural Approach to a Literary Genre*. Trans. Richard Howard. Ithaca, N.Y., 1975.

Trumbach, Randolph. "London's Sodomites: Homosexual Behavior and Western Culture in the Eighteenth Century." *Journal of Social History*, 11 (1977–78), 1–33.

———. *The Rise of the Egalitarian Family*. New York, 1978.

Turner, Victor. *The Forest of Symbols: Aspects of Ndembu Ritual*. Ithaca, N.Y., 1967.

———. *The Ritual Process: Structure and Anti-Structure*. Chicago, 1969.

Walford, Cornelius. *Fairs, Past and Present*. London, 1883.

Walford, Edward. *Old and New London*. 6 vols. London, 1878.

Walpole, Horace. *Correspondence*. 39 vols. Ed. W. S. Lewis et al. New Haven, Conn., 1937–79.

Ward, Edward. *The History of the London Clubs*. London, 1709.

———. *The London Spy*. London, 1698–1700.

Watt, Ian. *The Rise of the Novel*. Berkeley, Calif., 1957.

Wilson, Harriette. *The Memoirs of Harriette Wilson, Written by Herself.* 2 vols. London, 1924.

Wollstonecraft, Mary. *A Vindication of the Rights of Women*. Ed. Miriam Kramnick. New York, 1975.

Wright, Thomas. *Caricature History of the Georges; or, Annals of the House of Hanover*. London, 1868.

Wycherley, William. *The Complete Plays of William Wycherley*. Ed. Gerald Weales. New York, 1966.

Young, Edward. *Poetical Works*. 2 vols. London: Bell and Daldy, n.d.

Zall, Paul M. "The Cool World of Samuel Taylor Coleridge: Elizabeth Inchbald; or, Sex and Sensibility." *The Wordsworth Circle*, 12 (1981), 270–73.

Sources of Illustrations

The chapter-opening art is from Dover Publications, *Catchpenny Prints: 163 Popular Engravings from the Eighteenth Century* (New York, 1970). The other illustrations in this book are reproduced by courtesy of the following institutions and organizations:

Sources of Illustrations

The Barber Institute of Fine Arts, The University of Birmingham: 32
Virginia Museum of Fine Arts, Richmond: 33
Christies, London: 34
Private collection, taken from a reproduction by Gordon Fraser Ltd.:
  35
Fine Arts Museums of San Francisco: 37
The Walters Art Gallery, Baltimore: 38

Index

Index

Abelard and Héloïse, 300–301
Accomplished Rake; or, Modern Fine Gentleman, The (Davys), 358
Addison, Joseph, 2, 9, 50; comments in *Spectator*, 5, 28f, 32, 34, 38; *Remarks on Italy*, 12–13, 114; *Guardian* essay, 37, 47–48, 55, 66, 286
Adultery, 44, 251, 344
Adultery plot, in English fiction, 172, 221, 241–42
Adventures of Peregrine Pickle, The (Smollett), 117
After the Children's Ball (Ludovici), 335
Alexandria Quartet, The (Durrell), 340
Allegory, 203, 246; in Fielding, 190–93; representation of character in, 193–95; iconographic tendency of, 362
Allen, Ralph, 198
Almack's assembly-room, masquerades held at, 2, 10, 70
Ambassadors, The (James), 233n
Amelia, see under Fielding
Animal disguise, 23, 67–68; in popular ritual, 23–24
Animals, at masquerades, 67–68
Anti-masquerade writings, 3, 7–8, 41–44, 46, 79–86, 93–94, 95

Anti-theatrical writings, attacks on masquerade in, 79–80
Aristotle, 246
Ashton, John, 99
Assembly-rooms, *see* Almack's; Carlisle House; Haymarket Theater; Pantheon
d'Aumont, Louis, Duc d'Aumont, 9, 90
Austen, Jane, 172, 342; *Jack and Alice*, 333, 367; *Mansfield Park*, 291, 341; *Pride and Prejudice*, 341
Author's Farce, The (Fielding), 22, 182

Bahoo (hood), 59, 354
Bailey, Nathan, 9n, 15
Bakhtin, Mikhail: *Rabelais and His World*, ix, 126; on masks, 75, 183–84, 185; on carnival, 76, 161, 183–84, 185; theory of carnivalesque, 126–27, 171n, 185, 333, 365; on women and carnival, 363–64
Ballo in maschera, Un (Verdi), 339–40
Balzac, Honoré de, 99, 335, 344
Baout (hood), 59, 354
Barber, C. L., 16, 19
Barish, Jonas, 79
Barthes, Roland, 78, 89, 152
Bataille, Georges, 299

387

Beckford, William, 121
Behn, Aphra, 358
Belinda (Edgeworth), 115, 333
Belle's Stratagem, The (Cowley), 85, 97, 111, 231, 319n
Bernardi, Francesco, 36n
Black Act, the, 92, 356–57
Black Domino; or, The Masqued Ball, The (Wilks), 358
Blake, William, 328
Bleak House (Dickens), 300, 365–66
Blithedale Romance, The (Hawthorne), 337
Bluebeard, 295, 324, 366
Blue Beard (Colman), 366
Blue Boy (Gainsborough), 68
Boaden, James, 48, 291
Body language, at masquerades, 37
Boismortier, Joseph Bodin de, 312n
Boswell, James, 3n, 95; at masquerades, 74, 355
Boulton, William B., 20
Bowen, Elizabeth, 233n
Boy Bishop, festival of, 22
Bradshaigh, Lady, 159
Breastfeeding, as carnival motif, 156, 360
Broadsheets, 70–71
Brontë, Charlotte: *Jane Eyre*, 280, 341; *Villette*, 334, 341, 366
Brontë, Emily, 291, 321
Brooke, Frances [pseud. Mary Singleton], 31
Brooke, Francis, 8
Brophy, Brigid, 340
Burke, Edmund, 53ff
Burnet, Gilbert, 112, 358
Burney, Fanny, 52, 94, 253–89 *passim*
—*Cecilia*, 37, 71, 73, 115, 120, 124, 290, 292; anti-romantic masquerade scene, 259–65, 270–75; use of Shakespeare in, 265–67; comic interpretation of, 267; anti-romantic nature of, 276–84; treatment of carnivalesque, 285–89
—*Evelina*, 115, 260, 269, 288, 299
Byron, George Gordon, Lord, 98, 99, 331, 332

Cable, George Washington, 338
Caillois, Roger, 53, 59, 104–5, 183f
Canetti, Elias, 271n, 309
Caprichos, Los (Goya), 336

Carlisle House, masquerades held at, 10, 98; figs., 67, 213. *See also* Cornelys
Carmilla (Le Fanu), 338
Carnaval moralisé, in Fielding, 190–93
Carneval in Rom, Der (Strauss), 340
Carnival: relation to English masquerade, 11–16, 26–28; described by English visitors to Italy, 12–14; traditional motifs, 26, 160; social functions of, 86–94; safety-valve theory of, 88–89; and popular insurgency, 89; waning of, 100–105, 332–33. *See also* Masquerade
Carnival blows, 37
"Carnival" (Dinesen), 340n
Carnivalesque, the, *see under* Bakhtin
Carnivalization: defined, 125–26; in *Pamela*, 161
Carnival King, 21–22
Casanova, Jacques, 10, 351
"Cask of Amontillado, The" (Poe), 337
Castle of Otranto, The (Walpole), 121
Castrati, 36
Catalogues, costume, 60–61
Cavell, Stanley, 313n
Cecilia, see under Burney
Centlivre, Susannah, 9, 94, 358
Champion, The (Fielding), 182
Character dress, 58, 68–71
Charades, in 19th-century fiction, 341
Charge Delivered to the Grand Jury (Fielding), 188–89
Charles II, King of England, 111
Childermass, festival of Boy Bishop, 22
Chudleigh, Elizabeth, 4, 41f, 73; figs., 42
Cibber, Colley, 111
Civilization and Its Discontents (Freud), 86
Civil War, English, 93
Clarissa (Richardson), 69, 366
Cleland, John, 49, 115, 296n, 300, 366
Clothing: as language, 55–57; Western view of, 56
Collection of Eastern and Foreign Dresses, A (Tinney), 60
Collection of the Dresses of Different Nations, Ancient and Modern, A (Jefferys), 60–61; fig., 69
Colman (the Younger), George, 366
Commedia dell' arte, 15, 70
Commercialization: of masquerade, 11, 27–29, 112–13; of popular culture, 27, 100

Conan Doyle, Arthur, 134n
Conduct of the Stage Consider'd, with Short Remarks upon the Original and Pernicious Consequences of Masquerades, The (anon.), 46f, 79, 85
Conrad, Joseph, 342n
Constant, Benjamin, 366
Cornelys, Theresa, masquerade impresario: early life, 10; Carlisle House masquerades, 24, 27, 41, 64; last years, 98, 332
Costume: in carnival tradition, 13 (fig.), 14–16; animal disguise, 23, 67–68; ecclesiastical parodies, 40, 63; sexual travesty, 46–49, 63–64; fancy dress, 58, 60–68; character dress, 58, 68–71 (fig., 69); Oriental dress, 60–62; supernatural disguise, 64–66. *See also* Dominos; Mask
Costume catalogues, 60–61
Costume warehouses, 58
Country-Wife, The (Wycherley), 39
Cowley, Hannah, 85, 97, 111, 231, 319n
Crane, R. S., 197, 362
Cromwell, Oliver, 93
Crowds, 271n, 344
Crowd scenes, in literature, 344, 368
Curll, Edmund, 40

Dance of Death, The (Rowlandson), 337–38
Danger of Masquerades and Raree-Shows, The ("C.R."), 79
Davis, Natalie Zemon, 22, 89
Davys, Mary, 358
De Beauvoir, Simone, 293
Defoe, Daniel, 28, 161; *Moll Flanders*, 366; *The Political History of the Devil*, 64n; *Robinson Crusoe*, 133; *Roxana*, 28, 115, 123, 162, 254, 296n, 309; *A System of Magick*, 64n
Descartes, René, 103, 185
Destabilization: associated with masquerade scenes, 117–24; in *Amelia*, 235–36, 239–42
Detective fiction, 134n
Devil, the, 64; figs., 50, 65
Diana, 310–12
Diane et Actéon (Boismortier), 312n
Dickens, Charles, 342n, 344; *Bleak House*, 300, 365–66; *The Pickwick Papers*, 334

Didacticism, undermined by masquerade scene, 124, 125–26, 242
Diderot, Denis, 185
Dinesen, Isak, 340
Disguise, *see* Costume; Masquerade
Disorder, rituals of, *see* Carnival; Inversion
Distressed Mother, The (Philips), 157
Dog and Duck Gardens, 2
Dominos, 58–59, 77–78, 354; fig., 58
Don Carlos (Schiller), 358
Don Giovanni (Mozart), 59–60, 339
Doody, Margaret, 131
Doublure, La (Roussel), 368
Douglas, Mary, 86, 88, 106, 251
Dragons, at masquerades, 24
Dryden, John, 110–12
Duenna, The (Sheridan), 111
Durrell, Lawrence, 340

Earthquakes, blamed on masquerades, 84, 96, 182
Eaves, T. C. Duncan, 131
Ecclesiastical parodies, 40, 63, 305
Edgeworth, Maria, 291, 365; *Belinda*, 115, 333
L'Education sentimentale (Flaubert), 335
Egan, Pierce, 333
Eliot, George, 288, 326, 342, 344
Eloisa to Abelard (Pope), 300
Embarkation from the Island of Cythera (Watteau), 109, 357; 108 (fig.)
Emblematic figures, 69–70
Emperour of the Moon, The (Behn), 358
English Civil War, the, 93
Enquiry into the Causes of the Late Increase of Robbers, An (Fielding), 29, 85, 188–89, 261n
Essay on Plays and Masquerades (anon.), 79, 84–85
"Essay on the Knowledge of the Characters of Men" (Fielding), 85, 192–93
Evelina (Burney), 115, 260, 269, 288, 299
Exhibitionism, at masquerades, 40–41

Faerie Queene, The (Spenser), 203
Fairs, 33
Fancy dress, 58, 60–68
Fancy-dress portraiture, 68–69; figs., 61, 311
Fantastic tales, masquerade scenes in, 335
Farinelli, Carlo, 36n

Faulkner, William C., 338
Faust (Goethe), 333
Feast of Fools, the, 11, 87
Female emancipation, masquerade associated with, 41–44, 253–56
Female Husband, The (Fielding), 47
Female Spectator, The (Haywood), 43, 45, 52, 85
Fielding, Henry, 21–22, 43, 47, 177–252 *passim*; satires on Heidegger, 21–22, 190, 195; views on masquerade, 47, 188–98 *passim*; portrait by Hogarth, 180, 181 (fig.); New Critical view of, 186, 360–61; career as magistrate, 188–89
—*Amelia*, 115, 118f, 172, 198–252, 296; generic instability of, 186–87, 246–47, 361; didacticism of, 198–201; narrator of, 200–201, 226–28; allegorical representation in, 203, 215–16, 236–42; and *psychomachia*, 203, 216, 236, 243; *partie quarrée* in, 209, 211, 242; masquerade scene, 223–26; influence on *roman larmoyant*, 241, 363
—*Tom Jones*, 22, 35, 44, 115, 117, 182, 233n, 296n; masquerade scene, 195–98
—other works: *The Author's Farce*, 22, 182; *The Champion*, 182; *Charge Delivered to the Grand Jury*, 188–89; *An Enquiry into the Causes of the Late Increase of Robbers*, 29, 85, 188–89, 261n; "Essay on the Knowledge of the Characters of Men," 85, 192–93; *The Female Husband*, 47; *The Masquerade*, 21, 31–37 passim, 47, 54, 73, 177–78, 182, 184, 190–91, 195; *Miss Lucy in Town*, 182, 231, 358; *Shamela*, 135
Film iconography, 233n
Flaubert, Gustave, 99, 248, 300, 326, 342, 344, 366; *Madame Bovary*, 335
Fledermaus, Die (J. Strauss), 340
Fletcher, Angus, 193, 246, 345
Folk characters, represented by masqueraders, 24, 70
Foreign costume, 60–62
Foucault, Michel, 353
Frazer, James George, 11–12, 27, 87
Freud, Sigmund, 74, 86f, 272, 363, 364
Frisch, Max, 358
Frye, Northrop, 187, 267

Gainsborough, Thomas, 68
Gambling, associated with masquerades, 26, 53

Gardens, pleasure, *see* Ranelagh gardens; Vauxhall gardens
Gargantua (Rabelais), 171n
Garrick, David, 95, 113
Geertz, Clifford, 87
Generic instability, associated with masquerade scene, 126–27, 171n, 246–47
Gentleman, Francis, 358
George II, King of England, 10, 21, 28, 95
Gérôme, Jean-Léon, 368; fig., 339
Geschichte des Fräuleins von Sternheim (von La Roche), 358
Gibson, Edmund, 7
Gilbert, William S., 300
Gluckman, Max, 88
Godwin, William, 284, 291
Goethe, Johann Wolfgang von, 26, 344; *Faust*, 333; *Die Italienische Reise*, 1, 26, 160; *Die Wahlverwandtschaften*, 241, 341
Goffmann, Erving, 39
Goldoni, Carlo, 138
Goldsmith, Oliver, 85; *Vicar of Wakefield*, 69, 115
Goya, Francisco, 368; fig., 336
Grand Hotel, 233n
Grandissimes, The (Cable), 338
Grand Tour, the, Italian carnivals part of, 12–14
Green Man, at masquerade, 24
Griffin, Benjamin, 29–30, 38, 66, 231, 311, 358
Guardi, Francesco, 15
Guardian, The (Addison), 37, 47–48, 55, 66, 286
Guardian/ward relationships, 299–300, 365–66
Gustavus III, King of Sweden, 340

Halloween, 357
Handel, George Frideric, 10, 339
Harlequin, 15, 70; fig., 30
Harlot's Progress, A (Hogarth), 40
Hawthorne, Nathaniel, 337
Haymarket Theater, 10, 25, 29, 37, 50, 65, 182; fig., 23. *See also* Heidegger
Haywood, Eliza, 161; on masquerade, 43, 45, 52, 85; *The Masqueraders: or, Fatal Curiosity*, 3, 114, 214
Heidegger, John James ("Count"), opera and masquerade promoter, 2, 9–10, 23 (in fig.), 25, 27, 36n, 109, 332; presentment against, 10, 96; associated with

Carnival King, 21–22; satirized by
  Fielding and Hogarth, 23, 97, 182; as-
  sociated with Mother Needham, 31.
  See also Cornelys; Haymarket Theater;
  Masquerade
Henry VIII, King of England, 19, 68
Hercules, 206; fig., 97
Hervey, Lady, 73–74
Heteroglossia, 359
Heuberger, Richard, 340
"High-Life Men," the, 138
History of the London Clubs, The (Ward),
  46
Hitchcock, Alfred, 233n
Hoadly, Benjamin, 113
Hobby-horse games, 22
Hoffmann, E. T. A., 335
Hogarth, William, 2, 180–81; *A Harlot's
  Progress*, 40; *Marriage à la Mode*, 36n,
  112 (fig.), 259; *Masquerades and Operas*,
  2, 64, 65 (fig.); *Masquerade Ticket*, 2, 23
  (fig.), 37f, 67, 182, 196
Holbein, Hans, 68
Holidays, traditional, associated with
  masquerades, 21
Hollander, Anne, 56, 354
Hollar, Wenceslaus, 68
Homosexuality: at masquerades, 41,
  45–50; Foucault on, 353
Hoodening games, 22
"Hop-Frog" (Poe), 337
Howe, Susannah, 341
Hugo, Victor, 344
Hypocrisy, masquerade as emblem of, 85,
  119, 184

Iconography, 68–71, 196, 205–6, 233n,
  310–11, 362; 70–71 (figs.). *See also*
  Hogarth; World Upside-Down
Iconologia (Ripa), 69
Ilinx (vertigo), 53; fig., 54
Impresarios, masquerade, *see* Cornelys;
  Heidegger
Incest, associated with masquerade, 81,
  363
Inchbald, Elizabeth, 253, 258–59, 290–
  330 *passim*; in male masquerade costume, 48, 94; *Lovers' Vows*, 291; theatrical career, 291; Catholicism of, 291,
  329; literary reputation, 291–92; *Nature
  and Art*, 308n
—*A Simple Story*, 115, 124, 256, 259; as
  fiction of transgression, 292–93, 326;

treatment of space, 295, 323–24; representation of female desire, 303–7;
  masquerade scene, 308–12; romance
  structure, 317–20, 324–25; carnivales-
  que internalized in, 325–27; Edge-
  worth on, 365
Incongruity, as masquerade theme, 81–84
Individualism, and demise of carnival,
  103–5, 342–43
Internalization of carnivalesque, 325–37,
  341–42
Interpretation of Dreams, The (Freud), 272
Inversion, as carnivalesque motif, 75–79,
  86–88. *See also* Rites of reversal; World
  Upside-Down
Iolanthe (Gilbert and Sullivan), 300
Italian carnivals, 12–14
Italienische Reise, Die (Goethe), 1, 26, 160

Jack and Alice (Austen), 333, 367
James I, King of England, 19
James, Henry, 233n, 291, 326, 342
Jane Eyre (C. Brontë), 280, 341
Jarrett, Derek, 100–101
Jefferys, Thomas: *Collection of the Dresses
  of Different Nations*, 60–61; fig., 69
Johnson, Charles, 40, 358
Johnson, Samuel, 2, 85, 185, 355–56
Jones, Inigo, 19
Jubilee Masquerade of 1749, 4, 14, 21, 42,
  90n, 182; figs., 16, 20, 82. *See also*
  Ranelagh gardens
Justine (Sade), 304

Kelly, Hugh, 358
Kimpel, Ben D., 131
King Lear (Shakespeare), 313n
Kinkead-Weekes, Mark, 132
Kleist, Heinrich von, 335
Kundera, Milan, 342

Lamb, Charles, 89
Lecherometers, 38, 352–53
Lee, Sophia, 358
Leeson, Margaret, 94, 96, 312n
Le Fanu, Sheridan, 338
Lennox, Charlotte, 85
Lermontov, Mikhail, 358
Le Roy Ladurie, Emmanuel, 89
Lesbianism, 47f, 353
Letters from the Grand Tour (Spence), 13,
  331
Levey, Michael, 109, 357

Lévi-Strauss, Claude, 78, 251, 255
Lewis, Matthew, 305
Life in London (Egan), 333
Life of Pamela, The (anon.), 135
Lisbon earthquake, blamed on masquerade, 84, 96, 182
Locke, John, 103, 170, 185
London Spy, The (Ward), 39–40
Longhi, Pietro, 15
Lord of Misrule, 18, 21; Carnival King, 21–22
Louis, Duc d'Aumont, 9, 90
Lovers' Vows (Inchbald), 291
Lucifer (the Devil), 64; figs., 50, 65
Ludovici, Sr., Albert, 335

MacLaren, Archibald, 358
Madame Bovary (Flaubert), 335, 342
Malcolm, James Peller, 99
Mann, Horace, 13
Mann, Thomas, 233n
Mansfield Park (Austen), 291, 341
Mardi Gras, 338, 357
Maria; or, The Wrongs of Women (Wollstonecraft), 285
Marivaux, Pierre de, 300
Marriage à la Mode (Dryden), 110–12
Marriage à la Mode (Hogarth), 36n, 259; fig., 112
Marriage plot, in English fiction, 172
Marsh, Ngaio, 341
Marx Brothers, 233n
Mary, Queen of Scots, 68
Mask: erotic uses of, 39–40; as sign of intrigue, 59–60; in carnival tradition, 75; Bakhtin's theory of, 75, 183–84, 185; modern conception of, 104, 183–84; Fielding's treatment of, 177–83. See also Carnival; Costume
Maskarade (Nielsen), 340
Masque, distinguished from masquerade, 19–20
"Masque of the Red Death, The" (Poe), 337
Masquerade: as rite of reversal, 5–6, 86–89; English bishops on, 7, 84, 96; first appearances in England, 7–10; etymology of, 8–9; commercial aspects of, 11, 27–29, 112–13; mingling of social groups at, 28–34; sexual behavior at, 38–51; and female emancipation, 41–44, 253–56; associated with sublimity, 53–55; cognitive functions of, 76–79; and theater, 79–80; as political threat, 93–94; attempted suppression of, 95–96, 97 (fig.); gradual disappearance of, 98–109
Masquerade (Howe), 341
Masquerade, The (Fielding), 21, 31–37 passim, 47, 54, 73, 177–78, 182, 184, 190–91, 195
Masquerade, The (C. Johnson), 40, 358
Masquerade, The (Lermontov), 358
Masquerade intelligence, 3
Masquerade; or, An Evening's Intrigue, The (Griffin), 29–30, 38, 66, 231, 311, 358
Masquerade; or, Folly Exposed!, The (MacLaren), 358
Masquerade; or, The Devil's Nursery, The (anon.), 81, 358
Masquerade; or, The History of Lord Avon and Miss Tameworth, The (anon.), 358
Masqueraders; or, Fatal Curiosity, The (Haywood), 3, 114, 214
Masquerades and Operas (Hogarth), 2, 64; fig., 18
Masquerade scenes: in comic drama, 110–11, 358; in fiction, 114–29, 333–39, 341–45; in opera, 339–40. *See also individual works by name*
Masquerade squeak, the, 35–36
Masquerade Ticket (Hogarth), 2, 37f, 67, 182, 196; fig., 23
Maypole dancing, at masquerades, 21; fig., 18
Melville, Herman, 342n
Memoirs of a Woman of Pleasure (Cleland), 49, 115, 296n, 300, 366
Milton, John, 66n
Miss Lucy in Town (Fielding), 182, 231, 358
Moll Flanders (Defoe), 366
Monk, The (Lewis), 305
Montagu, Elizabeth, 41
Montagu, Lady Mary Wortley, 9, 14, 94f, 136
Morley, Thomas, 8
Morris dancing, 24
Mourners Below (Purdy), 368
Mozart, Wolfgang Amadeus, 59–60, 339, 340
Murder Must Advertise (Sayers), 341
Mysteries of Udolpho, The (Radcliffe), 115

Nacht in Venedig, Eine (J. Strauss), 340
Narcissism, 256–57, 286–87, 363

Nature and Art (Inchbald), 308n
Needham, Elizabeth ("Mother"), 31, 64, 254
Nielsen, Carl, 340
Night Thoughts (Young), 337, 367
Nouvelle Héloïse, La (Rousseau), 241, 300
Nozze di Figaro, Le (Mozart), 339

"Old English" dress, 68; 69 (fig.)
Old Maid, The (Singleton), 31
120 Days of Sodom, The (Sade), 304
"On Narcissism" (Freud), 363
"On Negation" (Freud), 87
Onomastics, 220, 322
"On the Masquerades" (Pitt), 30–31, 34, 83–84, 129
Opera, 36, 157–58; masquerade scenes in, 339–40
Opernball, Der (Heuberger), 340
Oriental costume, 60–62
Ovid, 312n

Pamela, see under Richardson
Pamela's Conduct in High Life (anon.), 135
Pantagruel (Rabelais), 126–27, 171n
Pantheon, the, 2, 10, 98; fig., 91
Pantheonites, The (Gentleman), 358
Paoli, Gen. Pasquale di, Boswell's appearance as, 3n, 74
Paradise Lost (Milton), 66n
Parodia sacra (ecclesiastical parodies), 40, 63, 305
Parrish, Maxfield, 338
Partie quarrée (heterosexual quartet), in *Amelia*, 209–11, 242
Paulson, Ronald, 23, 186, 342
Peau de chagrin, La (Balzac), 335
Peregrine Pickle, The Adventures of (Smollett), 117
Perjur'd Husband: or, The Adventures of Venice, The (Centlivre), 358
Pestilence, masquerade associated with, 84–85
Philips, Ambrose, 157
Physical contact, at masquerades, 37
Picaresque tradition, masquerade scene in, 116–17, 342
Pickwick Papers, The (Dickens), 334
Pictorial tradition, influence on masquerade costume, 68–71
Pierrot, 70, 368; fig., 339
Pilgrim's Progress, The (Bunyan), 203
Pirandello, Luigi, 358

Pitt, Christopher, 30–31, 34, 83–84, 129
Play, Caillois on, 104–5
Plot: masquerade scene as catalyst of, 120–24; relation to cultural spaces, 116, 233n; adultery and marriage themes, 172, 221, 241–42
Plumb, J. H., 101
Poe, Edgar Allan, 337–38
Political History of the Devil, The (Defoe), 64n
Pollution effects, 86
Pope, Alexander, 2, 9, 44, 237, 300
Popular culture, 16–19; and rites of reversal, 5, 86–89; reform of, 18, 100–101; influence on masquerade, 18–21; commercialization of, 27, 100. *See also* Carnival
Pornography, role of mask in, 40
Pregnancy, as carnival motif, 155, 160–61
Prévost, Abbé, 300
Pride and Prejudice (Austen), 341
Prinzessin Brambilla (Hoffmann), 335
Privatization, 150, 341
Prometheus Unbound (Shelley), 321
Promiscuity, as theme of masquerade, 80–82, 84
Prostitutes, 39–40; at masquerades, 31–33, 49
Proust, Marcel, 300
Psychomachia, in *Amelia*, 203, 216, 236, 243
Punchinello, 15, 70
Purdy, James, 339
Puritanism, 18; associated with masquerade, 93
Pym, Barbara, 301

Rabelais and His World (Bakhtin), ix, 126
Rabelais, François, 103, 126–27, 171n
Radcliffe, Ann, 115
Rambler, The (Johnson), 85
Ranelagh gardens, 2, 12, 27, 98; Jubilee Masquerade of 1749, 4, 14, 21, 42, 90n, 182; figs., 16ff, 82, 329
Rape of the Lock, The (Pope), 2, 44
Rationalism, role in demise of carnival, 102–6
Rawson, Claude, 248
Rebellion, rituals of, *see* Rites of reversal
Remarks on Italy (Addison), 12–13, 114
Reynolds, Joshua, 68
Richard III, King of England, 68
Richardson, Samuel, 159, 286; *Clarissa*,

69, 366; *Pamela*, Part 1, 133, 136; *Sir
Charles Grandison*, 29, 115, 118, 123,
142n, 296
—*Pamela*, Part 2, 36, 115, 117n, 118f, 124,
199, 296; masquerade scene, 130–31,
158–59; failings of, 131–32; relation to
Part 1, 135–39, 167–70; carnival imag-
ery, 160–61
Ripa, Cesare, 69
Rites of reversal, 5, 86–89. *See also* World
Upside-Down
Robinson Crusoe (Defoe), 133
Rococo art, Bakhtin on, 103–4
Roman larmoyant, 241, 363
Romanticism, survivals of masquerade
theme in, 335f, 340
Romeo and Juliet (Shakespeare), 265–67
Rosa Fielding: Victim of Lust (anon.), 300
Rosenkavalier, Der (R. Strauss), 340
Rousseau, Jean-Jacques, 241, 300, 303–4,
344, 366
Roussel, Raymond, 368
Rowlandson, Thomas, 337–38; figs.,
287, 338
Roxana (Defoe), 28, 115, 123, 254, 296n,
309; masquerade scene, 162
Rubens, Peter Paul, 68
"Rubens' Wife" (masquerade character),
68, 354; fig., 69

Sade, Marquis de, 167, 304
Sartorial signs, instability of, 56–57
Satan (the Devil), 64; figs., 50, 65
Saturnalia (Roman), 11, 87
Sayers, Dorothy, 341
Scaramouche, 70; fig., 30
Schiller, Friedrich von, 358
School for Wives, The (Kelly), 358
Seasonable Apology for Mr. H----g--r, A
(anon.), 22, 31, 43, 81, 184
Seasonal festivities, relation to masquer-
ade, 20–21. *See also* Popular culture
Sedgewick, Owen, 85
Sennett, Richard, 343
Sequels, 133–34
Sexual behavior, at masquerades, 38–51;
homosexuality, 41, 45–50; trans-
vestism, 46–47, 63–64; promiscuity,
80–82, 84; incest, 81, 363. *See also*
Women
Sexual travesty, *see* Costume; Trans-
vestism
Shadwell, Thomas, 111

Shakespeare, William, 48, 265–67, 313n
Shakespeare Jubilee Masquerade of 1769,
2, 3n
Shamela (Fielding), 135
Shaw, Peter, 89
She-male, 22. *See also* Transvestism
Shepherd, Jack, 18
Sheridan, Richard, 111
Simple Story, A, see under Inchbald
Singleton, Mary (Frances Brooke), 31
Sir Charles Grandison (Richardson), 29,
115, 118, 123, 142n, 296
Sisters, The (Lennox), 85
Smollett, Tobias, 115, 117
Snow Ball, The (Brophy), 340
Space: relation to fictional plot, 116,
233n; in *Pamela*, 149–51; in *A Simple
Story*, 295, 323–24
"Special Type of Object Choice Made by
Men, A" (Freud), 364
Spectator, The (Addison), 5, 28f, 32, 34, 38
Spence, Joseph, 13, 331
Spenser, Edmund, 203
Splendeurs et misères des courtisanes (Bal-
zac), 335
Squeak, the masquerade, 35–36
Starobinski, Jean, 346
Steele, Richard, 24, 64, 157
Stendhal [pseud. of Marie-Henri Beyle],
300, 344, 366
Sterne, Laurence, 171n, 185, 342
Stonewall riots, 89, 356
Strachey, Lytton, 128, 291
Strauss, Johann, 340
Strauss, Richard, 340
Sublime, the, associated with masquer-
ade, 53–55
Sullivan, Arthur S., 300
Sumptuary laws, 92, 356
Supernatural imagery: in costume, 64–
66, 77; in masquerade scenes, 121–22
Suspicious Husband, The (Hoadly), 113
(fig.)
Swift, Jonathan, 9n, 171n, 185
Sydney, William Connor, 99
*System of Magick; or, A History of the Black
Art, A* (Defoe), 64n

Tanner, Tony, 115, 142n, 152, 251, 344
Tender Husband, The (Steele), 157
Thackeray, William, 334, 341
Theater, linked with masquerade by crit-
ics, 79–80. *See also* Haymarket Theater

Index

Thomas, Keith, 16, 18
Ticket prices, at masquerades, 29, 351
Tied Up in Tinsel (Marsh), 341
Tinney, John, 60
Todorov, Tzvetan, 120–21
Tolstoy, Leo, 326, 342
Transvestism: in popular ritual, 22; at masquerades, 46–47, 63–64; of Horace Walpole, 64, 73–74, 354
Travesty, *see* Costume; Masquerade
Tristram Shandy (Sterne), 342
Trollope, Anthony, 301
Turkish costume, 60; figs., 61
Turner, Victor, 86f
"Two Emilys, The" (Lee), 358
Typology, of masquerade costumes, 58

Universal Masquerade; or, The World Turn'd Inside Out, The (Sedgewick), 85

Van Dyke, Anthony, 68f
Vanity Fair (Thackeray), 334, 341
Vathek (Beckford), 121
Vauxhall gardens, 2, 98
Ventilsitten (safety valve) theory of carnival, 86–89
Venus, 109
Venus in the Cloyster; or, The Nun in her Smock (Curll), 40
Verbal behavior, at masquerades, 34–37
Verdi, Giuseppe, 339–40
Verschwörung des Fiesco zu Genua, Die (Schiller), 358
Vertigo, rituals of, 53–54
Vicar of Wakefield, The (Goldsmith), 69, 115
Victorians, on masquerades, 20, 99
Vie de Marianne, La (Marivaux), 300
Villette (C. Brontë), 334, 341, 366
Vindication of the Rights of Women, A (Wollstonecraft), 287, 293
Virginity, threatened by masquerade, 43–44

Virtuoso, The (Shadwell), 111
Voltaire, 185
Von La Roche, Sophie, 98, 358

Wahlverwandtschaften, Die (Goethe), 241, 341
Walford, Edward, 20
Walpole, Horace: on masquerades, 3, 16, 34, 90, 92, 107; on Mrs. Cornelys, 10; on Jubilee Masquerade, 14, 21, 28n, 90n; dresses as old woman, 64, 73–74, 354; description of Pantheon, 98; *The Castle of Otranto*, 121
Walpole, Robert, 184
Ward, Ned, 39–40, 46
Warehouses, costume, 58
Watt, Ian, 133
Watteau, Jean-Antoine, 109, 312n, 357
Wharton, Edith, 338
White Rose of Memphis, The (Faulkner), 338
Wild, Jonathan, 18
Wilkes, John, 90ff
Wilks, Thomas Egerton, 358
Wilson, Harriette, 44, 94, 331
Winter's Tale, The (Shakespeare), 313n
Wodewose, at masquerade, 24
Wollstonecraft, Mary, 257, 285, 287, 293, 329
Women: at masquerades, 33, 41–45, 94, 253–55; Bakhtin on, 363–64
World Upside-Down, the, 89, 200, 205–6, 250, 254. *See also* Carnival; Rites of reversal
Wuthering Heights (E. Brontë), 291, 321
Wycherley, William, 39
Wynne, William Watkins, 68

Young, Edward, 337, 367

Zoffany, Johann, 68
Zola, Emile, 344